PORTRAITS OF HOPE

ARMENIANS IN THE CONTEMPORARY WORLD

Edited by
Huberta von Voss

Translated by
Alasdair Lean

Berghahn Books
New York • Oxford

First English edition published in 2007 by
Berghahn Books
www.berghahnbooks.com

© Huberta von Voss

Translated from the German
Porträt einer Hoffnung: Die Armenier. Lebensbilder aus aller Welt.
Mit einem Geleitwort von Yehuda Bauer
Published by: Verlag Hans Schiler (Berlin)
© Verlag Hans Schiler 2005

Library of Congress Cataloging-in-Publication Data
Porträt einer Hoffnung. English.
  Portraits of hope : Armenians in the contemporary world ; biographical portraits from around the
world / edited by Huberta von Voss ; with a preface by Yehuda Bauer ; translated into English by Alas-
dair Lean.
     p. cm.
Translated from German.
Includes bibliographical references and index.
ISBN 978-1-84545-257-5 (hardcover : alk. paper)
  1. Armenia--History. 2. Armenians--History. 3. Armenians--Foreign countries--Biography. 4. Arme-
nia--Civilization. I. Voss, Huberta von. II. Lean, Alasdair. III. Title.

DS175.P6713 2007
909'.0491992--dc22

                                                                                                            2007013875

British Library Cataloguing in Publication Data
A catalogue record for this book is available from the British Library

Printed in the United States on acid-free paper

ISBN-10: 1-84545-257-7 ISBN-13: 978-1-84545-257-5 hardback

Dedicated, with love, to my daughter Valeska

* * *

Caminante, son tus huellas
el camino, y nada más;
caminante, no hay camino,
se hace camino al andar.
Al andar se hace camino,
y al volver la vista atrás
se ve la senda que nunca
se ha de volver a pisar.
Caminante, no hay camino,
sino estelas en la mar.

Antonio Machado, 1917

Wanderer, it is your tracks
And nothing more, that are the road;
Wanderer, there is no road:
The road is made by walking.
By walking is the road made
And, on looking backwards,
One can see the path
One will never tread again.
Wanderer, there is no road,
But only wakes upon the sea.

Translated by Alasdair Lean

ILLUSTRATIONS

Illustration on back cover: a very rare Caucasian *kazak sevan* from the year 1891, probably from an Armenian church, as it has two crosses in the medallions and the first letters of the word "God" in Armenian. The inscription means "Holy Carpet" [by kind permission of Nalbandian-Tapis d'Orient, Beirut-Ashrafiyeh].

Spine: Bishop's crosier with six dragon's heads in the shape of serpents. The serpent, as a symbol of wisdom, is a frequent figure in Armenian art. Van, eighteenth century.

Frontispiece: a *kashkar* (Armenian cross sculpted in stone), Cilicia, 1723.

CONTENTS

Words

Faith

Arts and Architecture

Epilogue

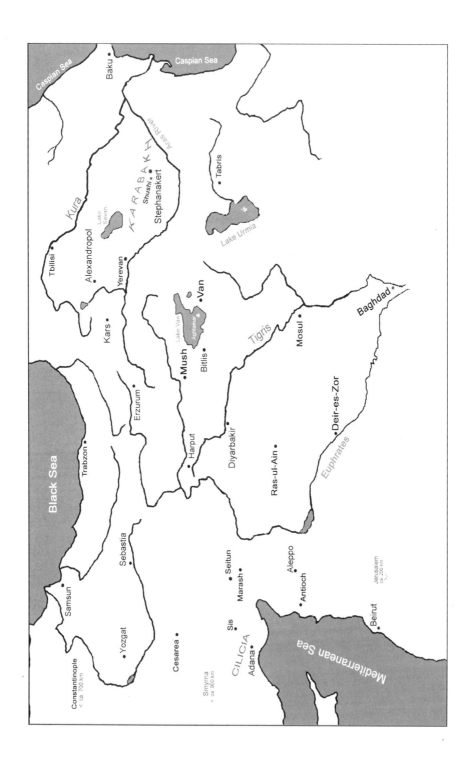

PREFACE

The Armenian genocide in Ottoman Turkey, mainly during World War I, was a historical tragedy of vast significance. This book is an attempt not only to describe the facts and consequences of the genocide but also, and perhaps even principally, to present the Armenians to the foreign reader: their culture, customs, and society—matters the non-Armenian public is hardly acquainted with.

Indeed, present-day Armenian society, both that of the diaspora and that of the independent Armenian state, is marked—one might even say branded—by the memory of the genocide; nor is this surprising. Parallels exist with other ethnic groups that have been victims of massacres and genocides that, in the same way as the Armenians, suffer a collective trauma: Jews, Tutsis, the Roma ("Gypsies"), and others. The only way to deal with this trauma, apparently, is to face it and elaborate what has happened with as much realism and objectivity as possible. The fact that modern Turkey rejects responsibility for the genocide perpetrated by a former, very different, imperial Ottoman Turkish government—they continue to deny it, in the face of great masses of documentation—makes the task of elaborating the trauma considerably harder. Other nations do not necessarily deny a genocide committed by previous generations. Present-day Americans talk openly of the genocide of the American Indians. Not only do the Germans recognize the National Socialist regime's accountability for the Shoah and the genocide of Gypsies and Poles, but the one carried out by imperial Germany against the Herreros in present-day Namibia at the beginning of the twentieth century is also openly discussed. Cambodia recognizes the mass slaughter carried out by the Pol Pot regime, and there are other examples.

The Armenian genocide, as Vahakn N. Dadrian constantly reminds us, was thoroughly tried by a Turkish military tribunal in 1919. But, since then, Turkish governments—which are actually based on the rejection of the Young Turks regime, which led the country not only to the genocide but also to a national catastrophe—have embarked on an official campaign in Orwellian fashion to brand the historical events enemy propaganda. One hopes that perhaps we are today on the threshold of a new era in which Turkish society no longer fears recognizing reality as such. For as long as this does not take place, there is no question of a modern, liberal Turkish society developing; to reject denial, then, is fundamental for Turkey itself.

This book, so to speak, has the obligation to talk about the genocide, but also tries to describe the past as well as the present, without fear of exercising self-criticism. Present-day Armenia, a tiny country, poor, and torn by internal strife, is described in detail and with great critical sympathy. The typical customs and traditions of the Armenians are presented here, perhaps for the first time in a Western language. One realizes that the Armenians are one of the most ancient nations in existence, who settled in large state-like communities in parts of present-day Anatolia and the southern Caucasus more than three thousand years ago. Christianity took hold there at the beginning of the fourth century, earlier than in many other parts of the ancient world. Thus the Armenians can legitimately claim to have been the first people to accept the new religion. Armenian script was invented at that time, and Armenian literature developed over the ages, in which Armenian civilization alternated between flourishing and decaying periods.

All this is reflected once more in the world of today, and the chapters of this book speak not only about the civilization of the past but also about the hope for a new advance. This is not something simple. The great majority of Armenians live in the diaspora: in the U.S.A., Europe, and elsewhere. Armenia is poor and underdeveloped, in part a consequence of long years of Soviet domination. In addition, a conflict has arisen between Armenia and the Azeris for control of the territory of Karabakh, and the two states, Armenia and Azerbaijan, are hostile to each other. The Azeris speak a language related to Turkish, which does not help at all to tackle the bilateral problems. But for the diaspora, Armenia would scarcely be able to rise out of its poverty; yet, even with the help of the diaspora, it is not finding it easy. More and more intellectuals seem to leave the country, and financial aid in itself is insufficient. In spite of all this, present-day Armenia constitutes the core of Armenian national consciousness, and the hopes of many Armenians are centered on that small mountainous country.

Still, this is not enough. This book depicts the diaspora and seduces the reader with the taste of Armenian dishes, memories of childhood places, and the ambitions for a future that will hopefully be better. The biographical sketches of intellectuals, artists, journalists, and others are most interesting, and produce a complicated kaleidoscope of a divided but lively people that is trying, once again, to rediscover its ethnic coherence. Armenian civilization does not consist solely of stories about a far-off past, but also of traditions and a national consciousness suggestive of a future that will transcend the present.

The solution is not to consign the genocide to the past, even though it took place more than ninety years ago and there are hardly any living witnesses of it left. To avenge it on present-day Turks, who are not to blame for what happened at that time, would be criminal, senseless, and counterproductive. But to arrive at an understanding with the Turkey of today can only be achieved after a recognition of the historical realities. In the meantime, life goes on, and one should neither forget history, nor allow oneself to be dominated by the trauma.

Development of a distinctive culture, promotion of their own language and script, and the willingness to coexist amicably with different peoples and cultures, very much including the Turkish people, seem to be what this book is trying to promote. The attempt being made here to make this clear to an international readership is extraordinarily important and, let us trust, also productive.

Yehuda Bauer
Jerusalem, Winter of 2005

PROLOGUE

Levon Dai was a man everybody envied. Whenever the Armenians from Smyrna got together in the evening at Uncle Pousant's restaurant in Manhattan, the conversation was about him. The fugitive from the Young Turks turned into an American industrialist, and this is how it happened: one sad September morning in 1919, he suddenly turned up at the home of his relatives in New York. His entire luggage was a leather suitcase containing fifty-one tins of sesame oil. From Smyrna to Jerusalem, then to Cyprus, Egypt, France, and New York he carried that suitcase, minding it like a life-insurance policy. Here he sold other refugees the traditional oil brought from his lost homeland at a big profit. Very soon he was able to leave New York with the unwavering intention of importing sesame oil to the United States. So he boarded a train to Chicago, where even then the Armenian community was much bigger than in New York. On the train he met Mrs. Slater, who found Levon Dai's dark eyes very exotic and was thrilled at meeting a genuine Armenian: one of those 'starving Armenians' from the Ottoman Empire that Americans had donated so much money for! Mrs. Slater, much enthused, persuaded the reluctant Levon Dai to go with her to Council Bluffs, Iowa, and give a talk on his "fascinating life" for the local bigwigs. "I do hope you'll wear your turban, Mr. Levonian," said the lady on the evening of the talk, "and your sari—isn't that what you call the long white garment your people wrap around themselves?"

Levon Dai corrected her. "My dear lady, I believe you are referring to a *charshaff*, which is something quite different from a sari. Indians wear saris. Turkish women wear *charshaffs*. Armenians, Mrs. Slater, wear suits, just like the Americans. I have no turban nor have I a *charshaff*." But Mrs. Slater was not to be put off from her intention, and so that evening in 1919 Levon Dai, fitted out with a turban and an improvised sari, brought the fifty people in the audience to tears. At the end of the session he was offered a job in a chemical dry-cleaning company, which was the cornerstone of his giddy rags-to-riches career "among the savages"—the Americans.

"There was once, or there was never..." is the way Armenian fairy tales begin. Levon's narrative was different in that it was one of those modern tales written by the twentieth century. Marjorie Housepian Dobkin, a delicate lady in her eighties with the energy of a twenty-year-old, wrote down this story for us. She is one of the many Armenians this book will be talking about. In her autobiographical novel, *A Houseful of Love*, from 1954, she writes about her childhood in New York among the Armenian refugees and describes—with much irony directed at her-self—what it meant for this first generation of émigrés to lose their old homeland and build a new life in a totally alien culture: homesickness and nostalgic exalta-tion, trauma and dreams, success and failure, misunderstandings and common-places, clinging to one's own culture, but also giving up old identifications. This volume expands that story. Forty-one Armenians from around the globe—some of them for the first time—tell about their lives, which the twentieth century with its many conflicts has fittingly turned upside down.

Armenians are one of the oldest ethnic cultures on earth. Yet, in many places, not a lot is known about them. What do we know about their history, which goes back three thousand years? Who are the Armenians today, ninety years after the Young Turk regime murdered up to a million and a half of them and drove hun-dreds of thousands into exile in the lee of World War I? How do they handle the denial of their fate by a Turkey on the way to joining the European Union? To what extent does the genocide determine the identity of that nation and the political situation in the southern Caucasus? Why are so many Armenians fight-ing for recognition of the historical facts? Isn't it 'just' history? And what does April 24, the day Armenians all over the world remember the beginning of the genocide, mean to the younger generations, who often no longer speak the lan-guage of their ancestors?

The thirty authors of this book have searched for their traces. Their portrayals are part of the jigsaw puzzle of Armenian reality, from Beirut through Jerusalem to Cairo, Alexandria, Istanbul, Deir-es-Zor, Tabriz, Moscow, Paris, Venice, Vienna, Brussels, London, Berlin, New York, Los Angeles, Pasadena, Toronto, Sydney, Buenos Aires, and Madras to Yerevan, Echmiadzin, and Karabakh. They are stories of famous Armenians like Charles Aznavour and of less well-known Armenians with extraordinary lives, such as Madame Anahit, the street musician of Istanbul. The editor considered it wise not so much to compile a *Who's Who* of the forty most relevant Armenians of today as to present in all its variety a kalei-doscope of the diaspora and the national state. Writers and historians, journalists and intellectuals, lobbyists and prelates, monks, painters, musicians, film direc-tors, photographers, philanthropists, politicians, and diplomats make up this por-trait. Apart from these fields, individual destinies are just as important as personalities, such as that of Monte Melkonian, the Armenian arch-terrorist and Karabakh fighter, or that of Armen Petrossian, who owns the caviar empire of the same name, or Rosita Youssefian, the teacher from Buenos Aires, and many oth-ers. Their lives all reflect a piece of the living reality of Armenian history and the present. The portraits are complemented by a few memorable places with a pro-nounced symbolic value in the Armenian consciousness, such as Deir-es-Zor, the end point of the death marches through the Mesopotamian desert, or the resist-ance at Musa Dagh, to which Franz Werfel raised a literary monument.

As Professor Yehuda Bauer has indicated in his preface, this book is one of crit-ical sympathy toward the Armenians and of respect for their rich and often tragic history. The people of *Hayastan*, as the Armenians call their country, consider themselves the heirs of the vanished Urartu Empire and descendants of Noah, whose ark came to rest "on Mount Ararat" according to the story of the Creation (Genesis 8: 4). Maybe the Biblical myth of the survival of mankind infused in them a powerful will to survive that overcame all natural adversities and political dangers while, all around them, empires rose and fell. The tiny country between Mount Ararat and the Caucasus lies on an Asian plateau as on a serving tray. Surrounded by weighty regional powers, it has endured innumerable invasions, occupations, devastations, and massacres. Whether Persians, Byzantines, Arabs, Seljuks, Mongols, Ottomans, or Tsarist or Soviet Russians, the Armenians managed to withstand their generally unbenevolent governments. United by the Christian faith within a mainly Muslim environment and by their own alphabet, throughout most of their history they have had to submit to foreign domination.

Still, they relied on their identity built on religion, as their literary and musical richness shows. The 1915–16 genocide, with which the Young Turk government tried to expel the Christian Armenians from their ancestral lands, is inextricably interwoven in the Armenian identity. This experience of violent expulsion shapes the collective memory, from Yerevan to the furthest confines of the world. Even more serious than the loss of their homeland is the traumatic experience of the systematic and brutal butchery of men, women, and children. To this day, the responsible political heirs of the perpetrators deny that it happened. In this way, the genocide remains an open wound that cannot heal and that leads to mutual hatreds. The road to reconciliation is yet untrodden. It can only be traveled by common accord.

Scientists, politicians, and representatives of human rights groups today agree that the dangers and the history of genocides must be brought out into the light, both as a precaution and as prevention.[1] A follow-up analysis is also thought to be crucial to understanding the character of mass murder aimed at the extinction of entire groups organized by a state. However, a gap remains between theory and practice, meaning that not all countries exert political pressure on Turkey to acknowledge its past and establish a relation with the Armenians that would rest on a new foundation and have a view to the future. Prevention includes public recognition of the crimes by the perpetrators or their heirs. The nongovernmental organization Genocide Watch defines denial as "the final stage of a genocide."[2] This division into stages was suggested by Deborah Lipstadt, whose studies of the denial of the Shoah opened the way to many researchers' public protests against the continued negation of the Armenian genocide.[3] "Denial of genocide— whether that of the Turks against the Armenians, or the Nazis against Jews—is not an act of historical reinterpretation. Rather, it sows confusion, by appearing to be engaged in a genuine scholarly effort," writes Deborah Lipstadt. It is an attempt "to reshape history in order to demonize the victims and rehabilitate the perpetrators."[4]

Survivors of the Armenian genocide, together with those of the Shoah, published a sensational declaration in the *New York Times* on June 9, 2000, in which 126 leading Holocaust researchers demanded that Western nations recognize the

Armenian genocide, also in order to promote democracy in Turkey. Among the numerous renowned signatories were the scholars Yehuda Bauer, Israel Charny, and Elie Wiesel.[5]

Not only is denial a crime, so is forgetting, claimed Nobel Prize-winner Elie Wiesel.[6] Thus it is not only the role of the perpetrators and the behavior of their descendants that matter, but also those of the spectators and their descendants. "We have all been bystanders to genocide. The crucial question is why," writes American Pulitzer Prize-winner Samantha Power.[7] The Armenian genocide did not take place without public knowledge. Imperial Germany, an ally of the Ottoman Empire in World War I, knew perfectly well what was going on—through abundant consular dispatches. Their Allied enemies were equally well informed. Yet no one intervened.

The Polish jurist Raphael Lemkin coined the term genocide in response to the extermination of the Armenian people and the Shoah. After many years' struggle, he succeeded in getting the United Nations to sanction the Genocide Convention in 1948, which, however, has not proved to guarantee protection for groups in danger of being massacred. Since the foundation of the UN in 1945, there have been fifty-five genocides and political mass murders. Altogether seven million people have lost their lives in this way—more than in all the wars of the last sixty years.[8] As usual, nothing, or very little, was done to prevent genocides or to react against them or threats that they might happen. The twentieth century has repeatedly been called the "century of genocide." It was also the bystander's century. And it also became the century in which many peoples willingly traveled the hard road to reconciliation by courageously facing the truth.

The 1.5 million Armenians who died in marches or by torture, shooting, starvation, exhaustion, drowning, or burning have no graves. On a commemorative plaque in Venice's old Jewish quarter, a French soldier wrote: "Your sad holocaust is engraved in history, and nothing shall purge your death from our memories, for our memories are your only grave."[9] However, for the descendants of those who forever lost their loved ones in the deportations, it is not only a matter of the dead resting in peace. The biographical portraits in this book show that, for many Armenians, the memory is still a mortuary. "Remembrance is the only paradise from which we cannot be expelled," wrote German poet Jean Paul. For many Armenians, this is not reality, but remains a hope.

It is the hope of restoring honor to the dead, but also of counterpoising the burdensome past with the relief of a new future—the hope of reconciliation with present-day Turkey, of an end to the mutual hatred. For the people of the Caucasus, the hope of a stable peace in the region is also an unfulfilled task. Irreconcilable and divided, Armenia and Azerbaijan face each other in an unresolved conflict over Karabakh, that portion of territory inhabited by Armenians but separated geographically, like an island, from the mother country. Both Turkey and its ally, Azerbaijan, keep their borders closed for this reason. The situation is unbearable for the expelled in both camps. The conflict clearly shows that a future based on mutual trust can be glimpsed only if the wounds of the past are given a chance to heal. In this respect, denial of the genocide not only generates stronger identification but also paralyzes present political decisions.

This book is meant as a contribution on the hard road to reconciliation since, just as we Germans know practically nothing about the Armenians, the Turkish stance is also based on ignorance. Turkish sociologist Taner Akçam, who has long been studying the genocide and is now a lecturer in the U.S.A., explains in his essay the difference between the ideas of Turkish people and the unyielding position of their government, which for a long time has rejected an open discussion of its own history. Increasingly, European and non-European states have enacted resolutions urging modern Turkey to take responsibility for the crimes of its political forerunners and place the archives at researchers' disposal. And so we find ourselves in the absurd situation in which to deny the Holocaust is a criminal offence in Germany, whereas in Turkey the term "genocide" in connection with the occurrences of 1915–16 has always been censored. The near future will show whether joining the EU will help those brave Turks, like the scholar Halil Berktay, who refuse to accept denial and insist on speaking up, to the acclaim of a growing Turkish public and press, who do not want any more censorship.

Western countries also use history to serve their own interests. Yet what makes them notably different is that new interpretations are not subject to traditional modes of thought or taboos. The European mentality includes the possibility of questioning itself. Our fundamental rights in Europe include freedom of opinion and of science and research and the protection of minorities. Such rights define us as Europeans and set the tone for the EU, founded by Western democracies. These guidelines must therefore also be accepted by countries wanting to join the Union. Thus, French historian Jacques le Goff is in no way essentially opposed to Turkey's joining the European Union, but he considers it an unthinkable step "so long as Turkey does not crave the Armenians' forgiveness."[10] The contest in schools that the Turkish education ministry organized on the untenability of Armenian demands for a correction of historical facts, sounds particularly cynical in this context and hardly lends credence to the Turkish state's modernization projects. Even Armenian schoolchildren are forced to deny the massacre of their ancestors. "Leave our Children in Peace!" said Hrant Dink, editor of the Turkish-Armenian newspaper *Agos*, in an angry headline.

Hrant Dink was shot dead on a sunny morning, 19 January 2007, by a seventeen year old ultra-nationalist, in front of his office in Istanbul. Cui bono? He was condemned to death because he claimed the right to openly say what he thought: that Turks and Armenians should accept that they are brothers instead of foes and that wounds cannot heal without honest respect for each other. In his eyes this acceptance should involve acknowledging the past, using the appropriate terms for the events, and also confronting any kind of guilt for which the Armenians were responsible. Not everybody liked such an independent position and few people stood up to defend him until he had been killed, with the odd exception such as the Nobel Prize winner Orhan Pamuk.

He was charged four times under the infamous § 301 of the penal code for allegedly insulting Turkishness. But where does it say in the paragraph that those people who are fighting against freedom of speech and dialogue are insulting Turkishness? Many European partners are demanding that the Government in Ankara abolish the disputed paragraph but whether this will actually happen is still unclear. The strong reaction to Dink's death has made one thing clear: the rift has deepened in Turkish society between those that identify with European values and those who still cling to the old nationalist pattern of excluding non-Turkish minorities.

A burning question in relation to Turkey's wish to join the EU is Germany's position on the Armenian genocide. In contrast to France and other states, it has always been Germany's policy to steer clear of expressing an opinion on the subject; to a great extent, this is probably because of the large number of Turkish temporary workers and immigrants in the country. What may seem on the face of it to have influenced Germany's refusal is the strategic importance of Turkey, a NATO member, and the two countries' close commercial ties, particularly because Turkey always seems ready to impose sanctions. Yet, deep down there is another reason for refusing to confront German involvement in the Armenian genocide: Germany's responsibility for the Holocaust and the fear that devoting attention to other genocides might be interpreted as an attempt to relativize the crimes of National Socialism have long led to great discretion. The reluctance to publicly analyze the issue goes to the very core of historical research. Nonetheless, it was the Imperial German state that had the fullest information on the Armenians' sufferings, and it regarded them with indifference. The moral guilt of not having acted in response to the occurrences is compounded by the active collaboration of German officers in the Ottoman army. German theologian Johannes Lepsius, from Potsdam, was commissioned by the government of the period to compile consular reports on the events. Despite the existing censorship, he left an essential source of information for researchers.[11] It was the German medic Armin T. Wegner who, as an eyewitness, took photographs of the death marches and thereby created decisive documentary material.[12] It was the Austrian Jewish writer, Franz Werfel, who wrote the national novel of the Armenians on the eve of the Shoah. The names of Lepsius, Wegner, and Werfel are engraved in Armenian history. However, although there are important collections of documents housed in the Foreign Ministry archives and although these sources are at researchers' disposal, few German scientists have looked into the matter. Why is this? This is a simple question for which there may be no simple answer. Have we chosen to read Franz Werfel's epic novel, *The Forty Days of Musa Dagh*, only to lay the subject aside as "mere" literature? Is it not high time that we Germans dealt with our role in the events of 1915–16? The growing interest of the German media and public in the Armenian genocide proves that we have reached a turning point in 2005 with the ninetieth anniversary of the event. The controversial debate on the German parliament's recent motion calling on Turkey to come to terms with its past has been very helpful in this respect. Let us hope the topic becomes part of the educational program in schools and universities as well.

Many Armenians of the diaspora have never been in the country of their fore-fathers, and some of them who do go there come away disappointed. The Soviet republic has left its traces in the people's mentality. Corruption, shady deals, and poverty are daily facts. And yet the Armenians, never mind where they are from, share a yearning for a thriving place of their own. William Saroyan, the best-known American-Armenian writer, has made a wonderful story of this attitude in his book, *My Name Is Aram* (New York, 1944). It is about his uncle Melik, "just about the worst farmer that ever lived," and his attempt, in the middle of the desert at the foot of the Sierra Nevada range, to establish a pomegranate planta-tion. "He was too imaginative and poetic for his own good. What he wanted was beauty. He wanted to plant it and see it grow." The uncle plants seven hundred expensive saplings of the best quality, most of which die. The uncle also wanted to see peach, mulberry, and apricot trees bloom in the desert. When he thinks of the last, his mouth waters: "A tree I knew well in the old country," he recalls, because the apricot—*Prunus armeniaca* in Latin—is native to Armenia. And that is what he is looking for: the past must appear before his eyes like a mirage in the desert, that empty space for dreams. It must blossom once more. After years of effort, he harvests the first two hundred meager fruits. Uncle Melik sends them to a wholesaler in Chicago. When he gets no answer, he makes a costly long-dis-tance phone call. The dealer wants to pay him a dollar per box. Melik demands five dollars. But the wholesaler is not interested and tells him that his customers do not know the fruit and he himself has not found it especially tasty. "You're crazy," yells Uncle Melik, gets his eleven boxes back, and has paid seventeen dol-lars for the call. And so the dream comes to an end. Years later, as uncle and nephew traverse the withered orchard in which cactuses have long since recovered their natural ascendancy, they say nothing. "We didn't say anything, because there was such an awful lot to say, and no language to say it in."[13]

Portraits of Hope tells of many attempts at a new start, of searches for a new lan-guage, of looking for continuity in a national history full of ruptures, of the sur-vivors' silence, and of the insecurity of their descendants. These are stories seen from a wide variety of angles. What they have in common is the search for the sig-nificance of Armenia—*Hayastan.*

Huberta von Voss
Berlin, February 2007

Notes

1. This finally became clear at the international conference Stockholm International Forum: Preventing Genocide: Threats and Responsibilities, which was held from January 26 to 28, 2004, in the Swedish capital, on Prime Minister Göran Persson's initiative. See web page *www.preventinggenocide.com.*

2. See *Genocide Watch. The International Campaign to End Genocide*'s web page: *www.genocidewatch.org.*

3. Deborah Lipstadt, *Denying the Holocaust: The Growing Assault on Truth and Memory*, New York, Toronto 1993.

4. Quote from Peter Balakian, *The Burning Tigris: the Armenian Genocide and America's Response*, New York 2003/London 2004, p. xix.

5. "126 Holocaust Scholars Affirm the Incontestable Fact of the Armenian Genocide and Urge Western Democracies to Officially Recognize It," *New York Times*, June 9, 2000.

6. See Elie Wiesel's preface to the French edition, *Les 40 jours du Musa Dagh*, Paris 1986, p. 7, quoted in Hans-Lukas Kieser and Dominik J. Schaller (eds), *The Armenian Genocide and the Shoah*, Zurich 2002, p. 6.

7. Samantha Power, *A Problem from Hell: America and the Age of Genocide*, New York 2002, p. xvii.

8. See *www.genocidewatch.org.*

9. Inscription by André Tronc at the Scola Mesulhamin, in the historical Jewish ghetto of Venice.

10. See "Die Grenzen Europas" [The borders of Europe], interview with Joachim Fritz Vannahme, *Die Zeit*, No. 50, December 7, 2000.

11. See the web page set up by Wolfgang and Sigrid Gust, with the censored and uncensored versions of Lepsius's reports: *www.armenocide.de.*

12. On this, see Martin Tamcke: "Zum Beieinander von Shoah und Völkermord an den Armeniern bei Armin T. Wegner," in Kieser and Schaller, *The Armenian Genocide*, pp. 481–500.

13. William Saroyan, *My Name Is Aram*, New York 1944, pp. 35–55.

ACKNOWLEDGMENTS

This book would never have existed but for my friend Ruth Keshishian. In her wonderful Moufflon Bookshop I found refuge from the Cyprus sun in countless books about her people, the Armenians. For her generosity and patience in fulfilling my every wish over the years I offer her my deepest thanks.

Without the generous financial support of Sara Chitjian (Los Angeles) and others, who promised their help to Professor Dadrian, this book would not have been translated into English. I am deeply indebted to all of them. I would also like to thank my translator Alasdair Lean (Buenos Aires) for the pleasant cooperation, as well as Mitch Cohen (Berlin) and the Oxford Office (Berghahn Books) for revising the text with a lot of care. Margaret Last has done a wonderful job as a copy editor.

On the way to this book I came upon a multitude of queries. I would like to express my gratitude to everyone that helped me find answers. The numerous discussions, hints, and encouragements were of enormous help to me. I am greatly indebted to His Holiness, Catholicos Aram I (Antelias), whose valuable advice and help accompanied me throughout the project. I am also most grateful to Prof. Vahakn N. Dadrian (Zoryan Institute, Cambridge, MA) for his faith in the idea when it was still in its initial stages. He opened many doors, gave many indications, and always encouraged me. I thank Dr. Tessa Hofmann (Berlin) for her corrections. I am grateful to Ralph Giordano for his encouragement as also George Shirinian of the Zoryan Institute (Toronto) for his kind help.

For his confidence in my book, I thank Jorge Vartparonian (Buenos Aires), who made its translation into Spanish possible.

Above all, however, I hold a debt of gratitude to Nouritza Matossian (London) and Garo Keheyan (Nicosia), who were present for me for three years each. Both persuaded me, with their creative energy and contagious enthusiasm, to finish the book despite a host of obstacles.

There are people and places that don't figure in this book. From the moment that there are some 8 million Armenians in the world, of which more than half live strewn around it, it was impossible to include every country and every interesting personality. But there were others, though very few, who didn't want to figure. Their wishes were respected. All the portraits in this volume are based on conversations the authors held with the people in the articles. I thank all those depicted in the portraits for their trust in us authors.

I also express my gratefulness to all the authors who participated in the book, and very specially Rainer Hermann (Istanbul), who was a very important adviser for me. Several of the authors had had no prior contact with the subject, and each went to great trouble to carry out their task. Without their generous readiness to collaborate in the book, despite their other professional duties, this work would not have been possible. Above all, I thank Prof. Yehuda Bauer (Jerusalem), Prof. Taner Akçam (Minnesota), Greg Sarkissian (Toronto), and Wolfgang Gust for their valuable support.

The authors were fortunate in having Patricia Ober as a proofreader. A hearty word of thanks to her for her extraordinary work in the name of all the collaborators in this book. I would also like to thank my German publisher Hans Schiler (Berlin) for his courage in publishing the book as well as for his friendship. My agent, Roberto de Hollanda (Bonn), was also a great help to me.

Last but not least I would like to thank Dr. Marion Berghahn as well as Mark Stanton for their good cooperation as well as for the high professional standard with which they are producing books. It was a pure pleasure to be part of that process.

For their practical aid I must remember Marine and Nazareth Karoyan (Yerevan), as also Zarouhi Isneian and Aiga Strazdina, without whose help with my three children I could never have finished this work on time.

Greater than all other help was that of my husband, Peter Wittig. But for his unlimited patience and his keen interest in the project, it would have been impossible. My daughter Valeska accompanied its writing with many intelligent questions. It is to her that, with love, I dedicate it.

Huberta von Voss
Berlin, February 2007

Part I

Introduction

1

BETWEEN ARARAT AND THE CAUCASUS: PORTRAIT OF A TINY COUNTRY IN FIVE LESSONS

Tessa Hofmann

Two Points of Reference: Between Ararat and the Caucasus

Armenian history teaches us historical relativism. In this land, where one tends to think in terms of centuries, conjuring up "eternal" values, nothing is long-lasting. The whim of history, that is, that of Soviet Russia, resulted in the country's most sacred mountain, Ararat, being attached to Turkey. Its name was changed, as happened with almost all Armenian place names, so as to conceal its real connection and ownership: the mountain, known worldwide as Ararat, and which the Armenians call Massis, is officially Ağrı Dağı in Turkish, the Mount of Sorrows or Woes, and since 1921 towers beyond the frontier.

However, the mystical connection of the Armenians with the Massis and their mountain cult has not changed on account of this. Not only the local inhabitants but also visitors, on either side of the border, perceive the mountain's magical presence, and can tell of experiencing visions of the Ararat that seems to beckon Armenians back home after their long absence. This is especially true of those that come from the Ararat plain, for whom the majesty of the mountain's imposing profile is often in view. On the fertile, though arid, plains between the volcanic giants, Ararat and Aragats, was the northern center of Armenian culture. The southern one was in the region of Lake Van, in present-day eastern Turkey. Both arose centuries before the sixth BC, when the shah-in-shahs of ancient Persia as well as Greek historians began calling the highlands of Asia Minor Armenia, two millennia before the first Turks appeared in the region in the eleventh century.

The change of names and geographical configurations indicate always changes in political reference values and their related points of view. Since World War I, when the borders of the Armenian plateau were bloodily erased by genocide and, even abroad, the name of eastern Anatolia was introduced instead of western Armenia or Turkish Armenia, what remained of Armenia became part of the Transcaucasus for seventy years, together with Georgia and Azerbaijan (officially termed "sister republics") as, from the European and Russian point of view, these countries lay on the other side of the Caucasus. After the dissolution of the USSR, the designation of Caucasus or southern Caucasus was adopted by Europe and the U.S.A. for the region, a new and neutral configuration in appearance alone. In fact it is owed to nationalist Turkish political thinkers of the early twentieth century, who, in this way, hoped to change the concept of the Armenian plateau, or that of Transcaucasia, as used from the European and Russian point of view. For the Turks Armenia, Georgia, and Azerbaijan made up, together with the northern Caucasus, or Great Caucasus, a unity, despite the fact that the Great Caucasus mountain range is not visible from any part of Armenia and despite the existence of marked differences between the early Christian cultures, on the one hand, and the tribal societies of the Caucasus, on the other.

The post-Soviet inclusion of Armenia in the (southern) Caucasus is thus due to a political program rather than to geographical, cultural, or historical facts. Armenia's acceptance of its placement in the southern Caucasus, as Europe and the U.S. wish, requires pragmatism and the renunciation of history on the part of the Armenians. Also, like other members of parliament of the German Federal Republic, Christa Lörcher (SPD), then the president of the parliamentary Commission for the Caucasus, defined in a document of the year 2000 the insistence of the Armenians on an explicit international recognition of the genocide of one and a half million of their ancestors as a factor that "possibly impeded dialog between Armenia and the neighboring countries, mainly Turkey." Besides, the danger exists that "the Armenians attach themselves so much to history that the need to deal politically with the problems of the present and the future, and specially to a more intensive collaboration with the neighboring countries, is not receiving the attention it requires."[1]

The Armenians' sight persists to be focused on Ararat, the country's most characteristic landmark. Whoever beholds it looks back on the past without meaning to. They see a continuity of almost three millennia of foreign domination, expulsion, and extermination, of loss and pain, but also the capability of surviving natural and man-made afflictions under the most adverse circumstances. This view is connected, in accordance with the Judeo-Christian tradition, with the hope of reconciliation. For Ararat and Noah's salvation in the book of Genesis stand as a symbol of God's promise of forgiveness to humankind. Since 1921, Ararat is unreachable from Armenia, but it remains imposingly visible. Not so, however, the Caucasus. The myth of the rebellious bringer of culture, Prometheus, developed by the Greeks, belongs to Europe, not the Near East. In the Armenia of the Near East, the eternal subjects of guilt, atonement, and salvation from destruction are dealt with.

The Most Ancient Existent Christian State

Armenia is in no way the most ancient Christian state but, in contrast to the earlier ones in Mesopotamia and the Aramaic-Hellenistic city-state of Urhoy/Edessa/Urfa, Christianity has endured in the Biblical land between Ararat and the Caucasus. Two of Jesus' apostles, Thadeus and Bartholomew, are said to have preached in Armenia, where they were martyred. According to ecclesiastical tradition, it was declared the official state religion by King Trdat the Great in 301, after he had been converted by the nobleman Grigor "Lussavorich" (the Enlightener). Grigor, in whose honour the Armenian Apostolic Church is also known as the "Gregorian," was its first spiritual head (Catholicos).

A century later Christianity also took hold as the religion of the people. Even the remotest regions, in which the ancient faith of Iranian Mazdaism persisted, were converted. A precondition was, that the Armenian script, supposedly laid aside in the euphoria of the second missionary phase due to its being considered pagan was "rediscovered" and perfected in 405, with the Bible being translated into Armenian in 433. Catholicos Sahak Partev (the Parthian, also known as the Great, *c.* 348–439) and King Vramshapuh (401–408/9) commissioned this task to the monk and former Court Secretary, as well as military commander, Mesrop Mashtots (362–440).

Modern linguists praise the Mesropian Bible as "the queen of translations." That the characters originally constituted no more than a means of translating the *astvatsatsundsh*, the "divine breath," into the vernacular, was almost forgotten due to the Armenians' unique veneration for script, since they not only canonized the creator of the "holy script," but elevated the writing itself to the rank of a continually worshipful object: graven in stone, cast in metal, carved in wood, woven in carpets, painted on paper and silk, embroidered on cloth. Armenia lies there where its sacred letters are seen, into which many languages of the world can be transcribed, but which hardly anyone who is not Armenian can decipher.

No other event in Armenian history, so rich in events, had such an influence on this people as its conversion to Christianity. This religion lived through Armenia's loss of independence in 428, thanks to the consolidation it was given by Mesrop's extraordinary theologico-philological feat. For centuries the only integrating institution was the Armenian Apostolic Church. It was the church that kept the Armenian identity alive during foreign rule, and which to this day preserves unity among Armenian communities disseminated around the world. It acquired its definite position as the national popular church after the Council of Chalcedon (451), which divided Christianity into two unequal camps. The Armenian clergy, whose church followed the rules of the older Syriac-orthodox one, together with the Copts and the Ethiopian church, fell into the anti-Byzantine camp. Armenia paid for this decision with isolation, since its church was treated as schismatic by both Byzantium and Rome. Within universal Christianity it became the national church which, from the seventh century on, renounced any mission whatsoever and in which ethnic and religious identity coalesced as in Judaism.

The second independent Armenian Republic[2] gave the Armenian Apostolic Church a special status as the national church as a sign of respect, in spite of the separation of state and church. If the church had maintained national and religious identity intact in previous centuries, even under the conditions of the diaspora and minorization, its present dominance in almost monoethnic and religiously united Armenia exerts a nearly overwhelming influence over other religions and denominations. This is felt particularly by members of the so-called "non-Apostolic" churches, such as the free evangelical ones, whose intensive mission has earned them the suspicion and rejection of the Armenian Apostolic Church. However, the leaders of these churches based in the U.S.A. have obviously understood the need of making the Armenian government realize that a constant oppression of these congregations would lead to palpable reductions in the funds with which the U.S. government aids Armenia.

With approximately 96 percent, the Armenian Apostolic Church is dominant in the country, number wise. A mere 2 percent of the population belongs to non-Christian religons, to wit, the Yezidi cult and Judaism. Some 10 percent of Armenians worldwide consider themselves Catholic, the majority of these living in the Middle East and the north of Armenia. The total figure of Catholic Armenians in the Republic of Armenia and in the Armenian region of Javakheti (Georgia) is about 200,000. Since 1742, patriarchal see of the Armenian church connected with Rome is located in Beirut, and the united Armenian episcopal see for Armenia, Georgia, and all eastern Europe, in Gyumri (Armenia) since 1991. Armenian evangelical communities have existed since the nineteenth century. Today the majority of the descendants of Armenian Protestant refugees from the Ottoman Empire live in the U.S.A. and Canada, and are grouped in the Armenian Evangelical Union of North America (AEUNA). Well-known Protestants occasionally branded as "non-Armenians" by fanatics of the "mother church" were, for instance, the Armenian American author William Saroyan (1908–1981) and Soghomon Tehlirian (1897–1960), worshiped as a national hero, who in 1921 assassinated in Berlin the former Home Minister of the Ottoman Empire, Talaat Paşa, the man most responsible for the Armenian genocide.

As a Phoenix from the Ashes?

The public buildings constructed in great numbers in Armenia during the Soviet period seem too large for the tiny country which, with a land surface of 29,743 square kilometers, is the size of Brandenburg, the fifth largest state of Germany (smaller than Maryland, though larger than Hawaii). In the Soviet era cinemas, congress halls, sport and youth palaces, and airports were built with imperial vigor, and nowadays fall into disrepair from disuse. In that period everything was *mets masshtabov*, on a grand scale. Marked by officially decreed historical optimism, the Soviet Armenians imagined that, after the fall of the Empire, everything would work even better since, as everyone hoped, important decisions would no longer be made in far-off Moscow, but in the Armenian capital and by an Armenian parliament. A desire cherished over generations seemed about to come true: after five hundred years of foreign domination, Armenia achieved its independence, albeit reduced to one tenth of its historical territory.[3] But little by little its inhabitants began to realize that in this way they were falling into isolation and insignificance. When on February 19, 2004, a 27-year-old Azeri, a member of the armed forces, participated in Budapest in an "Partnership for Peace" NATO exercise and, due to racial hatred, decapitated a sleeping Armenian comrade of the same age with a hatchet, the incident hardly merited a line in the international press. The rescue of a bear threatened by flooding at the Yerevan zoo at that same time possessed the necessary quota of "human interest" to appear on television around the world.

Dreams of national blossoming have long since turned into post-Soviet depression. Armenia is by no means like the fabulous phoenix reborn resplendent from the ashes of its destruction. It was left adrift in international politics with no previous preparation or lessons as to how to manage its affairs, and it must deal with an environment which, in the best of cases, is neutral. Among its immediate neighbors, it maintains really harmonious relations only with Iran. The Karabakh conflict makes its relations with Azerbaijan difficult, and with Turkey the genocide is the stumbling block. Both states refuse to establish diplomatic relations.

In order to counteract its geopolitical isolation, Armenia has decided to participate in all international structures. It carries out a multilateral foreign policy, and has realized the Karabakh problem can only be solved in the long term. Slowly and efficiently it has built its credibility, joining international organizations. Since 1992, it has been a member of the OSCE (Organization for Security and Cooperation in Europe), since 1995, of the United Nations, and since 2001, of the European Council. At present Armenia's foreign policy is more successful than its domestic policy, in which much is improvised and shortsighted. For its foreign politics a state does not need any great infrastructure, whereas for its internal life it requires a healthy basis, a functional and popular administration at a national, regional, and local level. Nothing of the sort exists in Armenia. The result is a sharp alienation between voters and the elected.

The social and cultural successes of the Soviet regime were modest, but reliable. A free health service, the right to work and to receive a stable salary, cheap rents and electricity, virtually free telephone service—citizens can only dream of these now. The change to a new social and economic order was experienced as a loss of all security. Most people lost all their savings and literally had to sell grandma's jewels. Nearly all factories and companies shut down in the first half of the 1990s. Still, it is only a tiny minority that wants to go back to Soviet rule. But the imperfection of the free-market economy and democracy has perceptibly dampened enthusiasm, giving rise to a dangerous political apathy. Citizens' distrust of the government, which existed since the time of the tsars and the

Soviet regime, is still there, and accentuated by corruption and administrative inefficiency, which are no longer owed to the authorities in Moscow but to members of the national, post-Soviet elite.

"Only tribes will survive!" This maxim already applied under the tsars and Soviets. In the poverty of Armenian society it becomes a survival tactic. Without being part of a network of social or tribal relations, without practicing the Latin motto *do, ut des* (I give, so that you give), without nepotism, the buying of offices, and bribery, no one in Armenia can keep his head above water. For this reason, of the three powers, the executive is the strongest, and the weakest is the legislative. In any case, unwritten laws have more power in Armenia than those that come from the legislature.

Over a hundred political parties and groups are registered, of which only seven actually participate in decision-making. All of them share a common feature: the program is far less important than the founder's personality. Splits are the most frequent cause for the formation of new parties. As a general rule, political opposition is a euphemism for breaches among the political elite or, as an Armenian observer put it, "Those that struggle for power are still hungry. The leaders defend their position with all the means at their disposal, without having learnt it's far more sensible to share a bit of the cake." These dividing struggles for power always give the population a chance to articulate their dissatisfaction and their desires—until the next time.

Since 2003, Armenia's readiness to follow the neo-liberal teachings of its masters in the World Bank led to stunning results: The Armenian GDP grew by 14 percent in 2005, and its inflation rate is lower than Japan's. But the social indicators are less convincing, and are obviously not influenced by the improved macroeconomic conditions.

The current economic transition exacts huge costs from those least able to bear them: children, single elderly, disabled, women, unemployed people, urban households, etc. The worst effects of this situation have been attenuated through coping mechanisms instituted through (e)migration in search of work, informal sector activity, and remittances from the Armenian Diaspora and a considerable sense of family solidarity, which has been the focus of the Armenian family through centuries.

The U.S. State Department human rights report for 2005 starts out from the fact that around 43 percent of Armenia's population lives below the poverty line – 55 percent according to the Armenian Economy Ministry and the Brussels Base NGO *International Crisis Group* – that is, earns monthly about 60 U.S. dollars (30,000 AMD) or less, and that an estimated 15 percent must be considered as extreme poor. For the elderly, average pensions are rated at 9.91 dollars (5,800 AMD) per month, and with a quarter of its population at the age of retirement, Armenia is one of the fastest "aging" countries in the world. The cost of the monthly minimum food basket is approx. 59 dollars (2006) per person, according to official estimation. However, average salaries are only about 35 dollars (AMD) 20,745). Whole professions, such as the chronically underpaid teachers, but also hospital staff, endured non-payment or delayed payment for years. Staff of private hospitals works unpaid or underpaid and subsequently seeks compensation from the patients. The official unemployment rate was 10.9 percent in 2004, according to more reliable estimations twenty percent with further 50 percent under-employed. The monthly unemployment benefit, paid for 12 months, was about 7 dollars in 2004.

Mid-term results of Armenia's impoverishment show in poor health and declining national education:

Studies on poverty in Armenia and its effect on health were carried out by UNICEF in 1998, and updated by the World Food Program in September 2000 and April 2001. This study proved that in the southeastern province of Sinnik a quarter of the children showed growth retardation, including cases of dwarfism, and nearly 17 percent of the elderly inhabitants were undernourished. In Gerarkunik province the percentage of children with retarded growth was as high as 32.4. The Refugee Council and the Norwegian honorary consul established in the year 2002 that there was a whole series of cases in which breast-fed babies died of hunger due to their mothers' being undernourished. Though the families do everything humanly possible for their children, those that suffer most are the aged, invalids, and the sick. Altogether, according to the UNICEF study of the year 2000, around 55 percent of the population is unable to cover its basic food requirements. According to figures of the United Nations bureau in Armenia, the average daily calorie intake is 2,040, compared with the international minimum guideline of 2,100 calories a day. It was possible, the Armenian Social Ministry, cynically explained in the summer of 2002 to representatives of the Austrian Red Cross, to return Armenian emigrants to their country, knowing the local authorities were under the obligation of taking care of them. Yet, if anyone was interested in the long life of the people in question, it was better for them to stay in Europe.[4]

General poverty is what leads many families, above all in rural areas, to cut short the obligatory ten years of schooling. As the young people are needed to work on the now privatized farms, their attendance in the final years of secondary school is very irregular. Out of each one hundred youths, only fifty-eight completed high school in 1995. According to Ministry of Defense data, this figure had gone down to forty in the year 2000. And, to make matters worse, the number of enrollments in elementary schools has also sunk noticeably. According to reports of the A. D. Sakharov American Human Rights Center, on account of poverty only half the children of primary age can attend school. The catastrophic financial situation and also the nonadaptation of the school system to the new conditions of life result in the present degree of learning at schools being only 30 or 40 percent of the basic material. One out of six teachers is now at retirement age, and one out of four has never sat for any exam at university level. With a monthly salary of 20 to 30 dollars, teachers belong to the population groups living below the poverty line.

Spyurk: A Constant, Thousand-Year-Old Armenian Story

Since the eleventh century Armenia has had permanent diasporas or communities established abroad. At present the estimated 8 or 9 million Armenians mostly live outside Armenia. Exactly how many cannot be known due not only to practical difficulties. Many distrust the post-Soviet censuses as much as the previous ones: instead of the 3 million that resulted from the October 2001 census, the real figures are presumed to lie between 2 and 2.5 million. "Dead souls," as intellectuals suspect, ever distrustful of the government, are used by the latter in manipulating election results. Economic data are also somewhat less dramatic when calculated according to a smaller denominator. The manipulation of statistics obviously gives rise to a conflict between the economy and politics, and, in the opinion of many commentators, a reasonable estimate would be a mean population of 2.5 million, with a falling tendency.

The relationship between Armenia—*Hayastan* in Armenian—and its diaspora—*Spyurk*—is not free of misunderstandings and mutual projections. In the Soviet era, *Hayastanziner* and *Spyurkahayer* declared themselves to be the guarantors of the country's survival. As a Soviet republic, Armenia became the ethnically most homogenous of all. The mutual of minorities from Azerbaijan as much as from Armenia has intensified this, so that the country today, with an Armenian population of around 97 percent, is almost monoethnic. In comparison, the diaspora feels threatened by assimilation and loss of identity in the industrialized countries. For instance, the loss of the national language is already complete by the third generation.

The diaspora is a product of Armenia's very varied history. Since late antiquity, the Persians and Byzantines depopulated entire regions through relocation. They deported Armenians by the tens of thousands to Crete, where there stands the oldest Armenian church in Europe, to the Balkans, and to Iran. The fall of the Armenian kingdoms of Shirak and Vaspurakan, as well as the Seljuk invasion in the eleventh century, set in motion the first Armenian mass exodus in history. Armenian communities established themselves even in the lands farthest from the ancestral homeland: in India, China, Ethiopia, Egypt. Still, not all the Armenian colonies persisted, such as those of China and India, as well as that of Manchester, which continued in existence until the 1930s. Its fate was closely linked to the rise and fall of the English textile industry. The production, manufacture, and marketing of silk, and later other textile raw materials, were an Armenian "specialty." Foreign trade in silk, precious stones, spices, incense, and other Oriental products from Iran through Russia was in the hands of Armenians for centuries, to such an extent that the commercial route along the Volga was known as the "Armenian road." From the time when the Byzantine military command sent Armenian units to the Crimea in the eighth century, the Armenian presence grew in the east and south of the peninsula, first with the approval and support of the Mongols, later that of the Genoese and Ottomans, and finally of the

Russians, so much so that many Western sources called Crimea *Armenia maritima* and the Sea of Azov *Lacus armeniacus*.

The history of the Armenian commercial colony in Moscow goes back to at least the year 1390, when the presence of a "certain Armenian named Avram" was documented in the commercial suburb of Kitai-gorod ("Chinatown"), which already had an Armenian street at the time, and an "Armenian trading company" in the sixteenth century. The fostering of Armenian commercial colonies in the Russian Empire in the seventeenth and eighteenth centuries, but, above all, the successful combination of Russian commercial interests with the Armenian yearning for the liberation of their country, favoured Armenians' careers in the Russian state as interpreters, diplomats and, in the nineteenth century, even as ministers in the industrial, cultural, and educational areas. The first silk merchants and manufacturers to be promoted to the nobility belonged to the Lazarian family (Lazariev in Russian) which, in the eighteenth century, moved from Iran to Moscow. Other noble families were the princes Abamelek and Argutinskiy and the counts of Loris-Melikov.

When the fall of the USSR produced the largest Armenian exodus in history, around half a million *rossiyanye* of Armenian origin lived within the Russian Federation. They were joined by Armenian refugees from Azerbaijan, Georgia, and Central Asia, but also emigrants from Armenia—a heterogeneous lot, of very diverse mentalities, background, and political interests. Despite the diversity of the Armenian community in Russia, a Union of Armenian Communities of the Russian Federation was formed as a centralizing organization. Today, the largest Armenian community abroad is the Russian one, with two and a half million members, one million of these in the Moscow area. Next in numbers is that of the U.S.A., with over a million, of which half live in the state of California. Politically it is the most active and influential foreign community, but it is also divided, being represented by two central organizations, the Armenian Assembly of America, and the Armenian National Congress. The most numerous Armenian community in Europe is that of France, with which there exists a very special relationship, from the time of the Crusades and thanks to the protection the Crusaders afforded the little Armenian kingdom of Cilicia, which prospered from the transit of goods. In the Near and Middle East there are traditional communities in Iran, Syria, and Lebanon.

The Armenian diaspora frequently regards the Armenian state with skepticism. It feels impatience at independent Armenia's rate of development, but also shows little understanding for those *Hayastanziner* that seek a materially and socially easier life in the diaspora. The *Spyurkahayer* reprove Armenia for looking on the diaspora as a mere milch cow. The 300 to 400 million dollars of private money sent annually to Armenia comes in great measure from the large diaspora communities in France and the U.S., and surpasses the Armenian national budget of 350 million dollars. Needless to say, this foreign financial aid from the diaspora to the motherland is indispensable. The basic principle of self-help, which is looked on as something very different from alms-giving, is also an expression of the most impressive virtues of the diaspora. The Franco-Armenian *chansonnier* Charles Aznavour has raised commitment to Armenia and Karabakh to the level of a characteristic feature of Armenian identity abroad. "Ancestry and religion are important. But if you're Armenian, then help Armenia, as the Armenians of France and the U.S.A. do."

A young *Hayastanzi* suggests another definition of patriotism: "Armenia doesn't need us. For the land, for the mountains it's the same who lives here. But we certainly need Armenia!" Is this true? In Mariam's view, patriotic sentiment is expressed in readiness to live in the country. This is what she says, but she lives in Berlin. Her brother has also come to live there, and has married a German from Russia. And her mother comes to the Spree for extended visits. At some point she is going to want to stay. Nevertheless, Mariam often speaks of Armenia and her wish to go back there. She lives spiritually with her bags packed, and she is not the only one. The nostalgic accounts of nearly every *Hayastanzi* are a picture of inner conflict and the yearning for a romanticized homeland, which the majority would only go back to as visitors, without ever fully arriving in their country of residence.

The entrepreneurial commitment, artistic creativity, and organizational know-how of Armenians living abroad are just as essential as the diaspora's money. The most interesting and successful shops and localities in Yerevan, such as Saltzsack, the arts and crafts shop on the traditional Abovyan Street, the much frequented international rendezvous Artbridge, on the same street, the typical restaurant in Pushkin Street, Dolmana, equally popular among foreigners—with impossible prices for the majority of the locals—were put up by foreign Armenians, mainly from the U.S. In this way they not only create jobs, but also considerably foster the cultivation of traditional crafts and industries, such as carpet-making. One of the first of these foreign Armenians, James Tufenkjian from the U.S.A., founded a company for the manufacture of carpets of traditional and modern design. In 1997 Garbis Jafalian, born in Aleppo and resident in Valence, France, founded a European-Armenian modern carpet workshop, Hemag, which has since been producing carpets in Sevan, Abovyan, and Ijevan with Armenian wool, and natural dyestuffs manufactured in Holland. With motifs taken from Armenian history and book illustrations, the Bible, European art deco, the signs of the zodiac, and floral designs by the French-Armenian painter Sir L., of which only seven specimens are made at a time, they have created a colourful and original universe of carpets. Each carpet sold at Hemag feeds two women for two months.

It is precisely this sort of active support that Grigor Magistros Pahlavuni (approx. 990–1058), a philosopher, author, scientist, politician, soldier, and Byzantine statesman—a man of many —praised in his fable of the lark. On noticing the sky was threatening to fall, the little bird lay on his back and stuck his legs upwards. Many scoffed at him. "What a ridiculous little bird you are! Do you expect to become a supporting beam with your needle-thin legs and your mood as whimsical as the sea?" And he answered, "I do what is within my powers."

An Attachment (or Not) of Armenia: Karabakh

Dressed in their Sunday best, they remained in the village's municipal building for hours, awaiting the delayed international delegation due to arrive in Baroness Caroline Cox's entourage to celebrate the feast day with them. However, behind the 2,483 meter Sissian Pass, the highest in Armenia, a dense fog had fallen. In winter the pass, through which the main highway to Karabakh runs, becomes an obstacle rather than a route. Even now in May, a rainy month, fogs impair visibility, forcing traffic to move at walking pace.

By radio the mayor finds out that the guests of honour have also had a chat in the middle of Berdzor (formerly Lachin), the capital town of the Kashatagh district. Lady Cox, as she is respectfully called there, is not only the deputy spokeswoman of the U.K. House of Lords but, principally, a nurse. She never misses the chance of trading news and opinions about medicine with her Karabakh-Armenian colleagues. And the hospital director, who lives in Berdzor, Artsakh Buniatyan, has known her for years and from numerous humanitarian interventions. For the deeply religious Scotswoman committed herself to this remote region, since no aid organization was active there except her Christian Solidarity Worldwide. From 1992 she transported relief supplies to Karabakh, first of all in dangerous plane flights, and then by road, along which Karabakh-Armenian units were engaged in open combat: baby food, medicines of every kind and, finally, the elements for a treatment center in which adolescent or adult victims of landmines and war casualties were taken care of, either as out- or in-patients. She furnished schools and kindergartens with writing implements, and brought British Halo Trust specialists to clear away the numerous mines placed in the area by both sides. In her entourage there were always motivated foreign journalists, clerics of diverse churches, Members of Parliament, human rights activists, and other opinion-makers from Europe and the U.S.A. This aid far exceeded the usual measure of foreign help. It was directed to connecting Karabakh with the outside world, and neutralizing one of the greatest traumas Armenians have, and not only in Karabakh: the experience, backed by history, of being left on their own by God and the world. In this sense the baroness' intervention has not been limited merely to caring for visible war injuries, but has given the Karabakh Armenians courage at a time when, for their survival, they needed foreign solidarity and comprehension with the same urgency as food, bandages, and medicines. It is no surprise that Caroline Cox has earned the rank of a national heroine in the Karabakh Armenians' memory and hearts—and that in an area where that title is not granted to just anyone, having produced its own heroes in quantity. When the baroness and her group finally lurched near in their jeeps and Volgas along the unpaved mountain road, there was a feeling of enormous relief.

The village schoolmistress describes the reason for the commemorative feast as an eye-witness. "Soldiers surrounded our village. Then the Turks began looting and murdering. I saw my neighbors die. I got hold of my baby and hid in the garden, in a pit covered with dead leaves. I kept my hand on my baby's mouth, just so that she wouldn't cry!" Turks and their close relatives, the Azeris, are very often considered as the same thing by the Armenians. They are convinced that, after the extermination of their compatriots in Asia Minor, there also exists a plan for the total elimination of the Armenians of the eastern Transcaucasus. Although the horrors in the village had taken place ten years earlier, the memory of them brings tears to the mother's eyes. "I knew they wanted to kill us!"

But her twelve-year-old daughter's look, with her rosy cheeks, such black eyes, and as healthy as her mother, proves that this intention failed. They both survived and, after the capture of the historical capital, Shushi—which the people here refer to as the liberation—they returned to their native village with other survivors. Now they stand under a thin drizzle in the village square, respectfully listening to speeches by Baroness Cox and other guests of honour. Whenever the fog lifts for brief moments, one is awestruck by imagining the extraordinary beauty around this mountain village, which overcame Operation Ring. From April to August 1991, the Azeri authorities attempted, with the support of the central Soviet Interior Ministry troops—later with the Third Division of the Fourth Soviet Army stationed in Azerbaijan—to expel the inhabitants of the twenty-five villages. The modus operandi was typical. In the beginning, electricity was cut off, and then the village was surrounded by tanks and armoured cars, with helicopters flying above them. Under this cover, members of the Interior Ministry troops and civilian officials came in; they looted, raped women, and terrorized the inhabitants, until they "voluntarily" signed their agreement to leave the place. They were then transported to the Soviet Armenian border and left to their fate.

At a press conference on May 22, 1991, an Azeri speaker in Moscow claimed that it was necessary to relocate 32,000 people in Karabakh—possibly a boastful exaggeration. Other reports give between 5,000 and 10,000 evicted. Between 140 and 170 Armenians died in this brutally implemented "ethnic cleansing," or later from their wounds. More than 600 were taken as hostages, or kidnapped and sent to prison as alleged terrorists. Nearly all of them were tortured.

Yet this was by no means the high point of what the Soviet press described as the "Nagorno- (meaning mountainous) Karabakh conflict." Crass human rights offences which owed as much to the late Soviet authority's arbitrariness as to the hatred toward Armenians already fostered in Azerbaijan during the Soviet era, were followed by a military attempt in late 1991 to subjugate that insubordinate region. Azerbaijan was specially upset that, a few days after the Azeris declared independence from the still existent USSR, Nagorno-Karabakh in its turn declared itself independent, and ratified this decision through a referendum in December 1991.

The officially undeclared, unequal war between Azerbaijan and Karabakh ended on May 14, 1994, with the mediation of Russia and Kyrgyzstan. The conflict that existed from 1988 on had uprooted almost a million people, after 18,000 Azeris and 20,000 Armenians had lost their lives, according to their own estimates; the latter were largely civilians killed in air raids. The border areas of the east, west, and south of the previous Autonomous Republic, were evacuated. Many war refugees and displaced persons—their exact number is debatable—live until the present day in temporary camps in the most miserable hygienic and social conditions—on purpose by the Azeri political leaders? Is this a way of preparing a fertile ground for interethnic hatred? At times of internal crisis and during electoral campaigns, the Karabakh question is useful to Azerbaijan as a patriotic stimulus, and aggravates the danger that the conflict, frozen since 1994, might enter another hot phase.

Since no lasting peace agreement has been found over the last twelve years and sporadic outbreaks of military violence occur despite an OSCE monitoring, experts disagree as to whether the conflict must be considered as frozen or even acute. At the former line of the front, monitored by the OSCE, there are constant mortal clashes due to Azerbaijan's attempts to invade territory under Armenian control. The difficulties of achieving an agreement are to be found mainly in the historical and juridical opposition of the two points of view. That the importance of Karabakh is different for both nations was something already noted by Russian Nobel prize-winner and human rights champion Andrej Sakharov (1921–1989), who accurately said shortly before he died, "For Azerbaijan the Nagorno-Karabakh question is one of ambition; for the Armenians it is a matter of life or death."

In not inconsiderable measure the Karabakh conflict goes back to the tense relations of the eastern Transcaucasus with Russia, and the latter's policies regarding local nationalities. After the collapse of the Armenian kingdom in the 11th century, no dominant sovereign nobility was left, except in the eastern provinces of Siunik and Artsakh on the Armenian plateau. Artsakh was ruled by five princes, who, from the sixteenth century on, were called *meliks*, the usual title for the Persians' local vassals. In this same period Artsakh began to be called by its Turkish name, Karabakh, which comes from *kara bakhche*, black garden. In the late seventeenth century, when Iran was weakened by internal and external crises, the Artsakh *meliks* joined in an armed pact against both Persians and Turks. They were able, until well into the eighteenth century, to remain semi-independent from the neighboring powers, thanks to the highly developed Karabakhi defense system, as well as the diplomatic skill of its princes. From early on the local Christians of the Transcaucasus sought to become allies of the Christian Russians, and the five princely families of Karabakh willingly put themselves at the tsar's service, backing the Russians in their southward expansion in the Transcaucasus, so that by 1804 Artsakh was already under Russian domination, a quarter of a century before the Armenian khanates of Yerevan and Nakhichevan. However, Armenia was deceived in its hope that Russia would make a political unity of all the Armenian areas, as the yearned-for core of the rebirth of Armenian sovereignty. In the times of the tsars Karabakh was not included in the Armenian fold or under the later administration of Yerevan, but in the Caspian region, in the government of Elizavetpol (in Armenian, Gandsak, today Gyanje) established in 1868. In times of crisis, when the central Russian power shook or simply collapsed, brutal ethnic conflicts would arise in the Empire's Transcaucasian periphery when the Armenians tried to improve their situation, and their Azeri neighbors massacred them by the hundreds. This is what happened in 1904–05 during the first Russian social revolution, even worse when the tsarist empire fell, and then again from 1988 to 1990 when Mikhail Gorbachev's reform projects gave the decrepit Soviet Union its *coup de grace.*

Azerbaijan bases its claim to Karabakh on arbitrary administrative rules, as they first existed under the tsars, and then the Soviets. One faction of the Russian Communist Party, in no way validated by the people, decided on July 5, 1921, to grant Karabakh to Soviet Azerbaijan "in virtue of the indispensability of national peace between Moslems and Armenians"—when that same faction had decided, the day before, to grant it to Soviet Armenia. The revision of the decision in favour of Azerbaijan was the result of the obstinate pressure by the president of the Azeri council on the people's commissar, Narimanov. He had already threatened anti-Soviet uprisings in the case of the Armenian region of Nakhichevan, should Armenia be favoured. Needless to say, so far no Azeri politician has appealed to the principle of self-determination, and with good reason: in 1921 around 90 percent of the population of Karabakh was Armenian.

The Armenians' legal basis starts out from the fact that Karabakh did not belong territorially to Azerbaijan in the period when this republic was created, and the legitimate representatives of Karabakh at no time recognized a lasting rule by Azerbaijan. When the limits of the Karabakh Autonomous Region were settled in 1923, it enclosed only the central third of the ancestral Armenian province of Artsakh, an island of only 4,400 square kilometers instead of the original surface of 12,000, divided by the Soviet army by means of the Lachin corridor.

The comforting promise in the communist decree of annexation of July 5, 1921, guaranteeing Karabakh "far-reaching regional autonomy" was nothing but pure fiction. The list of Karabakh Armenian grievances over abuses at the hands of the Azeri administration is long, from cultural and political repression and starvation to setting up social and economic-political obstacles, including the unilateral exploitation of natural resources. Above all it was feared that, as a result of these measures against the Armenians, the Armenian majority would once more retreat, and at the same time Turkish-speaking ethnic groups would settle in Karabakh. In the autumn of 1991, when Karabakh declared its independence from Azerbaijan, of its approximately 180,000 inhabitants, 75 percent were Armenians and the rest Azeris.

During the Soviet era, Armenia was forced to forget about Karabakh. There were hardly any points of contact. The Karabakhis that wanted their children baptized by the Catholicos of Echmiadzin—for not a single priest was allowed to practice in Karabakh, nor did any church exist for religious ceremonies—had to make a wide detour through Kirovabad (Gyanje), as the direct connection via Lachin was interrupted. Hardly any Soviet Armenian ever visited Karabakh.

The low opinion of the supposedly hardheaded, boorish Karabakh Armenians sprouted into a passing patriotic enthusiasm only in the 1980s, when the

Karabakhis' complained against being forced to be part of Azerbaijan in a few months found a response in an Armenia weary of communism. This wave of enthusiasm for Karabakh carried the national democrat opposition to power, which immediately backpedaled. In view of the probable rejection on the part of the international community, neither of the governments of the second Armenian Republic ever dared to carry forward its original claims for reunification. Instead, Yerevan limited itself to backing Karabakh, guaranteeing it the right to self-determination. This readiness became from then on a *conditio* sine qua non in Armenian politics, at least among the intellectual opinion-makers. President Levon Ter-Petrossian had to resign in 1998, after he had signalled his readiness to negotiate a conflict settlement below the independence of Karabakh. The then influential league of veterans, Yerkrapah, struggled for the support of Karabakh to be kept as a decisive patriotic criterion. This organization represented the interests of some 5,000 citizens of the Armenian Republic, it acted as unsalaried border guards from 1988 on, then fought and suffered as a volunteer corps in Karabakh.

Many see Karabakh today as the cause of the appalling standard of living, without bearing in mind that, there, the situation is even more difficult. Still, Karabakh depends unconditionally on Armenia's goodwill, political stability, and economic aid, even if its inhabitants are happy at not being administrated from Yerevan as the eleventh province of Armenia, but govern themselves from their capital, Stepanakert.

The speeches in the village square that damp, foggy afternoon in May 2001, were inevitably followed by a reception for the visitors at the mayor's house. In the narrow room with its long table it was soon warm. Cognac and vodka flowed, and fresh herbs, fragrant bread with herbs, roast chicken and pork, the tastiest cold and hot salads, and preserved and pickled vegetables were lavishly offered to the visitors. In these regions hospitality is a must, even to the point of being left penniless. Between the formal toasts, speeches, and official replies, the talk became ever more relaxed on the wings of warmth, alcohol, and affection. The survivor teacher finally dared to ask the foreigners an important question: "What do you suppose is going to become of us? Will our little republic finally be recognized?" And, without waiting for the answer, she said, "It's all the same. One thing is clear: we will never live under a Turkish regime, never, as long as we live. We'll be free, or dead, or expelled. But, in the meantime, is it possible that the world will accept our existence? There are many here who think that each year we exist is one more step toward recognition."

Notes

1. Quote from a letter by Christa Lörcher of March 22, 2000, to the president of the *Gesellschaft für bedrohte Völker* (Society for Threatened Peoples), Tilmann Zülch.
2. The first republic was established at the end of May 1918, as a product of the fall of the Russian Empire, with a brief unification of the three Transcaucasian states. Its government handed over power in late November 1920 to a military revolutionary

procommunist committee, in order to prevent total occupation and probable massacre by Kemalist Turkey.

3. The historical region of settlement of 300,000 square kilometers, extended from the Little Caucasus to the middle of the length of the Euphrates in the west. The area known as Little Armenia or Armenia Minor by the (eastern) Romans was added to this. Armenia achieved its greatest extension in the first century BC under its king Tigran II Artashian (the Great, who ruled 95–55 BC). At that period the north of Syria, Cilicia, Lebanon, and Palestine also came under the Armenian sphere of influence.

4. Stübinger, Martin: *Reisebericht Armenien* (Travel Account, Armenia), July 15–21, 2002, Vienna, ÖRK/ACCORD, September 2002, p. 32. Internet: www.ecoi. net/pub/ms86_acc-arm0902.pdf

2

THE ARMENIAN GENOCIDE: AN INTERPRETATION

Vahakn N. Dadrian

The year 2005 was the ninetieth anniversary of the Armenian genocide, the first major genocide of the twentieth century. It began with the arrest of the leading intellectuals and community leaders in Constantinople on April 24, 1915, the date on which Armenians all over the world remember their murdered forebears year after year. Up to 1.5 million Armenians of the Ottoman Empire lost their lives in a brutal way. To this day, this decisive experience shapes the historical memory of the nation, which inhabited the fertile land enclosed by the Bosporus, the Euphrates, and the Tigris many centuries before the Turks. The mass murder of Armenians carried out during World War I is still important, for a number of reasons.

To begin with, this genocide was the climax of a series of previous massacres. Before 1914, the most serious were those of 1894 to 1896, instigated by Abdul Hamid II, known as the "bloody Sultan," in which 200,000 Armenians lost their lives. On July 23, 1908, the Young Turks overthrew the Sultan's regime by *a coup d'état*, forcing the sultan to restore the constitution of 1876. For the Armenians, this was a day of rejoicing, because the constitution protected them from the sultan's despotic rule. The sultan's supporters, however, did not peacefully acquiesce to the loss of power, but staged a counter-coup in early 1909. During this period of tensions, another great massacre occurred in Cilicia, in which some 25,000 Armenians died.

The Young Turks came out the winners in this struggle. For the Armenians, this regime offered great hopes, because the so-called Committee of Union and Progress (Ittihat ve Terakki Cemiyeti) flew the banner of the French Revolution, promising liberty, equality, and fraternity to all the inhabitants of the Ottoman Empire. It looked as though century-long despotism would give way to a constitutional system. As the largest Christian minority, the Armenians placed great hopes in this new elite, which seemed oriented toward Western values. The days in which the local Christians counted as third-class citizens thus appeared to be a thing of the past. But the Ittihadists very soon jettisoned their founding ideals and instituted a policy of radical Turkification in order to arrest the Empire's progressive decline. Under this plan, the Christian minority did not even enjoy a third-class position. The page of history would finally turn. The heads of the new government thereby became the fateful link between the massacres of the previous regime and the present one, which, under the cover of World War I, ended in the wholesale extermination of the Armenians.

Thus, the Armenian genocide is the final result of a long development marked by tensions, oppositions, and the bloody persecutions that ensued. The analysis of the Armenian genocide within the framework of historical persecutions and massacres belies the argument that it was a more or less natural result of World War I, arising from the needs and the crisis produced by it. Likewise, the widespread opinion that the genocide was the result of its authors' "being misguided" must be discarded.

In order to understand the upsurge and the scope of the conflict, it is necessary to take into account the tradition of impunity accompanying genocidal crimes in that period. The massacres of the time of Abdul Hamid were committed without the institution of a subsequent criminal prosecution on either the national or the international level. The rival powers undertook to guarantee, through numerous agreements and treaties, the improvement of conditions for the Christians of the Ottoman Empire. But the agreements reached at the 1856 Paris Conference and the Berlin Congress of 1878 were non-binding. Thus there was no intervention in the constantly repeated massacres. This principle of impunity no doubt exerted an influence on the Ottomans' decision to set in motion a draconian action against the Armenians during World War I, who found themselves trapped in the throes of extinction.

Neither preventive measures nor retaliation was initiated by the foreign powers in the face of the murder of hundreds of thousands of Armenian men, women, and children. This encouraged the perpetrators to resort to a radical solution of the problem the Armenians supposedly posed. The unpunished massacres of the prewar period thus prove to be not only a cause, but even more a precondition of the subsequent genocide. The consequences of the principle of impunity must be taken into account when analyzing the genocide. Moreover, there is often an inner link between impunity and denial of the crime.

The whole gamut of denial that, even ninety years later, the Turkish state continues to uphold and foster with the same deliberateness gives the Armenian genocide additional meaning. For decades the Turkish elite has tried to hide the crimes under a shroud of silence and to prevent all public and political discussion of the subject. Researchers are still barred from some of the archives. The main weapon in the denial of the genocide is the classification of the Ottoman secret files as "proofs" that supposedly neutralize the accusation of genocide. The fact is that there is no possibility of examining the soundness of these "proofs," nor is the entire material at the complete disposal of the public. In order to make this denial campaign official, a so-called think tank was created at Ankara in April 2001 to give it all an air of legitimacy. At the Institute of Armenian Research, a branch of the Center of Euro-Asian Studies, about a dozen people are officially employed in the work of denying the genocide. They organize series of conferences, courses, and interviews. Publications and a quarterly periodical are used to proactively contest all claims of genocide. Even in the U.S.A., the Turks have managed, thanks to funds allotted for this purpose, to buy chairs in renowned universities and exert their influence there.

The Ottoman archives contain a multitude of official Turkish reports that must be put at the disposal of the public. But the fact that these sources are still not available has not prevented scholars from pursuing objective research using sources on the Armenian genocide, since the German Foreign Ministry archives have been open to anyone who wishes to examine the war files of the German Reich, Turkey's ally during World War I. To these must be added innumerable U.S., British, French, and Swiss documents sent by diplomats to their governments from Constantinople, as well as those of consuls and missionaries from the most far-flung outposts of the Ottoman Empire. The examination of these sources readily shows the cynical naming of the death marches as "relocation," which, according to present-day Turks, was simply a way of protecting victims from excesses. Whole villages and cities, Armenian for centuries, were evacuated, and their women, children, and elderly people transported along dusty roads to their death in the Mesopotamian desert. The Turkish general Ali Fuad Erden, who, as Chief of Staff of Cemal Pasha, the Commander-in-Chief of the Fourth Army in Damascus, could observe the columns of deportees, marching toward the nearby deserts of Mesopotamia, said: "No preparations have been made, nor have organizational measures been taken to shelter the hundreds of thousands of deportees."[1] That was the alleged "relocation." The pattern of denial arose even during World War I, while the genocide was in unrelenting progress.

Shortly after the war, between 1919 and 1921, due to Allied pressure some of the culprits were brought to trial and suffered punishment. Even here it was clear that the ethnic massacre of the Armenians—the term "genocide" was not created until quite some time later—was no fluke of history, but a crime organized on the state level and set in motion by zealous officials and unscrupulous militias. The military tribunal was not able to implement retributive justice, because most of the leaders had escaped abroad at the last minute—often to Berlin. Notwithstanding this, the evidence in the transcriptions of the trial show that the wholesale deportation of the victim population was no more than a means of liquidating the Armenians under the cover of the war. The incriminatory files of the tribunal later disappeared with the establishment of the Kemalist regime. Only "insiders" have any knowledge of the whereabouts of these historical documents.

The object of this essay is to examine how the Turks, months before going to war, conscripted Armenians of military age, which for the majority proved to be tantamount to a death sentence, since they were rapidly eliminated. The strategic process of getting rid of the remaining population will be explained by means of the example of Trabzon, on the Black Sea, and of Erzincan, south of the Pontic mountains.

Some Historical and Political Keys to the Genocide

At the core of the historical conflict between Turks and Armenians lies the struggle of the Armenians to eliminate the inequalities arising from the theocratic foundations of the multiethnic Ottoman Empire. The continual rigid prescriptions and prohibitions of Islamic canon law, codified in the Koran and the Sharia and interpreted and enforced by the Ottoman elite, led to a dichotomous political system, within which non-Muslims were assigned an inferior position (*milleti makhume*) and were thus treated by the Muslim majority (*milleti hakime*) as subordinates.

The Armenians' strivings for reforms and freedom were based on the ideals of the French Revolution and the success of the Balkan peoples in achieving independence by means of a gradual liberation from Ottoman domination. This emancipationist movement also inspired the Armenians. Their revolutionaries reacted more and more, and openly, to oppressive taxation and the constant overall injustice. The Ottomans' response was massacres, aimed at breaking the backbone of the Armenians' liberation movement. This precarious situation characterized the final decades of the nineteenth century. It was within this framework that the first Balkan war erupted in 1912.

The catastrophic defeat of the Ottoman army at the end of 1912 gave new encouragement to the Armenians' emancipationist aspirations. The decay of the Ottoman Empire also worried the "Committee of Union and Progress." News of the Armenians' reformist successes was consequently a shock for the Young Turks. After the 1908 revolution, the Young Turks (Ittihadists) staged a further one in January 1913. The torchbearers of this coup-like revolt took over the seat of the Ottoman government, the Sublime Porte, and overthrew the regime of the opposing "Liberty and Union" party (*Hürriyet ve Itilaf*), setting up a new government in its stead.

The coup led to a profound change in the structure of the Ottoman state. Key government positions were taken over by the top echelons of a political party organization whose philosophy was to monopolize state power. In addition, the Young Turks assured the steadiness of the support they needed from the distant provinces; they also consolidated their influence in the armed forces. The main founders of the party, Ismail Enver and Mehmet Talaat, became Defense and Interior Ministers, respectively. These managers of the internal and external politics of the state increasingly came to dominate the public and secret party programs.

As a result of the Balkan War, the Young Turks left their general headquarters in Saloniki and moved to Constantinople, where, in 1913, they held their annual party congress. By this time, the government was concentrated almost completely in the hands of the "Committee of Union and Progress." Ittihadists held all the key ministries. The party congress was a signal for the intensification of a nationalist policy, with Behaeddin Şakir and Mehmed Nazim gaining influence as top party leaders. Both were physicians by training. They were joined by the ideological guru of the Young Turks, Zia Gökalp. Together they led the party and the government, both in the public eye and behind the scenes, to a new stance toward the diverse non-Muslim peoples of the Ottoman Empire. Even the party leaders Enver and Talaat were influenced by them. The powerful trio of Şakir–Nazim–Gökalp became in time the central engine in the organization of the Armenian genocide. Their method was invariably influenced by nationalist objectives. The idea of a multiethnic Ottoman Empire was laid aside in favor of extreme pan-Turkism, according to which the non-Turks of the Empire did not even have the right to exist. In their effort to preserve what was left of the Empire, whose Balkan provinces had already become independent, the Turkification of the Empire became the central item on the political agenda. That this was directed principally against the Armenians was no coincidence: with a population of about 2.1 million, they were the most numerous Christian minority. Their area of influence was largely on the Empire's eastern frontier, which was geostrategically important as the border with the Empire's Russian rivals. To make matters worse, a conflict had been brewing for some time because of the Armenians' ambitions for emancipation. All this turned them into the principal target of the liquidation and expulsion set in motion in 1915, which was also intended as a weapon to deal with the Pontic Greeks, the Arameans, the Syriacs, and other Christians of Asia Minor.

However, to carry out the intended extermination of the Armenian people, the legal, organizational, and methodological conditions had to be created first. The destruction of large groups of the population, spread out over extensive territories and numerous cities, towns, and villages, often in mountainous areas, was no easy matter. The rule of "economy in lethal violence" also applies to mass murder. In this sense, the deportations during World War I were the acme of efficiency in murderous intent. The method proved functional, enabling the perpetrators to concentrate large portions of the population for targeting while disguising the real purpose of the measures: the extermination of the deportees. In their party congress of 1913, the Ittihadists, in accordance with article 12 of their party program, decided on a slight modification of article 36 of the Ottoman constitution, which article had already been altered in 1909. With this, the Young Turks created the legal preconditions to carry out forced deportations of large portions of the population pursuant to the authority's decrees. This legal manipulation allowed the cabinet to enact emergency laws. An essential prerequisite was the need for prompt action—a clause that afforded the Ittihadists ample freedom of maneuver. The original clause of the constitution, relative to the promulgation of emergency laws, by contrast, stipulated an emergency situation in which "the State must be defended from dangers and public security protected."

The outbreak of World War I provided the necessary opportunity to put the plans into practice. Just a few hours after Germany declared war on Russia, the Young Turk leaders signed a secret military and political pact with Germany. Shortly thereafter they dissolved Parliament for an indefinite period. This gave the Ittihadists and a handful of the party's central committee the power of decision in matters of war and peace. Finally a small group of ministers—Enver, the War Minister, Talaat, Minister of the Interior, Jemal Akhmed, Minister of the Navy, and Halil, the President of the Chamber of Deputies and later Foreign Minister— led the country to war. By means of a preemptive attack against Russian warships in the Black Sea, the Ottoman Turks took sides with the Germans in World War I after maintaining a status of armed neutrality for three months. Although there was a long series of reasons for making this aggressive decision, the Ittihadists admitted that the goal of solving the Armenian Question had been a major factor in their decision to declare war. It was not only Enver who hoped, under the cloak of the war, to put an end to the Armenians' reformist strivings: Navy Minister Jemal stated that widespread massacres were unavoidable if the reformist movement was to succeed. He said the "Committee of Union and Progress" had entered the war to prevent the success of the Armenian reformers. The preparations for this end were nearly completed.

The First Step of the Genocide: Recruitment and Elimination of Armenian Conscripts

Part of the strategy of the "economy of lethal violence" consists in rendering the victim population as defenseless as possible. A few hours after the secret military and political pact had been signed with the German Reich on August 2, 1914, the Ittihadist regime decreed a general mobilization. Every man fit for military service—Armenians included—was conscripted into the Ottoman army, beginning with the 20- to 45-year-old age group, then the 18- to 20-, and finally the 45- to 60-year-olds. When, in the course of the genocide, the Ottoman authorities constantly claimed that the mass deportations were unavoidable for reasons of military security, German and Austrian functionaries began to send dispatches questioning this pretext. As political and military allies, they were well enough informed to see through the Turks' feeble arguments. The German consul of Aleppo, Walter Roessler, wrote in his report of July 27, 1915, to Berlin: "In the absence of menfolk, nearly all of whom have been conscripted, how can women and children pose a threat?"[2] The German colonel, Stange, commander of part of the so-called "special" troops in eastern Turkey, questioned the Turkish military authorities' excuses that this was a military necessity aimed at preventing the constant threat of an Armenian uprising. In a report to his military superiors, Stange to the contrary said: "Save for a small fraction of them, all able-bodied Armenian men were recruited."[3] Therefore there was no valid reason to fear any serious uprising. Another high-ranking allied official, Major General

Pomiankowski, the Austrian representative in the Ottoman general staff, was even clearer: the Turks "began to massacre the able-bodied Armenian men ... in order to render the rest of the population defenseless."[4] The U.S. ambassador to the Ottoman Empire, Henry Morgenthau, noted, with regard to the scenes of the mass killing of the Armenian conscripts, that "in almost all cases the procedure was the same" and was carried out "in summary fashion." His opinion was emphatic: "Before Armenia could be slaughtered, Armenia must be made defenseless." In this sense, the ambassador reported to Washington on July 10, 1915 that "all the men from 20 to 45 are in the Turkish army."[5]

There are numerous eyewitness reports of the liquidation of Armenians fit for military service and of the subsequent massacre of the Armenian civilian population, which, compiled by Viscount Bryce and Arnold Toynbee, were published in London in 1916. Two of them will be constantly mentioned in this book. The Kavass of a branch of the Ottoman Bank in Trabzon, a Montenegrin, saw how "five hundred Armenian soldiers were disarmed, [and] then deported and massacred on the [road]." Subsequently the mass murder of the civilians began. "The river Yel Degirmeni brought down every day to the sea a number of corpses, mutilated and absolutely naked, the women with their breasts cut off."[6] Another report, by British missionary William N. Chambers, gives information on the situation at Adana, on the Mediterranean coast. On December 3, 1915, more than six months after the beginning of the planned deportations and massacres, he wrote: "The enormity is not so much in the torture, massacring, outrage, etc., as in the intention and effort to exterminate a nation. The Armenians in the past have endured massacre and outrage and persecution and oppression; this however shatters all hope for life and a future."[7]

The practice of wholesale butchery of Armenian recruits is confirmed by innumerable documents in the German Foreign Ministry archives. The vice-consul of Erzurum, von Scheubner-Richter, wrote in a report to Berlin on December 4, 1916, that General Halil, the uncle of War Minister Enver, ordered the "massacre of his Armenian ... battalions."[8] Halil's policy of exterminating Armenian soldiers is confirmed in the report of a Turkish officer who was part of his First Expeditionary Force: "All of the Armenian officers and soldiers of our Force were massacred by order of Halil Paşa." And further: "Halil had the entire Armenian population (men, women and children) in the areas of Bitlis, Mus, and Beyazit also massacred without pity. My company received a similar order. Many of the victims were buried alive in especially prepared ditches."[9]

This region in the vicinity of Lake Van, which today belongs to Turkey, had been the home of the ancient Urartians, the original eastern ancestors of the Armenians, many centuries before the Christian era. An Armenian lawyer named Gregory Tchalkhouchian has provided additional details. By means of a "Red Book" he compiled, he tried, in his own words, to lay bare the lies of the "White Book" the Ottoman authorities had published during the war. He wrote: "Upon orders of General Halil, 800 Armenian and another time 1,000 soldiers, officers, and MDs in his Expeditionary Force were disarmed and killed by the Turkish soldiers of that Force."[10] Halil was the commander of a number of different units of the Turkish Ottoman army, among them the Fifth Expeditionary Force, the Fifty-second Division, the Eighteenth Army Corps. In his war memoirs, he boasted of having killed "300,000 Armenians altogether," and added, "It can be more or less. I didn't count."[11]

The Turkish authorities maintained that the "neutralization" of the Armenian recruits was carried out due to cases of sabotage or the treason of individuals who joined the enemy camp. There were undoubtedly a few such cases. However, the preventive measures, consisting in separating and isolating the Armenians from the other recruits, were set in motion long before the beginning of the main fighting. Even the plan to disarm them and put them in work battalions was initiated weeks before Turkey entered the war. Armenian forced laborers also contributed in considerable measure to the construction of the Berlin–Baghdad railway. To be noted is a Turkish official document containing a ciphered telegram sent by General Hazan Izzet, then the supreme commander of the Third Army, with headquarters at Erzurum. It proves that by September 24, 1914, the decision had already been made to disarm the Armenians, that is, seven weeks after the secret alliance signed by Germany and Turkey and five before Turkey declared war. General Izzet's order, of which a copy was sent to the Ottoman General Staff, required "the disarming of the Armenians from this moment on, and as generally as possible." War Minister Enver issued a similar order shortly before putting his ill-fated offensive against Sarikamiş in operation. This order foresaw the formation of "militias," for which Muslims who had not been mustered as conscripts were to be recruited. Both the renowned Turkish scholar of political science, Tarik Zafer Tunaya,[12] and Arif Cemil[13], the representative of the Special Organization, declare that the militias were no more than gangs of convicts and "bandits." These were the "operational" elements of the Special Organization. These gangs of murderers were the Ittihadists' most important instrument in the anti-Armenian plan.

German sources also confirm the disarming and liquidation procedures. Due to the deficient organization of the Ottoman army, the objectives were not carried out everywhere in the same way or to the same extent.

There were unusual cases in which the actual annihilation was postponed when, for instance, the disarmed Armenian soldiers were needed immediately for forced labor, as also happened with the 2,000 or 2,500 Armenians of Sivas. It was only in the summer of 1916, that they were bound together with special ropes and murdered in the Kizildere valley near Gemerek, northeast of Kaysen. A brave Turkish commander, General Vehib, sent the two main perpetrators to the gallows after a court-martial.

As the war went on, new possibilities arose to increase the anti-Armenian measures. In this respect, two important events in the war against Russia in eastern Turkey must be mentioned that accentuated the conflict between Turks and Armenians. In both cases, the Armenians were involved as fighters, and in each the Turkish offensive suffered equally serious setbacks, as did the political-strategic plan that gave rise to them. The first was the shattering defeat suffered by the Turks at the hands of the Russians at Sarikamiş in January 1915. According to some reports, Armenian volunteers contributed measurably to the Russian victory. The other example was the Armenian uprising at Van from April 20 to May 17, 1915. Before the Armenians at Van revolted in despair of escaping the butchery that awaited them, numerous villages in the province had already fallen victim to bloody massacres. The pertinent reports of German and Austrian envoys can be read in the archives. These statements by foreign observers have been confirmed by two Ottoman provincial governors. In his postwar memoirs, the governor-general of Van province disclosed that the Ittihadists had goaded the Muslim population into attacking the Armenians.[14] The governor-general of Erzurum, who had been the governor of Van before the uprising, complained of these happenings to Talaat. "I swear the Van uprising would never have taken place, and never needed to happen. We are to blame for it, having done everything possible [to provoke the Armenians] and this is how we brought about an insurrection that we can no longer control."[15]

There is no doubt that a number of Armenian soldiers deserted from the Ottoman army as soon as they were within reach of the enemy lines. This also happened in some battles against the Russian Caucasus army in eastern Turkey. The constant ill treatment that Armenian recruits suffered from their Muslim peers contributed to this decision. Essentially, the desertions reflected a deep longing for liberation from the heavy burden of a tyrannical system. It is also true that there were individual cases of spying and sabotage. These incidents, however, were not restricted to Armenians, but were especially frequent among the Muslim Kurds and even among some Turks. The sporadic cases were blown up by the Turks and used as a pretext for a campaign of extermination against the Armenians. The experiences of Sarikamiş and Van as well as the desertions of individual soldiers and isolated cases of espionage served as catalysts. The extermination campaign was soon extended to the whole population. In this respect, the events at Erzincan and Trabzon are revealing.

The case of Erzincan will be described below, where a certain type of deadly experiment prepared the ground for medical murders, which would later become an element of the Armenian genocide.

Erzincan: Murder in the Name of Medicine

Each genocidal campaign follows its own logic. In the case of the Armenians, an unusual factor involved a perverted practice of epidemiology, which led to a very particular form of preventive medicine. The leaders of the Special Organization, who were central in developing this program, defamed their Armenian victims as "microbes" or "tumors" that, in their opinion, were devouring the Empire. With such a contemptuous attitude toward people, their cohorts devised medical experiments with lethal results, in which young Armenian men served as guinea pigs.[16]

The opportunity appeared at the beginning of the war, when various epidemics and contagious diseases were spreading. The already miserable sanitary and hygienic conditions took a turn for the worse during the war, leading to illness-induced deaths in the army ranks. A noted Turkish military historian also blamed sanitary conditions and lack of vaccines for the losses sustained by the Third Army,[17] whose defenseless soldiers had been exposed to the effects of the devastating epidemics. Relying on statistics, he stated that, in the course of World War I, the Third Army alone suffered a total of 128,698 deaths on account of this deficiency. An official Turkish doctor also referred to this problem, stating that even before the onset of major battles, such as Sarikamiş, "the typhus epidemics had wreaked havoc in the army, causing the death of tens of thousands of soldiers."[18]

The chief of the Third Army's Sanitation and Health Service, physician Tevfik Salim (who later adopted the surname Saglam), then issued orders for studies on typhus, with the aim of discovering a serum against it. The experiments were carried out at the Central Hospital of Erzincan, some 180 km south of Trabzon. Two groups of young Armenian men were selected for them. One, a fairly numerous group, consisted of disarmed Armenians who were being used for various types of labor; the other group, of around 200 Armenians, were enrolled in Erzincan's two military schools. In order to discover a typhus vaccine, a large portion of the Armenians being trained at the reservist school and, along with them, the labor battalion soldiers were subjected to experiments, which were ultimately fatal. The physician Behaeddin Şakir, one of the main architects of the Armenian genocide, was also indirectly involved in the lethal project. He was able to secure the transfer of Dr. Hamdi Suat from his job at the Istanbul University Medical School in order to travel first to Erzurum and thence to Erzincan, where he would carry out his deadly experiments at the Central Hospital.

Hamdi Suat (Aknar), who had studied in Munich, was a Professor of Pathology at Istanbul University Medical School. His research was directed at finding antibodies that would produce a certain immunity to typhus. To this end, he injected hundreds of Armenians with typhus-contaminated blood. He employed the defibrination method, which consists in separating the denser and lighter elements by centrifugation, in order to obtain an injectable serum. With these experiments the professor hoped to determine the diverse effects of the serum on the different body organs, such as the heart, brain, and liver. Dr. Suat's Turkish colleagues openly acknowledged that the experiments had been lethal, because Dr. Suat had purposely bypassed the method of "deactivating" the infected blood.[19] When these facts were made public after the cease-fire and groups of experts were commissioned by the Turkish military tribunals to look into the case, Professor Suat was undergoing psychiatric treatment for "acute psychosis" at the Medical School clinic. Despite all this, he is nowadays honored in Turkey as "the father" of bacteriology in Turkey.[20] A commemorative museum erected in his name on the grounds of the University of Istanbul in Beyazit bears witness to this honor.

In an extensive study in 1990, German medical historian Helmut Becker investigated these experiments carried out by Hamdi Suat, pointing out that both Süleyman Numan, Chief Medical Officer of the Ottoman Armed Forces, and Talaat's Interior Ministry had approved them. But there were also protests against the experiments from within their own ranks. Becker establishes with abundant detail, on the basis of documents at the Bavarian Central Archives (section IV of the war archive), the fact of the protest by Professor Georg Mayer, Süleyman Numan's German deputy, as well as that of Marshall Liman von Sanders, Chief of the German Military Mission in Turkey. Both of them had unsuccessfully tried to prevent the experiments carried out on the Armenians. What is more, War Minister Enver, the de facto Commander-in-Chief of the Ottoman Armed Forces, did not comply with the numerous requests for him to intervene and forbid "these injections, which can infect even monkeys, and which are not only devoid of scientific merit but are unconscionable as well." According to Becker, Professor Mayer first heard of the deadly experiments from the German consul at Erzurum. The German consul of Trabzon also reported sixty-five men dead on account of the infected injections. Without mentioning the Armenians directly, Professor Mayer expressed indignation at sacrificing young cadets at the Erzincan Military School. He found it hard to explain why the experiments had been carried out. The governor general of Erzurum province thanked Talaat for his support for the experiments. It is more than likely that he felt obliged to do so "in order to cover up the unhappy outcomes."[21]

To understand the genocidal nature of the fatal experiments, it is necessary to bear in mind the course of events. While the Turkish authorities were still engaged in taking to court those responsible for the deportations and massacres of Armenians, an Armenian doctor who had survived disclosed details of the murders carried out in the name of medicine. In an article called, "The Turkish Physicians Too Are Complicit," he documented the active participation of a host of Turkish military physicians.[22] He offered to identify the culprits in a properly instituted juridical venue and to testify against them. The ministry's health service promptly denied the charge. The shamelessness of this official denial caused two Turkish doctors who had first-hand knowledge about these experiments such indignation that they appealed to public opinion, offering information, including the names of the doctors who had carried out the experiments. One of the two doctors who protested, the surgeon Cemal Haydar, criticized the habit of denial, "customary among the Turkish authorities," in the Istanbul newspaper *Türkce Istanbul* of December 23, 1918.

In an open letter to the Interior Minister, Dr. Haydar wrote:

> The blood of typhoid fever patients was inoculated into innocent Armenians without rendering that blood "inactive." The subjects were duped [*igfal*] into believing that they were being inoculated against typhus. The experiments were of the kind whose

application medical science allows only for animals slated for vivisection. When publishing the results of these criminal experiments, of which I personally was a close witness, the esteemed professor simply stated that the subjects were men condemned to death, without identifying them as Armenians whose sole guilt was that they belonged to the Armenian people.[23]

After identifying the two chief physicians of the Erzincan Central Hospital and the Red Crescent Hospital as authorities with intimate knowledge about these tests, Haydar declared, "I am able to furnish the requisite explanations on the matter" and sought the help of the Interior Ministry's Commission of Inquiry of Misdeeds.[24] This commission had been created to gather all the evidence from pretrial oral and written statements, as a result of which those responsible for the "Armenian deportations and massacres" were made to appear before the military court. Seeking help, he appealed to the authorities' sense of honor and conscience. He further declared that the tribunal should also be empowered to demand the handing over of the hospital records, in which the doctors should have registered the names of the patients they treated, and thus prove that those innocent victims had not been criminals. Surgeon Dr. Haydar denounced the fact of allowing these deeds to sink into oblivion as unscrupulousness. He said, "The barbarities committed against the Armenians were not only an administrative but a scientific crime as well and as such they constitute a stain on the medical profession."[25]

Dr. Haydar's declarations were seconded by Dr. Salaheddin, the chief physician at the Red Crescent Hospital in Erzincan. His statement was published the following day in the same Turkish newspaper. He lamented having known about the experiments that were carried out at the Erzincan Central Hospital and said he was more than ready to help in having those responsible punished, which would relieve his conscience and remove a great burden from the dishonored medical profession and Turkish society itself. The Armenians, Dr. Haydar went on to say, obviously terrorized by the atrocities that were going on around them, were victims of experiments for which only laboratory animals such as guinea pigs or rabbits are used. They were based on an unproven theory and were very risky procedures.

> [A] large number of Armenians succumbed to these inhuman experiments, they hardly contributed to the health of others ... No positive results whatsoever were obtained. The unfortunate Armenians, whose existence was relegated to levels lower than that of animals, were victimized in the name of certain obscure points of science. As far as I remember, the blood taken from these typhus-infected Armenian subjects was used to inoculate Erzurum's Governor Tahsin—after having been rendered "inactive," as required by the ad hoc rules of medicine.[26]

When the Ministry of Defense denied these allegations, surgeons Haydar and Salaheddin each published a second letter. Haydar stated once more that "hundreds" of young Armenians had been killed by experiments with typhus serum, by which the good name of Turkish medicine was stained forever. He felt ashamed that so many medical schools and doctors continued to remain silent, in the false belief that in this way they would preserve the honor of their profession.

The Defense Ministry denied only the existence of an order or authorization for the experiments to be carried out, but not that they had taken place. As for Dr. Salaheddin, he stated that, "to his surprise," he had been pressured into keeping quiet about the whole affair, while many "ignorant doctors" were readier to conceal the facts than to reveal them.

Professor Hamdi Suat and his accomplices were lucky and escaped their rightful punishment, as did many others responsible for the Armenian genocide, from the initiators to the executors and even the bureaucrats involved. Suat was even able to publish the results of his experiments in the German *Zeitschrift für Hygiene und Infektionskrankheiten* (Journal of Hygiene and Infectious Diseases) in 1916 and, in 1918, in the Journal of Military Medicine (*Ceride-i Tibbiyi-e Askeriyye*). Had these medical murders been merely an isolated case, perhaps the delirium of a mentally ill or inhuman professor, they would be of little importance in the framework of the Armenian genocide. But Dr. Suat worked within a system. He had superiors, assistants, and, above all, colleagues, who insisted on keeping quiet. In fact, some of these did not hesitate to exert all kinds of pressure upon the two courageous chief physicians who demanded justice in the name of the victims and the honor of their profession.

Historical research has shown that Professor Hamdi Suat—who carried out the lethal experiments—was no more than a cog in the machinery. Genocides begin by dehumanizing the victims. From the analysis of political speeches it is already clear that the Armenians, from being a tolerated minority, had been branded a nefarious pathogen in the body of the Ottoman Empire.

A U.S. State Department document states that Armenian doctors at the Aziziye hospital in Erzincan were also victims of the planned extermination, according to the testimony of Greek physician Dr. Vassilaki. The victims also included Armenian pharmacists and dentists. Erzincan is just one example among others. Two nurses, one American and the other German, who worked at the military hospital at Bitlis, hundreds of kilometers away, reported the killing of all Armenian nurses, pharmacists, and sanitary assistants. "It mattered not that they were the most intelligent and faithful helpers and that there was no one left to prepare medicines for the Turkish patients—all had to go."[27]

Trabzon: Medical Killings of Babies and Toddlers

The Turkish state still upholds the official thesis that the deportation of the Armenian population of the Ottoman Empire was a self-defense measure necessitated by the war. However, even supposing every Armenian male of military age had been a revolutionary, deserter, or spy, how could defenseless children be a threat to the state? The murder of babies and infants in the city of Trabzon clearly shows that the Ottomans' objective was the annihilation of the

Armenian nation. The happenings in the picturesque town on the Black Sea coast demonstrate the extent to which professional physicians can become involved in criminal acts.

Dr. Ali Saib was the Director of the Trabzon Public Health and Sanitation Services, which means that he had authority over the Red Crescent hospital. When the Armenians were deported from Trabzon in the summer of 1915, he ordered the murder of many Armenian patients, but especially of many children. The Istanbul trials after the war brought innumerable proofs of these deeds into the open. The tribunal sent Health Service inspector Dr. Zia Fuad to interrogate the medical staff there about Dr. Saib's actions. In the "Fuad Report," included in the protocol in April 1919, Dr. Saib is accused of having poisoned several of the Armenian patients. In general, the poison was administered to the patients in their drinking glasses, telling them it was a vaccine. Whoever refused to drink was forced to do so, according to eyewitnesses. Just as in the Mesopotamian desert and in transit camps, it was common for them to receive injections of morphine and other lethal substances.

Hundreds of orphan children in Trabzon were also victims of this ruthless doctor. There were at the time three thousand orphans in the care of the Greek Metropolitan who, however, could shelter them only temporarily. Those who were not distributed among Turkish families were taken to the Red Crescent hospital and some schools. Father Laurent, the French Capuchin Father Superior in Trabzon, testified at the Istanbul trial that he had personally seen the bodies of poisoned children squeezed into big deep baskets. They were later thrown into the Black Sea.

Another Turkish physician, Dr. Adnan, the director of the Trabzon Public Health Services, launched his own investigation and wrote a report. It too was read into the record at the military tribunal in Istanbul. The "Adnan Report" confirms the poisoning of the children at the schools and their "disposal in baskets." Besides poisoning, other methods were used in the schools. Dr. Saib had sterilizing chambers procured from the army, in which babies and infants were killed with superheated steam.[28]

The Extermination of Women and Children by Drowning

Most of the Armenian population was exterminated by means of "deportations," but the method of drowning was also used, mainly for women, including pregnant ones, as well as children, the sick, and the aged. On December 2, 1918, the former general and several-times minister, Çürüksulu Mahmud Paşa, branded the former provincial governor-general, Cemal Azmi, during a parliamentary debate, as the main culprit in the drownings. He was acting on orders from the party's CUP Central Committee. In December 1918, Deputy Hafiz Mehmed declared in the parliament:

God will punish us for what we did ... the matter is too obvious to be denied. I personally witnessed this Armenian occurrence in the port city of Ordu [about 155 km west of Trabzon]. Under the pretext of sending them off to Samsun, another port city on the Black Sea [about 255 km west of Trabzon], the district governor loaded the Armenians on vessels and had them thrown overboard. I have heard that the governor general applied this procedure [throughout the province]. Even though I reported this at the Interior Ministry immediately upon my return to Istanbul ... I was unable to initiate any action against the latter; I tried for some three years to get such action instituted but in vain.[29]

The governor of Ordu, Faik by name, personally oversaw the drownings. A Turkish trader declared in May 1919 at the Trabzon trial series: "I saw Kaymakam Faik one afternoon load two barges with women and children, supposedly to take them to Samsun. But the boats, which needed two days for the journey, returned in two hours instead, as the corpses of the victims began to be sighted near the shoreline."[30] The military court's verdict specifically mentioned the crime of the drownings. The Austro-Hungarian consul of Trabzon, Ernst von Kwiatkowski, wrote about the drowning of women and children out at sea in his reports. Even the German consul, Heinrich Bergfeld, who was pro-Turkish in his general attitude, informed Berlin that he and his colleagues were in agreement that what was going on amounted to "mass murder."[31] The German Colonel Stange, who played an active role in the Turkish army, informed his superior, Marshall Liman von Sanders, about the happenings at Trabzon:

At Trabzon Armenians were transported out to sea, and then thrown overboard ... The military reasons for this were very secondary. It was rather the case of a favorable opportunity, when protests from abroad were not likely, to carry forward a long-cherished plan of substantially weakening the Armenian population, if not to exterminate them outright. Military reasons and seditious tumults in different locations provided handy pretexts.[32]

Conclusions

The Armenian genocide in the Ottoman Empire was anything but a byproduct of World War I. It was the first great planned genocide of the twentieth century. Its methods, degree of organization, and brutality were the forerunners of many other genocides that spelled disaster for other victim groups, usually defenseless ones. What makes it even more unbearable is that present-day Turkey, the legal heir of the Ottoman Empire, denies the great catastrophe. It was Turks themselves who accused, tried, and sentenced the main culprits in the courts-martial at the end of the war. Still, with the exception of a few courageous Turks, all this seems to have been forgotten. A veritable industry of denial appears to have taken its place, whose deliberate aim is to sow doubt about the historical facts, inside and outside Turkey. Political pressure is brought to bear on foreign governments not to recognize the truth. Yet the weight of historical evidence is so overwhelming that Turkey will not be able to go on denying this dark chapter of its history. More and more parliaments around the world, but mainly impartial Western specialists and historians, see it this way, and urge Turkey to recognize the Armenian genocide, in order to clear the way to a possible reconciliation.

Notes

1. (General) Ali Fuad Erden, *Birinci Dünya Harbinde Suriye Hatiralari* (Memoirs of the First World War in Syria), vol. 1, Istanbul 1954, p. 122.
2. German Foreign Ministry archives (FM), Turkey 183/38, A 23991.
3. FM, Embassy in Constantinople (BoKon) 170, No. 3841, "Secret" Report, August 23, 1915.
4. Joseph Pomiankowski, *Der Zusammenbruch des Ottomanischen Reiches* (The collapse of the Ottoman Empire), Graz 1969, p. 160.
5. Henry Morgenthau, *Ambassador Morgenthau's Story*, Garden City, N.Y., 1918, pp. 302ff. See also his report of July 10, 1915, U.S. National Archives, RG 59, 867.4016/74.
6. James Bryce (ed.), *The Treatment of Armenians in the Ottoman Empire, 1915–1916. Documents Presented to Viscount Grey of Fallodon by Viscount Bryce*. Compiled by Arnold Toynbee, London 1916. New ed.: Princeton 2000, Document 74, p. 319.
7. Bryce/Toynbee, ibid., Doc. 128, pp. 511ff.
8. FM, Turkey 183/45, A 33457.
9. "Les massacres d'Arménie d'après un témoin oculaire" (The massacres in Armenia according to an eyewitness), in *La Voix de l'Arménie* (The voice of Armenia), Vol. 1, No. 26 (15/XII/1918), p. 901.
10. Gregory Tchalkhouchian, *Le Livre rouge* (The red book), Paris 1919, pp. 43ff.
11. Halil Pasha, *Bitmeyen Savas* (The unending struggle), ed. M.T. Sorgún, Istanbul 1972, p. 274.
12. T. Z. Tunaya, *Türkiyede Siyasal Partiler* (Turkish political parties), vol. 3, Istanbul 1989, p. 282.
13. Arif Cemal, *Ici Dünya Savasinda Teskilât-i Mahsusa* (The Special Organization in World War I), Istanbul 1997, pp. 44, 58.
14. Ibrahim Arvas, *Tarihi Hakikatler* (Historical truths), Ankara 1964, p. 6.
15. Hasan Tahsin, "Kasem ederim ki Vanda ihtilâl olmazdi. Kendimiz zorlaya zorlaya su içinden çikamadigimiz kargasaligi meydana getirdik." See Archives of the patriarchate (Jerusalem), Series 17, File H, Doc. 571, 572.
16. For more detail, see Vahakn N. Dadrian, "The Role of the Turkish Physicians in the World War I Genocide of the Ottoman Armenians," in *Holocaust and Genocide Studies*, vol. 1, No. 2, 1986, pp. 169–192.
17. (General) Fahri Belen, *Birinci Cihan Harbinde Türk Harbi* (Turkey's war during World War I), Ankara 1966, p. 194.
18. Dr. Rifat Gözberk, in *Hürriyet* (a Turkish newspaper), June 28, 1969.
19. *Türkce Istanbul*, December 23–24, 1918.
20. Türk mikrobiyolojisinin Babasi.
21. On what follows, see Helmut Becker, *Äskulap zwischen Reichsadler und Halbmond* (Aesculapius between the Reich eagle and the crescent), Herzogenrath 1990, pp. 152ff.

22. Mihran Norair, "Turk Pushisgnern Al Mechsageetz" (Turkish Physicians Foo one complicit) in *Ariamard* (also *Azadamard*), December 15, 1918. The French translation of the article appeared in *Renaissance* (French newspaper of Istanbul), December 16, 1918, and once more in Turkish in *Yeni Gazete*, December 17, 1918.
23. *Türkce Istanbul*, December 23, 1918.
24. Tedkik-i-Seyyîat Komisyonu.
25. *Türkce Istanbul*, December 23, 1918. See also Dadrian, "Role of Turkish Physicians", pp. 177ff.
26. *Türkce Istanbul*, December 24, 1918, and ibid., pp. 178f.
27. Grace Knapp, *The Tragedy of Bitlis*, London/Edinburgh 1919, p. 54.
28. On this, see also Vahakn N. Dadrian: "The Armenian Genocide: An Interpretation," in Jay Winter (ed.), *America and the Armenian Genocide of 1915*, Cambridge, MA, 2003, pp. 77–80.
29. *Meclisi Mebusan Zabit Ceridesi* (Transcription of the minutes of the chamber of deputies), 3rd electoral period, 5th period of sessions, 24th session, December 1, 1918, p. 299.
30. *Hadisat* (a Turkish newspaper), May 7, 1919.
31. FM, Botschaft Konstantinopel/Embassy in Constantinopel (BoKon) 169, No. 7, Folio 135 (4002), June 29, 1915.
32. FM Turkey 183/38; (BoKon) 170, No. 3841, "Secret" report, August 23, 1915.

3

THE TURKISH DENIAL OF THE ARMENIAN GENOCIDE IN ITS EUROPEAN CONTEXT

Taner Akçam

The European Parliament has recognized the Armenian genocide through several resolutions. The first and most important was "Towards a Political Solution of the Armenian" Question of June 18, 1987. In it, recognition is established as one of the preconditions for Turkey's acceptance into the European Union. This made clear at the same time that the matter was not purely historical but also political. On February 28, 2002, the European Parliament reaffirmed by a wide majority its requirement that Turkey recognize the genocide before it can become a member of the EU. This position gives rise to a number of questions: Should recognition be a precondition for Turkey to be accepted, when the country is going through radical changes? Is it possible to build a democracy without accepting historical facts? What is more important, democratization or recognition of history? Is the ruling elite honestly interested in the internal dynamics of the move toward democracy put in motion by the aim of joining the EU? Or are the barriers slowing down democratization welcome, as this would entail a loss of their privileges? We will try and answer these questions in what follows.

Not only the European Parliament but also the parliament, of almost twenty nations have enacted, from 1965 on, resolutions, decisions, or laws whereby the Armenian genocide must be recognized according to the UN Genocide Convention of 1948. Among these countries are the U.S.A. (House of Representatives, 1975) and Russia (National Duma, 1995), as well as Canada (2004) and the parliaments of EU members, such as Greece (1996), France (1998/2001), Sweden (2000), Italy (2000), and Poland. Most recently, the German Bundestag voted a motion in which Turkey is asked to come to terms with its national history. They all seem to have become a battleground in the Turkish–Armenian conflict. If the EU considers the Armenian genocide an important issue, it cannot be dealt with only in the parliament, but also in other forums, and with a view to elaborating long-range conflict-solving strategies. At the same time, the EU must respect the fact that this is a problem of the Turks and the Armenians, and attempt to promote a solution that will lead to a more harmonious coexistence of the two countries. It has to bring about conditions that will allow the two countries to come face to face in a productive way. This leads us to the subject of resolving conflicts, and the relevant role third parties can play.

How do Outsiders See the Conflict?

Seen from the outside, there are two parties in the Turkish–Armenian conflict: on one hand, the Turkish state and its nationalist interpretation of history, which disregards all consideration of the historical context of World War I—particularly the genocide; on the other, the Armenian state and the diaspora, whose position has been adopted, to a large extent, as a reaction to the Turkish state. Both sides seem to be waging a political and psychological war, in which the options are apparently either to affirm or deny the genocide. The Armenian diaspora, helped by the intervention of the Western powers and public opinion, are trying to oblige Turkey to recognize the facts. Turkey, instead, makes use of its political and military power in the region to keep third parties out. It is no exaggeration to say that both sides make use of history in their present relations. It is a long time since the historical facts were discussed without reproach. History has rather become an instrument in the present-day debate.

It is clear that the Turkish position, with its insistence on not recognizing the existence of a historical problem, has led to this division into two camps. The Turkish state feels strong enough to set the rules of the game in the debates, absolutely rejecting every Armenian claim regarding the genocide. This leaves the pressure of third parties as the only possible way out for the Armenians.

That the Armenians place such significance on the Turkish recognition of the genocide is owed to several reasons. It is well known that victims of such humanitarian catastrophes suffer a "second traumatization" when their original suffering is not recognized. Armenian identity is also menaced by living in the Diaspora. In this sense, the genocide becomes a unifying element among Armenians spread out across the world. Thus, the genocide has become an essential factor in Armenian identity. One of their main common objectives during the last decades has been to get the support of third parties in their struggle for Turkish recognition.

In turn, Turkey has responded to this strategy by making use of abundant resources and the strategic position of the region to prevent those international organizations from recognizing the genocide, by means of lobbies and investments of millions of dollars.

In short, it can be said that both sides have put in operation a strategy of convincing third parties. Public opinion, parliaments, and other international institutions have been turned into fundamental arenas in which to ventilate the Turko-Armenian conflict. The relevant questions here are: Can this conflict be resolved by unilaterally convincing outsiders? Does such a strategy work as a solution to the problem, or does it simply create additional problems?

The Advantages and Disadvantages of Unilaterally Convincing Third Parties

It is possible to see certain advantages and disadvantages in the strategy of convincing third parties. Recognition by national parliaments is a kind of surrogate in the face of Turkish nonrecognition. In addition, the diaspora Armenians, as citizens of those countries, are naturally and democratically entitled to request it. It is the only means by which Armenians manage to keep the matter alive. The fact that it is only talked about in Turkey when it comes up in other parliaments proves this.

Its airing in national parliaments results only in Turkish rage and hate toward others and, specially, against the Armenians. But this is also what leads to its being debated in Turkey itself. Unfortunately, it is the only opportunity for internal critics to be listened to and for the Armenian community to express its grief. I feel that, notwithstanding the Turks' negative reactions, it also has salutary effects, as ever more Turks are beginning to ask questions about the true facts.

As convincing as our arguments may be against the resolutions of other parliaments, we must acknowledge that this is the only way the matter can be kept on the front burner in Turkey so long as it is impossible to talk about it publicly. The Turkish state does not wish the issue to be brought out into the open, which is why it is against its treatment by other parliaments. The Armenians worry that it may be forgotten unless it is debated in foreign parliaments, which the Turks' behaviour so far justifies.

In view of this, it is no use simply to reject the resolutions and interference of outsiders, or to yell and rage against the resolutions of their parliaments. It would be better to look for alternative means and forums since, otherwise, parliamentary resolutions are the only resource the Armenians have at their disposal. I do not think it is decisive whether parliaments recognize the genocide or not, but some way should be devised to defuse the conflict through constructive debate. This will only happen once the Armenians feel their claims and their grief are paid due attention.

On the negative side, there are also disadvantages in recognition coming exclusively from foreign parliaments and third parties. Each party in the conflict is obviously ready to give whoever it wishes to convince unlimited opportunities, yet this position can never be neutral, and so it will not lead to a solution. Even outsiders tend to use the problem for their own benefit—and in this way the problem is extended, besides producing additional difficulties. The second drawback is that the adversaries waive the possibility of solving the problem on their own, and in this way recognize and give others to understand that they themselves are part of the problem. This renders them not only vulnerable to others, but also susceptible to their demands.

The strategy of involving outsiders is also costly in economic terms and effort, producing additional problems and often backfiring. (The clearest example was the French government's attempt to bring the subject of the genocide into play in order to sell Turkey helicopters.) One final disadvantage is that both parties will look on the other as an enemy, giving rise to stereotypes. All these inconveniences do nothing more than worsen relations between the conflicting parties.

It is not my intention to impugn with this the intervention of outsiders when the opponents are unable to solve the problem on their own. The key question is how they should intervene. It is essential that the opposing parties feel that whoever intervenes has constructive intentions. Thus both sides must agree on who is to mediate for it to be effective. To this end a program must be devised that will enable mutual understanding, so that the two sides can solve their problem. This is something that so far has not happened in the Turko-Armenian conflict.

What Is the Cause of the Problem?

The parties in conflict generally consider the root of the problem to be the disagreement as regards the historical occurrences. Yet this is so only to a certain degree. If it were just a question of discussing history, the true facts would very soon be established on the basis of the more than sufficient official and nonofficial documentation that exists. These documents, however, are in diverse languages and places. What must then be done is to set up a "Truth Commission" that will study the documents. These must be available to everyone so that a serious debate can take place. In other words, the first step is the creation of a common body of knowledge.

Such initiatives have never prospered, especially in Turkey, which indicates problems beyond the discord itself. Thus the relationship between the two sides is as important as events of the past, if not more so. These are used to reinforce mutual prejudices. Each side is only interested in pointing at the other, or backing up existing points of view with new evidence. That shows that both are preventing reconciliation, increasing the "trauma-guilt account" in order to use it in the next discussion.

Owing to this behaviour each side has developed a very negative idea of the other, which it resorts to at all times. As a general rule, dehumanized images of others exist in the depths of the mentality of opposed ethnic or religious groups, including the belief that the "other side" is the enemy, deceitful, aggressive, and incapable of improving. This is also true in the Turko-Armenian conflict. In referring to the events of 1915, each party has evolved its own vocabulary, which exacerbates animosity. Thus, "the other" seems to hinder the solution of the conflict. The opposing sides indeed have a differentiated self-awareness, while regarding the other as a stereotype. For as long as these attitudes, impressions, and mentalities remain unchanged, a solution is unthinkable.

As I see it, it is necessary to clearly point out the distinction between the problem itself and the way it is dealt with. So far, the way it has been handled has resulted in additional problems. One special complication lies in the fact that we are talking about events almost a century old. Why regard the other side—and this goes especially for the Turkish state—as an enemy instead of giving it the chance to cooperate in the solution of the problem? Even a hundred years later, both camps seem caught up in the psychological tangles of 1915.

There is yet another reason for the persistence of monolithic, stereotyped images, as the parties are more interested in hanging on to the problem than in solving it. Both sides, particularly their nationalist circles, have developed their points of view and their identity in opposition to an imagined enemy. In the case of Turkey's ruling elite, these pursue an anti-Armenian policy so as to bolster up Turkish society's national identity. If the Turkish state changed its stance toward the genocide, it would have to rewrite its entire history. Certain Armenian circles also find the image of the Turks as barbarians and savages useful. They maintain, for instance, that the tendency to commit massacres is hereditary in Turks. In other words, the nationalists of each side use hatred to gather their countrymen around them.

In order to clear away this obstacle, party interests must be left aside, which can only happen if both sides sit down at the conference table and so develop a realistic image of the others. The first step in solving the conflict is to give up the stereotyped image of the other side, on the basis of alternative information being available. For this reason, it is vital to bring about a change in public opinion. However, it must be made clear that political belief systems are extremely resistant to change, above all when they are reinforced by an intensive victim psychology. The solution of long-lasting conflicts must be brought about by means of a change in the value judgments in the collective points of view, whereby a modification in public awareness will come about.

Turkish Society Has No Part in the Ongoing Conflict

One of the essential questions is why Turkish society has never questioned the official version of the events. Where does the origin of the deep rift between state and society in Turkey lie?

The Turkish Republic has inherited, in great measure, the traditions, politics, and administrative structure of the Ottoman Empire. In contrast to the West, the Ottoman-Turkish modernization process has not led to a widening of the power base, which would have given access to new social classes and groups. The motor of modernization was the ruling class. Instead of giving new groups access to power, the very opposite has happened. Changing to a republic did not essentially modify either the structure or the influence of the ruling classes.

The Ottoman idea of power and conception of a state came from an archaic imperial tradition. According to this idea, power legitimates itself exclusively. The state is sacrosanct. It is not that the nation has a state, but that the state has a nation. According to this philosophy, the state is independent from society, and organized against it. The state was regarded as a bulwark against the dangers of imperial decay when changing over to republicanism. Whoever really wishes to understand Turkey must regard the state as a brake on the progressive collapse of the Empire. The feeling of being threatened was the consequence of the following historical events:

1. The great powers planned several times, in the nineteenth and twentieth centuries, to share out the Ottoman Empire among themselves.

2. As a reaction, pan-Islamic and pan-Turkish concepts arose, so as to rescue the state structure. These ideas were laid aside owing to the defeat of the Ottoman Empire, the ally of Germany, in World War I. Plans for territorial expansion turned into fear of total destruction.

3. Certain ethnic groups in the Ottoman Empire attempted to become independent from the Ottoman state.

4. The metaphorical image of the "sick man of the Bosporus" that arose in Europe in the nineteenth century produced a general social psychosis, which increased in the aftermath of Sèvres (1920). According to this treaty, Turkey was to be partitioned among the great powers. The Turks would be left with nothing but a skeleton state, with Istanbul as the capital. The Armenians were promised an independent state in eastern Anatolia. The fact is that the treaty of Sèvres was not implemented, but the result was that the Turkish state felt itself constrained to defend Anatolia against its "enemies." In this way the concept of "threat" became the republic's basis of legitimacy.

Even today the legitimacy of the Turkish state derives from the existence of internal and external "enemies," who are attributed with the permanent design of destroying Turkey. Thus, for instance, the National Security Council, which is the most important constitutional organ, regularly publishes "Black Books," with lists of the gravest threats to the state, according to their significance. In Turkey we call this psychology—fear of partition and fear of threats—the "Sèvres syndrome."

The generation of Turkish founding leaders came mainly from the bureaucracy and the army, with a strong imprint of military values, and it wanted to create a homogenous Turkish republic. Very soon this project came up against the challenges of a pluralistic society, with the result that the latter became a barrier to carrying out this state conception. As a complement to the idea of the "external enemy," there arose that of the "internal enemy." In order to take away all influence from them, the founders hit upon an easy way out: they denied the existence and forbade the discussion of every social group that got in their way. It could be said that our republic is built on five taboos:

1. No social or economic classes exist in Turkey.

2. There are no Kurds in Turkey. Kurds are mountain Turks.

3. Turkey is a Western state. Thus Islamic values and culture have no influence.

4. The genocide of the Armenians never happened.

5. The military's authority and protective role are untouchable.

These taboos became the fundamental principles of the republic. In other words, the Turkish state was built on the basis of denying its own social reality and the existence of different ethnic, religious, and cultural groups. These groups were seen as "problems" and "threats" to the republic's safety. Political changes have lifted the taboo against talking about these groups. The role of the military has also been questioned. For the same reason the Armenian genocide has also become an important item on the national and international agenda. No doubt this taboo will also cease to exist, but this will require some time, as it is a most painful subject for the Turkish state.

Is "Negationism" an Exact Description of the Position of Turkish Society?

"Negationism" is the international term for the position of the Turkish state and society toward the Armenian genocide. As for the state, I consider it correctly used. The position of society, instead, must be described differently. In this case it is more a matter of ignorance, apathy, and silence.

To understand this we must consider the lack of historical awareness in Turkey as a social phenomenon. I would call Turkey a country that suffers from social amnesia. The inability to remember is not only referred to World War I but also to the events of the 1960s and 1970s, which have long since passed into forgetfulness. There are different reasons for this. Initially, the Turkish state has introduced a nationalist version of history in the educational system, which has led to a lack of knowledge. This is specially noticeable in everything related to the passage from the Ottoman Empire to the Turkish Republic. The official version has ignored, or falsified, not only the Armenian genocide, but also the history of other ethnic and religious minorities. This has led to collective amnesia.

The reform of the alphabet in 1928, when the Arabic script was changed to the Roman, has also contributed to this. The common people in Turkey, thus, lost the possibility of reading documents from before 1928 and so drawing their own conclusions. The reform, and the purification of the language connected with it, gave the Turkish state control over the access of society to its own past, as only texts that were convenient to the state were transcribed.

As for keeping quiet, one of the essential characteristics of Turkey is that it does not possess any common collective identity, but rather consists of a multiplicity of identities of ethnic and religious groups. Each of these has developed its own versions of history, transmitted orally. Despite all the existing differences, certain common traits can be seen: in contrast to postwar Germany, where the Holocaust was covered up with a "We didn't know anything about all that," in Turkey the different groups spoke openly about the Armenian genocide. Some said, "They deserved it," others, "It should never have happened. It was shameful." What is noteworthy about these opposing viewpoints is that they are never expressed in public, but only in private. Although wide sectors of Turkish society do not share the state's negationist policy, they never actively question it, but approve of it in public. In other words, what people say in public is very different from what they say privately. As criticizing the state's position in public was not allowed, and was punishable, there are two different versions in circulation: the official one imposed by the state, and the forbidden, private one of the different subgroups.

The discrepancy between an official historical tradition and a private one has led to Turkish society's having no real access to its past. In this way the private versions cannot be elaborated either. The nationalist version of history imposed by the state has not taken into account the points of view of the diverse ethnic and religious groups, and this is how the state has not been able to produce a unified social identity. Society has never questioned the imposed identity, based on ignorance, historical amnesia, and fear. The existence of two contradictory versions of history illustrates the schizophrenic position toward the Armenian genocide and other disputed "truths" in Turkey.

So far Turkish society has contributed nothing to clear up the Turko-Armenian conflict, and it is precisely this that must change. So long as Turkish society and the historical versions that exist within it do not play an active part in solving the conflict, this will carry on existing. This is why it is essential for platforms to be created so that Turkish society can make itself heard.

What Must Happen?

Both sides have to develop a concept of how future relations should be. If we cannot manage to link the historical conflict with an idea for the future, no solution is possible. Reconciliation means breaking the vicious circle of mutual recriminations in order to make dialog possible. Turkey and Armenia are in permanent contact due to their regional closeness, so the idea of the coexistence of the two states must include this consideration.

Both parties must have the chance of articulating their trauma, their grief, and their memories, but also their self-awareness. International experiences show that commissions of historians and truth commissions create a space for such a dialog. A common version of history must be created; sources that have so far been restricted must be put at the public disposal. Nevertheless, it is not enough just to dare to know the truth: the way to a new beginning must also include a feeling of compassion. If forgiveness is not asked for, and if there is not the courage to give it, there can be no reconciliation.

The European Union should begin to take its role as mediator in this conflict seriously, having so far seemed to deal with it superficially.

Europe must appreciate that the Turko-Armenian conflict is an essential component in its extension to the Near East and the Caucasus. Such a role can only function by preventing confrontation, and getting the two sides involved to sit down at the conference table. Parliamentary resolutions are insufficient for this.

4

THE SILENT PARTNER: IMPERIAL GERMANY AND THE YOUNG TURKS' POLICY OF ANNIHILATION

Wolfgang Gust

There was something that did not quite tally with Uncle Willi. Each time we visited him and his wife, my father's cousin, in the first years after World War II, the atmosphere I, a boy of eleven or twelve, sensed was one of strange tension every time we talked about political problems. My father seemed less calm than at other times, my mother hummed and hawed, and even Uncle Willi often tried to avoid them. It was like this for years, until the explanation popped up at last: Willi was interned in a concentration camp during the war for listening to BBC news bulletins, which was forbidden. Uncle Willi, the only socialist in our lower middle-class family, had opposed the Nazis in his own way, and was a minor hero. My parents, however, instead of being proud of him, were ashamed.

There was something that did not quite tally in Peter Balakian's grandmother. The American poet of Armenian origin noticed this early on, and it was a long time before he finally discovered the truth, which he described in his fascinating book, *Black Dog of Fate*. His Armenian grandmother was a survivor of the Armenian genocide of 1915–16. She had never spoken of the subject. It was only after her death that he was able to reconstruct the facts from accounts of his aunts'.

There was something that did not quite tally in so many Turkish families. Frequently, it was a grandmother or great-grandmother that kept some secret. Many young Turks only found out many years after emigrating that their grandmother was not really Turkish but Armenian. Probably hundreds of thousands of Armenian girls and young women saved their lives during World War I by being adopted by Turkish families or ending up in harems, often as slave housemaids, but also frequently becoming honorable family members. Even without Granny, the genocide is part of Turkish families' history, claim "insiders," in contrast to the Germans, who, after World War II, did all they could to locate any Jew that they had been kind to at some point, finding them only very rarely.

And in Germans there is also something that does not quite tally, for instance, myself. I had already passed my fiftieth birthday without once having heard of the Armenian genocide. One day I read a book about a destiny I found all too familiar: in order to survive, a refugee, who could not reveal his identity, rushed around in his own country, always on guard against the persecutors. The difference was that, in this case, it was not a Jew trying to save himself, but an Armenian escaping from his Turkish persecutors. I began to understand from reading *Le Ciel était noir sur l'Euphrat* (Black Was the Sky over the Euphrates), by Jacques Der Alexanian, that before the Holocaust there must have been another genocide. Reading this pertinent book gave rise to a whole series of articles in *Spiegel* magazine. Since then the subject has enthralled me.

During World War I, Germany was the most important ally of the Ottoman Empire, where the Young Turks had taken power some years previously. Austria-Hungary and, later, Bulgaria were also Turkish allies. Yet neither of these had so much influence as Imperial Germany, which had just equipped Turkey, financially as well as militarily, for a full-scale war. In eastern Turkey, the most important settlement of the over two million Ottoman Armenians, Germany was represented by consuls in Erzerum and the coastal area, and by missions in the interior, so that in that area it was often Germans who witnessed and reported on the genocide.

The United States, which has never been to war with Turkey, maintained a presence in the east, with even more missions than Germany. However, only the Germans were accorded privileges, which the Austrians never enjoyed: they could send their reports to Constantinople and Berlin in code. In this way, the German Foreign Ministry archives are the best proof of the Armenian genocide, as historical sources go.

In 1919, Johannes Lepsius published a selection of these files as *Deutschland und Armenien 1914–1918* (Germany and Armenia, 1914–1918). Lepsius was the Armenians great friend in Imperial Germany: he had become acquainted with them during a trip to Jerusalem following the footsteps of his father, a famous Egyptologist. The professional theologian gave up his pastoral post at that moment, founded, together with several other German Christians, societies to aid the victims of Sultan Abdul Hamid's massacres of Armenians from 1894 to 1896, and made the information on this crime public in Germany. At Urfa he later founded an important mission, which the Swiss Jakob Künzler directed, where there functioned an attached carpet factory in which many Armenian widows found employment.

The Foreign Ministry files published by Lepsius, together with the eyewitness reports published in 1916 by Lord James Bryce, became immediately after the war, the essential documents that served as proof of the genocide the Turks committed against the Armenians. Johannes Lepsius's personality seemed to guarantee that everything had been carried out with German precision. Still, there was something that did not quite tally in Lepsius's material. It is years since genocide scholars such as the American-Armenian scholar Vahakn N. Dadrian pointed out the existence of incongruities and omissions. A systematic comparative study my wife and I carried out of practically all the published documents has shown that both Lepsius and the Foreign Ministry not only selected the documents, but also altered the text. Many names of those responsible for the genocide were removed, as well as ugly racist comments of German officials about the Turks (and also the Armenians). And more: the German role in the genocide was not merely justified, but simply faked.[1] The documents give a clear indication of Imperial Germany's role in the genocide.

Included in this are the activities of the German military, which, as might be supposed, do not stand out in the diplomatic files. However, the different hints and indications are already important for this reason, since the military documents themselves were to a great extent destroyed in a bomb attack at the end of World War II. Shortly before World War I began, the position of the German military in Turkey was stronger than ever before. In the nineteenth century Germany had already trained Turkish officers. German officers occupied posts in nearly every section of the high command, and some Turkish armies had German commanders. The two main warships of the Turkish navy were renamed German vessels, whose crews were made up of German officers and sailors. These two ships, which were only nominally Turkish, got Turkey to declare war as Germany wanted by bombarding the Russian coast by German order.

And German officers also played an important role, for instance the artillery officer Count Eberhard Wolffskeel von Reichenberg, struck out in all the documents published by Lepsius. This officer shelled, at the end of March 1915, the cloister of the Armenian fort at Zeitun, in which Armenian (and also Turkish) deserters had taken refuge. Shortly after, the first deportations began from there. At the prompting of the military, the German consul of Aleppo, Walter Roessler, had previously been expressly forbidden to travel to Zeitun. Wolffskeel persecuted the Armenians that sought shelter on the mountain called Musa Dagh and were later rescued by Allied ships, which is the basis of Werfel's novel, *Die vierzig Tage des Musa Dagh* (The Forty Days of Musa Dagh). The German artillery officer subsequently destroyed the Armenians of Urfa, who had entrenched themselves in their quarter. The male survivors were hung, and the women and children were sent to the nearby Syrian desert, where nearly all of them starved to death. None of the actions had anything to do with military operations. Consul Roessler asked his ambassador whether it was "fitting that a German officer should take part in an expedition against an internal enemy of Turkey."

Another German officer that went astray was Lieutenant-Colonel Boettrich, responsible to Turkish general headquarters for the railroad system and as such also for the many Armenian employees of the Baghdad railroad, Germany's biggest foreign investment. Boettrich signed deportation orders, equivalent to death warrants, against the Armenian railroad employees. "Our enemies will pay a lot for this document," predicted the Baghdad railroad's vice-director, Franz Günther, on sending one of the orders signed by Boettrich to the Foreign Ministry in Berlin, "for with the signature of a member of the military mission they will be able to prove that, not only did the Germans do nothing to prevent the persecution of the Armenians, but some of the orders to that effect are due to them, that is, are signed by them." It was with a "malicious smirk" that the Turkish military commissioner "pointed with his finger at Herr Boettrich's signature," said Günther, "since this document with a German signature and not a Turkish one, which will give a lot to talk about, is also valuable to the Turks." Günther had no way of knowing that none of these documents would be known publicly in the visible future, the same as supposedly many other testimonies of German military actions against the Armenians.

The center of the German Foreign Ministry files are, of course, the diplomatic activities of the Imperial diplomats. They are limited to feeble protests of the ambassadors against the Armenian massacres, warnings by the consuls, or documents related to the almost constant turning down by the Turkish authorities of requests for some Armenian employee at German missions or diplomatic legations to be excepted. The publication of the genuine files since then shows that something did not tally in the Imperial Germans and the genocide.

The most critical view of the German position came from the U.S. ambassador in Constantinople, Henry Morgenthau. On returning to his country, he attacked in his book *Ambassador Morgenthau's Story* not only the German military but especially the German ambassador, Baron Hans von Wangenheim, who had exerted great influence in the Turkish capital in his time. Had Wangenheim wanted, claimed Morgenthau, the Armenians could have been saved.

That the Germans, though not their diplomats, were in a position to save the Armenians, is proven. On November 8, 1916, the Turkish authorities arrested and deported hundreds of Armenians from the coastal town of Smyrna, today Izmir. The Young Turks committee was behind the action, as the German chargé d'affaires in Constantinople, Radowitz, informed the German chancellor. He added, "I consider it impossible to have this measure countermanded, even presenting the case before the High Porte." The German general in charge, Liman von Sanders, forbade the deportations without further ado, and the Turks complied with his decision. No doubt Liman acted so as to guarantee supplies for his troops, which would have been at risk with the deportation of the Armenians and the equally cornered Greeks.

Morgenthau specifically criticized Wangenheim for his many remarks on not wanting to lift a finger for the Armenians, and for the Germans having as their only objective to win the war. Actually Wangenheim tried once, in 1913, to interest his superiors in the Armenians, and put the latter under the protection of German consuls. They were the most industrious people of the Ottoman Empire in his opinion, and part of them lived in a region called Cilicia, today practically identical with the province of Adana, which the Germans eyed as a future German colony—a colony that was to extend to the very Persian Gulf. Wangenheim's superior, Gottlieb von Jagow, was not against Germany's colonial intentions, but imagined this would cause the Turks great indignation, so he immediately disallowed the plan.

Notwithstanding, this alone would not have led to Wangenheim's firm anti-Armenian stance. Another seriously mutilated document in Lepsius's edition perhaps explains it. In December 1915, when the Turks' extermination machinery had already liquidated a great part of the Armenians in their own territory, the German ambassador Count Paul Wolff-Metternich requested by means of an article in the official government newspaper, *Norddeutsche Allgemeine Zeitung*, that Turkey be reproached, with much tact, for its policy of extermination. The undersecretary of state, Arthur Zimmermann and secretary of state, Jagow, did their part in making this formulation as soft as a plum, even softer. However, Chancellor Bethmann-Hollweg found even this too much. In his opinion a gentle rebuke to "a wartime ally was an unheard of measure at any time in history." He added, "Our sole objective is to keep Turkey on our side until the end of the war, whether the Armenians die or not." This strict refusal to do anything for the Armenians was told by the chancellor to Wangenheim a few months earlier in Berlin when the latter, now mortally ill, went there to receive new instructions. Back in Constantinople, he answered Morgenthau in practically the same words.

But Morgenthau also mentions another expression of Wangenheim's, which he hardly believed. Germany, the German ambassador told the American, was not responsible for the massacres of the Armenians. The statement, not only of the Armenians but also of many Turks, as to Germany being the original instigator of the genocide led the German diplomats to make use of special maneuvres. They did not firmly protest to the main Turkish politicians against the genocide, but against the insinuation of their complicity. There was also something that did not quite tally in the German politicians, as there existed an unquestionable German complicity, as becomes apparent from the numerous files published since then.

Replying to requests of the German embassy, the Turkish government repeated on December 22, 1915, that the measures against the Armenians were an exclusively internal affair of Turkey. Each country, as it said in the reply, was entitled "to take necessary measures to neutralize subversive activities that might take place in it." This view was endorsed by the German embassy, thus suggesting that the actions carried out against the Armenians in the eastern provinces were legitimate from a military and self-defence point of view. Germany, goes the gist of the Turkish document, supposedly requested for military reasons the Armenian population's deportation from the whole of the Empire, not just Anatolia.

The recipient of the letter, Wolff-Metternich, showed his total agreement with that position in his report of April 3, 1916, to the imperial chancellor. He added, that "the relocation measures have taken place not only in the eastern provinces but, as we admitted, in the whole of the Empire." This proves the Germans had been in agreement with the deportations from the eastern region. According to this document they were not the authors of the idea, as Wangenheim told Morgenthau on the German role, but the German Empire undoubtedly was an accomplice by its approval of the genocide.

Later, in a brief passage, Max Erwin von Scheubner-Richter expressed the Young Turks' real intentions after being many weeks in the company of important Turkish leaders as an officer of a mounted expedition to Persia, and having the chance to have long talks with them: "A large portion of the Young Turks' Committee favours the idea that the Turkish Empire is to be built on purely Mohammedan and Pan-Turkish foundations. The non-Muslim and non-Turkish inhabitants are to be converted and Turkified by force, or otherwise be exterminated," wrote Scheubner-Richter in his report to the chancellor.

> To put this plan in operation, these gentlemen consider the present time ideal. As the first point of their program came the settling of the Armenian problem. Turkey's allies were made to believe that a supposed revolt of the Dashnaktzagan party was ahead. Local uprisings and attempts at self-defense by the Armenians were exaggerated and used as a pretext to deport those of the menaced frontier areas. On the way the Armenians were murdered by Kurdish and Turkish bands, and partly by gendarmes, at the behest of the Committee.

In the document on German toleration of the deportations it does not figure how or when this agreement was arrived at. But it is proven that, early on, in late December 1914, the friend of the Armenians, Johannes Lepsius, and a close collaborator influenced the Armenians so that they remained loyal to the Turkish government. "Measures" were also talked of at that time, yet this did not then mean deportations, but other measures.

However, on June 17, 1915, when the first columns of deportees were under way, Lepsius sent the Foreign Ministry a letter that he had written six days earlier to Ambassador Wangenheim, in which he explains: "Harsh measures against the Armenian subjects, apparently to repress espionage and local unrest, are only of episodic import, and have no relation with our German interests." The most critical passage in the letter to Wangenheim was: "I do not consider tragic the War Minister's measures against Armenian schools, the press, and so forth. Even the deportations would be inoffensive if the technique of administration (as the Circassians demonstrate) did not generally result in the deportations ending in death."

The use of the term "deportations" by Lepsius must strike one as strange, and can only have originated in the forced resettlement of tens of thousands of French and Belgians, including women and children, apparently recommended by Lepsius, who had been in favour of the annexation of part of Belgium, and changed the name of the great German project from "Berlin–Baghdad" to "Antwerp–Baghdad." Even more amazing is it to find a passage of the *Deutsch-Armenische Korrespondenz*, of which he was the editor, of November 25, 1918. According to this, the deportation plan had been authorized by the German general Colmar von der Goltz, and Lepsius commented, "In its official version it seemed quite harmless."

A deportation harmless?

He authorized Turkish military commanders to "evacuate, on an individual or mass basis the inhabitants of villages or cities and resettle them in other places, in the case of military necessity and in the case of their being suspected of espionage or treason." This supposedly harmless order which, according to Lepsius, was "in tolerable consonance with the military measures of civilized states," resulted in massacres in the very first days of its implementation, which not only von der Goltz must have known, as Lepsius accused him of, but the latter must also have known. By the look of it, there was something in Lepsius that did not quite tally.

A mere week after his letter to Wangenheim, Lepsius made a complete turnabout. In the following weeks he carried out an exemplary work of exposing the crimes in Turkey, and wrote his most important work—which appeared after the war as *Der Todesgang des armenischen Volkes* (The Way to Death of the Armenian People). Copies of this report on the Armenian genocide were distributed to some 20,000 Protestant pastors in the summer of 1916.

The Armenians had no lobby among the German elite besides Lepsius and a few others, like Paul Rohrbach, and this has an explanation: that among the leading German thinkers during the World War I there was something that did not quite tally. Whereas German writers and intellectuals had enthusiastically espoused the ideas of the French Revolution in 1789, they gradually moved away from the West after the Citizens' Revolution of 1848. The German intellectual elite found the "ideas of 1789" diametrically opposed to the German "ideas of 1914." Democratic parliamentary society with a basically cosmopolitan, supranational outlook was at odds from then on to the world of experiences and feelings of complacency among the mass of the people. World War I, known as the "Great War" right from the beginning, produced among intellectuals and artists an enthusiasm that is today hardly understandable. "How was the artist not to praise God for the collapse of a world of peace which he was sick of, so thoroughly sick?" wrote Thomas Mann, who later won the Nobel Prize for Literature.

Only by means of war, according to one of the fundamental axioms of these circles, could German culture conquer the world, in which there was little room for intellectuals, journalists, democrats, cosmopolitans, and individualists in general. On October 24, 1914, ninety-three German intellectuals issued their manifesto, *An die Kulturwelt* (To the World of Culture), declaring that German militarism had been derived from German culture in order to protect it. A "surprising self-prostitution of the German intellectual world in the face of international lust for conquest," as the Germanophile president of the American University of Columbia, Nicholas Murray Butler, called the pamphlet. Nearly four thousand German professors, practically the entire academic world, backed the proclamation.

The inventor of the "ideas of 1914" was the political science professor Johann Plenge. "In us," he wrote in 1933, "is the twentieth century. We are the exemplary people. Our ideas will become Humanity's life objectives." In those ideas, Plenge saw the "unequivocally clear anticipation of the National Socialist idea, with all its basic requirements." The Swede Rudolf Klellén, one of the spiritual fathers of National Socialism, based the ideas of 1914 on duty, order, and justice; and the Berlin philosopher of religion, Ernst Troeltsch, contrasted civilization with "German freedom," which was based on the supra-individual community. The co-founder of sociology in Germany, Werner Sombart, denounced in his book, which had the symptomatic title of *Händler und Helden—Patriotische Besinnungen* (Merchants and Heroes—Patriotic Intimations) "the hollow culture of English shopkeepers," against which he opposed German heroes, who defended the "last dyke of contention against the muddy flood of mercantilism." Paul Rohrbach praised the "German war" as the struggle for German values like honesty, meekness, and altruism, as opposed to English materialism and individualism.

This German mixture of irrationality and self-centerdness, hardly comprehensible to a foreigner, based on arrogance and the right of the strongest, was fatal for the Armenians. "Parasites in the body of the dominant people," the Brunswick geographer Ewald Banse called the Armenians. These "Jews of the East," as they were called in numerous documents, had lived for many years in the West, especially in the United States, were educated at excellent American missionary schools according to Western democratic values, and seldom had access to German culture. "It is to be noted that, even among the Armenians educated in Germany or at the German missions, we have few friends," wrote Scheubner-Richter from Erzurum in May 1915.

The Armenians were marked out for special suffering by the ideology of "merchants or heroes," as they embodied the commonplaces of being cunning Levantine businessmen oriented to Roman legal culture, and enemies of Germany. Wangenheim wrote in 1913: "In Germany we have become used to seeing the periodically repeated [*sic*] Armenian massacres as nothing but a natural reaction to the bloodsucking system of Armenian merchants." Even Consul Scheubner-Richter, who sympathized with the Armenians, mocked their "commercial ability verging on unscrupulousness." In his view, the Armenians, "thanks to their innate commercial talents, can take over the whole of commercial life in which, the same as the Jews, their role is often useful, but not always desirable."

German diplomats opposed the distorted merchant image, rejected in the popular culture of Germany, to that of the honest, down-to-earth worker. Says Vice-Consul Hermann Hoffmann, "If every Armenian were, as we hear and read from the German side, essentially a usurer and no more, one could not talk of any loss for the Empire." He added, "The truth is that hundreds of thousands of Armenians of working age are industrious and capable craftsmen, and energetic, assiduous, and enterprising farmers."

"The Armenians have been called the 'Jews of the East,' and with this was left aside the fact that in Anatolia there exists a strong agricultural community of Armenians, which has all the traits of a healthy rural population," wrote Wangenheim; and Hoffmann added, "Bodily healthy, productive, mentally active, and enterprising, they are too valuable an element for the economic development of the abandoned lands."

The Armenians' destiny was not determined by the opinion of diplomats but that of the highest German military circles. The embassy pastor, Count Lüttichau, complained at the end of the war that many of them "had consented to the evacuation measures for military-strategic reasons." Swiss historian Christoph Dinkel quoted the former chief of the operation section of the Turkish General Headquarters, Otto von Feldmann: "It must not and cannot be denied that German officers—and I am one of them—were obliged at certain times to advise clearing Armenians out of certain areas at the rearguard of the army."

This was especially so for the top German officers, who directly advised War Minister Enver. Among them was the highest German officer of the Turkish Army High Command, General Fritz Bronsart von Schellendorf, who issued orders which were signed by Enver; and also Felix Guse, who was described by the chief of the German military mission in Turkey, Liman von Sanders, as the "soul of the Supreme Command" of the Third Army, and in whose jurisdiction the greatest number of deportations took place. Dinkel collected quotes by these two German officers. They spoke of the Armenians as "stingy" or "greedy," "parasites," "bloodsucking enemies of the state," "usurers" who "fed on the marrow of other nations" and were "rightfully hated more than the vilest Jews," even "nine times worse in usury than the Jews."

According to Bronsart, the Armenians had not only had a "purely military effect against the flank and rearguard of the Turkish army of the East operating on the Russian front," but "simply annihilated the Muslim populations of those areas." Thus, "the entire ministry took the grave decision of declaring the Armenians a danger to the state and immediately clearing them out of the frontier regions to resettle them in an area distant from the war zone, sparsely inhabited but fertile, in the north of Mesopotamia."

With this stab in the back, that very German way of criminalizing a political opponent, he referred to the Van uprising of April 20, 1915, which even today is considered the event that unleashed the genocide among the Turks and some Germans. The highest German authorities also accepted this version, and the absurd numbers quoted by the Turks. The undersecretary of state at the Foreign Ministry, Arthur Zimmermann, told the president of the Society of Editors of German newspapers, Friedrich Faber, that "a blood bath" took place in Van, and stated that "countermeasures were put in motion only after the Armenian uprising had begun, behind the Turkish troops that were going towards Azerbaijan, which produced more than 150,000 Muslim victims." In this way the Armenians would have murdered the whole Muslim population of the province of Van (120,000 Kurds and 30,000 Turks), as Lepsius already mentioned during the war. Zimmermann, however, was better informed by means of his consuls. Scheubner-Richter spoke of 400 wounded and 200 dead Turks, a figure he later corrected to 1,000; Consul Holstein mentioned 200 Turks dead. Even Turkish Interior Minister Talaat mentioned to the Germans the number of 400

Armenians and several hundred Turks dead. The supposedly high number of casualties must have resulted from the flight before the Russian advance, for which the Armenians can hardly be held responsible.

Even the German Christians were fooled systematically. A short time before his sentencing the Armenians to destruction, Chancellor Bethmann-Hollweg formally assured them: "The Imperial German government considers it its major duty, as in the past so also in the future, to exert its influence so that the Christian populations do not suffer persecution on account of their religion. German Christians can rest assured that I will do everything within my power to bear in mind the worries and wishes they have expressed to me." He did nothing, and the official in charge of the Turkish section of the Foreign Ministry, Frederic von Rosenberg, cynically stated he did not believe "the persecutions are due to religious reasons."

As a preventative measure against the accusations that were to be expected in the sense that Germany had sacrificed the Armenians, by August 4, 1915, Undersecretary of State Arthur Zimmermann prepared a "White Book" (German documents meant for self-justification used white as the chosen colour, like blue with the British and orange with the Russians), in which were listed German verbal efforts to save the Armenians. Alexander von Hoesch, a future ambassador in Paris and London, compiled the work, which was later replaced by the more objective one by Lepsius, *Deutschland und Armenien*, and thus it never appeared.

During the war Lepsius travelled to Holland, allegedly to rest, but in fact to carry out political actions as the representative of his new employer, even without the Foreign Ministry's knowledge, which, as a result, thought of asking the Dutch government for Lepsius's expulsion. The latter worked in Holland for who would later be the foreign propaganda chief, Hans von Haeften, the right hand of the new strong man in German politics and later Hitler supporter, Erich Ludendorff.

As von Haeften's representative, Lepsius also evaluated English newspapers in Holland, but above all worked with Kurt Hahn, the last chancellor, Prince Max of Baden's, right-hand man. He acted as a liaison with the British Union of Democratic Control, a confederation of radical-liberal and socialist politicians working to reach a reasonable peace settlement with Germany. Among the Union's members were several defenders of the Armenians, like Lord James Bryce and Arthur Ponsonby, with whom Lepsius had had good contact before the war. However, the British would not accept an unconditional peace as almost all German politicians and Lepsius himself favored.

In the latter stages of the war, with the advance of the Turkish army to the Caucasus, Lepsius once more found himself in a position to set the Armenians in play, as Ludendorff wanted unconditional access to the Baku oilfields, whose soviet, however, was under Armenian control. In this way a political struggle arose between Germans and Turks—with even some skirmishes—in which Germany at least courted the Russian brothers of the murdered Ottoman Armenians, though without being able to prevent the massacre of many tens of thousands of Armenians. Germany's total defeat also forced the retreat of the Turkish troops.

That there was something that did not quite tally with the Germans after losing World War I is shown in the figure beyond all suspicion of Johannes Lepsius. He fought, like almost all Germans, with every means at his disposal, against the Treaty of Versailles. "The gods of the Entente, who govern the world, wish to impose a Promethean life on us, and wrench out our liver according to the guidelines of Versailles," he wrote to Aage Meyer Benedictsen, the Danish Lepsius, who kept his needy German friend's family afloat with packets of sausages at the end of the war.

The Danish defender of the Armenians was specially shocked at his German counterpart, who, in a conversation they had, described precisely the work of the intellectual father of the Pan-Germanists, and later the Nazis, Houston Chamberlain, as "great, great!" The Dane answered:

> I'm a man of the world enough to understand foreign rights, and sufficiently Danish to feel that our suffering at having Germany on top of us as our ruler, setting standards, and goading us forward was something we found not only disagreeable but utterly repellent and hateful, surely as we knew by instinct that it was like having a cannon pointing straight at our heart. As I see it, a malignant demon took possession of Germany, gradually poisoning every soul, first of all the naturally stupid and evil ones, and then little by little taking over the most noble and well-meaning.

Lepsius' answer? Silence.

The Dane said:

> I remember how, formerly, we talked about everything and how I, yet young and credulous, hoped the German people would see the injustice and the stupidity, and that a change would take place as soon as they understood. Later I no longer believed that. The crude trust in power penetrated ever more deeply in the people, and that God, that is to say, real Goodness, always sides with the strong.

Yet again Lepsius said nothing.

"You never answered my letter of quite some time ago about the Danes and Germans in Schleswig," Aage Meyer Benedictsen thus closed the attempted dialog, "but I realize how hard it must be for you to find the time and the mood to interchange abstract opinions when passion does not drive one to it, and I forgive you."

Lepsius had two further moments of stardom: his declarations as an expert in the trial against Talaat's murderer, Salomon Teilirian (also Soromon Tehleryan), whom his German judges, to the amazement of the world—and to the Danish friend's great joy—acquitted by reason of insanity, according to Article 51 of the Criminal Code, in June, 1921; and later his role in providing the ideas for Franz Werfel's great novel about the Armenians. He was only able to offer limited help to the Armenians dispersed during the war. When the war finished it was mainly the Americans who took charge of this, earning Lepsius's admiration and contempt in equal measure.

In the Germany of the Weimar Republic, the curtain finally closed on the Armenian genocide, as that of the Holocaust opened and the "world war culture" again took hold in Germany. On March 21, 1934, when Hitler and Hindenburg shook hands for the first time in Potsdam, the garrison chaplain described the day as of "the rebirth of the spirit of 1914," which had had such baleful effects for the Armenians. Whether Hitler's phrase a short time before the outbreak of World War II, "Who yet remembers the Armenians?" was said at Obersalzberg or elsewhere, its internal logic is so great that it has entered history.

That the treatment given the Holocaust was different from that of the Armenian genocide was no German merit. No writer of what was considered the real opposition in Germany—the so-called inner emigration—took up the subject of the Holocaust at the end of the war. This was left to the emigrated and Jewish writers. It was only with Eichmann's trial and the Auschwitz process in the 1960s that it reached the collective memory of Germans. Since then, whoever was interested in genocide worked on the Holocaust. In this, Germans found the individuality of the Shoah of far greater help, on account of the founding of the state of Israel in those first decades. They ignored the fact that the Holocaust had been preceded by the extermination of the Hereros and Nama in southwest Africa at the beginning of the nineteenth century. And they ignored until recently the Armenian genocide. The elaboration of these two genocides before the big Holocaust is likely to bring Germany to the disturbing realization that the basis not only of the Nazi regime, but also that of the Shoah, had already been laid before, and during, World War I.

And the Turks? There is also something in them that does not quite tally. "Why then do you not hang that trio of Enver, Talaat, and Jemal?" Mustafa Kemal, the father of modern Turkey, asked French correspondent Maurice Prax. When the postwar Turkish government—at Britain's prompting—in 1919 began prosecuting and sent a handful of war criminals to the gallows, the new Turkish government granted the remainder a generous pension, and Atatürk raised ever more Young Turks to the highest official positions, since they provided him with the elements for his struggle against the Turkish "Versailles." Kemal dissolved all the military courts, had some of the judges sentenced, and on May 23, 1923, the new father of the people finally amnestied all the murderers of the Armenians. This "congenital defect in the Turkish Republic," as the scholar Taner Akçam, an associate professor in the United States, calls it, has determined everything to do with the discussion of the genocide in Turkey—still surrounded by many taboos—till this very day. However, polls show that 60 percent of the population favors making the facts clear.

At Iğdir, on the border with the Armenian Republic, stands a huge monument, as visible from Yerevan, the Armenian capital, as the sacred mountain of the Armenians, Ararat, also on Turkish territory. It commemorates the victims of the genocide—not the Armenian ones, however, but the Turkish victims of the genocide perpetrated by the Armenians against them. Imagine it: a monstrous German monument at the Czech or Polish border for the victims of the expulsion of Germans. On April 14, 2003, Turkish education minister Hüseyin Celik issued an order to all teachers—therefore, including the few Armenian teachers left in Istanbul—to deny the Armenian genocide and work on the subject of "the Armenians' baseless allegations." Imagine a similar instruction being issued in German schools to Jewish teachers that the Shoah is a "baseless allegation," and obliging them to promote neo-Nazi ideas.

European politicians are asking themselves if Europe can adapt to 70 million Turks. The French, British, Dutch, and Danes may wonder if Europe can stand 150 million Germans and Turks that are not able, or not willing, to elaborate a crime against humanity of major proportions. Only a very, very open discussion on the Armenian genocide will be able to prove to the victims that both countries are seriously engaged in exorcizing the demons of their past.

Note

1. I have tried to clarify the degree to which the Foreign Ministry at the time or Johannes Lepsius himself manipulated the documents in my article "Magisches Viereck" (Magic Square), which can be consulted on the internet at *www.armenocide.net*, where all the manipulations are laid bare in detail, and there are some 500 further documents never published heretofore.

Part II

Portraits from Around the World

History

5

THE INVESTIGATOR: VAHAKN N. DADRIAN, GENOCIDE SCHOLAR (CAMBRIDGE, MA)

Huberta von Voss

"I would like to talk to you about the Armenian genocide. Allow me to start off by explaining my scientific method to you. The sources I use must fulfill four criteria: pertinence, incontestability, explicitness, and verifiability."

His thought unfolds resting as it does on these four columns. This man knows that the ground he has been cultivating for half a century is shaky. His talk on the Armenian genocide is to last sixty minutes and it actually will deal with the significance of the historical sources and the seriousness of his method of investigation. On the podium of the packed Intercollege Conference Hall in the Greek part of Nicosia sits a man who has devoted his life to investigating the genocide against his own people. For decades he has been fighting for that crime's recognition by the world of scholars. Today his unassailable monographs appear in large editions and his articles in the most respected journals, for instance the Turkophilic *International Journal of Middle East Studies*. The most prominent member of the Zoryan Institute for Contemporary Armenian Research and Documentation of Cambridge, Massachusetts, he receives invitations from all over the world to give talks. Nevertheless, he begins his usual conferences in the role of a novice who must prove that his methods are scientific before expecting to be listened to. Eighteen times in recent decades he has devoted weeks to browsing in the German Foreign Ministry archives, rooting out from diplomatic and military dispatches proofs of his thesis that the mass extermination of the Armenian people was in no way a collateral effect of World War I, conditioned by circumstances, but a deliberate and planned genocide whose goal was the annihilation of the Armenians. "German and Austrian sources are indispensable for the study of the genocide, for it is inconceivable that a war ally during that very war should want to discredit a confederate," he notes. However, even when Dadrian speaks before an audience as critical of Turkey as Greek Cypriot students are, he changes nothing in the structure of his richly documented conference. The

speaker is someone who knows that, in the Armenian case, the burden of proof is on the Armenians, in contrast to other victim nations.

During the conference, Dadrian looks at a fixed point in the hall, emphasizing his words with his right hand. He wears a sort of episcopal ring on it, which he himself bought. His American English is immaculate. An Armenian claims he has a Turkish accent in his pronunciation of the sound "oo."

This would be no surprise. Dadrian was born in Istanbul after World War I, the son of a wealthy lawyer and landowner, Hagop Dadrian. Hagop was deported with all his family, but was able to evade the general massacres thanks to his great influence. At a little convent school, young Vahakn learned European languages. This is how he can today quote, without notes to prompt him, sources in Turkish, German, French, English, and Armenian to illustrate the points he makes. His stupendous memory is an aid in this. "Tell me all the German synonyms of 'rapid,'" he suddenly says the first time we meet. And, before one can answer, he rattles off, "rasch, eilig, hurtig, behende, fix, schleunigst …" and many more. A slight, satisfied smile spreads over his face. "At the Jesuit school, classes began at 6 a.m. It was no fun. But the lessons stuck," he assures his listener.

On moving to Berlin at the end of World War II to study mathematics, he had already broken his inner ties with Turkey. His father died early. "In Turkey my chances for the future were nonexistent. So I left," he says laconically. In devastated Berlin, Dadrian read *Faustus*, and was fascinated by humanity's vacillation between good and evil. "I love German, Goethe's language," he says enthusiastically, and quotes long passages of the text as if he had just read them. Kant, Nietzsche, Ranke, Max Weber, and other great German thinkers also impressed him at the time, and even now enrich his repertoire of quotes. When he read Franz Werfel's monumental work, *Die vierzig Tage des Musa Dagh* (The Forty Days of Musa Dagh), in its original version, he knew in what direction his professional career would run. In no small measure because of his polyglot ability, he feels called to assemble a coherent general picture from the parts of the puzzle. But before he could do this, more years of study ensued in Vienna at the history seminar. Then he went to Zurich to study international law.

This was at the time when the great flowering of the social sciences began, and Dadrian emigrated to the United States, where he earned a doctorate in sociology at the University of Chicago. He taught sociology at the State University of New

York from 1970 to 1991. There was a period of postdoctoral research at Harvard University, and then he was a guest lecturer at the Massachusetts Institute of Technology (MIT). At the start of the 1990s, he decided to devote all his time to investigating the Armenian genocide, and the Guggenheim Foundation named him director of a far-reaching research project on the subject. Some years later the results appeared: *The History of the Armenian Genocide: Ethnic Conflict from the Balkans to Anatolia to the Caucasus*, which has gone through six editions since 1995. In 1996 he published a new in-depth study, *German Responsibility in the Armenian Genocide: A Review of the Historical Evidence of German Complicity*. In later works, he goes more deeply into the causes of the Turko-Armenian conflict, and analyzes the Turks' strategy of denying the historical facts. Then there are two studies in which Dadrian looks into the Armenian genocide and the Holocaust from the angle of international law. Both essays were published in the *Yale Journal of International Law*. Since then he has been going around the whole world as a guest lecturer expounding the results of his scientific investigations. The universities of Munich, Berlin (Free University), Parma, Turin, Zurich, and Uppsala count among his visits.

He has worked very hard for the academic recognition of the Armenian genocide and the result is there to see. In 2000, he was invited as the main speaker at a Holocaust conference in Philadelphia. "There I protested against the concept of the Holocaust's singularity," he says in his warm, high-pitched voice. Yehuda Bauer, director of the International Institute of Holocaust Research—Yad Vashem, publicly stated at the end of the conference that he planned to move away from the concept of the singularity of the Jewish Holocaust. "I expected to encounter hostility. The opposite was the case." In his conferences, Dadrian does not refrain from saying things in a way that freezes the blood in your veins. "At least, the majority of Jews died within 45 seconds, gassed. Instead, Armenians were hewn to pieces with hatchets, swords, sickles, and hoes." What a terrible sentence. He must hit hard to breach the wall of silence surrounding the planned murder of his people.

At this conference, Dadrian used the advantage of the moment to present a declaration on the Armenian genocide, immediately collecting the signatures of 126 of the best-known Holocaust scholars. Besides Yehuda Bauer, the signatories included Israel Charny, Saul Friedman, and Nobel Laureate Elie Wiesel. The *Jerusalem Post* and the *New York Times* published the document. This was his breakthrough in academic circles. Israel Charny, director of the renowned Institute of Holocaust and Genocide in Jerusalem and currently President of the International Association of Genocide Scholars (IAGS), has since become a close research collaborator. "Even Elie Wiesel showed me respect for my scientific work after the conference. Although he tends to shy away from endorsing petitions, he signed my declaration," Dadrian recalls, passing his finger along the inside of his shirt collar, as if needing to loosen a rope that is strangling him. He repeats this unconscious gesture often.

Yet how does he feel about Turkey's refusal to recognize and assume some responsibility for the crime? And what does he think of its war ally of the time, Germany, whose language he has mastered with the best; who reads, respects, and knows the great German poets and thinkers, but not a single one of whose scientific papers has found a publisher in Germany? Does this man, who lives on his own in a small American town, researching and writing to the music of Bach and Beethoven turned up loud, feel bitterness?

"Not at all. I am—and this I say with all modesty—at the peak of my career. I'm invited, consulted, published; my books sell," he says. In 1995, the House of Commons of the British Parliament invited him to speak on the occasion of the eightieth anniversary of the genocide. Yet, behind his mild, cultivated manner there undoubtedly hides a corresponding portion of fury and contempt. "Many, many Turks," he says categorically, "haven't yet attained the Germans' level of civilization with regard to working through and bravley confronting their own history. In this sense they are still half savages."

He also believes there is a Turkish tradition of bluffing, which one should not allow oneself to be unduly impressed by. "The Turks are prone to feint—and so they frighten. But if things get nasty they soon lay aside their bluster." Foreigners are not aware of this trait of the Turks, he says, and so let themselves be intimidated. The proof is in the rescue of the Armenians of Smyrna, present-day Izmir. The German general Liman von Sanders, then the commander of the Fifth Army, prevented the imminent deportation and massacre of the Armenian minority, threatening to defend the people with his own troops. This bold act served its purpose. "This shows that the German soldiers serving in Turkey were in a position to save the Armenians," maintains Dadrian. He finds it utterly incomprehensible that no German historian has ever investigated Germany's role in the Armenian genocide and that silence in this respect still prevails in German historiography. "When one considers the high degree of German culture and civilization—I refer, for instance, to the tradition of a Max Weber's scientific objectivity—it's impossible to understand it." Thoughtfully he takes a sip of herb tea, searching for a word. "The Germans played a secondary role in the Armenians' annihilation. They aren't the main culprits, but they are moral accomplices. However, even that seems a bit much for some sensitive souls. The Germans are simply sated with their own Holocaust and therefore want nothing to do with the genocide of the Armenians." There is this tacit unwillingness to take on the moral responsibility in yet another genocide. "This is understandable. There is probably also a problem of marketability for books on the subject," he says amiably, sounding cynical, perhaps without wishing to. Around seventy publications make up the list of Dadrian's essays, studies, and monographs, of which only three have appeared in German, one of them commissioned by the German Armenian Society.

For years he has investigated German complicity in the archives. His verdict is hard, but recognizes distinctions. "The Kaiser was quite cold-blooded and indifferent toward the Armenians' fate. When William II received a report on the massacre at Adana in 1909, he wrote in the margin, "What do we care?". Commercial interests, like building the Berlin–Baghdad Railway, had priority. Among the soldiers and military diplomats, some, for instance, General Bronsart von Schellendorf, Marshall Goltz, and Ambassador von Wangenheim, were personally to blame. "I've discovered many reports indicating that General Bronsart von Schellendorf, as Chief of the Turkish General Staff, gave direct orders for the Armenians to be deported. He used the actual Turkish word *shedide*, meaning stern measures, which in the orders was the code name for massacre."

However, Dadrian also recognizes that many "less Turkophilic" Germans showed humanity, such as the consul at Erzurum, von Scheubner-Richter, and the pastor, Lepsius. While Dadrian talks about the German role, he quotes by heart long passages from consular reports, correspondence, military orders, and dispatches.

When at a loss for a word, he shuts his eyes until he remembers the entire quotation with its date, place, and file number. Dadrian is aware of the risk in being a harbinger of bad news, especially because he is a member of the victim nation, which condition inevitably casts the suspicion of partiality upon him. As if wanting to apologize for what he has said, he quotes Goethe: *"Zwei Seelen wohnen ach in meiner Brust,* (Two souls, ah! dwell in my breast.) There is this ambivalence in the psyche of the Germans."

Nevertheless, he is against making any concessions to Turkey. He does not avoid telling the truth in order to create a suitable climate for dialog. This criticism also extends to those Armenians, mainly American, who, within the so-called Turkish–Armenian Reconciliation Committee, have been trying to establish ground rules acceptable to both parties in the presentation of the historical facts. "The genocide was a crime against humanity. That's not negotiable," he says with conviction, and for a moment his voice loses its warmth. As a NATO member, Turkey feels no urge to recognize its guilt. "Besides, the Turks are afraid of the stigma. They don't want to be compared with the Nazi Germans." An additional fear is that material and territorial compensation will be demanded from them.

He shares the viewpoint of Max Weber, who said that, to enhance one's analytical capabilities, one must ask hypothetical questions from time to time, for instance, "What would Europe be like if Napoleon had won at Waterloo? What would the situation of the Blacks in America be if the South had won the Civil War? Or, what position would the Jews be in if Hitler had won the war?" He shrugs with annoyance. "They'd have the same problem as the Armenians have with the Turks. The victorious Nazis would say, 'Holocaust? What's that, Holocaust?'" But the Germans were defeated, and had no choice but to face the truth. The Turks also lost the war but, thanks to the disunity of the Allies, Atatürk was able to promote Turkey's interests as well as to impose her will at, and after, the Lausanne Conference.

"Recognition or denial," says Dadrian with a firm voice, "are both a function of power. Whoever has power can permit himself to lie, and Turkey is strong owing to its strategic position. This is why there is a long legacy of denial. However, the longer it carries on denying, the harder it will become to recognize the truth."

And he adds a self-criticism. "We've lost eighty-five years during which the most we did was publish propaganda material to insult the Turks. We should rather concentrate on the cultivation and dissemination of scientific knowledge." Dadrian picks up his cup of tea and looks upward. "Some time in the future we're going to succeed," he says, once again affable, and nods.

6

A Foundation of Facts and Fiction: The Poet and Writer Peter Balakian (Hamilton, NY)

Huberta von Voss

Peter Balakian's parents' home on Dickerson Road has a delightful front yard with bushy hydrangeas and a generous porch. On weekends fathers trim the privet hedges, while mothers go to the hairdresser to have their hair permed, and children polish Buicks and Chevies. In the evening an aroma of barbecued meat wafts from house to house. The Balakians' shish kebab smells exactly the same as the neighbours' steaks. Through the open porch doors one hears the commentaries on Channel 11: "Yankees score, Home run!" In the 1950s the inhabitants of Teaneck, on the outskirts of New York, have plenty to look forward to. Peter and his three siblings, Pamela, James, and Janet not only have typical American names but are typical all-American kids. Still, something marks them off from the other kids on Dickerson Road: their surname is not Blumenthal or Goldfischer or Liebowitz.

On Saturday morning, when Peter looks out of his window on to the street, he goes green with envy. The neighbours' families pass by in long processions with their numerous offspring in front of Dr. Balakian's house on their way to the Jewish center, where there is *schul* today. Perplexed, the lad views himself in the bathroom mirror. His image in the mirror, with its dark brown eyes and hair, is like a question mark. "Why can't I be Jewish?" One day, Peter happily attends his friend Lenny's bar mitzvah. But then a friendly question from Lenny's aunt puts

Peter in a very embarrassing situation: "Are you Reformed or Conservative?" Peter nods helplessly and stuffs so much pastrami sandwich in his mouth that he can hardly open his lips. "Reformed," he mumbles. Straight away he gets up to wash his hands, so as not to admit he does not belong there.

It is precisely this feeling of not belonging that Peter's parents, grandparents, and aunts did their utmost to prevent. All of them were survivors of the genocide. Of the banishment. When they fled to the United States, every door closed on the past, which had turned into a house of mourning. The key was buried and lapsed into oblivion. New York held opportunities open for each member of the family. Father became a doctor, Aunt Anna a lecturer in French literature at New York University, and Aunt Nona a prestigious literary critic for the *New York Times Review of Books*. Even grandmother Nafina successfully leaps across the abyss to a new life, is a fan of the Yankees, knows the results of every match, and by speculating on the stock exchange makes enough money to spoil her grandchildren at the elegant Saks department store on Fifth Avenue. OK, granny doesn't call them honey, but *iavrey (iavrig)*, which comes from Turkish and means little dear. Or she says to him, *hokit sirem*: let me love your soul. But woe betide anyone else speaking to him like that, or in front of his friends! When the identification with his Jewish friends gets too pronounced, his father buys a house in another area, to his son's disappointment.

Yet his father does worry again about the boy's development when he turns into a teenager and plunges into American youth culture, with petting sessions in drive-in cinemas. Gerard Balakian is infuriated by this decadent atmosphere. "You've turned into a creature of rock-and-roll!" he grunts in disgust, and bugs the boy from then on by threatening to send him to a private school. Some day Peter will have to write a paper on some Middle Eastern culture as a social studies project at school. "It's a perfect opportunity to learn something about Armenia!" deems his father.

And so it was that the youngster engaged in a classical research project in the pre-Internet era, choosing volume A of the encyclopedia in the TV room. Just around 200 words on Armenia—hardly enough for a sociological essay. Peter then remembers Armenia had been where Turkey is now, so he selects volume T. This is already somewhat more promising, with photos, maps, export statistics, and any number of stories about the sultans and Atatürk. Armed with bibliographical data, he finds material at the public library. He begins to wonder at the fact that, in the books, Armenia is never mentioned, whereas American books do mention the Indians, who, after all, happen to have been there before the conquerors, just like the Armenians. But a school assignment is a school assignment, so he ends up writing about Turkey.

"So, what have you found out about Armenia?" asked his father with excitement a few days later at the dinner table. "I wrote about Turkey," replies the youngster. His father stares at him in disbelief, and there is a roaring stillness round the table. "You wha-at?" His father's voice quivers with rage: "You were supposed to …" "I know," his son cuts in, "but I couldn't find anything." His father begins to rant. "Don't you know what the Turks did to us?" "Of course," answers the lad, but in fact he knew nothing, as no one had ever spoken to him on the subject.

"Would your Jewish friends write about the Germans like this?" his father carries on, goading him. "Maybe." Saying this, the boy gets up from the table so that no one will see the tears welling up in his eyes. Why was there no picture of Ararat on the walls of the Balakian household, like the one of Milan at their Italian neighbours'? Why did no one ever talk about the past? It was only as a grown-up that he held in his hands the legal claim his grandmother sent to the U.S. government in 1920 against the Turkish state. Two whole generations of his family, with few exceptions, had died during the deportations. The survivors kept this under a shroud of silence.

Peter Balakian was thirteen when this episode took place, which he relates in his autobiographical book, *Black Dogs of Fate*, for which he received the 1998 PEN award. His son, James Gerard, is not much older today. He and his sister, Sophia Ann, grew up with a father who wanted Armenia to figure in history books once more, a father that broke the family's conspiracy of silence and built a foundation of facts and fiction for his children, so that their home should have no provisional character. As a poet he began his search for the silent, suppressed fatherland, triumphed as a writer and, as a lecturer on American Studies, presented a historical investigation about the great humanitarian interventions of America on behalf of the Armenians. *The Burning Tigris* catapulted him to the *New York Times's* best-seller list in a matter of weeks.

While on a reading tour of his *Black Dogs of Fate*, more and more people offered him correspondence from the period, and other unpublished documents. An article on the Hamidian massacres, by Clara Barton, the American founder of the Red Cross, unleashed the avalanche. "This is enormously important," he thought to himself. "I began to investigate, and realized American commitment towards the Armenians over the decades was the first international human rights movement in the U.S.," he reflects with his deep voice, unhurriedly, leaning back in his chair as someone very sure of his facts.

A mere 500 pages long, with unpublished material from private archives, the book offers his compatriots the moral choice: either the positive tradition of Theodore Roosevelt, who described the Armenian genocide as the greatest crime of World War I, in accord with American public opinion; or to go along with Roosevelt's successor, Wilson, who considered relations with Turkey more important than feeling sorry for the Armenians. Roosevelt did not fail to point out that he looked on Wilson's nonintervention as fatal.

No international issue of 1915–16 was given such coverage in the *New York Times* as the massacres. Close to 150 articles appeared during the months of the genocide, most of them on the front page. The reports made it quite clear that the so-called deportations led nowhere. Writers like Ezra Pound denounced these events. It was the American people—and not their government—that helped through humanitarian actions, as far as they were able. The American Red Cross, under the energetic leadership of Clara Barton, had declared the fate of the Armenians a priority after the massacres of 1894 to 1896 under Sultan Abdul Hamid. The first international U.S. care package was sent to "the starving Armenians." This expression became part of the everyday language in the States.

"Eat your food—think of the starving Armenians …" For the Armenian immigrants, however, this image became a hated stigma.

Balakian describes in his thoroughly researched book the pathway historical truth took in the U.S. after World War I, or rather the general idea of it. He shows how, piece by piece, truth was corrupted and sacrificed to strategic interests. Whoever holds power determines the truth. Whoever has oil, or access to it, can dictate the clauses.

From the early 1920s on, feelings shifted in favor of the Turkish version of history. In the following decades Turkish emissaries in the United States began to fight every attempt at political, scientific and artistic elucidation. When Metro-Goldwyn-Mayer bought the rights to film Werfel's epic, *The Forty Days of Musa Dagh*, the Turkish ambassador, Munir Ertegun, intervened personally, threatening to call for a boycott of American movies in Turkey. The State Department negotiated with MGM, who shelved the project. The success of this threatening gesture caught on. The more time passes since the events, the more funds Turkey pours into financing university chairs or pseudoscientific institutes that engage in publicly discrediting researchers who bring archival material out into the light of day.

This is what happened to the renowned American historian Robert J. Lifton, whose book *The Nazi Doctors* so irked Heath Lowry. As the director of the Institute for Turkish Studies in Washington, financed by Turkey, Lowry wrote the Turkish ambassador a long memorandum on why Lifton's book ought not to be left without an official denial. In the book, Lifton drew parallels between the less than holy role of doctors in both the Armenian genocide and the Holocaust. Lowry dutifully drafted a letter to Lifton, which Turkish ambassador Nuhzet Kandemir was supposed to sign and send off on officially headed letter paper. And so he did. When Lifton opened the envelope, the memorandum and Lowry's draft fell out. This unfortunate bureaucratic error in early 1995 gained the whole country's attention because, instead of answering the ambassador, Lifton and his equally committed colleagues, Roger Smith and Eric Markusen, published an article on "Professional Ethics and the Negation of the Armenian Genocide" in the respected *Journal of Holocaust and Genocide*.

Since then the climate has been gradually changing. Balakian documents and comments on all these steps in his book. "I'd like to keep reminding people that denying the genocide is its final stage. It is the attempt to demonize the victims and absolve the perpetrators. The fatal message of this is that genocide entails no moral responsibility. And that is fatal." The Armenian genocide became the pattern for all subsequent genocides in the twentieth century. "Hitler was encouraged by the collective absence of memory that had already taken over in the 1930s. This shows how important memory is in setting moral boundaries."

Shortly before leaving his home in Hamilton, in New York state, with his wife Helen, to travel to London, where the William Heinemann publishing house was launching the British edition of his book, the British ambassador in Yerevan denied the Armenian genocide. Many newspaper editors asked Balakian for contributions. Several days later he was still fuming. "The denial of the perpetrators is immoral and, for us, traumatic. But the denial by third parties who were bystanders is unforgivable. It shows the moral cowardice we face even today when crimes against humanity aren't stopped."

Balakian demanded the recall of the ambassador—who, however, remained in her post, with her government's blessing. Maybe Balakian should send her one of his first poems, called "History of Armenia." It shows how the trauma of the events is transmitted to descendants who, otherwise, have enjoyed a happy childhood in sunny suburbs:

One woman carried
the arms of her child
to East Orange last night
and fell on her uncle's
stoop, two boys came
with the skin
of their legs
in their pockets
and turned themselves in
to local officials;
this morning sun
is red and spreading.

If I go to sleep
tonight, she said,
the ceiling will open
and bodies will fall
from clouds. Yavrey,
where is the angel
without sword, Yavrey,
where is the angel
without six fingers
and a missing leg,
the angel with news
the water will be clear
and have fish.

Grandpa is pressing
pants, they came for him
before the birds were up—
he left without shoes
or tie, without shirt
or suspenders.
It was quiet.
The birds, the birds
were still sleeping.

(Selection of poems from the anthology *Sad Days of Light*, 1983)

7
THE MEMORY OF CILICIA: CLAUDE MUTAFIAN, HISTORIAN AND MATHEMATICIAN (PARIS)

Dorothea Hahn

The algebra exams are over. The Professor has finished correcting the last pile of papers and clears them off his desk. Retirement lies ahead for him, after four decades as a mathematician, finally at the University of Paris XIII, but he is not sorry. The vast field of the Middle Ages awaits him. Since the summer of 2004, Claude Mutafian has been a full-fledged historian, a career that has taken him to the southeast corner of the Mediterranean, to Cilicia, the last Armenian kingdom.

"I made my money with maths, and now I'll spend it on Armenia," says the 64-year-old lecturer. In his office in a half-timbered house in the Quartier Latin of Paris, there are books stacked up to the ceiling. Many are about the Middle Ages, in particular those 177 years of the Armenian kingdom of Cilicia's existence, from 1198 to 1375. For Claude Mutafian this brief kingdom was a Golden Age of Armenian history. "Because of the intermingling," he explains. "Before that the Armenians were wedged in between two powerful neighbours. Instead, in Cilicia they were at the crossroads of many different cultures. They had contact with all of them."

Cilicia became a kingdom at the time Greater Armenia, a mere 1,000 km to the northeast, was running into trouble. Before the flood of Seljuks and Mongols, increasing numbers of Armenians, including noble families, fled towards the Mediterranean, where they founded the kingdom of Cilicia. The Crusaders from Northern Europe took advantage of them in their struggle against the Muslim Orient. They used the strategically favorable territory as a bastion for their expeditions of conquest in the neighboring Holy Land.

Cilicia's international network became evident in 1198, when many representatives of European royalty traveled there for the coronation of its first Armenian king, Levon I. A few generations later, one of the most powerful rulers of Europe, the French king Philip VI of Valois, graciously called the king of Cilicia, Levon IV, "my Armenian cousin."

In their new territory amid the Taurus, Antitaurus, and Amanus mountains the Armenians experienced their last period of splendor. They built castles and monasteries, minted the first Armenian coins and, by means of the seaports they now controlled, traded throughout the Mediterranean. Their partners stretched from the four Levantine kingdoms and the Arab emirates through Byzantium and the Italian maritime cities to far-off Catalonia. As Greater Armenia had vanished from the map, the lords of the Cilician capital, Sis, regarded themselves, in the thirteenth century, as the kings of all the Armenians.

As the Armenians of Cilicia were militarily weak, they made up for this by diplomacy, not only with the European Crusaders but also with the powerful Mongols. In 1254 the Armenian king Hetum I traveled to the Mongol capital, Karakorum, thousands of kilometers away, where he struck an alliance with the Mongol Emperor Mongka Khan, whose troops were preparing the conquest of the West. More than seven centuries later Claude Mutafian admires him for this initiative. "A brilliant idea," he says enthusiastically, "based on the understanding that my enemy's enemy is my friend. And this is how he bought himself fifty years of tranquility."

Mutafian sports a full beard and waist-length hair, and a Caribbean guayabera shirt outside his trousers, a style he has followed since the late 1960s. At that time he was a guest lecturer at Princeton University and witnessed how American society, including students, was in favor of bombing Hanoi. He rescinded his contract and joined the other camp. From 1969 to 1971 he taught maths at Havana University. He is convinced that humanity had two enemies, the United States and religion. "The States since the twentieth century, religion from the start."

Till today Mutafian avoids the USA. If he happens to travel there he stays only for a few days. Among other things he blames Washington for its pro-Turkish policy toward the Armenian question. "If it wanted, the U.S. could force Turkey to recognize the Armenian genocide." Mutafian's atheism does not prevent him from working with the churches, the Armenian as well as the Catholic. Commissioned by the Catholicos of All Armenians, Karekin I, he organized an exhibition at the Vatican in 1999 on the relations between Armenia and Italy, which was Mutafian's biggest exhibition. He jointly inaugurated "Roma–Armenia" with Pope John Paul II, an event commemorated by a large photograph hanging in his Paris office, but, for Mutafian, the head of the Catholic Church is "an old scoundrel."

Mutafian is a loner. He does not belong to any party or any Armenian club. He does not accept money for his work on Armenia. "That gives me freedom of action," he says. He is as little interested in Armenian folklore as in religion. What are his interests? "To guarantee Armenian culture its place in history."

In order to do this he accepts every invitation he gets from scientists and laymen, schools and museums. One Saturday afternoon in March 2004 he gave a talk to children at the Armenian Cultural Center in the ninth *arrondissement* of Paris. Most of the children, between eight and thirteen years old, had never been in Armenia, either in Turkey or the republic. Some of them knew Armenian from their parents, others attended Armenian schools in Paris. Mutafian showed slides of cloisters and castles with the projector, reproductions of religious images and coins, and emblems of the ruling dynasties, going through the ages at great speed. He spoke of battles and coronations, of Frederic Barbarossa, who had been in Cilicia, and Richard the Lionheart, of "beautiful"—needless to say—Armenian princesses, as well as the French family of Lusignan, who married into the royal family. From that time on, French was also spoken at the already multilingual royal court at Sis.

Mutafian speaks to the children in Armenian, but reverts to French from time to time. "How did King Levon travel?" he asks. "He had a horse," yells a young child in French. A grandmother whispers something in his ear.

As a child, in the Paris suburb of Clamart, Mutafian never thought of considering himself Armenian. "I was French, and I in no way wished to be anything else." That his parents came from Asia Minor (they never said Turkey) he already knew, and that they had gone through big trouble could only be guessed. Like many survivors, the Mutafians never talked about that. It was only at his father's death that Mutafian found out what had happened to him at Samsun, on the Black Sea, in April 1915: that at seven years old his father had saved his life under the bodies of his parents and brothers and sisters; that neighbors had taken him with them on the march to Syria; and that on the way in Malatya a Kurdish tinsmith took him out of the column. "He wanted him as a slave in his workshop," said the son, "but that saved his life." Mutafian's mother was also from Samsun. Her father was shot at the city gates when she was only four. Her mother bribed Turkish officers to save herself and her four children.

Mutafian is sketchy in telling about his family's life in Samsun, with fewer details than about the kings of Cilicia who had reigned many centuries ago. He already took an interest in the Middle Ages as a school student, and in Latin and Greek as languages. He became acquainted with the Armenian Middle Ages a lot later. In 1977, he travelled for the first and, so far, only time to the land of his forefathers. "At some point you have to know where you're from." He visited Samsun with his French wife, and then the frontier region with Syria: Cilicia. And that is when he was taken over by his passion. He learnt Armenian intensively; he read; and he gradually replaced his mathematical research with historical studies. His last book on algebraic equations appeared in 1980, in France. Since then he has devoted himself to articles, essays, and books on Cilicia. He found out that the last Armenian king of Cilicia, Levon V, was a descendant of the French family of Lusignan. During the last year of his reign, Cilicia was conquered piecemeal by the Mamelukes from Egypt. In 1375 Sis, the capital, finally fell, the kingdom collapsed, and in 1393 the Armenian exile with French ancestors died in Paris.

Exactly 600 years after the death of the last Armenian king, Mutafian organized his first historical exhibition. "We French love anniversaries." Two presidents inaugurated the exhibition, "Les Derniers Rois d'Arménie" (The last kings of Armenia), that of France, François Mitterrand, and the Armenian Levon Ter-Petrossian. It was the first exhibition on the vanished kingdom of Cilicia, and Mutafian became internationally known.

The Turkish authorities have also heard of his work on the 177-year kingdom. In the region of Cilicia they had let the remains of Armenian castles and monasteries fall into ruin. The local inhabitants know nothing about the origin of the buildings. The Armenian era is no longer talked about. In the early 1990s border guards prevented Mutafian from entering the Turkish part of Cyprus. Since then he has not returned to Turkey, just in case. "An accident happens quickly."

Instead of visiting Cilicia, Claude Mutafian studies its history at libraries in Vienna, London, Rome, and Paris, as well as during his periodical trips to the ex-Soviet Caucasus. This is where, a millennium earlier, those that were to become the kings of Cilicia emigrated from. In 2001 Mutafian visited the Lachin corridor. In a forest he came closer than ever to the origins of "his" kingdom. A stone marks the place from which the Hetumids came from. Hetum I, the king Mutafian admires for his diplomacy, comes from that dynasty.

When necessary, Mutafian also connects with the present. During the transition to the end of the Soviet era he wrote articles on the Armenian minorities in the Caucasus. He participates every year in the April 24 ceremony commemorating the genocide, which in Paris starts out from Komitas's monument on the banks of the Seine. As for the matter of Turkey's joining the EU, he is in favour of conditioning acceptance upon Turkey's prior recognition of the genocide. Nevertheless he doubts Turkey is about to do that: "Negationism is one of the cornerstones of the Turkish state."

That France should have recognized the genocide in spite of Turkish threats is a result in which Mutafian had his share. He feels relieved about the step having been taken in 2001, even though he does not have any illusions as to the underlying reasons: "300,000 French Armenians exert a certain electoral pressure," he says. He explains Germany's reticence with the same mathematical logic: "Millions of Turks live in Germany. Berlin doesn't want trouble."

At the end of the 1990s Mutafian organized a campaign that made it to the front pages of the media. He wished to prevent Gilles Veinstein, an expert on Turkish and Ottoman history who refuses to call the persecution of Armenians in 1915 "genocide," from being accepted by the Collège de France, the Olympus of French science. He kept politicians informed, wrote articles and petitions, and almost prevented the election. To discredit Mutafian, who at that time was still a maths professor, his opponents branded him a "weekend historian."

Mutafian reacted as passionately as when he was a young mathematician in the U.S.A. By 1999, this "weekend historian" had begun working on his thesis. Three years later he earned his doctor's title in history. The subject of his dissertation was Armenian diplomacy from the twelfth to the fourteenth century. It is soon to appear as a book.

8

LORD OF THE BOOKS: VARTAN GREGORIAN, PRESIDENT OF THE CARNEGIE CORPORATION (NEW YORK CITY)

Huberta von Voss

Where is the garden of Eden actually located? Where did the tree of knowledge stand, from which Adam and Eve plucked the apple in defiance of God's commandment, signifying the end of our innocence and our initiation into the knowledge of good and evil? British archeologist David Rohl believes he has identified the spot, 15 km from the industrial town of Tabriz, in northwest Iran. The sources of four biblical rivers reveal the place where humans began their quest for truth and their struggle for survival.

When Vartan Gregorian was born in the Armenian quarter of Tabriz in 1934, the dusty city was certainly no paradise. Neither was his childhood; but that tree of knowledge was like a compass to him, steering him to the summit of the academic world in the United States. There he now runs the Carnegie Corporation, whose president he is, from the twenty-sixth floor of an office building on Madison Avenue in New York, handing out millions of dollars for philanthropic purposes. He has a professor's title, fifty-six honorary doctorates, and the same number of prizes and decorations, and is an adviser to the Aga Khan and Bill Gates foundations.

The small man who rose so high in the world does not send his secretary to receive me. "I am Vartan Gregorian," he says simply, with a warm smile.

When he was five, his well-to-do grandfather was arrested and, on the eve of World War II, tortured to death for alleged weapon smuggling. His beloved mother Shushanik died shortly after. The family was impoverished. Vartan and his sister Oyik were left with their absent father and their kind grandmother Voski, who, as an illiterate, equipped them with adages such as, "The reason you have a house with walls is to keep the family news inside. Don't make a private matter a public one." Vartan Gregorian has remembered the lesson well. Even today, absolute discretion is a rule for him. It is one of the secrets of his success.

Worry over the family situation made a voracious reader of him. The Armenian community library became his refuge. In his parents' house with mud floors there were only two books: a bible and a history of the world in English. At the community library he devoured Armenian translations of novels from Russian, German, Polish, French, and English literature, becoming a knight, a king, or a lover for a few hours. He found Victor Hugo's *Les Misérables* moving. Instead, the school playground and the street were less romantic for Vartan, who was short and owned a single pair of shoes that had to do for him from one Easter to the next. "You had to know the entire spectrum of Armenian, Russian, Persian, and above all Turkish cuss words," he writes in his memoirs. Only those that were quick-witted and had the necessary verbal agility stood any chance. In those days the later expert and historian of Islam learnt all that was necessary in order to understand the Muslim mentality, including the lesson of never trying to make an opponent loose face or attack him in front of women.

He finds Americans' incapacity of understanding the character of the Islamic world, and the general lack of historical knowledge, infuriating:

> One has to know each nation's etiquette, or else one will make big mistakes. We're now going through, above all in the States, a historical period, but without a historical view of the facts. Lack of knowledge isn't limited to Islam, but also includes American history. People live exclusively in the present, without any particular reference to the past. That's dangerous, because it leads to impromptu solutions. Then comes the awakening: one realizes how complicated things are.

A number of examples follow to illustrate the idea. When the president of the foundation speaks he quickly turns into the impassioned professor that has taught and worked for almost forty years at the best US universities, finally as president of the renowned Brown University. "Let's take the example of Iraq and the American attempt to create a new Iraqi flag." It is self-evident that he stresses the initial "i" in the country's name. Until the first Gulf War the Iraqis had a secular flag. Later they added the motto, "There is no God but God, and Mohammed is His prophet." In the model favoured by the Americans, this motto is missing. "For religious Iraqis it's obvious this phrase can't be eliminated, while Iraqi nationalists see it as an attempt to erase the past." Worse still, they have chosen a blue that reminds one of the Israeli flag, "and then Americans are amazed that there is such resistance to a new flag!" he says with incomprehension, and a brief mocking laugh. He has been American for a long time, and is grateful to his adopted country for all the opportunities it has offered him. But he keeps his prudential distance.

Gregorian wishes to fight against general ignorance by means of a great project planned by his foundation: all the fundamental Islamic and modern texts, on Islam and science, international law, progress, and minorities will be compiled and placed on the Internet so that the debate on the Islamic world acquires the substance which, in Gregorian's view, is lacking. "Religion is today also very important in the political area. We must understand this and deepen our knowledge of religions." The thing is to get rid of prejudices. "The name of the Virgin Mary appears more often in the Koran than in the Bible," he says, for one to think about this. Gregorian follows the footsteps of Andrew Carnegie who, as an indigent immigrant to the United States maintained: From knowledge comes understanding, and from understanding, freedom. The Scottish immigrant's portrait beams at him with paternal benevolence. "There's a lot that joins us. When we were young, neither of us had money to buy books, and we both thirsted for knowledge," he says, surrounded by dozens of untidy piles of books, monographs, and manuscripts.

Amid the creative chaos of his office, where he works fourteen hours a day six days a week, there is a giant photograph of his American wife, Clare, to whom he has been happily married for forty years. She also supported him during the hard times. When his hope of being made the president of Pennsylvania University was quashed in 1980, he said farewell to the state and got a somewhat discouraging job in Manhattan: to rescue the moribund New York Public Library on Fifth Avenue from its impending collapse. Idyllic times were left behind in the Pennsylvania countryside. The august board of the NYPL, as it was known to the mere ten million visitors a year to the magnificent building inaugurated in 1911, put the professor in the balance and found him weighty enough. Dr. Gregorian was now called "Greg." The boy that had had no money to buy himself books became the man who was to lord it over 29 million volumes in 3,000 languages and dialects, with a head office and 85 branches in Manhattan, Bronx, and Staten Island. "A library is a sacred place," he stated in an interview. "We contain the unique and the absurd, the wise and fragments of stupidity. We mirror the world in all its folly and wisdom." Each week 10,000 new volumes arrive. You find everything there, from the Warsaw telephone directory from the time of the Holocaust to historical maps of the remotest corners of the earth.

That the long tables in the reading rooms, tall as church naves, always have hundreds of readers at them at all times of day is owed to Gregorian's prodigious effort. When he began the salvage operation in 1981, New York was going through a difficult stretch. Cash boxes were empty, criminality was on the rise, and there were no funds available for public libraries. "I was in the right place at the right time. New York's full of chutzpah. So am I," he says, looking back.

During weeks he had meetings with each of the Board members, looked into the diverse sections of the library, sat down personally at the loan counter, and answered the information telephone. Then he came up with his master plan to rescue the sinking ship. By means of exhibitions, glamorous fund-raising dinners in the company of the stars of American literature in the sacred halls, and readings of books by their authors, he got the NYPL back into the headlines. His visit to the *New York Times* editor brought about the big change. Hardly a day went by without the newspaper carrying news on the library.

And then came the big breakthrough: the Vincent Astor Foundation donated 10 million dollars. New York City suddenly came up with a further 27.6 million. From that moment on, funds streamed in from all sides. More than 400 million dollars reached the library coffers. Once more it was "trendy" to help the NYPL. "I think he's the strongest-willed person I have ever worked with," is his former assistant, Joan Dunlop's, opinion. "People find it hard to say no to him. People think his power lies somewhere in his personality and his charm, but actually it's something else. It's his ability to make people think differently, to alter their perspective."

After rehabilitating the NYPL, in 1989 he became the president of Brown University, which belongs to the venerable Ivy League. In 1997, came his appointment at the Carnegie Corporation. All at once he fell very ill. "Till five years ago I was never once ill in my life. I've never been in hospital. I wasn't even born in one," he says. He decided to write his autobiography, specially for his three adult children Vahe, Raffi, and Dareh. "I'm very sociable, but very reserved at the same time," he reflects. It is clear he also extended his discretion to his children, never having talked to them about his needy childhood. "All my life I've poured out all possible enthusiasm around me, and I've never been antisocial, but I've always been very sparing in talking about my past. The most difficult was to write about my father. I took months to write that bit, as I had to break every taboo to do it. But I wanted my children to know."

He is happy with the long way that has brought him from Tabriz to his student days in Beirut and then to the U.S.A. In all this process he has always been restless. When the *New York Times Book Review* asked him what character in literature he would like to have been, he immediately answered, "I would like to be Voltaire's Candide. For Candide, with his deep concern for humanity, embodies a critical rationalism; a healthy skepticism; and a realistic optimism about mankind and the human condition." Vartan Gregorian will be cultivating his garden for a long time yet.

Words

9

SHADOWS AND PHANTOMS: MICHAEL J. ARLEN, WRITER AND MEDIA CRITIC (NEW YORK CITY)

Huberta von Voss

A heavy summer shower is falling outside. Thunderclaps drown out the din of horns from the yellow cabs, doing a roaring trade today. Beneath the elegant canopies outside the entrances on Fifth Avenue wait the local inhabitants with their expensive shopping bags or their thoroughbred dogs, until they can rush back into their apartment buildings. There are few outsiders in this area. This is where refined New Yorkers are in their element. Lightning flashes above the lake in Central Park. Michael J. Arlen suddenly gets up from his seat and briefly looks out the window. The storm raging outside is hardly audible in the perfect elegance of the drawing room. His wife felt like going out for a walk in the park across the way. He glides back onto the thick ivory-colored cushions graced with scarlet blossoms. Decorated with exquisite tapestries from India and China, English antiques, and books by Marcel Proust and other great writers, the sand-colored room resembles an oceangoing ship of which those onshore cannot say whether it is approaching or departing.

With his Roman head, Michael J. Arlen's aristocratic origin would be noticeable even downtown at the *New Yorker* office where he worked for many years. People like him simply move differently: more calmly, more self-consciously, like panthers. Whoever writes regularly for the *New Yorker* has made it, is part of intellectual New York, and sometimes even makes the rules beyond the Big Apple. Arlen has shaped attitudes toward the effects of television. His essays on the Vietnam War are still quoted today, each time images of new wars appear on the screen at dinnertime in the living room, when distant men die in salvos of bullets and men at home open another can of Coke. His expression "living room war" has become a regular element in the American vocabulary. Everyone in the U.S.A. who thinks about media esthetics and the violence of war does so with Arlen's collections of essays, *Living Room War* (1967) and *The Camera Age* (1981).

Thus the *New Yorker* applies to the war in Iraq what he wrote thirty-seven years ago on the Vietnam War:

> The cumulative effect of all these three- and five-minute film clips, with their almost unvarying implicit deference to the importance of purely military solutions ... and with their catering (in part unavoidably) to a popular democracy's insistent desire to view even as unbelievably complicated a war as this one in emotional terms (our guys against their guys), is surely wide of the mark, and is bound to provide these millions of people with an excessively simple, emotional, and military-oriented view of what is, at best, a mighty unsimple situation.

No man whose judgments are simple writes that way.

Whoever delves into Arlen's biography might feel that his reflections on the reality of images have to do with his childhood and, doubtless, with his parents, the question being whether one is who one pretends to be and how an artificial image affects the viewer's life. *Exiles* is the name of the book in which the author, then forty years old, took up the quest of his already dead parents. Both raised questions and both provided quiet answers to the question of who they had really been.

His beautiful mother, Atalanta Mercati, was born on a cold February day in 1903, the daughter of a highly decorated Greek baron and an American mother, who abandoned her husband and children for an Austrian aristocrat. Following the king's forced abdication, Atalanta was exiled with her father from their palace in Athens to a small Greek island. She spent her formative years among goats and olive trees, before the tides of time swept them into a new life between Paris and Saint Moritz. Or Cannes, where his grandmother lived, remarried to a wealthy Serbian prince, Alexis Kara-Georgevitch, whose independent country had disappeared from the map and who drowned in a hydroplane accident.

Finally, Michael Arlen senior (1895–1956), one of the first international literary stars, who earned a huge fortune with his novels about English society. He was born of Armenian parents in Rushuk, Bulgaria, in 1895 but grew up in England and expunged his original name when he began to be successful. Dikran Kouyoumyian is an almost ridiculously complicated name, he later told his son, whenever he had to write thank-you letters to his uncles in Manchester and

Argentina. A classy father who used to drive with his family in a canary-yellow Rolls Royce along the Côte d'Azur, his chosen place of residence. Who was a friend of Hemingway and Somerset Maugham's and was eternalized as Michaelis in his mentor D.H. Lawrence's novel *Lady Chatterley's Lover*. In London in 1924, when he was just thirty, he wrote *The Green Hat*, the definitive novel of a whole generation that, to the blare of jazz, tried to forget the horrors of World War I and the reality of the world economic crisis. The famous father, whose successful novel of 1929 was filmed as *A Woman of Affairs* with Greta Garbo, the "goddess," the first female Hollywood legend. The distant father, the shadowy figure, who emigrated during World War II to the United States and fell silent in his new residence on renowned Park Avenue in New York.

Who he—Michael J., born in 1930—is in all this tangled sequence of events is a precarious question, like a trunk he has been lugging along behind him but has never opened. When, in 1939, the door to a carefree childhood, brightened by the light of the Mediterranean, shut behind him and, to elude the approaching war, he was sent alone to a boarding school in Canada on the other side of the big puddle, he thought he knew one thing with absolute certainty—that he was English. Until one day, at the table, the headmaster's charming wife mentioned his famous father as an Armenian writer. This was not only embarrassing for the boy but also—and this is something he declares categorically—untrue, because his father was English and his passport proved it.

"Har-meenian?" his little Scots roommate MacGregor asks him in surprise after dinner. "What kind of sports do they play there?" "I don't know," replies Michael. "I've never been there. Probably the same sports as here." "Not cricket," answers MacGregor categorically. "Yes, cricket," says Michael. "Anyway, I'm English." "You can't be English," says MacGregor.

Soon, the question no longer needed to be answered, because the whole family was together once more in New York, and they became naturalized American citizens. His father traveled to Hollywood as a scriptwriter, where—like the majority of European literary émigrés—he would never feel happy. In a material sense, the boy's youth carried on without hardships and, like other smart upper-class boys, he studies at an expensive New England school. Yet he was missing something irrecoverable that is needed on the threshold of adulthood if one is to weigh anchor and travel to new shores: a harbor, a firm anchorage in childhood. Maybe this is why his writing style seems so intense today, as though he is trying to sail through straits with all his strength against the wind, with an economy of movement, toward his home.

Some years after his book *Exiles* was nominated for the prestigious National Book Award and raised him to the rank of a writer in the estimation of critics and journalists, he traveled to the land many diaspora Armenians refer to as the "old country," even if their families have lived elsewhere for generations: Armenia, at that time a tiny but vital Soviet republic in the Transcaucasus. *Passage to Armenia* is the name he gives the book, as it was no simple journey but rather a sort of transition through a space dividing the New York intellectual from his undiscovered roots. This book was his literary breakthrough: it won the National Book Award.

With heavy luggage, he and his wife flew from Moscow to Yerevan. He had armed himself with all sorts of books documenting the 3,000-year history of the Armenian people. His people, he writes—as though he needed to recognize that what he was experiencing was significant. His origin, as he points out at the beginning of the book, was often a burden to him. "That association of difference, one's own difference, with something deeply degrading, with sin," unconsciously prevented him from elaborating everything related to his Armenian provenance. Because his father had kept quiet about everything to do with the family roots, the son's identity took on a dual basis. "Something always lay between us—something unspoken and (it seemed) unreachable. We were strangers."

Michael J., the American, with an American wife and four American children, is disconcerted by the Armenian diaspora's extreme reaction to its past, which he, more by chance than intention, experiences in the U.S.A. He tells the story of the two old people who spend their time recalling the past and so forget to live in the present. "My father had committed no crime," one of the old men sobs time and again, and remains bound even decades later, bewildered, to his father's violent death. Nevertheless Arlen also relates the story of two Armenian brothers who succeed in the building trade and are unable to understand how their host (not Arlen) has so many books on the genocide. "What do you read this for? Haven't you read enough of such things?" asks one of the brothers. "Yes, it's all ancient history," says the other. How is he himself to feel, then, in whose veins also flows that blood, far from the sacred Mount, when he comes in contact with the people of Ararat?

His encounter with the trauma almost produced a great rejection in him. "Those damned massacres, I thought. That chauvinism, such a chauvinism of misfortune," he writes. Thirty years later, amid the impeccable elegance of his home, he repeats these words, which he originally jotted down amid the walls of Soviet buildings. In Armenia a man called Sarkis guided him around museums and galleries and apparently wanted to convert Arlen into a dyed-in-the-wool Armenian within a few days. One night the New Yorker said, "I hadn't realized the Armenians were so European." "We're not European, we're Indo-Europeans. That is not the same thing," said the other with finality. But, replied Arlen, there was interchange, at least, with the Crusaders. "There should have been a kinship, but there was not. For one thing, Armenia was so far away. For another, don't you know, we were the rug merchants, the traders." Sarkis laughed in a relaxed manner, while Arlen felt such a sudden rage at these seemingly casual remarks that he could hardly speak.

The memory of old insults, some big, others trifling, welled up in him. "Now don't get taken in by any of those wily Armenians," a friend called out laughingly when he left.

Wily Armenians! Rug merchants! Traders! What in hell did those things matter, I thought, trying to be more rational about it. But something had been let loose inside me: a shame, an anger. And I knew suddenly how it mattered. It mattered because it was supposed to matter. It mattered because I had said that it couldn't, mustn't matter. It mattered because my father had said that none of it existed.

He was still furious when he visited a museum of Armenian art objects.

I remember staring dumbly at an enormous orange-colored wine jar, peering at it studiously, and thinking, My secret is that I have always hated being an Armenian. I haven't ignored it or been shy about it—I have hated it. Because I was given the values of the Europeans and they despised the Armenians. And I have hated my father not, as I have thought all these years, for being too strong a figure or too authoritarian but because he, so to speak, stepped back and gave me to the Europeans.

As I remind him of these words from his book *Passage to Ararat*, he disowns them. "I never said I hated being Armenian. I wasn't even aware I was one," he says in a pleasant but categorical tone. Time cures all ills, smoothing cutting edges that are too painful when one hurries past them in memory. Mild is the man who has stopped writing for quite some time because he has begun to repeat himself, and so it is best to keep quiet. He has set dozens of photos of his children under specially prepared sheets of glass out on the table in the carmine dining room, in the luminous kitchen, and even on the shelf at the entrance, as if he wanted to break the spell and direct paternal regard outward, paying attention to his children and not losing sight of them. Pictures of cute little girls who all turned into stunning beauties. Images of an unspoiled world.

10

THE ASHES OF SMYRNA: MARJORIE HOUSEPIAN DOBKIN, WRITER (NEW YORK CITY)

Huberta von Voss

Some people inherit a gold pocket watch from their grandfather. Or a silver cigarette case with a monogram. Marjorie Housepian's inheritance from her grandfather is a dented brass cup. It was not willingly given. She found it when she was disposing of her mother's flat. A yellow label stuck on the goblet was written in her mother's handwriting:

> My father's cup. He was holding it when a Turkish soldier smashed his skull with his rifle-butt on the pier of the port of Smyrna, as he attempted to embark on a Greek ship with my mother. He lay dead in front of her. She had to leave him there. She took the cup out of his hand on 22nd September, 1922, the only property my mother took with her, apart from the clothes she wore.

Marjorie Dobkin, as she is called today, is a dainty lady of around eighty. Her fingers, instead, are anything but. They are fingers that have written a lot. They now hold the cup of her grandfather, who died in Smyrna when Atatürk's Turkish army set the legendary town on the Ionian coast in flames. Her grandfather was one of the 100,000 victims who, in September 1922, suffered a horrendous death. "It was the final chapter of the genocide," says his granddaughter. She has recorded it: *The Smyrna Affair* was first published in 1971, in the U.S.A.[1] Almost forty years later her extensive study still counts as the standard work on "The Catastrophe," as the Greeks call the burning of Homer's alleged birthplace. Another legend maintains the city was founded by Amazons, who furnished it with special survival features. Yet Smyrna, one of the most important port cities of Asia Minor, the city of Greeks and Armenians, Assyrians and Jews, fell and vanished from the map. Izmir was built on the city's ruins. Where Greek temples once stood there are factory smokestacks today. From Samos, Khios, and Lesbos the Greeks can discern, on clear days, the new outline. Less than a hundred kilometers separates them from a place which, since antiquity, was a part of their colonial history in Asia Minor. Now it belongs to the

Turks. "One of the keenest impressions which I brought away with me from Smyrna was a feeling of shame that I belonged to the human race," wrote George Horton, the American consul at the time. Twenty-seven Allied warships, among them three U.S. destroyers, received orders not to go to the rescue of the fleeing population, mostly Christian. The butchery, which went on for many days, put in motion by the Turkish soldiers before the fire, occurred under the eyes of the whole world. When the heatwave became too intense, the ships retired from the coast.

By 1923 the West had already begun propping up the young Turkish republic as a strategic partner. Consul Horton's words slipped into oblivion. The "Smyrna affair" evaporated from the public memory just as the town did off the face of the earth, until in New York a pretty woman with bleached movie-star waves, whose literary debut drew a lot of attention, set out to find witnesses. Her research, lasting years, was not motivated by the fate of her own family, about which, as was so customary, little was said, but was the result of a long journey through Europe. In the course of it she also visited Saloniki (now Thessaloniki), where numerous refugees from Smyrna lived. They told the young American with a New York accent and full of *joie de vivre*, how the Turks had set fire to the city. Marjorie traveled on to Izmir, where the Turks told her the exact opposite: that the Greeks themselves had set it on fire when it was conquered by Atatürk. And this is the way it figures to this day in Turkish history books.

Back in New York she looked it up in the *Encyclopedia Britannica*. In the fourteenth edition of that revered book of reference she found the Turkish version of the events. A look at the names of the authors showed why. They were three Turkish professors from Istanbul University. Curious now, Marjorie began investigating microfilms of what the *New York Times* published during those days of September 1922. On September 15, the title was: "Smyrna Burning, 14 Americans Missing. 1,000 Massacred As Turks Fire City. Kemal Threatens March on Capital. Our Consulate Destroyed. Fire Starting in Armenian and Greek Quarters Is Sweeping City."[2] Next day it said, "Smyrna Wiped Out. Killings Continue."[3]

Marjorie married at a young age an American marine who came back from Pearl Harbor with battle shock and mental confusion. Her knowledge of the navy led her to the idea of investigating the names of crew members in the logbooks of American ships. She found out which of them were still receiving a pension. By chance she also came upon Dr. Ralph Harlow, who had been a teacher at a boys' school belonging to the American mission in a Smyrna suburb.

Two members of the Jewish community of Smyrna were added to the twenty or so eyewitnesses still living. A long period of work began in the archives, during which Marjorie happened upon Admiral Mark L. Bristol's report, among others, in the Library of Congress in Washington. Bristol had sent an on-site report on the happenings to the State Department. This documentation also contained the official report of the Smyrna fire chief, Paul Grescovich. Fundamental in her study were the book by George Horton, *The Blights of Asia* (New York 1926), and Esther P. Lovejoy's *Certain Samaritans* (New York 1927). Both authors were eyewitnesses. From these and many other sources Marjorie Housepian reconstructed the days of the conflagration. "A contribution to modern history of distinct value," Lord Kinross, Atatürk's British biographer, said in praise. "Only now, 50 years later, does a writer ... dispel the clouds of smoke from the ashes of Smyrna. Proves that truth, in the hand of a skilled craftsman, can indeed be more compelling than fiction."

With her book Marjorie Housepian, whose second husband was an American Jew of Russian origin, touched the heart of the big community of Greek immigrants in the United States. But also the tragedy of the Assyrians, who were likewise expelled from Smyrna, found its place in history books by her offices. She is often invited to give talks by descendants of the victims. In this way, it is not easy to get hold of the lively, jovial authoress. Whoever wishes to invite her must wait till, among all her engagements, she can find a little gap in her agenda. Her apartment has been too big for her since her husband died, but she will find it hard to take leave of it, and this not only because she grew up in the area around Columbia University and watched her three sons grow up in that dwelling. From the drawing room's ample windows her sight sweeps the northern edge of Central Park. The setting sun sends its warm beams into the room, from which there is a wide view. It is no surprise that Marjorie still has many projects. Comfortably reclining on her armchair, she lucidly observes the world.

Her mother survived the genocide because she went to a mission school in Constantinople. The remaining family was deported from Izmit, on the Sea of Marmara.

> Her parents, brothers and sisters, and cousins were loaded on cattle vans in Izmit and sent to Konya. My grandfather was a very intelligent man. Each time there was a departure from Konya, with the promise that whoever arrived first at the destination would receive the best land, he and his family would remain at the end of the queue. One day some Turkish cavalrymen arrived and read names from a list. Everyone trembled. Those families had to report.

The list had been drawn up by her great-uncle, who, despite being Armenian, was part of the Turkish administration. Thanks to this list numerous families were saved. "They were sent to Smyrna in sleeping carriages." This is how Marjorie's grandparents found themselves in the port of the city in 1922, when the last page of the genocide was turned over.

Marjorie rises and walks, a little bent, to another room. She comes back right away with an old notebook. The light-coloured leather covers show the marks of time, and the pages easily come unstuck.

My mother's youngest uncle got his title of Doctor in Agronomy in Germany. The boys in the family had all learned German, because the schools were considered the most demanding. He was the only person in Turkey with this professional qualification. He became a member of parliament for a rural area. When the genocide began he protested as often as he could. They told him, "You talk too much. Take care, or they'll take you as well." He had assumed a Turkish name, Onnig Ihsan. "Make me a list," said Talaat, by which he meant, of his relatives. But my mother said uncle wrote down the names of everyone he could remember.

After her mother died, Marjorie came across this leather folder containing annotations that looked like names. "I personally can't read handwritten Armenian, so I took the notes with me to Nice, where I visited my aunt every year. 'Aunt Navart, can you read this?' Aunt murmured, 'I can't understand what it's about. It's just a lot of names.'" Marjorie's mother had never spoken to her about her uncle's act of rescue. When it finally got too dangerous for him to stay, he escaped to the U.S.A. "The end of the story is that Atatürk asked him to go back and direct an important school of agriculture. My uncle, who spoke French, Turkish, German and, needless to say, Armenian, was never able to pick up English. So he went back." Only when Izmet Inönü took power did he leave Turkey once more.

No one in the family talked about the events, just like in Peter Balakian's. If they ever mentioned them they spoke in Turkish so we kids wouldn't understand. But my grandmother could swear very well in Turkish. "Go to the darkest hell" is one example. We children picked up the words after a time, but we couldn't understand the connection.

One day she picked out a book from her parents' library, *Ambassador Morgenthau's Story*. "This is how I began to get into the subject." Years later Peter Balakian, a generation younger, read the same book and began contacting eyewitnesses of the genocide. "It shook me and greatly impressed me. I really didn't know anything about all that." But the history of her people in the "old country" did not become her literary theme straight away.

When I got back to New York I got a job as secretary to the president of Barnard College at Columbia University. I didn't really want to do that, but she was so lovely. Each time I wanted to resign she'd persuade me to stay. I didn't have to take down shorthand, and I could take my son with me. I did an evening course at Columbia on the other side of the street, in short story writing. Mine was nominated.

She recalls with pride her first steps as a writer. Finally, three stories resulted, about an Armenian family that owned a restaurant. They were immediately published. "The Random House editor called me. That was the best publishing house at the time. Anyway, I was very impressed with myself," she says chuckling ironically. He invited her out to dinner, whipped a contract out of his pocket, and made her a generous offer. "I hadn't a clue what to do. Each time I hesitated he'd raise the offer," she laughs. "Finally I got 3,500 dollars as an advance." That was an enormous amount of money for the recently separated thirty-year-old. "And I had no idea what I was going to write about. So I spent the money on a nice trip to the Middle East, just to increase the pressure to make up my mind what to write about." A little later her first novel, *A Houseful of Love* (London 1954) appeared. This autobiographical narrative on the beginnings of her family in the United States became an overnight success. The whole of New York was peopled by refugees of the Holocaust and other tragedies. More than 12 million immigrants arrived in the U.S.A. through the needle-eye of Ellis Island between 1892 and 1954. Marjorie gained a ready readership with her ironical observations about her family, who found Americans as strange as the Americans found the immigrants. "The *New York Times* owner's mother wrote to me, 'My family in Tennessee found it exactly the same.'" She received an offer from Broadway to turn her book into a musical. John Steinbeck's agent accepted her. "Once the script was ready and just needed a final polish, I went to a house for artists at Pyramid Lake. Two other writers were there, Arthur Miller, who shortly after would marry Marilyn, and Saul Bellow. We had our meals together, but otherwise each of us worked in our separate rooms."

In 1965, before the fiftieth anniversary of the genocide, the archbishop of the Armenian church in New York called her. "Your book's a best-seller. Write something and we'll make it to the newspapers. This is something we've never managed. We just talk to ourselves." So she wrote an article for the Sunday issue of the *New York Times* about the relationship between Armenians and Turks half a century after the events. But the article did not appear. The editor of the Sunday edition rang her up to say he was very sorry but, by orders from above, the story had to be shelved. "Until recently the *Times* has always tried to be nice to the Turks on account of Israel. Turkey always threatens," she says laconically. Finally the article appeared in the prestigious publication *Commentary*. "It was the first time something was published on the Armenian genocide in an international medium. With that, the ice was broken." Marjorie Housepian is proud of this. Nowadays younger authors ask for her advice.

Notes

1. First by Harcourt Brace Jovanovich, New York. Then, in 1972, by Faber & Faber, London. Since then, as *Smyrna 1922, The Destruction of a City*. 4th ed., Newmark Press, New York 1998.
2. Quoted in Marjorie Housepian Dobkin, *Smyrna 1922: The Destruction of a City*, 4th ed., New York 1998, p. 6.
3. Quoted in *ibid*.

11

THE TRACKER: NOURITZA MATOSSIAN, WRITER AND ACTRESS (LONDON AND NICOSIA)

Huberta von Voss

The June sun beats down pitilessly on the parade ground. Only a faint breeze ruffles the tips of the tall palms in front of one of the most luxurious hotels of the eastern Mediterranean—the Ledra Palace. Every one of rank and honor in Cyprus is seated on the grandstand. The island is still undivided. The British will retain their colonial power until 1960. This year like every other, the ambassadors' wives visited Alice Raphaelian, the best milliner in the little British colony. The great white plumes of the governor's ceremonial hat rise majestically above the scorched lawn. The brass bands blare. Her Majesty's soldiers stand to attention. It is the Queen's birthday, and the Empire parades past its subjects' gaze. On the other side of the square, surrounded by its Venetian walls, are the limits of the Old Town of Nicosia. Here, in the Zarah Sokak, live mostly Armenians. Even the milliner has her atelier there.

Nouritza is a pretty little girl with waist-length blonde hair and big brown eyes. She stands next to her parents on the balcony high above the moat, where she can watch the great parade. Alice has lent her an especially pretty hat for the celebration. All at once a soldier falls flat on his face from his position of attention. Smack! The summer heat has hit hard again. Secretly, all the children have been waiting for this moment, and start to count the number of soldiers who faint from the heat. Nouritza still laughs about it today. We are standing outside her aunt's house, back in the place of her childhood. Thirty years have gone by since she left. Since then, the Greek and Turkish frontier soldiers have been face to face, irreconcilable.

The neat English lawn of the parade grounds has become a wild meadow. Tennis socks and vests flutter, drying in the sun, on the stone balconies of the Ledra Palace. The high society guests have been replaced by United Nations soldiers now. The once grand hotel is now in the middle of no man's land. Its yellow sandstone façade is pockmarked by bullets from the civil war in 1974, which led to the partition of Cyprus. Zarah Sokak has also been abandoned. Swallows swoop in and out of the broken windows. The sandstone balconies have collapsed and the wind has unhinged front doors. The Armenians who had sought refuge here from the Turkish genocide of 1915 have had to flee yet again, this time because of the fierce struggles between the island's Greeks and Turks. Nouritza's family had also escaped at that time.

Just as in continental Turkey, Anatolian immigrants have been settled in Armenian houses, but near the border most of them are vacant. The Armenian quarter on the Green Line cuts the town in two with a ghostly feeling. Only someone like Nouritza is able to bring the ghosts back to life, populating the abandoned alleys with the power of her memory. We see her grandmother feeding baby chicks in the enchanted inner yard of the house; her aunt trying on a hat in the lofty workshop ornamented with Ottoman motifs; her mother taking out honey-colored baklavas from the stone oven. "We children always scurried back and forth, from house to house, with overflowing bowls. When my mother baked, she would put a big hunk on a dish and say, 'Take this to Alice.' She in turn would send us back with a pudding she'd just made. The dishes must never be returned empty," she recalls. We see Nouritza with her friend, Ruth, on their way to piano lessons. "It was torture," she moans, turning up her almond eyes. With her voice and her words, that are like color and spices, Nouritza rekindles the past. With her deep laugh, which encompasses the lightheartedness of childhood and a woman's wistfulness, she conjures up the melody of the past. And with her swinging gait evoking love and youth, the vital atmosphere is reestablished in which the Armenian community of Cyprus once flourished.

Nouritza, now a well-known writer and actress in London, stands outside her grandmother's house, now tumbledown and derelict. Her son Vahakn points the camera at his mother. Her elder son, Hagop, is by her side. Both grew up in London where it usually rains on the Queen's birthday. This is their first visit to the place where their mother was a girl. Nouritza, afraid of bursting into tears in front of her two grown-up sons, smiles and tells stories, and a lost world opens up before the boys' eyes. A car slowly goes by and the driver looks at us. Hagop gently draws aside his mother, engrossed in her tales of the past.

At the end of Zarah Sokak, high on the ramparts of the city's old walls, there is a park that borders the Greek sector of the city. On weekends young Turkish Cypriots go there to stare through the barbed-wire fence at the colorful activity.

A tin of the local Bixi-Cola and Marlboro cigarettes have replaced their free movement for decades. "We all learned to walk here," says Nouritza. "At that time no one had their own garden." A young Turkish woman passes by us leading by the hand her little daughter, who practices her first steps. Below the toddler's bright red frock her nappy can be seen. There are no longer Armenians in the northern Turkish Republic of Cyprus. Now it is little Cypriot and Anatolian Turks that learn how to walk in the park.

We turn into Tanzimat Street, where the parental house stands. The tension rises in Nouritza's face with every step we take. "Guess which of these houses your grandparents built," she invites the boys—but they already know, for their mother has stopped as though spellbound, looking at number 80/82. "Your grandfather had a commodities business, and kept mountains of spices in the cellar. There was always a smell of cumin wafting through our home." She has them take her picture on the entrance stairs of the house. An old red Opel comes round the corner and stops in front of us. The driver wears dark polarized Ray-Ban glasses with a golden frame. "You no take photo here!" he barks, and slowly drives on. Nouritza loses control of her feelings. The impressions have overwhelmed her. In a trance, she videos and photographs ceaselessly, as though wishing to prevent these last vestiges of the past from disappearing from the earth. She goes into the garden, now a virgin wilderness, and looks up. The yellow sandstone glares in the sunshine. "When I visited Aintab I realized my father had built his new home just like the ones over there." Close to the present Syrian border, Aintab was one of the big Armenian strongholds in the Ottoman Empire. We return to our car to leave the Old City. Suddenly the man with the dark glasses is there. He signals us to pull over and wait until his superior arrives. The warning is clear: no one is to delve into the past here. We are ordered to leave the Old Town.

"I've been an exile since I was born." What is said is said. This is how Nouritza's lecture 'On Art and Exile' begins at the Goethe Institute in Nicosia—on the other, the Greek, side of the city. "I wanted to go to Britain, to discover my identity." At the age of twelve the self-assured girl resolved to leave home. She had a hard time persuading her father to send her to boarding school. "But all that business of finding a new identity was merely an illusion. Over there we were third-class citizens." Since then Nouritza has not given up her quest, learning languages without rest, perhaps to finally come upon a magic alphabet. This is how she acquired nine languages, German and Turkish included. "I speak as best I can. I don't worry about making mistakes," she quips, like a child with the future still stretching out ahead. The experience of homelessness also shapes her interests as a writer. Both biographies she wrote are about artists whose work can only be understood from the viewpoint of an exile.

Her first book deals with the Greek composer Iannis Xenakis, born in Romania in 1922 (died 2002), who went to boarding school on the island of Spetsai and spent his student years in Athens in the Resistance against the Nazi occupation. In 1945, he was wounded by shrapnel from the British Liberation

Army and imprisoned. He managed to escape but was sentenced to death *in absentiae* by a war tribunal. He worked in Paris as an engineer with the architect Le Corbusier, soon becoming one of his chief designers. The parallels between architecture and music led him to modern composition. He found a teacher in Messiaen, who encouraged his application of chaos theory to musical composition. "For years Xenakis was ostracized by the musical world. But he made a path for himself, because he composed independently of the others, and believed in himself." Nouritza, who at that time was studying philosophy and music at London University, and at Darmstadt, in Germany, was fascinated by this outsider and, in the early 1970s, travelled to Paris. "He wanted to invent a new musical language," says Nouritza, who became his confidante. After a decade of research and collaboration with the composer, she published a detailed biography of this obsessive genius with the renowned Paris publisher Fayard in 1981. Nouritza also gets obsessed when she becomes fascinated by someone. She tirelessly gathers information, visits the places where they have lived, allows light, space, and sound to have their effect on her, speaks to people they knew, until a visual psychogram of the person emerges. "Who are you—Sherlock Holmes?" asks Xenakis gruffly, as she jots down an observation on one of the innumerable slips of paper she pulls out of her bag.

After taming Xenakis, a biography on American artist Arshile Gorky was on her mind. "A hard nut to crack," she admits, and works for twenty years. Gorky, alias Manoug Adoian, was born in 1902, at Khorkom, on the shore of Lake Van, at the easternmost end of present-day Turkey. On Nouritza's first trip to Turkey, she visited the birthplace of her own grandparents, whose elder daughter Satenig died of shock during the deportations. Nouritza's mother was given the name of her dead sister. "The journey to Van was the most moving I've ever made," she remembers. Only by going there, where hundreds of thousands of Armenians had lived since pre-Christian times, whose traces have been rubbed out almost competely by the bloody persecutions, could she understand the origin of Gorky's surrealist paintings. "The circle came to a close. I had found him." Each of his paintings originated in the tragic story. Fatherless since before the genocide, young Manoug fought in the siege of Van, walked the 150 mile march past Mount Ararat to Echmiadzin. In Yerevan, his beloved mother Shushan died of famine, and this forced him to emigrate to the U.S.A. as a young man. "For the first time I fully understood in Van, just how much the Armenian race had lost: not only vast territories, cities, lives but its history, its memory." In America Gorky succeeded in the Boston and New York world of art, turning into an idol of contemporaries like Willem de Kooning and Mark Rothko. Yet he never managed to ovecome the loss of his home and the impossibility of returning to Van. "Kneeling on the far-away soil of suffering, my soul is drinking the wounds of twilight," Gorky wrote in one of his first poems published in *the Grand Central School of Art Quarterly*. He didn't disclose his Armenian identity to others though. His soulful dark eyes and towering height allowed him to pose as Arshile Gorky, nephew of the celebrated writer, Maxim Gorky (or Gorki). In the 1920s, everything Russian was "chic" for New Yorkers. Armenians were regarded as "starving Armenians," as Nouritza writes in her stunning biography, *Black Angel: A Life of Arshile Gorky* (London 1998). "Gorky no longer wished to carry on identifying with his birthplace, which had vanished from the map." A loner who never adapted to the United States, he took his own life in 1948.

On traveling to Van in search of Gorky, Nouritza also discovers the origins of her own family. "My childhood was replete with horrific stories about the Van massacres," she recalls. For many years the inveterate traveler was unable to summon up the necessary courage to visit the root of their common destinies. When she finally did, she was able to bring to a close a decade of research and interpretation. The well-known Canadian film-maker Atom Egoyan was so impressed with the book that he made a film inspired by Gorky, basing his female lead character, Ani on Nouritza, in great measure to elaborate his own Armenian roots. *Ararat* drew attention at the 2002 Cannes film festival for breaking the taboo on the Armenian genocide.

After the great success of the biography, Nouritza organized a traveling exhibition and wrote a theater piece on Gorky, from the viewpoint of four women who were important in his life, his mother, sister, sweetheart and wife. Since then she has toured this moving solo performance with music and images at the London Tate Gallery and the Edinburgh Festival, as well as in New York, Beirut, Yerevan, Nicosia, and Teheran. A chair in the middle of the stage is her only prop, while an apricot scarf, sometimes wound round her head, sometimes round her hips, does for a change of a costume. Nouritza's self-assurance is strong enough to act the parts of the four women in public, with only images, music, and lights. Her drama studies at the Dartington College Theatre Department prepared the multi-talented artiste for this venture.

But bags are already packed for a new track-finding voyage. This time it is the German poet and travel chronicler Armin T. Wegner that Nouritza wishes to portray. Wegner became an eyewitness of the genocide while serving as a Red Cross nurse in the German Army based in Turkey. He took dozens of photographs, which he spirited out of the country at great risk to himself, so as to inform the German public of the crimes. Today they hang in the commemorative museum at Deir-es-Zor, the final point of the death marches, as well as in the Genocide Memorial Museum in Armenia. Over the years these photos have become the Armenians' main evidence in their toilsome task to obtain international recognition for the historical accuracy of the genocide. Wegner, whose travel books sold in huge numbers, nevertheless lost his writer's voice after the traumatic events of the German persecution of the Jews. A "burnt-out poet," he retired to Positano, Italy, where he spent the rest of his life writing a four-volume novel on the Armenians, called *Die Austreibung* (The Expulsion), which was never to be completed. Opinions about him differ greatly. Some consider him a talented poet and tragic hero, others a conceited military tourist with a tendency to use self-aggrandizement or a very middling poet. Nouritza calls these contradictory opinions simply "fascinating!" From the jigsaw of her impressions on Wegner she means to put together her own picture.

When we left the Old Town of Nicosia, we went toward the sea to look for a little sandbank where, as a girl, she used to bathe on weekends. A few meters from the beach a gigantic monument that looks like a rocket launch pad rises to the sky. The Turks of the island call it the "landing monument," for Turkish troops arrived here in 1974 in support of their "blood brothers." After the ceasefire, and despite the presence of UN troops, they stayed on. Instead the Greeks called the monstrous concrete structure—in accordance with their version of history—the monument of "invasion." Down at the seashore, we perch on a low wall. She feels it's too cold to go into the water. Next day she will perform her piece on Gorky, and wishes to give her voice a rest. But she finds it hard not to dive into the water like her sons, who swim to the islet in the tiny cove and climb onto the rocks. "I wonder whether children still call it Snake Island as we did?" she asks in a low voice

Dreamily she contemplates the little island, humming the poignant Armenian melody she will sing next day in her show. Her face lights up with relief at not having lost control of her feelings in front of her sons during this return to her childhood. They have supported her, wordlessly, catching her hand, putting their arm round her shoulder every time it was needed. "Oh, what is the point of crying over spilt milk? It's too late go back now," she says with finality. She jumps from the wall and hurries down to the sea, letting the waves lap around her legs. Her red blouse flutters over her light skirt. She wades through the shallow water. And suddenly she starts to run, to jump over the waves, changing back into the little girl who first learnt to swim there.

12

DIFFICULT TRUTHS: NANCY KRICORIAN, WRITER (NEW YORK CITY)

Hrag Vartanian

By her own admission, Nancy Kricorian is an intellectual. A recognized poet, she is more popularly known as a novelist, with two books that give voice to some distinctly Armenian American realities. A native of Watertown, Massachusetts, she's an unlikely New Yorker, who first arrived in the great American metropolis in 1984 and slowly fell in love with a place she first considered dirty, noisy, and crowded.

Today, she bucks the traditional adage that New York is no place to raise kids, and has settled with her family in the city's academic heartland that circles Columbia University. She is part of the American literary tradition, which takes for granted that America has been woven with the threads of varied cultural narratives.

Kricorian, like her writing, is taut and rhythmic and has a tone that is distinctly American. Yet there is also a recognizable Armenian voice in her writing and thinking, one that comes across as innate, something I can only think to describe as cosmopolitan. It is a sensibility that seems to permeate her life in every aspect.

As a poet, Kricorian is cultivated and doesn't shy away from images that jolt her readers. In her poem entitled "My Armenia" she writes:

"Armenia is a country where someone is always crying,
Women punch in and out on the clock, grieving in shifts.
1895, 1915, 1921, the thirties, 1988, 1992, 1993, 1994 ..."

Her humor is black, vintage, but chillingly precise.

Unlike the cinematic quality of her poems, her novels chart emotional journeys in which her main characters, who have huge appetites for the world and a naivety that allows them to explore it thoroughly, partake.

Her first book, *Zabelle* (1998), took six years to finish and emerged as part of an explosion of American novels at the end of the twentieth century that confronted the legacy of the Armenian genocide. As if to make up for lost time, Kricorian's book, along with Carol Edgarian's *Rise the Euphrates*, Peter Balakian's *Black Dog of Fate*, and others, was poignant and powerful. Already in her first volume you see a developed voice with strong contrasts—intense and casual, sensitive and pragmatic, cautious

and uninhibited. In *Zabelle*, Toros Chahasbanian is afflicted by a memory that almost consumes him in his old age. He admits to his wife, Zabelle, how he witnessed Turks dragging away an Armenian neighbor, "I watched the whole thing, and did nothing. God will never forgive me," he confesses.

Kricorian's second novel, *Dreams of Bread and Fire* (2003), released five years later, follows a rebellious half-Armenian half-Jewish young American woman, with an almost superhero sounding name—Ani Silver.

Kricorian's third novel completes an unofficial trilogy that grapples with a difficult century, one that has been particularly tumultuous for Armenians. Set in Nazi-occupied Paris during the 1940s, the story centers on the Armenian neighborhood of Belleville.

As the middle tome of her trilogy, her still unnamed novel is according to the author about some simpler questions that don't have straightforward answers.

> What was it like to be an Armenian who survived the genocide, started this new family and your next door neighbors are Jews? You wake up this morning, July 16, 1942, and the French police come and are dragging all the Jews out of your building, and you live in Belleville and half of the people in your building are Jews. What do you think about that?

Kricorian is mining the complex history of a time that pitted communities against each other and its citizens against themselves. The dilemma at the core of her third novel is typical Kricorian.

The history Kricorian is unraveling in her new novel is difficult and highly politicized. Half a century after the fact, she is at times still uncomfortable discussing all the peculiarities for fear that some people will claim she is being partisan. One woman she interviewed in Paris urged in a chilling tone, "You must be kind." Kricorian didn't understand at the time what that meant, but now she realizes what her interviewee must've meant—it is a story tangled into many tight knots.

In her novels, moral dilemmas are carefully dissected but they always become fragments of larger systems, which does not make for easy morality. Kricorian's characters don't dally or navel gaze, they are sometimes curt, often direct, and always emotionally present, even when they are confronted with something as horrific as genocide—all qualities that seem to emerge from the author's own personality.

"I write from my obsessions," she admitted at a recent book-reading for young Armenian students and professionals in Manhattan. "Right now I am writing about Armenians because that stimulates my imagination."

Kricorian lives with her husband, screenwriter and film producer James Schamus, and her two daughters in Morningside Heights, where they recently relocated after years on the more pastoral Riverside Drive.

While her writing receives the brunt of her creative passion, more recently she has become an active organizer in the New York chapter of Code Pink, Women for Peace—an activist group with a progressive agenda.

"I devoted the six months leading up to the 2004 U.S. Presidential to unseating the junta," Kricorian says referring to the shorthand many in American leftist circles use to describe the Bush administration—it was a project that temporarily sidetracked her latest novel. As talk drifts from literature to politics, the relaxed conversational manner, which Kricorian spikes with laughter and anecdotes, shifts to something more dramatic and stark. She sees the need to fight against an aspect of American society that wants to deaden the public's interest in real change, particularly political, as much as possible. "They want us to watch TV and shop," she insists. Kricorian doesn't like playing dead.

"Part of the reason I'm feeling very politically engaged is because of the research I have been doing for my book," Kricorian admits about a process that began when she was writing about the Armenian terrorist character in *Dreams of Bread and Fire*. During that time, she came across a French documentary, *Des terroristes à la retraite* (Terrorists in Retirement) about the members of the French resistance pictured on the infamous *L'Affiche rouge* (red poster) which the Nazis plastered on the streets of Paris in 1944. This unlikely group, described by the fascists as "Jewish, Armenian, and other stateless terrorists," were predominantly Eastern European revolutionaries headed by the Armenian poet, Missak Manouchian—it was a major discovery for Kricorian.

When she began her footwork and appealed to friendly French Armenians for contacts, she was disappointed that they all ended up being intellectuals and other learned types. Kricorian sought out everyday people to understand the working-class milieu. It took a couple of trips before she was able to crack through the tight-lipped "resistance" community. Things started falling into place when she met Arthur Chakarian, one of the last living members of the Manouchian group.

While the story on the surface could easily be one that glorified the resistance of French Armenians in the period, Kricorian has glimpsed a fuller story, which includes some prickly and unflattering chapters that don't allow such a storybook retelling.

There is also an ironic fact that is not lost on the author: these were men—in the case of the Manouchian group—that were labeled terrorists by the Nazis and are now viewed differently through our contemporary prism. It is a fact that can gray ones perspective when the American government is busy making black and white assertions during their post 9/11 "war on terror".

Other digging revealed that some small sectors of the Armenian community shared Nazi sympathies and wanted to change the Nazi perception of Armenians as Semitic and, like Jews or "Gypsies," "nationless vermin."

One blonde, blue-eyed little French Armenian girl named Anahid Der Minassian was trotted around Paris to prove how Aryan Armenians supposedly were.

> One of the totally bizarre things is that there were different [Armenian] people fighting with the Nazis for different reasons. I met a guy in Paris who had been in the Soviet army and he was very young but I believe he was a commander of a group that included Chechens, Georgians, Armenians, Uzbeks—some of them were 18, 15, 60, some of them had no boots, they were a rag-tag kind of thing.

They were captured by the Nazis and put into a prisoner-of-war camp in Poland, where they were basically being starved to death with food rations that would keep them alive for only three years. So it was enough to keep the body functioning while the body slowly ate itself. Kricorian said:

> This man was in the camp and [the famous Armenian] General Tro came and said, "We don't know how this war is going to end, we don't know who is going to win, but we want you alive because Armenia will need you at the end of the war, so put this German uniform on." So he joined the Armenian battalion of the Wehrmacht.

Kricorian explained that his story was endemic of the few thousand Armenians that sided with the Nazis. But the tale doesn't end there and continues into a more Byzantine saga.

Some of the Armenian soldiers from that Nazi battalion ended up in Paris, where they met members of the city's Armenian community. The local leftist Armenians, which included the family of famous singer Charles Aznavour, played a role in trying to convince the soldiers to desert and offered them help to slip under Nazi radar into hiding.

While the theme of political violence permeates her third novel, like it does her previous two, the real story evolves in the resistance to violence. In *Dreams of Bread and Fire*, while Van is the most obvious example of resistance, it is Ani's story that is a true act of subversive resistance—the young woman carves out her own unpackaged identity. It is a resilience Kricorian seems comfortable with, as if it is part of the obsession that drives her writing.

It is a tribute to the author that her characters are palpable. Her literary style maintains a focused trajectory towards self-actualization and her characters travel that path wide-eyed and never cynical.

At the beginning of *Zabelle*, the main character says, "I remember what it was to be a child—you see the world in pieces." It is a crucial line that explains why memories jostle each other in both her published novels—and even her poetry—and open up into a fuller picture, but never without seams.

"I don't think [Zabelle] sees the world whole but as an adult you can make the connections between the different scenes and impressions that you can't do as a child," Kricorian explains. "This perception had to do with watching one of my daughters, who seemed to have a map of the world in her head that was quite sophisticated in some small patches, but there were gaping chasms between these areas of knowledge."

Kricorian's own books seem to construct a larger portrait of Armenian life in the twentieth century. It is a series of stories that are not easy to tell, and uncomfortable for some to hear. She says:

> I feel that even in the Armenian community, when I was working on my [second] book [and wrote about an Armenian "terrorist"] they were like, "Oh, the Turks say Armenians are terrorists, so you can't write about that, you are just playing into their hands.' I think that life is complicated, people are complicated, politics are complicated and there are all different kinds of people doing different things and its fascinating how people make the decisions they make, and I want to write about it.

She searches for an anecdote that demonstrates her defiance of rules, "One time when I was having a fight with my father and he said, 'Now don't you talk to me like that.' And I responded, 'I'm going to talk, and I'm going to talk and you can't stop me.' That is a kind of resistance, they are telling me to shut up, lie down, go shopping, no, I don't want to." For Kricorian, the alternative to resistance is a state of helplessness.

13

A SEEDBED OF WORDS: HRANT DINK, EDITOR-IN-CHIEF OF THE ARMENIAN NEWSPAPER *AGOS* (ISTANBUL)

Huberta von Voss

He was seven when the door closed behind him at the orphanage in Istanbul. That day marked the end of the carefree times of his childhood, when mother, father, and their three sons were happy in poor Malatya. But family life already began to cloud over when the family moved from the former Armenian stronghold in eastern Anatolia to the Turkish metropolis on the Bosporus. The couple split up soon after arriving there, and in this way their life with their children came to an end. A relative sent the boys to the orphanage. None of them ever saw his parents again. Childhood now meant living in a Turkish environment as the child of a repudiated minority, with neither fatherly protection nor motherly love. All that was left was a brother's hand. It is possibly this early existential experience of little Hrant's that today determines the political stance of the fifty-year-old editor of the Armenian newspaper *Agos*: the attempt to overcome loss and isolation by means of a fraternal attitude toward the Turks, and so guarantee future security.

There is heavy traffic in both directions downstairs on the long Halaskergazi Street, where dozens of old yellow taxis weave in and out, and the toot of buses covers the confusion of voices from the pavements. There, at 2 p.m., there is no sign of Oriental siesta drowsiness. People, like the traffic, stream in apparently uninterrupted columns to the little shops crowded together on both sides of the thoroughfare. Here, in the middle of the Osmanbey quarter, whose population is overwhelmingly Turkish, is where the thirty-five employees of the weekly *Agos* work. The location of the editorial office is like the paper's policy: to be inserted in everyday Turkish reality.

Agos is far from being the first Armenian periodical in Turkey, where a Turkish daily already published a supplement in Armenian as early as 1832. More than 450 newspapers, magazines, and yearly almanacs existed from then on, in which, besides community news, mainly Turkish news appeared translated into Armenian. *Agos*, "Furrow" in English, founded in 1996, now does the very opposite: it deals with Armenian community events in Turkey "in our neighbors' language," that is, in Turkish.

This idea arose among ex-bookshop owner Dink and a few friends. After decades of negative headlines and anti-Armenian propaganda in the Turkish press, they wished to give the public a different, more balanced image of their community. Until then the most numerous Christian minority was held to endanger state security directly or indirectly. The background was bloody attacks by the Armenian terrorist group ASALA, which left as its toll dozens of victims among Turkish diplomats abroad. The constantly stirred up suspicion that the Armenians backed the Kurdish PKK and number one enemy of the state, Öcalan, gave strength to this image of treachery. Dink and his friends decided to attack this ongoing hostility. "We wanted to sow something other than distrust." This is how the idea of the weekly *Agos* came about, which has already been tilling the ground of public opinion for five years.

Dink looks like a print from a neo-realist woodcut. His head is like an Otto Dix drawing. His powerful, clear features reflect his purpose of sketching reality in clear strokes, and freeing it from obscurity. Dink has the wide-awake and tolerant look of a zoologist, which is what he first wanted to be. Yet the basic questions about human existence took pride of place before zoology, and Dink studied philosophy on a Gulbenkian grant. But he never lost his penchant for precise observation of behavior patterns. If it is a matter of "eating or being eaten," be it an individual animal or whole species, the human world also has a lot to do with the survival of individuals, ethnic minorities, and nations.

The greatest danger for minorities, thinks Dink, lies in their isolation. "Our identity as a closed society is one of the fundamental reasons for creating *Agos*," he explains in Turkish, which he must manage brilliantly, as few Turks do. According to Dink, the origin of this isolation comes from the Treaty of Lausanne, which in 1923 established the legal bases for Turkey, endorsed by the European powers and the recently created republic. Amongst these were included the rights of minorities. After the deportations and mass killings from 1915 to 1922, there were some 300,000 Armenians left in Turkey, 170,000 in Anatolia and the rest in Istanbul. "Following the spirit of Lausanne, the officially equal minorities should and could float like icebergs in the great sea that was Turkey," notes Dink. Existence as a closed society was at first a relief for the Armenians, traumatized by the events, but mass emigration of compatriots made it necessary to redefine their identity. "After the 1980s our community had shrunk to 60,000. We realized we could not carry on living like an iceberg," says Dink, turning over the coin of the partly deliberate, partly enforced isolation. "We wished to leave aside our fear of melting and, instead, voluntarily turn into water with our own culture."

That the way of assimilation also calls for concessions is something Dink and his colleagues accept. As a Turkish citizen Dink cannot and may not share the international diaspora's often frankly anti-Turkish stance, whereby the Turkish state's recognition of the genocide is a precondition for any future dialog. "Armenians that parade every 24th of April are Armenians once a year. We're Armenians every day." Many diaspora representatives are not fond of the word dialog. "For them we are the people of the State par excellence," he says with an angry shrug. He describes his relation toward the diaspora with a caricaturesque image:

> You fell a tree and any number of people water the dead trunk with their tears. Only a handful kneel and dig down in the ground to find roots and new sprouts. I'm one of this last group. It's these roots that will one day grow and propagate the tree's life. The diaspora look at the past as a nostalgic element of their identity. Instead, we see in history a determining factor of our future.

He, too, considers Turkey should face its history, but outside pressure does not help in this respect. Foreigners have waited eighty-five years to protest against the injustice that was perpetrated, he says critically, and supposes the debate on the recognition of the "events" to be put in motion by countries' individual economic interests, as well as Turkey's interest in joining the EU—importunate as many European countries see it. "Can a tragedy in any way wait for good days or bad, in other words, a favourable moment, to protest against it?" For him, historical truth should not be subject to fashions. He himself often uses words he finds more striking than genocide, which in his paper—so as not to draw the censors' attention—he only writes in inverted commas. "When asked on a television program if I believe in the 'genocide,' I say, 'History isn't something you believe in. There are only facts that have taken place and others that haven't. And I know what happened.'"

Instead of getting angry at the restricted freedom of expression, he declares that the term is unimportant:

> No one has any right to tie me to any particular term, when history is a book of many pages. In 1914 there were more than two million Armenians living in what is now Turkey. At the time the republic was founded almost a decade later only 300,000 were left. Many of those that disappeared had died on the way to deportation. Others escaped or emigrated in time. Many became converts, some were sheltered by good neighbors, and many children were adopted.

Dink refrains from mentioning the abundant documentation proving the massacres of Armenians, and says instead, "It was a time of great distress. There were good stories and bad ones side by side. We must look at the whole of history. It's also a part of it to accept our ancestors' guilt," he says in a conciliatory tone. Self-flagellation instead of flagellation? Or the simple attempt of building a bridge that will not cave in on crossing it? In order to promote this point of view Dink, already recognized internationally, may travel abroad—the Turkish state accorded him a passport for the first time in his life only a few years ago.

Dink does not need to let himself be reproached for not promoting the internal Turkish debate on the injustice committed. Thus he wrote in an editorial of June 2001 about the day of remembrance, April 24: "Armenians the world over can participate in this commemorative date, except those of Turkey. The Armenian problem will only cease to be such when the Turks take part in the ceremony alongside the Armenians." The issue was immediately prohibited. "Some people found that a bit much," he says laconically, and sips his glass of tea.

Through his office window comes the incessant noise from the street. It is hot in his modest, though luminous, office at the end of the passage. There is no air conditioner to freshen the writers' sometimes minute offices. One lives, works, and manages with one's circumstances. In this run-down, early nineteenthcentury building one senses the hope of assuring the Armenians their future in the land of their ancestors in the twenty-first century, through dialog with their Turkish fellow-citizens.

They also want to improve relations between Turkey and Armenia. This commitment of these journalists is not merely a matter of goodwill. It has to do, to put it simply, with the survival of a minority that tilled the land of present-day Turkey as its first ethnic group. Hrant Dink, who shapes his words as if they were clay, thoughtfully rests his arms on his knees. Then he says, gently, "I'm no more than a drop, very far from the Armenian waters; and if a channel isn't built, I'll disappear."

I met Hrant Dink for the first time in the year 2002. He had never left his country by then. Shortly after, he, a Turkish citizen since his birth, was given a passport for the first time. Since then he has been traveling all around the world to promote his ideas on dialog. The Turkish government seemed to like this stance untill the day, the EU member states opted to open accession talks with the eager candidate from Ankara in early October 2005. To create further trust in the democratic standard of the Turkish society, Foreign Minister Abdullah Gül even supported in the very last moment the first ever held conference on the Armenian genocide at the Bilgi University in Istanbul, which took place in late September 2005.

Since then several Turkish intellectuals have been charged with insulting Turkish identity or threatening the security of the state as a result of their open remarks on the history of 1914–1922. The case of Orhan Pamuk, the best-selling Turkish author and Nobel Prize Winner of 2006 has made headlines all over the globe. Yet there are other cases that do not get the same international attention, like the ones of Hrant Dink, Ragýp Zarakolu, or Murat Belge. No matter what the sentences will be, this is a clear attempt to break the pen of those who speak up to a growing public of young Turks that are sick of the prevailing taboos in their society as well as to a growing crowd of nationalists that are allowed to openly threaten the accused. It is an attempt to scare people so that they refrain from asking questions or trying to find answers in an open debate. They may keep the concluding words of Hrant Dink's speech at Bilgi University in mind: "Do not fear."

Hrant Dink himself had plenty of reasons to be afraid: since 2005 there had been four trials pending against him for allegedly "denigrating Turkey" and "insulting Turkish identity." He was sentenced to six months of prison in October 2005, which was suspended. Since then, he has been constantly in the news. On four occasions the Turkish media covered the trials, often accusing him of being a "traitor." Each time the government in Ankara said nothing to stop this campaign. Hrant Dink subsequently became a prime target of the ultra-nationalists. Hundreds of hate mails were sent to him, he received death threats and people turned their heads when he was walking through the streets of Istanbul. He never wanted to be this sort of hero or anti-hero, but to live in peace in his native country. When he asked the government for protection, he was ignored. "I feel like a dove" he wrote in his last article – nervous, vulnerable, hated by some, and loved by others.

On Friday 19 January, 2007 Hrant Dink walked back to his office. The pavement was crowded as usual, but he loved this atmosphere and wanted to be part of it. He was approached by a 17-year-old boy from Trabzon who had travelled all the way down the Bosphorus to defend "Turkish honour" by killing a "traitor." Three bullets were fired at Hrant Dink's head. He died instantly. The assassin ran off after tucking his gun into his belt. Hrant Dink never ran away. Crowds gathered instantly. Hundreds turned into thousands. They brought banners which read in Turkish: "'We are all Hrant Dink. We are all Armenians.'"

Turks and Armenians were deeply shocked by his murder. Within minutes it became headline news around the world. Armenians held vigils outside embassies. In Istanbul, thousands flocked to the newspaper office to mourn him, on the very day of the crime. About 100,000 people followed his coffin some days later. "We are all Hrant Dink" was the message that could be read on thousands of placards.

Prime Minister Erdogan blamed the assassin for threatening the whole society. Yet who was willing to protect Dink when he needed it most? Will Hrant Dink's death bring about a profound change in the mentality? Will civil courage occur more often now? Will a visible crowd of Turkish citizens defend and protect those who are persecuted or still put on trial under § 301 and will they do it in time while they are still alive? Will more Turks now be able to identify with the situation of the minorities in their common country? These questions still remain unanswered.

Many people will remember the moving farewell speech that Hrant Dink's wife, Rakel, gave to a crowd of thousands who later followed the funeral car to the Armenian cemetery: "I am here with great honour and with great sorrow. Hrant has left the ones he loved, he has left my arms but he has not left the country which he loved more than anything." "Do not fear" – his words will continue to resound.

14

LA FEMME RÉVOLTÉE: HUMAN RIGHTS ACTIVIST AND PRESIDENT OF THE ARMENIAN PEN CENTER, ANNA HAKOBYAN (YEREVAN)

Rainer Hermann

She has always petitioned: in the Soviet Union, against injustice; in the Armenian Republic against antiquated behavior patterns. And, in addition, it was always for culture and freedom that she fought, she says. The small, buxom woman with short red hair restlessly moves back and forth on her chair, her hands gesticulating all the time to accompany her imperturbable thinking aloud. Preferably in French. She has lived almost exclusively in Armenia, but her mindset has a strong French influence.

"Camus wrote *L'Homme révolté* ("The Rebel") and I'm the *femme révoltée* (the rebel woman)," she says, laughing lightheartedly. Throughout her life she has spoken out every time her humanistic ideals were at stake. The human rights activist was born into a family of firm communist convictions, in Gyumri, the

second most important city of Armenia, called Leninakan at that time. Today the whole of her thinking is influenced by the French *hommes de lettres*, whereas her father used to recite the writings of Marx and Lenin. His bible was the *Communist Manifesto*, and his life was communism. His daughter never went along with this. "If communism is really so outstanding, why doesn't everyone struggle for it?" she asked her surprised father when she was a little girl.

Her father devoted his whole life to the ideas of communism. But that communism was utopian and unreal. Nearly his whole life, since in his old age even he understood, and his enthusiasm turned into disappointment. All of a sudden he saw through the corruption and injustice. "In his last years he said the system was rotten, and wouldn't be able to hold out for long," his daughter recalls. And he felt bitterness at having devoted his life to that system. His gifted daughter decided she was not going to repeat those mistakes.

Anna Hakobyan learnt dissent from her late father. Yet she was never a real dissident, she says, but was simply against injustice, and for culture, adopting a fairly moderate position. Instead, her husband was a born dissenter, fighting against the Soviet Union with his intellect and his pen. "You just can't stop him. He's like a bomb," Anna Hakobyan laughs, looking at her husband, Mikael Danielyan, even after decades of living together. He wears his dark hair in a ponytail, and at this moment is talking to his lawyer.

Their two children, a girl and a boy, follow in their parents' footsteps. They are both students, and neither thinks like the mainstream. "I'm glad about that, and sorry at the same time." Because demanding freedom and thinking freely are always hard in a country where, according to her, dictatorial practices are on the rise. She uses one word to describe her country's situation as to freedom of opinion and intellectual freedom: "Bleak. Bleak." Her husband was recently beaten up. "The state's behind that," she says darkly. "Maybe the president, maybe the Nagorno-Karabakh mafia," because Mikael was against the war for the enclave, and thinks the annexed region should be given back.

This is why he was seeking his lawyer's advice at that precise moment. He is not the first dissident to be thrashed since Armenia's independence. The people that put this in motion want to frighten him, make him keep quiet, not to kill him, she explains. "Nowadays I'm frightened, but he never is," she says, uneasy. Before the beating she was already worried something would happen to him or the family. Not so her husband, who always relied on his renown for protection. The international community recognizes him as the president of the Helsinki Association in Armenia. The International Helsinki Federation intervened promptly, writing more than 300 protest letters, including one from its head, to the president of Armenia, Kocharian—all of them asking what was going on in the country.

"Nevertheless, our authorities are insolent. They do as they please," says the fighting Hakobyan, sighing, almost a little resignedly. The popular opposition television channel, A1+, was closed down years ago. Magazines were banned. "There is nowhere left to air one's opinions freely," she says, shaking her red-haired head in anger. No, in Armenia there is really no intellectual discourse—and it is not as a nihilist, or because she refuses to see anything positive, that she says this. Her judgment is based on an example she knows very well, the Armenian Union of Writers. What goes on there is revolting and disgusting, she says. "They meet and applaud the government, just like in the Soviet era. The same methods, the same behavior." A boss is applauded, and no one contradicts. One is not entitled to one's own opinion. Even in independent Armenia the Armenian Union of Writers is like a Soviet organization, which receives money from the government.

"The debates that began in Moscow in the 1960s never got to Armenia," says the energetic woman indignantly. Because people were afraid. Pushkin himself remarked during his journey to the Caucasus that the Armenians were *poltrons*, that is, cowards. People still behave today as if they were slaves, asking what the point is in speaking out and banging their head against a brick wall, when they can live quietly.

In 1991, the year of independence, the PEN (poets, essayists, novelists) Center was founded in Armenia. In the Soviet Union this would not have been possible, as PEN Centers keep in touch with each other, and are very critical of governments, whereas in Armenia only communists became PEN members. Many were not even aware that the PEN had chosen them as members. In this way, no one did anything, no one criticized the government. All this changed when Anna awoke the Armenian PEN Center to a new life in 1999.

Restless Anna Hakobyan was elected president of the Armenian PEN Center, and has put a lot in motion since then. The Armenian PEN Center has several dozens of active members. With their limited resources they sponsor competitions, such as recent poetry, short story, translation, and essay contests. They publish yearbooks. Last year in Yerevan a conference of PEN International took place entitled "The Future of Poetry Through Translation." "And there are free discussions at our conferences. This is the only place where freedom of expression is enjoyed," she says proudly. In Armenia Anna Hakobyan has founded another organization, Tsovinar—Women against Violence, that is, domestic violence. The name of the organization is not accidental. Tsovinar is an Armenian mythological heroine, who, being subjected to physical and psychological violence, remains firm, rebellious, and just. Thus, Tsovinar embodies the first Armenian mutinous woman, who openly opposes the society. The general objective of the organization is to change the attitude of Armenian law-enforcement agencies and judiciary toward violence, and also to ensure protection of the rights and dignity of domestic violence victims for the sake of the formation of a democratic civic society free of violence.

Anna Hakobyan is a member of the Women's Committee, "Writers in Prison" Committee and Translation and Linguistic Committee of PEN International. In Armenia they draw up resolutions which they present at the General Assemblies of PEN International, where Armenia is invited, as a member of the European Council, to fall in line with international standards.

Today the PEN Center takes up all Anna Hakobyan's time. In former times chess and translating were of paramount importance, in other words, logic and literature. As a talented chess player, she was invited to Yerevan, the capital of

Armenia, while a primary-school pupil. Though tiny, Armenia has produced many first-rate chess players. While a high-school student, Anna became the chess champion of her Soviet republic many times and took part in Soviet Union championships. "But there was a lot of injustice there too," she says.

She played professional chess for fifteen years. At that time she began studying Romano-Germanic languages at Yerevan State University. From then she devoted herself to literature and translation. She translated from French into Armenian Albert Camus, Paul Valéry, Paul Eluard, Marguerite Duras, Saint-Jean Perse and many more. As she was a politically suspect intellectual, she was unable to publish her books in the Soviet Union. She would have had to be a communist for that. "That's something I never wanted to be." Other young translators were in the same position. When Armenia became independent, Anna Hakobyan decided to found a publishing house for translations. The name of the publishing house is "Anna&Mikael." A journalist of the left-wing Parisian newspaper *Libération* once told her he had never seen any comparable publishing house in all his travels round the world, that published French contemporary literature only.

Right after the fall of the Soviet Union, Anna Hakobyan was able to visit France for the first time, and they asked her when she had last been there. She was invited as a translator to the Saint-Jean Perse Foundation in Aix-en-Provence, where she, two years later, defended her doctoral thesis, entitled "Difficulties in Translating French into Armenian." In the Soviet Union and, even more so in Armenia, there had never existed a theory of translation. She finished her doctorate and till now is lecturing on the theory of translation at Yerevan State University.

She was already a professor and a publisher, but this was not enough for her. Thus, from 1996 on, she worked with her husband in the Helsinki Association. Mikael Danielyan has never been a member of any party, nor has Anna Hakobyan.

It was far too late, she says, and so she paid no attention in April 2004 to a few thousand demonstrators who congregated at the Opera Square demanding the resignation of the government. This should have been done earlier, in 2003, when it was shown there had been fraud in the parliamentary elections. And those responsible for shooting several members of parliament on October 27, 1999, had still not been made to answer for their action.

Everybody has a right to demonstrate, and she is also against the authorities, she says with certainty. But it is naive to expect a change of power through this. These demonstrations will not bring about any result, she forecast. And so it was. Armenians are always at loggerheads. Each one wants to be the leader. This way there can arise no strong opposition.

Yet, in her opinion, this should not bring one to "sitting on one's hands, twiddling one's thumbs" saying that it is impossible to change anything. Anna's credo is different: one should always be active, for she is a *femme révoltée*—a rebel woman.

15

VOCATION *AZGAYIN GORTSICH*. ZORI BALAYAN: AN INTELLECTUAL (KARABAKH-YEREVAN)

Tessa Hofmann

"Since my earliest childhood I've believed in the power of the printed word. This is why, when I became an adult I recruited into the ranks of the Fourth Power. At the same time I began to consider how I might best serve Justice and Truth." In the original language of this quote, Russian, nouns are capitalized only when one wishes to give them special importance. Zori Balayan wrote Justice and Truth that way.*

Zori Balayan, an Armenian from Karabakh, is connected with Siberia in many ways. His biography is marked by the dual character of the "slumbering land," as *Sibir* is called by its indigenous inhabitants; for the east of Siberia is both a place of exile and a refuge. The land of penal colonies was also the Eldorado of misfits,

adventurers, and daredevils, of researchers and freethinkers. "Russia is large, the Tsar is far away," as a proverb says of the free Siberian spaces, which are not limited by the central power in Moscow, but only by nature and geography, more than enough reason for young Zori Balayan to travel extensively and become acquainted with the wild, indomitable east of the Soviet empire.

In Siberia, Balayan's father was shot in 1937 as an "enemy of the people." His mother suffered in a prison camp there. Zori was two when his father was arrested following a denunciation. He was taken first to Shushi, the fortified city in the mountains, the historical center of Nagorno-Karabakh. Fifty-five years later Zori himself was to stand in cell no. 8 of the notorious Shushi jail in which his father, Haik, had been imprisoned. A photo shows the son next to a double bunk, his left hand holding a bunch of flowers, and his right fist clenched in his trouser pocket. Around this time, he wrote down his mother's report on the years of terror:

> I traveled … to Moscow to see Kalinin (Chairman of the Presidium of the Supreme Soviet of the USSR). I was doing it for your father's sake. Many wives acted in the same way then—they traveled to the Kremlin in Moscow, to stand up for the truth. I was thrown into a cell—they kept me there without water, without bread, for quite a few days. That was to show me I wasn't just the mother of two sons, but that I belonged to the family of an enemy of the people, not only that—I was the wife of an enemy of the people. Besides which, my whole family had been denounced as "kulaks,"[1] persecuted for having their own houses, their own cows and horses, and for working hard day and night. But if I had complained, I would never have seen my sons again.
>
> When I returned to Stepanakert, they had already had time to "legally" confiscate all our property behind my back. The children's clothes had gone, as well as your father's suits and handkerchiefs. There wasn't a single book left—and we had owned a real library. Some of the books were very valuable. He was the People's Commissioner for Education in Karabakh, in other words, the minister. Whenever he returned from anywhere, he would bring all kinds of books with him. And now there wasn't a single one.

Stalin later confessed that the bloody economicide of millions of farmers, who were more than 90 percent of the pre-Soviet population was "much more dangerous and dreadful a battle than Stalingrad."[2] The forced collectivization of the agricultural economy between 1928 and 1934, and the mass denunciations, arrests, deportations, show trials, and executions during the Stalinist "Great Purge" were traumatic for all the countries under Soviet domination at the time; but, coming a mere twenty years after the genocide in Turkey, this was a new nightmare for the Armenians in their long succession of nightmares. Many extraordinary intellectuals who had fled from the area under Turkish domination to the Transcaucasus fell victims to Stalin's thugs. Not even their having been well-known adherents of the world proletarian revolution, at least at a certain time, was good enough to save them. As a member of minority and a small, persecuted nation, the Armenian communists believed in changing the world, and that the triumph of socialism would once and for all put an end to all ethnic conflicts, massacres, and genocide. As alleged nationalists, the poet Yeghishe Charents and the writer Axel Bakunts, whose importance for the new Armenian literature is comparable to that of Vladimir Mayakovski and Anton Chekhov for the Russian, were murdered. Both were party members, and exuberantly extolled the friendship between nations in their works.

Moreover, anyone considered an enemy of the people was excluded from society. The relatives of an enemy of the people atoned vicariously. In the winter of the war and famine year of 1944, nine-year-old Zori was ejected from a bread queue because someone recognized him as the son of an enemy of the people. "That was the worst experience in my life," he remembers now, sixty years later.

Common sense, alongside truth and justice, is also a keyword in the ideals, thought, and behaviour of the children of such victims. Though he was a victim of Soviet violence on account of both his parents, Zori does not roundly condemn them for their communist ideals. He does not reproach his parents' generation for not having resisted the system more actively, or not having:

> tried to undermine the Lenin myth and to expose Stalin for what he really was. … No one can know the truth in its entirety, as its only criterion is what society does in practice. And practice has shown that people had to live and fight for life on the basis of common sense … It was precisely that attitude that gave us the opportunity to revive our national culture—to rebuild Yerevan, with its million inhabitants, with its valuable collections of ancient manuscripts, the *Matenadaran*,[3] and its metro system. To grow from seven hundred thousand orphans and poor people into a country of four million, where thirty thousand weddings were held every year and seventy thousand children were born.[4]

The victims' offspring nevermore took communism seriously. They joined the Party and in public paid lip service to it, but with a knowing wink. Behind the ever more rapidly crumbling façade they tried hard to revive pre-Soviet ideals. In this way the Soviet Armenian intellectuals successfully salvaged values that were officially disapproved of, such as love for one's homeland and patriotism. Born in the years between forced collectivization and the Stalinist terror, Zori Balayan became the *azgayin gortsich*. In the history of Armenian culture, as well as that of most Eastern European peoples, above all the Russian, *azgayin gortsich* refers to the intellectual, mainly a writer, who, thanks to the integrity of his thought and conduct, at the junction between journalism and pedagogy, gains an influence in the destiny of his nation that goes far beyond his literary profession. In this way the expression is perfectly translatable into Russian as *naródny déyatel*, but as "national activist" in English gives a somewhat wrong idea. The *azgayin gortsich* of the Armenian or Soviet variety creates a moral requirement in a society in which the citizen believes the authorities capable of every sort of roguery. An *azgayin gortsich* has no personal power at all, but does enjoy the greatest moral weight, for which reason the real authorities fear him, and indeed must, for he is no elite inhabitant of an ivory tower but an energetic spokesman of the people. His favourite weapons are the oral and written word. He enjoys the unlimited trust of every stratum of a society that is normally distrustful to the point of paranoia. The most important Soviet Armenian poet after the end of World War II, Paruyr Sevak (1924–1971), describes the *azgayin gortsichner* as "the great men of history":

> They are as harmless as sunburn,
> snakes without poison or wile
> and yet the State is afraid of them
> even when they loath it.
> In speaking to kings they treat them as equals
> (but only if the kings like it).
> They never fail to say what must be said. If they're not listened to
> they speak all the same, to God and the world.
> … But they fear neither punishment nor death:
> their life is hard, their death easy …

The day before January 4, 1992, when the parliament of Nagorno ("mountainous" in Russian)-Karabakh, as the second Armenian state, was convened, Zori Balayan was offered the presidency. He did not accept it. Instead, he went down to the basement of the parliament building in Stepanakert, where a makeshift maternity hospital had been set up, protected from the Azeri air raids. Down here women were giving birth while, upstairs, the birth of a mini-republic was taking place, cast into the world against its will. In the basement Zori was asked to name the first Karabakhi baby born in freedom. "I went back to the parliament session hall and thought to myself that naming newborn babies was something right up my street."

Zori Balayan has earned the trust of his compatriots by becoming the spokesman and nonofficial representative of his country, Karabakh. "If people only knew what it took to get the Soviet press to even mention Karabakh before! Each time I wrote something about my homeland, the editors would straight away receive letters of protest from Azerbaijan." On February 17, 1988, three days before the Soviet region decided to secede from the Soviet territory of Azerbaijan, so as to become a part of Armenia, Zori was in the U.S. as a member of a peace delegation, and made use of the opportunity to explain Karabakh's problems to a group of over thirty representatives of U.N. member-states.

The history of the Karabakh movement is interwoven with his personal biography. At the high point of this movement, when in February 1988 something like a million people made a peaceful demonstration in Yerevan in solidarity with their compatriots of Karabakh, for a brief period there existed ideal conditions: harmonious agreement and a feeling of unlimited patriotism among wide spheres of a population which, in general, lives amid constant conflicts. Taxi drivers ferried participants to the demontration venue for nothing, and even thieves solemnly pledged not to ply their trade during the march. Although opposed to this, Moscow was not able to ignore these mass movements. In the face of this, the poetess Silva Kaputikian and her colleague Zori Balayan were named representatives to negotiate with the highest circles of the USSR government and party. Armenia very often put its affairs in the hands of those whom it staunchly considered the best of its people—poets, writers, and intellectuals—although these idealist were seldom up to coping with professional politicians and diplomats.

On the evening of February 26, 1988, Mikhail Gorbachev and his adviser Yakovlev spoke for an hour with the two envoys of the Karabakh movement. Gorbachev made a vague promise to look for a "fair solution" to the Karabakh question. Though they had not obtained any real result, Zori and Silva agreed to a moratorium, and the next day were able to get the demonstrations in Yerevan to dissolve for the moment. The Soviet government, however, did not take advantage of the opportunity. As the demonstrators in Yerevan were leaving, gangs organized with the approval of the local authorities arrived in the Azeri industrial city of Sumgait, and fell on their Armenian neighbors there, massacring entire families. Among the victims, mostly Armenians from Karabakh, were two members of Zori Balayan's mother's family. The Soviet army intervened only on the third day of the pogrom. The alienation between the Russian center and the Armenian periphery grew rapidly.

When in the summer of 1990 a crippling blockade and embargo were imposed on Karabakh, and the infamous OMON[5] units occupied Stepanakert airport, through which Karabakh remains connected with the external world only by means of small planes, Zori Balayan, then deputy for Karabakh in the Supreme Soviet, the highest national institution of the USSR, went public and began an indeterminate hunger strike in protest against Mikhail Gorbachev's Karabakh policy. Four days later the outstanding scholar and internationally prominent astrophysicist Viktor Hambartsumyan joined the strike, as did other Armenian deputies. Although the Soviet media tried to minimize the action, tens of thousands of Soviet citizens expressed their solidarity. Numerous intellectuals and deputies asked Gorbachev to backtrack on Karabakh. At the end of a week of hunger strike, 82-year-old Hambartsumyan had to be put in hospital. On the twenty-first day of the strike, the Catholicos of All Armenians, Vasgen I (1908–1994) decided to join the strike. This put Zori Balayan in a tight spot. So as not to risk the life of the elderly head of the church and, also, in recognition that Gorbachev, heeding protests from all over the country, had withdrawn the OMON units from Stepanakert airport, Zori Balayan ended his hunger strike.

Yet this did not solve the conflict. A new phase of the Karabakh movement began in which, parallel to the crumbling power of the Soviet state, the new bases for a new state entity were laid—one that would have to defend itself before its official foundation. More than ever, it was a matter of gaining understanding and allies, and publishing their own interests internationally by means of the printed word. On May 22, 1991, Zori Balayan was the last speaker at a work group of the Sakharov International Congress in Moscow, led by Baroness Caroline Cox. This group's subject matter was serious human rights violations. At the same time as the Karabakh parliament was in session, Zori Balayan spoke about the terror methods employed in "Operation Ring": a forced resettlement of whole villages.

Caroline Cox reacted immediately, set up an international commission, and requested a visa, which Gorbachev personally accorded her. That was the beginning of an intensive collaboration between the "Scots granny," as the member of the House of Lords is known, and the *azgayin gortsich* of Karabakh.

Zori Balayan was not spared various episodes of violence in subsequent years, including the flight of thousands of his compatriots from the Azeri advance. "I felt like a wounded bird that found no refuge," he wrote in reference to his helplessness as a witness of events. In this period of mass flights his mother returned from Uzbekistan, where she had been exiled after her Siberian captivity, and together with her son she was present at the liberation of her native city, Shushi. "The Artsakhis were fated to win," said Zori Balayan on the amazing victories. "Not only their fate depended on their victory, but that of all Armenians. In this way the day of Shushi's liberation, May 9, 1992, was the happiest event in my life. I remember a similar feeling of happiness only when I received in the Far East, in distant Kamchatka, a telegram announcing the birth of my first daughter."

Notes

* The author points this out because, in German, all nouns are capitalized. (Tr.)

1. *kulak*—literally "fist" in Russian, a term used then to describe big and medium farmers, often used synonymously for a successful farmer, or just an independent one.

2. Theodor Shanin, *The Awkward Class. Political Sociology of Peasantry in a Developing Country: Russia 1910–1925*, Oxford 1972, p. 2.

3. *Matenadaran*, lit. "place where manuscripts are collected," with reference to the Yerevan manuscript museum, which, at the same time, serves as a research center and archive. With some 12,000 Armenian manuscripts (out of a total of 17,000) and many early prints, it is the largest collection of its kind in the world, formed since the nationalization of the monastic library of the Catholicosate at Echmiadzin, moved to Yerevan in 1939, permanently increased since then by donations and purchases.

4. In the 1980s the population of Armenia was almost 4 million, which decreased to around half that number after the collapse of the Soviet Union.

5. OMON = (Russian) *Otryad Militsiy Osóbovo Naznachéniya* (a special task force), a.k.a. "Black Berets." Created in 1980 for the Olympic Games in Moscow, and part of the anti-terrorist units of the Interior Ministry's (also engaged in anti-drug efforts since 1991), aimed at preventing a repetition of the criminal actions during the Munich Olympics (1972). During the period of dismemberment of the Soviet Union from 1988 on, they were used to intimidate and repress protest and independence movements in Armenia, Azerbaijan, Georgia, and Central Asia. From 1990 OMONS—Interior Ministry forces—were also created in the individual republics. Azerbaijan's unit had 4,000 men in early 1991.

Faith

16

THE CATHOLICOS OF ALL ARMENIANS: HIS HOLINESS KAREKIN II (ECHMIADZIN)

Rainer Hermann

The recently renovated Philharmonia is sold out, and the musicians of the Armenian Philharmonic Orchestra have taken their places at their music stands. The audience looks up at the balcony as the two principal representatives of Armenia, President Robert Kocharian and the Catholicos of All Armenians, Karekin II, arrive at the concert hall to a round of applause, one in the suit of an official, the other wearing black monachal attire, on his head a pointed *veghar* reminiscent of Mount Ararat, which, for church services, is replaced by the *teshteltak*, the three-part miter.

During pauses they go into a huddle to talk turkey. The political and spiritual leaders of the Armenians have business to deal with. They also do this outside the Philharmonia, as during the opposition's demonstrations in 2004, when the church leader volunteered to talk and mediate in order to guarantee the country's peace and stability. "Confrontation is not the solution," he said gently but firmly. On the other side, the state is also in favour of the Church. Kocharian and Karekin II finally resolved that Church history should be taught in schools. National history is hardly comprehensible without the history of the Church, the Catholicos explains, justifying his proposal. State and Church are indeed divided by constitutional law, but in practice they collaborate on a day-to-day basis. "So that people will be good Christians and good citizens, and so that we live in peace and prosperity," says Karekin II.

They work together, but their spheres of influence have very different extensions. The president of Armenia is limited to the republic, whereas the Catholicos is the spiritual head of the whole Armenian Apostolic Church. In this way his influence extends far beyond Armenia's borders, since more than two thirds of the church's members live disseminated around the world. It was more by a chance of history that the Armenians are autonomous, as they have lived under foreign domination for the most part. Echmiadzin, the Catholicosal see, was the spiritual home of all the Armenians during those dark periods, who were thus able to preserve a feeling of independence, says the Catholicos, somewhat proudly in spite of his humility. He holds that the Church's task consists in guaranteeing national culture and identity. "Finally our faith has furnished us with the strength for the resurrection to be for our people too."

Echmiadzin is without a doubt the spiritual home of the Armenians, and in the diaspora it is common to speak of "being willing to do something for 'Holy Echmiadzin's' sake." Thoughts center on Echmiadzin, and looks are directed toward it. The place, center of the Armenian Church, however, hardly allows comparison with the Vatican, or even with St. Peter's Cathedral. It possesses nothing to make a visitor feel insignificant. The altar below the dome, which rises at the center of the cross-shaped building, is within hand's reach, and during the religious service the Catholicos takes up position on one of its sides under a small baldachin.

The present Cathedral of Echmiadzin goes back to previous buildings, and to the year 303, when Gregor the Enlightener had the first church built on these grounds. Colorful historical mosaics have been uncovered only in recent years, and even earlier than that is King Tiridates' portal, from the year 301. Going through the simple arches of the portals one arrives at the Catholicos's residence, a modest building of dark sandstone, whose windows are adorned with elegant arches.

His Holiness Karekin II, the Catholicos's official title, gives his guests private audiences in a long office, furnished with valuable carpets. Small light fittings illuminate the room, and there is nothing that mars the discreet atmosphere. Unpretentiously, but with dignity, the Catholicos receives the visitor in a simple blue monk's habit. Only the great medallion on his chest gives away the Catholicos of All Armenians. The churchman's golden miter is painted on the wood-panelled wall behind his desk. On his left side stands the black pastoral staff, and to his right, an Armenian *khachkar* cross. Telephones are lined up on the desk one after another. No computer disturbs for now.

Karekin II speaks fluent German, having spent many years of his life in Germany and Austria. He was born in the village of Voskehat, near Echmiadzin in the Ararat valley, the biggest fruit plantation in Armenia, in 1951. Apricot trees grow there, whose fruit bears the Latin name *Prunus armeniaca.* Alexander the Great took them to Greece, and the Romans later spread them all over Europe. Karekin II was fourteen when he entered the Echmiadzin theological seminary. In 1971, he finished his studies with distinction. The following year he took his religious vows and continued his studies at Vienna University's Catholic theological seminary. In 1975, he moved to Cologne, where he became the single spiritual representative of nine Armenian congregations in Germany. Nowadays five priests minister to almost three times as many communities.

He has fond memories of Germany, he declares, where he spent valuable years of his life and his professional training. Above all, he let himself be influenced by the German mentality, and he is keen on the idea of visiting the country again.

He began his postgraduate studies at the Religious Academy of the Russian Orthodox church in Moscow in 1979. In 1983, he was ordained as a bishop, and in 1992 became archbishop of the diocese of Ararat. His election as head of the Church was already in the offing when he took over the management of the Church in 1993 as locum tenens of the seriously ailing Catholicos Karekin I, who died in June, 1999. On October 27, he was elected by the national ecclesiastical assembly as the 132nd Catholicos of All Armenians as Karekin II, his baptismal name being Ktrich.

The election took place at a turbulent time. On the one hand, President Kocharian, in office since a year earlier, wished for a Catholicos well versed in matters of internal politics. In this way, he was to be different from Karekin I, who was born in Syria, and when he was elected as head of the Church, was the Catholicos of Cilicia at Antelias in Lebanon. The Catholicos of Antelias, as well as the Patriarchs of Jerusalem and Istanbul, protested against this interference. Even the following year, tensions between the new head of the Church and the Catholicos of Cilicia fueled further conflicts. At the same time, Karekin's festive election was overshadowed by the bloody attack on the Armenian parliament on October 27, in which the prime minister at the time and seven other politicians were shot dead.

Karekin II wants to be the Church head, not a politician. He wishes to make use of the great tradition of the Church, which has kept all the Armenians of the diaspora united. "Faith was the basis of Armenian existence, and the Church was a Noah's ark for its people." No matter how grave the danger, the people congregated in and round the Church. In sum, it is the Christian faith that has kept Armenian culture alive. It has given shape to their thought and their inner life. It became their skin.

To a certain extent the Church came out unscathed from the Soviet decades. Even when the atheists set up barriers to the Church, people found a way to get through them, and grandmothers instilled the faith in their grandchildren. However, Karekin II admits the Christian faith did suffer in the Soviet Union. Yet after its dismemberment people flocked back to the Church in great numbers, though the Church was unable to satisfy all their hopes.

There is one change, however, which the head of the Church is not in the least happy about: that missionaries, mostly from the United States, should enjoy the same rights as the 1,700-year-old Armenian Apostolic Church. Even its name indicates it derives from the apostles. Two of them, Thaddeus and Bartholomew, brought Christianity to Armenia, where they were martyred. They were the first enlighteners of Armenia. The next was Gregory, who inspired King Tiridates III to declare Christianity the state religion in 301, even before the Roman Emperor Constantine did. Gregory was a Persian who became Christian in Cesarea, Cappadocia (presently in Anatolia). There he had himself ordained bishop of Armenia by the archbishop of that region, but he established himself at Vagharshapat (later Echmiadzin), at the foot of Mount Ararat, where he founded the line of the catholicoi. Since Grigor the Illuminator had received his education during exile in Caesarea, the links with this see remained close even after his death; Grigor and his descendents were consecrated by the archbishops of Caesarea. But the jurisdiction of the exarchate of Pontos was limited to those areas of Armenia, which were under Roman (Byzantine) rule, such as Satala or Nicopolis. Increasingly overshadowed by the Byzantine-Persian antagonism and divide, the ecclestical relations of Armenia with neighbouring Cappadokia and Pontos loosened towards the end of the fourth century, gradually fostering the already existing independence of the Armenian church, but also its isolation. While the Catholicos himself was participating in the Ecumenical Council of Nikaia (325), no Armenian representatives could be sent to the Council of Constantinople (381). At the important Council of Chalcedon (451), only clerics from the Byzantine parts of Armenia were present.

Today, the American missionaries are to enjoy the same rights as the oldest state church in Christendom. Jehovah's Witnesses and Mormons, in particular, have begun their proselytizing work in Armenia after independence. The Catholicos's opinion of them is unfaltering. He mentions two points. On the one hand, he accuses them of turning the Armenians into a nation with no further connection with their history and culture. They have a new cultural model in mind. On the other hand, he complains that they are trying to destroy moral concepts in that they hope to attract new believers not by their teachings but by taking advantage of people's social situation. In this way they will also undermine the moral foundations, as individuals learn they win by selling their faith.

Nevertheless, he is conciliating. He trusts that in time unity will once more prevail. His Church is working on this, and trying hard to satisfy the expectations of its flock. During the Soviet period one young priest might be ordained per year. "Now we have thirty-five to forty ordinations a year," he says with satisfaction. Thanks to gifts and generous benefactors it is possible to renovate and rebuild old churches, even the big one in Yerevan, consecrated to St. Gregory.

The Church is playing an increasing social role. It helps in the case of need, it organizes soup kitchens and help for orphans, it supports the poverty-stricken, and extends its spiritual work to prisons and the army. One of his dearest projects is to set up new Sunday schools: he considers it a central task, following the collapse of the Soviet Union, to teach his people Christian faith and national history through education. In collaboration with the international benevolent organization AGBU (Armenian General Benevolent Union), the Church has converted Soviet-era scout centers into modern youth complexes where young people are able to employ their talents. The Armenian Apostolic Church is recovering its place in society. That the president and the Catholicos of All Armenians should appear together and have common matters to talk over is an eloquent sign of this.

17

THE MODERNIZER WITH THE MITER: HIS HOLINESS ARAM I, CATHOLICOS OF THE GREAT HOUSE OF CILICIA (ANTELIAS, BEIRUT)

Huberta von Voss

Fast-moving traffic circulates along the multiple lanes of the coastal highway joining Beirut with the north of this country of noisy traffic. Traversing this highway to Antelias to meet his Holiness Aram I, Catholicos of the Great House of Cilicia, one is not moving away from the world toward a collapsed kingdom of yore. When in 1930 the Catholicos of Cilicia was expelled from Turkey and established his seat in this Beirut suburb, it was still an area of rural tranquility far from the city's boisterous port. Even the Armenians' commercial activity in Bourj Hammoud was a long way off. Today, the tumult of horn-honkers has become the rule around the fortress-like sandstone walls of the protected refuge, located directly on one of the exits of Lebanon's main highway. This has changed nothing in the historical awareness of the Catholical See, where one lives, prays, preaches, and publishes in the spirit of an age-old tradition.

This tradition began in the tenth century in Armenia with the Seljuk invasion and the emigration of great masses of the population to Cilicia, where the nation survived in a newly founded kingdom; the spiritual head established himself in its capital, Sis. For almost 400 years, the political, cultural, and religious Armenian center was not occupied Armenia, but Cilicia. When the little kingdom became the battleground of Seljuks, Mamelukes, and other powers in 1375, many Armenians returned to their old homeland. The catholicos, instead, remained at Sis to personally perpetuate the existence of the fallen kingdom. The faithful who arrived back in their old home at Echmiadzin, the Church's ancient seat, chose a new head, and so from then on there have always been two catholicoses. In June 1995, Aram Keshishan became the first "Lebanese" to receive the insignia of the Catholicos of Cilicia, also called the Catholicos of Sis.

His Holiness, whose assistant in monk's apparel kisses his emerald ring when handing him his pastoral crook, receives his guests with the amiable courtesy of a CEO. One does not have to cross a hall to reach this exiled king. He sits without his miter at an oaken desk full of books, surrounded by a fax machine, telephones, and carved religious objects. Behind him hangs the Cilician coat of arms; on his chest he wears three resplendent chains in the shape of the cross with his official insignia. Below his window, the Levantine coast spreads out against the expanse of the sea.

He has lived behind cloistered walls since he was thirteen, and has published more than twelve books in Armenian, English, and French since 1974. Whoever imagines him as an unworldly, purely cerebral cleric is in for a disappointment. "We are no relic of the past, but very much alive," the man in his late fifties declares, who can speak for hours in perfect English on the advantages and drawbacks of the Internet and globalization, as well as on the challenges of ecumenical dialog or the need for modernization in the Armenian Apostolic Church. Aram I is aware that, more than 1,700 years after Armenia declared Christianity its state religion, reforms are needed if the younger generation is not to be lost. Aram I wishes to employ the weapons of modernization and dialog to resist the inroads of assimilation. The catholicos's task as a figure of integration is not made easier by all the time that has passed since the expulsion from Turkey.

The first emigrants arrived in Lebanon in the first half of the nineteenth century. Many were Catholics, who fled from ill treatment at the hands of their "own" Apostolic Church in Constantinople. The Armenian language was very soon abandoned. Learning Arabic smoothed the way and enabled ascent in Lebanese society. In contrast to these "local" Armenians, the radicals who arrived in Beirut from 1880 to 1914 wanted to escape the reach of the Sublime Porte. Like tens of thousands of refugees of the later genocide, they remained "diaspora Armenians" for generations, opposed to each other according to their place of origin and political views, isolated from the Franco-Arabophonic environment in refugee camps, and to a certain extent rejected by Lebanese society. "In the camps, there was daily contact between the proud mountain dweller from Sassoon and the cosmopolitan moneylender from Smyrna; between the Armenian-speaking farmer from Van and the Turkish-speaking shopkeeper from Adana; between the Catholic fanatic from Ankara and the equally fanatical Apostolic from Erzurum," as Nikola B. Shahgaldian wrote in a study on the Armenian community of

Lebanon in 1983. The unifying element remained the Church, personified in the patriarchal catholicos since 1930. Nevertheless, the decades of integration and assimilation have weakened the appeal and cohesion of the Church. The same process is apparent in the language. Aram's father arrived in Lebanon in the 1930s and never learned English; his son lives, thinks, and works in Armenian, Arabic, English, and French. The next generations are equally polyglot. Armenian is often the only language missing.

"We must adapt the liturgy to this evolution," maintains Aram. He knows that, in this world of fast deals and mass social problems, young people in the Middle East no longer have the dedication to study ecclesiastic Ancient Armenian, which their parents still knew. The catholicos is thoroughly opposed to the growing assimilation of diaspora Armenians, and coins for it a strong term, for it: "white genocide," or also "disappearance by overassimilation." "But I favor renewal and integration. We have to keep up with the modern world, or evolution will leave us behind." Preaching in the local language of the faithful must be possible, along with the translation of biblical passages and prayers into modern Armenian. Also, in the offing is the elimination of hierarchies: "lean management" is the term used in economics. "We're advancing toward a boundless society," he says at a conference on globalization. "We can no longer run the Church as in olden times." He openly tells his audience how he sat in the VIP lounge in an international airport and made calls with his cell phone. All at once the waitress's cellphone rang. It was exactly the same model. He laughs. "I told my fellow priest, 'You see, that's modernity for you. The patriarch and the waitress have the same cell phone!'" For this very reason, the Church's structures and content need to be reformed and open up to believers, especially women.

"Today you're either in the game, or you're out of it." Aram I, lifelong catholicos, is 50-odd years old and wants to be part of the game—among other reasons, to be able to have a say in the rules. "We're all online," says the catholicos, who appears in public wearing a hood like the cupola of an Armenian church. He does not consider globalization a movement, but a worldwide system that, with the propagation of a Western monoculture, brings about the destruction of local identities. Especially threatened in his eyes is the Armenians' cultural identity, which, despite emigration over centuries, was able to preserve itself on the basis of its common elements. The three great unifying elements of the Armenian people are language, the alphabet, and religion.

He sees in particular a threat to the cultural identity of the Armenians, who, despite their centuries-old history of emigration, were able to endure thanks to the strength of their common language, script, and religion. "Today the survival of an entire nation in the diaspora is at stake." As ever more Armenians marry outside their communities and the children of these unions are educated in the language of the country, the knowledge of modern Armenian is retreating. He clearly also has misgivings about the increasing Westernization of the style of life. "I am a person of the Middle East," he says with confident pride.

At the 1,700-year celebration in Nicosia, the high priest of the Apostolic Church, wearing red and golden brocade, holds aloft a cross embossed with gems. For more than half an hour he preaches in Armenian to the faithful with extended arms. The word "*yekerezi*" is frequently heard, sometimes in an amiable tone, sometimes joyful, but always with earnest emphasis. "The Church" is the subject of his preaching, which he immediately repeats in English. "The Church is meaningless without the substance we give it. It can only rise from our concrete community, not from hierarchies or buildings." Christian faith is not abstract, but a vital reality factually experienced through the existence of Christ in human form. He wishes that churches will always be full and urges the community to ensure this—even though he knows that, except for the main festivities and visits, the congregation and especially youth remain at home.

"By nature I'm a man of dialog," says the catholicos, for years an active ecumenical leader of the World Council of Churches (WCC). He grew up with his five siblings knowing he was a "genocide survivor." Though born in 1947 in Lebanon, long after the traumatic events and outside Turkish frontiers, his exiled parents' humble circumstances gave definite shape to his national conscience. "My parents' wish was for us to feel at home in the foreign environment, but without forgetting our roots and, above all, the crime the Turks committed against our people." Like the catholicos of Sis, he says with conviction, "I am an exile of the genocide!"

His origin and ministry define his position toward Turkey, which he hopes will recognize the historical facts and apologize for them. "There can be no reconciliation unless the facts are recognized without reserve. Historical reality isn't negotiable," he says firmly, for this reason distrusting the so-called "Reconciliation Commission" of the Turks and mainly American Armenians. "I'm all for dialog with, not against, the others," he says, in the direction of Ankara. But, before this can be, he demands that the Turks "recognize the crime." That is, first recognition, then dialog. Nor should foreign states' parliaments subordinate their attitude toward recognition of the genocide to strategic interests. "Today, Turkey denies history; tomorrow others will do the same." Aram I, religious and political head of the Armenians of Cilicia, lowers his resonant voice, and his shiny dark eyes cloud over. "More than a crime against humanity, the planned murder of the Armenians was a crime against God. One can run away from history, but not hide from it."

18

REFEREE ON A SLIPPERY PITCH: HIS BEATITUDE MESROP II, PATRIARCH OF THE ARMENIANS IN TURKEY (ISTANBUL)

Huberta von Voss

From the window of the comfortable drawing room of his summer residence, His Beatitude, Patriarch Mesrop II, looks out across the flourishing palm gardens of the Isle of Princes, Kinali, toward Istanbul, 25 km away on the Asian coast. Just like the vista from his window, only less idyllic, is the existence of the Armenian community of 60,000 in Turkey. From having been the largest non-Muslim ethnic group of Anatolia, they have become a small island in a population of 64 million Turks of Sunnite faith. The picturesque, somewhat secluded vista certainly does not fool the spiritual and secular leader as to the mass exodus of Armenians from the time of the foundation of the state in 1923, increasingly confronting those that have stayed on with the problems of a fringe existence.

Around 300,000 Armenians still lived in Turkey in the early 1920s, after the systematic murder and deportations during World War I and shortly thereafter. But especially in the 1950s and the 1980s many packed up and left their home of centuries for Europe or across the sea, in fear of an increasing islamization of the country. Officially, Armenians enjoy equal rights, but in everyday reality they often feel the stain of belonging to a Christian minority. One of the patriarch's main objectives is to prevent the Armenians that are left from feeling like second-class citizens owing to the discrimination they are subjected to in their rights and in society, and thus leaving the land of their ancestors. He himself describes his mission as "not political," yet his whole intervention and thought function permanently in a political terrain.

It is a life among many fronts that Mesrop chose in 1998, when he was forty-five, and assumed the highest office among the Armenians of Turkey. "We live between two fires, and both are explosive," is how the patriarch, who seems of indeterminate age, describes the situation. On the one hand is the diaspora's burning wish for an official recognition of the historical facts by the Turkish state and, on the other, the flak from the Turkish side any time the taboo subject is mentioned. Mesrop, whose full pastoral beard and big spectacles give him the physical distance he needs as a mediator, weighs his words with care. He knows how easy it is to get one's fingers burnt. "Our way is a constant search for compromise between the irreconcilable requirements of the two factions," is his sober description of the situation. Where the ice of trust is thin, diplomatic skill cannot avoid its breaking even at the slightest jolt. "You go to the diaspora, and they tell you you're Turkish. You go to the Turks, and they say you're Armenian."

His loyalty—and that of his community—is naturally toward the Turkish state, which has never, as he repeatedly underlines in his conversation, interfered in the Church's affairs. The foreign correspondents writing from Istanbul do not confirm this. It is known there that not only do local authorities and the justiciary exert pressure on the Armenian community (for instance, in declarations of property), but Mesrop, formerly considered very progressive, found himself restrained by his own people, among which the conservative world of business, which is not interested in creating conflicts, just wants to keep things as they are. Friendly fire is not always easy to live with. Yet the patriarch feels the fundamental line of conflict does not run within but outside of his own community. On one hand are the Armenians of Turkey, whose number is steadily diminishing and, as a result, they feel the pressure to assimilate; and on the other the communities of the international diaspora, ever more self-confident, who promote their demands with renewed emphasis since some national parliaments recognized the genocide. "The diaspora Armenians have broken off with Turkey, and this is how they can do what they please." While the latter closed the door behind them, it is Mesrop's task to keep it permanently open for his ever-dwindling community, so that living with the Turks is as peaceful and free of conflicts as possible. In contrast to his colleagues in Jerusalem, Beirut, and Echmiadzin, Mesrop's office has to be looked at as "service toward reconciliation."

The churchman, who has traveled widely, went to secondary school in Stuttgart, and studied in Memphis, is not a man who refuses to look further than his nose. He originally wished to enroll in the United Nations' Peace Corps, on realizing that, above all, his own compatriots needed to foster peace and reconciliation. "This can only be so through dialog and prudence."

He considers Armenians' readiness to integrate in Turkish society as a minority's primary task. "Our children learn early on to strike an agreement between their Armenian origin and their Turkish nationality. Here we have Turkish neighbors and clients and social intercourse. Therefore it's perfectly natural we should try and get on with them." Besides, the special position of the Ottoman Empire's Armenian elite, due to its cosmopolitan education, like that of Jews and Greeks, no longer exists today. "The elite hasn't come from minorities since a long time back. Quite the contrary: there are umpteen Turkish youths that have studied abroad and have received a brilliant education." Though for centuries the Armenians were architects and bankers under the Sultans, nowadays they must prove their skill in a very different way. An added problem is the impoverishment of the rural Armenian population. However, in seeking the means to back it up, he must—even in the diaspora—fight against many prejudices. "They see every penny for us as money for the Turkish state." This attitude sickens not only him but also other active community members.

The patriarch has high hopes in Turkey's new foreign policy. The ever closer relations between the Turkish and Israeli governments have led, for instance, to an improvement in the treatment of Jews, who mostly live in Istanbul. Mesrop hopes the faint ties established between Turkey and Armenia will also result in similar consequences. Yet his greatest hope is in the process of integrating into the European Union. Turkey's negotiations in Brussels have already led to perceptible improvements for the minorities, with a growing respect for human rights and freedom of expression.

Whereas the wheel of Westward orientation has only just been put in motion, Mesrop thinks the diaspora is gumming up the works with its promotion of parliamentary resolutions on the genocide.

> In my opinion Turkey can apologize for the victims that died on the road to deportation, regardless of the definition. But a proper dialog on the question of guilt can only happen among the people that live together here. This conflict only allows a joint solution. This is why I think: Let's talk it over, not abroad, but here. The pressure from abroad doesn't make this easier.

The decades of negative propaganda in the media have left their traces, above all in the Turks outside the big towns. "In the provinces they distrust us." So what is recommendable is to hold one's breath for a good while and not be drawn into unnecessary arguments.

Born in Istanbul, Mesrop, whose father was a foreman in the building trade, learnt early on to work with energy to achieve his objectives in a tricky terrain. When he was sixteen he left his parents' home and spontaneously decided, during a trip to London he won in an essay-writing competition in English, to visit his aunt in Stuttgart. As he found that city to his liking, he immediately decided not to return home from that trip. He enrolled in the American High School and, two years later, completed his "Abitur." "Those were two wonderful years in the hippy era, hitchhiking across Europe, and going to pop recitals," he remembers fondly. On continuing his studies in the mid-1970s in the U.S.A. The came face to face—even taking into account the very modest means at his disposal—with the much greater needs of Armenian refugees from Lebanon. He founded a choir to gather the Armenians, and little by little he came to understand he wanted to dedicate his life to keeping the Armenian community united. After some time he gave up his studies in economy, and took up philosophy and sociology. He had to finance his studies himself, as his father was only able to help him during the first year. He worked at a bookshop, as a nightclub waiter, and as a football referee, as which he soon became well-known and was able to support himself with. "I was a good referee," he recalls with juvenile pride. That can be of use to him in his difficult task today.

19

WITH CELLPHONE AND HABIT ON LORD BYRON'S ISLAND: FATHER GRIGORIS AND THE NOVICE ARTOUR (SAN LAZZARO, VENICE)

Huberta von Voss

I stood in Venice, on the Bridge of Sighs;

A palace and a prison on each hand:

I saw from out the wave her structures rise

As from the stroke of the enchanter's wand:

A thousand years their cloudy wings expand.

Lord Byron's verses sound almost fatigued. He has just left his wife and child behind in England, begets another child, illegitimate, in Switzerland, and upon his arrival in Venice is captivated by his host's beautiful wife. Having escaped from his country's criticism and society, driven by political and human passions, as thirsty for life as he is melancholy, the handsome lame poet hires a boat one morning to row on the Venetian lagoons and leaves the attractions of the hundred islands behind. He does not seek the diversions of the big islands like La Giudecca, but the peace of some tiny cove and lands on the little beach of San Lazzaro.

The islet is still minute at this time. And yet a great monastery—calm and stately—stands on it amid cypresses, cedars, and olive trees. The shadow of its red-stained walls seems to reach almost to the sea. Not a sound issues from behind the green wooden shutters. The bell tower rises like an index finger, as though enjoining contemplation. He wants to stay here, thinks the poet, and knocks on the door. A beautiful unadorned cloister, resting on Doric columns, stands before him. In the middle of the courtyard there is an ivy-covered well. A pomegranate tree spreads its gentle shade, heavy fruits weighing its laden branches. Colorful

geraniums grace the yellowish sandstone. The year is 1816. The Mekhitarist brothers receive the poet, as depraved as he is talented, with the critical dignity of an intellectual elite. Lord Byron will thank them for this. He stays there, learns the language, and translates Armenian poetry into English.

Today, the order founded in Constantinople by Mekhitar of Sebaste (present-day Sivas), which he soon moved to the Peloponnese peninsula in historical Morea under the protection of the maritime Republic of Venice, is over 300 years old. When the Ottoman armies presented themselves in front of Morea, the monks fled from their monastery. After 150 years' struggle for dominance in Asia Minor, proud Venice finally had to give up Morea to the Ottomans. Mekhitar and nineteen fellow brothers sailed to the unlucky protector power, arriving in the city of the lagoons in April 1715. Two years later the Serenissimo's government granted them the minute hospital island of Lazzaro in perpetuity as a place of exile, which since then has been called San Lazzaro degli Armeni. Arriving there September 8, 1717, they found a couple of crumbling two-storey buildings lepers had once lived in, and travelers worried about the happy end of their quarantine.

The unfortunate site becomes the refugees' new home and, shortly after their arrival, the epicenter of the Armenian rebirth. Leo, alias Arakel Babakhanian

(1860–1932), one of the most famous Armenian historians, will later write, "The work of Mekhitar and his disciples had such influence on Armenian cultural life in the eighteenth century, that the whole of it could be called the Mekhitarist age of Armenian history." Devoutness, but scholarship above all, was the monks' task, so that only the most talented were accepted by the order. They would spread out to every land and all round the world, teaching the diaspora the fullness of Armenian culture, but also infusing their own culture with foreign influences through their various translations. Any time a permanent selection of the best European novels was found in community libraries, from Madras in India to Tabriz in Iran, it was most of the times due to the merit of the monks on the three hectare island in front of Venice. That the monks, on their journeys, worked for the Armenian Catholic Church and for recognition of the pope goes without saying. Nevertheless, their extraordinary importance is not limited to the 300,000 Armenian Catholics strewn around the world, since their educational work has never been restricted to believers of their own confession.

Their schools in Venice, Paris, Istanbul, Aleppo, Buenos Aires, and Alexandria are still considered elite institutes. The monks in the order have always had to be multi-talented, in full accordance with the humanistic educational ideal, possessing exceptional knowledge of mathematics and astronomy, the age-old history of their nation, philology, and languages. Whoever does not master Ancient Armenian, Greek, Latin and, if possible, Persian and Arabic—let alone modern tongues like Italian, French, and English—has always been, and is, in the wrong place here. There are over 4,500 manuscripts in the sacred halls, many still awaiting their scientific elaboration. This requires extensive linguistic knowledge, although the requirement of knowing numerous languages has slackened. Fitted out with modern air-conditioners, a newly built tower has for thirty years provided the manuscripts, dating from the years 862 to 1700, protection against the ravages of time. Only those that know the code are able to open the iron door, protected by an alarm, to the cloister's holy of holies. Behind it is what is probably the most valuable collection of Armenian biblical manuscripts in the world. Art historians would also enjoy the marvelous miniature paintings with which the monks always illustrated their biblical texts. However, the scope of the collection is even greater, possessing Sultan Ahmet's Koran from the year 1500, a medical treatise of 1281, down to an edict signed by Tsar Peter the Great in 1717.

It is the morning of Wednesday, June 10, 2002. Ferries are on strike in Venice—a good day for taxi launches. The trip by *vaporetto* from the terminal at the Piazza di San Marco to the island of San Lazzaro degli Armeni takes around twenty minutes. The motor launch blows its horn as it glides across the waters, and the young driver with the dark polarized glasses approaches the wooden pier with a deft turn. As soon as his passenger alights, he moves off at full speed.

The monastery is silent in the morning heat, and there is nobody around; only the deafening buzz of cicadas pierces the shimmering air. Concrete barriers prevent one from seeing the magnificent entrance courtyard. The entrance to the monastery is hidden along a side passage. One man in shorts cleans a dark room.

Another wearing a tracksuit trots by. No one looks at the visitor. A young man in a white Lacoste polo shirt and light-brown Prada-style shoes talks on a small modern cellphone in the archway. Where are these elitist monks in this honorable monastery? Where is one of those spiritual fathers with his white hair and balding pate, and an old manuscript under his arm? Have they died out? "Holiday today. Free dress," explains a taciturn monk. He invites me into the reception. One must await the abbot, Father Elia. Finally, the grumpy old brother in a black habit arrives, but he hardly knows English, and goes off soon after. He probably only knows dead languages. In place of him, Father Grigoris takes his time. He looks like a young professor at an elite university: scholarly, lively, ironical, polyglot. The novice Artour, the young man with the modern shoes, has come with him.

We look over the monastery's impressive premises. The hall alone, in which the 100,000 volumes of the Armenian library are tidily set out on delicate pear-wood bookcases, measures 40 meters. In an adjacent hall there are 50,000 volumes of the best European literature and social sciences. Through an open side window comes the fragrance of dry grass and rosemary into a small reading room. Lord Byron's portrait looks on from one of the walls. This was his room.

Spectacular paintings on the ceiling make one forget this is a cloister and not a Venetian palace. Even young Tiepolo left the monks a similar painting, *Pace e Giustizia*. The 30-meter-long Armenian gallery is also impressive. Monumental seascapes by Ayvazovski hang next to illustrations by the Armenian-French artist Edgar Chahin, Toulouse-Lautrec's famous contemporary, who, at that time, sold his work at a much higher price than his tragic colleague. The icon of Russian cinema, Sergej Paradjanov, persecuted throughout his life, left a testimony of his presence here. This comprehensive and, in part, valuable collection of paintings was the world's contribution to these hard-working servants of God. For wealthy Armenians, it is a tradition and a point of honor to send a piece of art, a liturgical object, or an archeological find to San Lazzaro. However, they much prefer taking them there personally, making a pilgrimage to the island at least once in their life and, at Mekhitar's grave, saying a prayer for the survival of Armenian culture, much as Catholic Christians pray for their dear ones' lives at Lourdes. Boghos Nubar Pasha, the founder of the biggest Armenian benevolent organization, AGBU, at the time he was the Egyptian prime minister in the nineteenth century, donated the mummy of Nemenkhet Amen, embalmed more than 3,000 years earlier. It is now part of the cloister's museum among Etruscan, Roman, Byzantine, Indian, and Armenian objects.

Father Grigoris—Robert in English—talks nonstop. There is a *graffito* in the corridor to the church. "Van," it says, at one time the largest lake in historical Armenia, in the middle of the Armenian provinces of the Ottoman Empire, now eastern Turkey. The island of San Lazzaro has always remained in the peaceful shadow of history. Even Napoleon left the scholarly monks, already famous outside Armenian circles for their book-printing and their erudition, in peace. Mekhitar's Armenian Thesaurus of 1742, which is constantly updated, is still an indispensable philological work. Sometimes the island is also called "Little

Armenia," where cultural continuity was possible, as opposed to other Armenian localities. The monks at San Lazzaro see themselves as the depositaries of Armenian culture and history. But they also want to be a bridge between Eastern and Western culture. Thus, Armenians can be thankful to them for important translations of European literature into Armenian, ancient or modern according to the origin of the text: Caesar, Virgil, Seneca, Dante's *Divina Commedia*, or Manzoni's "Betrothed." The criterion in the choice of texts is, more than anything else, their literary value.

Father Grigoris extols the monastery's valuable manuscript collection. When asked if the monks also go in for refurbishing the manuscripts, he answers mockingly, "Our clerics do not occupy their time in worldly matters. We send everything to a Benedictine monastery at Perugia. They know all about bee-keeping and restoring manuscripts." Artour grins. As we leave the church, his cellphone shrieks. The contrast between intelligent, talkative Father Grigoris and the quiet novice, Artour, who does not seem so monkish, is only apparent. Artour's way of speaking is also highly precise, his Armenian rich and very elaborate. Nevertheless, an intellectual hierarchy rules here, and the young novice is aware of his station.

At the age of sixteen he met a Mekhitarist in Yerevan, where he grew up. On finishing school, he decided to travel to Italy to study Catholic theology. When he arrived on the island there were thirty seminarists there. It was a fun group. Today, there are only ten. Most of them study in Lebanon, where the congregation is more numerous and the courses are easier to organize. Despite the apparently worldly lifestyle, traditional yardsticks still apply. The few postulants to the priesthood must prove their varied dedication, just like in modern "Accessment Centers." Yet the daily schedule follows the old rules for monks. The day begins at 6.30 a.m. with matins and, after a heavy program of intellectual and physical work, ends late at night with a prayer. Yet the times when a couple of dozen novices eager for instruction were tutored in their own school by outstanding professors seem definitely to be a thing of the past. The *Collegio* had to be closed quite some time ago owing to a dearth of pupils. The seminary building is there, disused. It will now be modernized, which may make the cloister more attractive. Even the famous printing shop at the monastery had to be closed down after two hundred years' activity.

Artour is not put off by these ups and downs. In 1512, the first Armenian book was printed in Venice. Nineteen other publishers turned the city of the lagoons into the center of Armenian literature. In 1789, the Mekhitarists finally set up their own printing establishment, with whose production the needs of diaspora schoolchildren were covered. Still, the 26-year-old with an open expression and a happy laugh seems as if he would like to work for an Internet provider. But behind the front hides a very serious young man, who has a great dream. "One day I'd like to go back to Armenia and put up a school of theology, at which Apostolics and Catholics could talk in an ecumenical atmosphere." His eyes brighten as he says this. At this moment there are some 180,000 Catholics and some 3 million Apostolics in his old country, according to official figures. In the diaspora the difference between the two confessions is even greater, the relation being something like 1:170. "So there's plenty to be done in order to improve this dialog," Artour knows.

A brother calls to lunch. At the head of the table sits the surly abbot. The midday sunlight comes in through the milky windowpanes. Like a veil float grains of dust in front of the wonderful fresco of the Last Supper covering the whole of the refectory's back wall. A monk says a brief grace, and a white-bearded old fellow brother with a spiritual look eats the vegetable soup in silence. Only he and the abbot wear monkish attire. They seem almost like outsiders in this happy circle. One of the friars, paunchy and wearing a black V-neck T-shirt and a thick gold bracelet looks like a sailor. Another, a young one, in a Nike tracksuit, looks as if he had been out on the town and could do with a good night's sleep. Father Grigoris sets off some intellectual fireworks, talking about his doctoral thesis, about Heidegger's concepts of space and time. Artour is quiet and listens attentively. He knows that here only those that really have something to say open their mouths.

But Artour will also leave, turning his back forever on San Lazzaro. When I asked many months later about his ordination as a priest, there was deep silence at the other end; then evasions and insinuations, as if someone had escaped from a fortress or should not be given away. Maybe energetic Father Grigoris finds it difficult to express what many must ask themselves: who will there be left living within the monastery walls in ten years' time and, more to the point, what will become of the manuscripts?

Arts and Architecture

20

SON OF AN AMAZON:
ASHOT BAYANDUR, PAINTER
(NICOSIA AND YEREVAN)

Huberta von Voss

"My mother comes from Shulaver, a big village in Georgia. One breathes a very special air there. Many of our greatest intellectuals come from there," says Ashot, the painter, son of the celebrated poetess Maro Markarian, and the nephew of internationally famous astrophysicist Benjamin Margaryan, the discoverer of "1,500 galaxies" at the Armenian observatory at Byurakan. However, anyone that imagines Ashot is interested in praising himself or his talented family through vanity is mistaken. Only little children boast about inventing great deeds and claim earnest recognition. Instead, big children, such as Ashot, do the opposite. They put a jester's cap on vanity, they invent stories instead of facts, and promote humor in place of seriousness. "When I went there I really got a fright," he says laughing. "They all looked like me: big eyes, a long nose, and huge ears. It was horrific!" His sister Anahit, a deputy and defender of human rights, would look like him, "except that she has no beard." And Ashot narrates one of his burlesque anecdotes, which make the listener not only laugh but also feel self-doubt. Why does one take this comical life so seriously?

> My three cousins, for instance, also look like me. They're very famous rustlers. One night they took me in their Volga pickup. We drove to near the border with Azerbaijan. They left me in a forest with the car and off they went across the green frontier. Three hours later I hear an Armenian soldier song, and then a torch shines. Out of the darkness come my three cousins, followed by the cows.

Ashot holds an imaginary torch aloft, imitates his cousins' song, and the swing of the cows' rumps. "Two wonderful, fat Azeri cows. Just like that, no need to drive them. I think they must've liked the song." The lively scene is easy to imagine. "It took us five hours to get the two cows into the little Volga," he adds.

Have people not also believed Münchhausen?

In his illustrations and drawings the laws of gravity also remain in abeyance: princesses fly like inflated balloons, knights wriggling helplessly in their armor, and dragons breathing fire from their mouths do anything but frighten. As he sees it, the world is the way one feels it is. "Life," he says in his soft high-pitched voice, "is wonderful!"

He spent all his childhood at the famous Byurakan observatory, where his uncle was able to solve the puzzles of the universe through science. Surrounded by his self-centered uncle's telescopes and his two debating and intellectual parents in Yerevan, the youngster grew up with the awareness that the key to the world lies in the power of one's own imagination and soul. "Every morning I woke up to the sound of an unworldly shouting match. My parents squabbled without end, but loved each other passionately until the end. My mother would recite her last poem to us in the morning. My father, an art critic, would immediately find fault with it, and my mother would go right off the reel." He laughs, his eyes shining in amazement at his temperamental mother who, until her most advanced age, was the feminine poetical voice of Armenia. "My mother was an Amazon. She always carried a drawn sword. I can imagine her riding a stallion, sallying forth to defend others. She always defended others, every day. That was her elixir of life." His mother was a simple villager, for whom life was replete with magic. "Maro turned everything into metaphor," he says tenderly. Her legacy is reflected today in her son's artistic sense, with less political commitment, but with the human element occupying a central position.

"Our education no longer teaches us to listen to our inner voice to be happy," he writes in a manifesto called *Everyone Needs Space, Everyone Needs Quietness, Everyone Must Be Himself,* in which he censures the attractions of the material world, above all the influence of the new media, which in his opinion destroy sensitivity. Man is born to acquire knowledge and develop and accept his own judgment. "This is why we must promote our own creativeness. Creation furnishes us with the weapons to protect ourselves: intuition, instinct, reason, doubt, and our inner voice."

Ashot's own dream of happiness is simple: to live at the edge of a big lake in a simple cabin, and to have a boat that can take him to the quietness of the waters. In Slovenia, where he paints with a group of artists two months a year, the fishermen already know him. In his artistic work Ashot also concentrates on the essential, which to his mind is numbers and letters. Time and again the number 12 appears, on a background of texts about life and art. How he came to paint the number 12 for years is something he no longer knows. But the figure suddenly captured him with all its symbolic force. "Twelve represents the masculine and feminine element in the universe, which turns chaos into life," he writes in his manifesto. After this obsession came an extended phase in which he invariably painted the first four letters of the Armenian alphabet. His backbone was to be language, and the first four letters the limbs that would support it. Numbers and letters are closely related in Armenian culture, as each letter also has a numerical value.

Ashot is one of those people that give themselves to a passion and allow themselves to be carried away by it, whose soul is lost in the game with the cheerfulness and natural trust of a child. Like an alchemist, he believes in the symbolical power of things, in the triumph of good as in fairy tales, which will happen if one only believes in it strongly enough. So it is no surprise that he has illustrated the principal Armenian epis, Davit of Sassoon. After the Babylonian epic of Gilgamesh, the heroic deeds of the house of Davit, a powerful lord of the Armenians, transmitted by oral tradition since the tenth century, are the second most ancient epic in the world. It was only written down in the nineteenth century. Davit possesses supernatural powers, like his grandfather Sanasar; but he is brave above all else, and defends his people from the encroachments of thieves and shameless tax collectors. "Davit," says Ashot, "gave the Armenians the self-confidence to be able to defend themselves on their own." Anyone that meets Ashot perceives that his fascination does not lie in the material content of the text but—aside from its poetical beauty—in the narrative structure. Here meek good triumphs against powerful evil, because it has confidence in itself. "To everyone" can be read on many of Ashot's paintings, meaning "We have all lost paradises and are driven by insignificant things. Yet we all have the possibility of being happy."

Ashot nimbly jumps up from the ground in the forest where we have partaken of a picnic. "This old gray-haired Armenian wants more wine," he says laughing, and he helps himself to some more. It is June. We are sitting under some olive trees in a village just outside the gates of Nicosia. Even the cicadas have ceased their song in the noonday heat. The children wish to draw with Ashot. The drawings are called "Spaceship," "Rocket," "Daddies Sleeping on the Moon," or "Two Flowers That Chat, and One Lonely Flower." As if spellbound, the children gather round him. At last! An adult who finds it perfectly normal that flowers should talk and can feel lonely, and that parents should have a nap in space.

We want him to recite one of his mother's poems. He balks at first, but finally decides to, and thus to keep his mother alive through her poems. "Be very quiet, children. I'm going to recite a poem by Maro for you." The four-year-old understands straight away what Ashot is going to do, and folds his hands. Ashot closes his eyes, pulls himself together, and begins to recite in Armenian: *Bolorn uzum yen ashkharkh pokhel/Voch vok chi uzum esksel irenits.* The children bow their heads and look at us in earnestness. They do not know a single word in Armenian but, just as Ashot understands them, they seem to understand him. Only we adults miss the sense. The translation is: "Everyone wishes to change the world. No one wants to begin with himself."

On June 12, 2003, Ashot Bayandur died of a heart attack in Slovenia at the age of fifty-six.

21

SEISMOGRAPH OF DIFFERENT WORLDS: PAINTER SARKIS HAMALBASHIAN (GYUMRI AND YEREVAN)

Huberta von Voss

Tightly huddled, as though sensing their Lord's coming sacrifice, the disciples throng for the last time round Christ, who seems to have already fixed his sight on another world. Before them is the bread of life. But it is not a whole loaf to be broken by the Lord as a symbol of their unity. The bread has already been handed out, on twelve plates painted on a separate sheet glued on to the canvas. At the very moment of their last joint act, the isolation of man has already begun. In the painting's blood-red background the future already lours. The F-541 pointing down is about to crash into the holy gathering. One can almost hear the droning arrival of this World War I propeller-driven plane. The aircraft is beautiful in each of its technical details.

This is but one section from the complex world of Sarkis Hamalbashian, who always insists he is not a storyteller, but has nevertheless created a cosmos perfectly his own, full of murmurs, in which past, present, and future are parallel, and seem as elevated as the superiority of the human world, which exists only by dint of its interrelation with that of machines, animals, and angels. The viewer is struck by a bizarre cosmic vision in primary colors, combining saints and whores, headless kings and podgy knights, obese popes and helpless angels; the fish, the lamb, hell hounds, and watchdogs, and many other creatures that serve man, symbolically or otherwise, menacing or blessing him. "I believe each person lives in a world very much their own," explains Sarkis, whose deep voice rumbles with an energy that is frequently reflected in his enormous figurative paintings. Humanity goes on sharing passions and weaknesses, desire and sorrow, greed and ideals, which, have endured throughout the ages. This is the putty in the eternal tragicomedy, which the introverted painter "unconsciously" blends, he says, out of impressions and memories. Oil paintings and ink drawings, old sepia photographs, numbers and letters reminiscent of ancient manuscripts, free brushstrokes, and the stencil-like recurrence of shapes flow into each other in him. He paints directly on the canvas, he says, as he compares the act of painting with the transmission process of an aerial that captures waves, transforms them into images, and emits them into the ether. His inspiration comes from the world of Christian images as well as the spiritual elaboration of "traumatic events" that have marked his life over the previous decade and a half.

When Sarkis appeared at 11.30 a.m. on December 7, 1988, at the central post office in Gyumri to meet a journalist friend on the first floor, he did not yet know that some minutes later the world was to collapse around him. His native town lay peacefully in the wintry morning light, which clearly brought out the outlines of the splendid nineteenth-century buildings. At Alexandropol, as Gyumri had once been called, before its name was changed yet again to Leninakan, the Tsar's garrisons had had their headquarters. Not Yerevan, but Gyumri had at one time been the intellectual and cultural center of Armenia. Many renowned artists, among them poet Avetik Issahakian and the esotericist and choreographer G.I. Gurdjeff, who later became famous in Paris, were born in this historical town. Sarkis's father, Dagdad, at the age of six, also found refuge here, together with his sister, at an orphanage on this plateau at the border between Georgia and present-day Turkey, after escaping on foot from the massacres at Ardahan in western Armenia, more than 100 kilometers away. Sarkis's mother, Herannush, came from a long-established family, whose men had been loyal soldiers and high officers in the Tsar's army.

Sarkis was thirty-two the day all traces of Alexandropol vanished from the map in twenty seconds due to an earthquake of unknown intensity, and had just participated in a first group exhibition of young Soviet painters in Moscow. "All at once everything started shaking, but we didn't worry: in our region we're used to earthquakes," recalls Sarkis and, despite his self-control, one gets an idea of how dramatic his memories are from the frequency of his deep sighs. The roar of the earthquake sounded as if a truck full of stones was going along a cobblestone street. Thereafter everything happened very quickly, and it became too risky to escape along the long corridor in the building. "We embraced and got under a door frame." Sarkis and his friend Hagop were lucky, and survived. When they finally ran out of the building, the world they knew had disappeared. "I'll never forget that sight," says Sarkis. He quickly went back home and found his wife Marianna with their two children, Vahagn and Tigran, four and two years old, standing distraught outside the front door. For 25,000 people in Gyumri help came too late that day. They were buried under the ruins. "I asked a policeman, 'Is Yerevan still there?' He didn't know. We remained totally cut off from the outside world for hours."

Yerevan still stood, and it was here that the family of four found lodging at Sarkis's parents-in-law's, together with their belongings and the paintings that had not been damaged. Painter friends offered their studios for his use, until Sarkis found himself and his paintings a new house. The quake was also a watershed in his artistic activity. "My style changed from then on. The collapse of the Soviet Union and Armenia's new independence, with its serious economic effects, also exerted their influence. His present studio is in an artists' building of the Soviet period, and, as he previously did from his "shattered home," he again looks on the movement in the streets from a fifth story. He sometimes observes passers-by in the street through a telescope he has at the big window of his studio. What he sees through the optical instrument is turned into the ironical-sarcastic brushstrokes with which the *voyeur* rather pitilessly exposes the tragicomedy of naked heroes.

The calm painter, obsessed with his art, loves the Renaissance. "Michelangelo, da Vinci, and Raphael are my idols, because they made humanity and beauty synonymous," says Sarkis in praise, and yet he does not seem to look for either the sublime or the beautiful in his own painting, but rather the abyss and the enigma of the human condition. Thus, the numerous angelical figures present in his paintings in no way resemble Raphael's sweet, childlike cherubs but rather Archangel Gabriel on tiptoe in Fra Angelico's Annunciation to Mary of 1432–33. But only as regards form.

While the Annunciation scene, frequently painted in the Renaissance, symbolizes the joyous hope of humankind's salvation, in Sarkis's paintings this 2000-year-old message appears frozen in a tender pose and disconcerted by worldly human endeavor. Where salvation was announced we now have a less than holy disorder; where man was offered salvation helplessness now rules. Unnoticed, but also not understood, the angels, whom Sarkis considers "mediators between the worlds," appear and seem to fulfill their task. "That's the way it is," says Sarkis. "There isn't a lot of hope in my paintings, but anyway that isn't their purpose. I just paint what I feel."

Like shoots sprouting in disorder from the ground, his feelings arise from his memories and observations, sensibly reacting to any change in the atmosphere. "I live in a region of constant tensions. The feeling of fear and insecurity is always there," he says, describing circles in the air. "We painters are like sensors of existing dangers regardless of the present situation." His painting of the Last Supper from the year 2000, in which an aeroplane flies towards the observer, shows that, after the devastating September 11 attack, in a political sense events simply prove him right. Today, the painting hangs in Washington.

22

FITZCARRALDO IN THE OLIVE GROVE: GARO KEHEYAN, PHILANTHROPIST AND IMPRESARIO (NICOSIA)

Huberta von Voss

Brian Sweeney, called Fitzcarraldo, is eccentric and obsessive. So is his life dream—to build an opera house in the Amazonian forest, play Verdi for the Indians in the jungle. As one needs money for that, he will trade in rubber—the gold of the jungle—and chop down virgin forest to get to the area of cultivation. Unfortunately, the river up to there has many rapids. So the steamer has to be towed over a mountain, by the Indians. Fitzcarraldo bewitches them with Enrico Caruso's voice played on an old gramophone.

Werner Herzog's 1981 movie with Klaus Kinski in the main role does not take place in Cyprus. But Garo Keheyan here lives like Kinski's double: Fitzcarraldo in the olive grove. Garo Keheyan also pursues the dream—or does the dream pursue him?—of building a great art center, devoted to the dialogue between cultures and art forms, in the village of Delikipos, between the capital, Nicosia, and the coast of Larnaka. "Delikipos means garden of fools," smiles Keheyan with satisfaction and, in accordance with the purpose of the center as a bridge between West and East, the name is made up of Turkish *deli* (fool) and Greek *kipos* (garden).

The construction of the ambitious project awaits government approval, although preliminary plans for a concert hall, center for contemporary art, 50,000 volume reference library and artists residencies have been drawn up by a Bulgarian-Turkish woman architect and a well-known acoustics consultant who designs the world's leading concert halls, who has visited the area. One of the best London and New York consultant firms, AEA, which also works for the Paul Getty Museum, has given the project a polish. The brainchild already has a name, the Pharos (*pharos*, Greek for lighthouse) Center for Art, Culture, and Global Dialogue. And yet, after years of dedication, there is still a long way to go to convince politicians and functionaries that Cyprus needs such a center, as a hinge between Orient and Occident. But the little island on the edge of Europe and at the doors of the Levant has other worries and interests. Its incorporation in the European Union has fulfilled an old dream, but the island is now losing its profitable offshore business. Tens of thousands of new tourists are to replenish the depleted coffers, and mass tourism is the policy at this moment. There is no room here in budgetary calculations for a high-quality artist village. Garo often feels irked by the lobbying and the red tape as he looks out of his office window onto the street, which leads to the presidential palace. Large paintings by the best Armenian artists garnish the wall and make the modern room look like a luxurious art gallery. "But I'm going to achieve my objective," he says, sighing, in his very best Oxford English. The numerous concerts by the most outstanding international artists he organizes every year—in 2006 alone there will be about thirty concerts, including a chamber music festival—compensate for his endeavor to obtain subsidies.

When Armenia became independent in 1991 he traveled in the winter to the spiritual homeland. The everlasting search for his own identity acquired a new orientation. "I identify with Cyprus, though I didn't go to school here. I was educated in England but I don't belong there," he says emphatically. When he was eight his parents sent him to a public school in England. At that time, in the early 1960s, the situation in Cyprus was tense. The family moved from the part of the capital with a Turkish majority and settled in the Greek part. This move was also a great change for his parents, Hagop and Stella, who were the second generation born on the island. They had both grown up in the Turkish zone, and were as familiar with Turkish as they were with Greek since their school days. Still, it was Garo, the child of the Mediterranean, who found the change most difficult. "To be an Armenian in England was exotic, and not always easy," he says of the atmosphere of the upper-class boarding school. As years go by it becomes ever more complex to give a simple answer regarding his origin. "I feel a stranger to this day," says Garo Keheyan, even being firmly inserted in Cypriot society.

While a student at Oxford, he came across a book on Armenian architecture at a secondhand bookshop. His notion of the far-off land of origin, which was then out of sight, half of it in Turkey and the rest in the Soviet Union, suddenly took shape. "Armenia existed in the territory of the imagination: medieval churches with ruined conical domes scattered over the empty Anatolian highlands. They looked so real, so very Armenian," he wrote in his book on Armenia, *Yearning for the Sea* (Nicosia 2000, Pharos Publishers).

The organic connection between man and nature, man and matter, is one of his favorite subjects. For his artist village at Delikipos he plans to have red tufa stone from Armenia shipped over, which blends well with the reddish soil of the area. A large rock from Ani, the metropolis in ruins whose street plan was once upon a time designed by Hannibal, adorns his dining-room table. The first time he visited Armenia in winter in the early 1990s, he saw clearly that the journey home remained a fragmentary one.

> The past is a foreign country. I stand with a permit in my pocket to view it. My eyes get cold, caught in a blank stare. Little remains of Ani's ramparts and thousand churches, of the former glory of that medieval city that equaled Constantinople and Baghdad. Consumed by feuding and decadence, and ravaged by the Seljuk and Byzantine armies, the Armenian project was given new birth in Cilicia. Now the desolate city is inaccessible, a stone's throw across a deep ravine on the wrong side of the Turkish border—an invisible, arbitrary line that divides Armenia from its own heritage. The past is in a foreign country.

When the border in no man's land between Turks and Greeks was opened up in Cyprus after thirty years, Garo Keheyan made another trip into the past. The fifty-year-old man's parents did not accompany him. For them the reencounter with the old places would have been too painful. On the coast of Kyrenia (Cyrene), one of the prettiest harbors in the Mediterranean, stands the dazzlingly white Yasmin Court Hotel. The lacquer on the five big stars on its façade is peeling off. Continental Turks and young Russian women now gamble there, which is forbidden in mainland Turkey. Business is good, except that its real proprietor, Hagop Keheyan, is not part of it.

Further west along the same coast road there is a big army camp in which Turkish soldiers carry out military exercises. Behind the gates, somewhere out of sight, is his parents' former summer house. "It was a spectacular house, in colonial style. My room was destroyed by a shell during the Turkish invasion." But Garo's journey took him elsewhere, to the picturesque mountain village of Lapithos, where, in the 1960s, young artists of the island converged to participate in all sorts of workshops, dancing, music, and painting meetings. At a certain moment Garo bought an old house here. In the summer he slept on the flat roof, and watched the sun set on the Mediterranean. On clear days the mountains of Cilicia, the vanished Armenian kingdom in continental Turkey, could be seen. "My house had disappeared. I found just land covered in weeds," he says. He did not bring back a single stone with him as a souvenir. "When you lose an arm, you can't put it back on again."

Back in Nicosia, he puts his Ottoman period town house in Ayios Kassianos at the disposal of the artists he tirelessly brings to the island. The little garden full of weeds borders the Green Line. At night the Turkish soldiers on patrol look up from a distance at the candlelit windows. Salsa music wafts out on the warm night air. The upstair rooms fill up with laughter. Guests stretch out on kelim cushions, while others dance till daybreak. The Keheyans have been connected with Brazil for decades as honorary consuls. At the crack of dawn Garo often has a swim in the sea at Larnaka or drives to his "land," as he calls the 44,000 square meter grounds at Delikipos. "Language, religion, ethnicity—all that can be transcended with nature, music, and art. I believe in the power of nature and of beauty. This is where wounds can heal."

He does not leave this process to chance. Now that Turks and Greeks can once more mingle after thirty years, since Easter 2004, he makes a telephone call. At the other end is Turkish-Cypriot horn-player Turgay Hilmi. He invites him to accompany the lied "Auf dem Strom" (On the Stream) in the Schubert Festival sponsored by the Pharos Trust. It is a love song, one of farewell, of unfulfilled yearning, but also one of overcoming the limitations of space.

Sieh, wie fließt der Strand vorüber
Und wie drängt es mich hinüber,
Zieht mit unnennbaren Banden
An der Hütte dort zu landen,
In der Laube dort zu weilen;
Doch des Stromes Wellen eilen
Weiter ohne Rast und Ruh,
Führen mich dem Weltmeer zu.

Behold, see how the bank is flowing
How strong towards it it does draw,
Pulls with bonds beyond all knowing
Of its cabin to go through the door
And there to linger in the arbour;
But the waves flow past such harbor
Onwards, with unceasing motion
Carrying me towards the ocean.

23

IBIS EYES: ARTIST AND POETESS ANNA BOGHIGUIAN (ALEXANDRIA AND CAIRO)

Huberta von Voss

"No one would call this city a happy place," wrote the English novelist Lawrence Durrell about Alexandria. And yet he was captivated, just like so many other poets and painters before and since, by the city interwoven with legends, founded by Alexander the Great on Egypt's Mediterranean coast. Cleopatra chose it as her place of residence. What is left is the magical, seductive power of the place. "Here our bodies were wounded by the rough, dry winds from Africa's deserts, and instead of love we had to invest a tenderness, more sage but so much crueler, which made us sink more deeply into solitude rather than freeing us of it."[1]

Painter and book illustrator Anna Boghiguian has devoted a large portion of her work to dilapidated Alexandria. Drawing pad and ink well in hand she illustrates, for many years on the tracks of those poets that sang and lamented the city, morbid and, at the same time, thirsty for life. While other young girls would read romantic novels typical of bourgeois "bobbysoxers," the daughter of the master watchmaker of Cairo devoured the somber quartet of Durrell's novels and decided to track down in reality that dark imaginary world. She was a young student of political sciences at the American University of Cairo when she traveled alone to Alexandria for the first time. "I wanted to travel back to the past, because it was more interesting than the present.

Life in Cairo was hard, although in those days Egypt was more open than now,"
says the fifty-odd-year-old woman, referring to the 1960s.

Years later Anna Boghiguian counterpoised, with her sensitive but savage
illustrations, a parallel world to the decadent, or already decayed, one that
internationally renowned poets like the Greek Konstantinos Kafavis and the
Italian Giuseppe Ungaretti evoked in their verses. Both poets were born in
Alexandria in the second half of the nineteenth century, the sons of immigrants
who sought their fortune in the large Greek and Italian communities of the port
city. With her very frequently allegorical drawings, Anna creates a dialog with the
text rather than simply illustrating it. For a whole year she sketches the shadows
cast by the hard Mediterranean light shining through the windows of Kafavis's
house of birth, and analyzes his verses. He warns the reader:

No new countries will you discover, nor new seas
The city will always follow you. The same streets
you will walk along, and grow old in the same quarter
with your hair going white in the same houses;
Wherever you will go to, your journey will end here.

It is his "extraordinary sensitivity" that spellbinds Anna for a long time. While
Kafavis remained irremediably seduced by Alexandria, Ungaretti returned to his
native city after twenty years' absence, and then left once more, to seek his
identity elsewhere.

Thus, through our fate,
my return and new departure,
in the twinkling of an eye
I excavate Time, I invent it
from the ground up to the crown of my head,
a fugitive like others
were, are, and shall be.

Yet, though the artist gets her inspiration from the poets' lyric power, she keeps
her distance. "No, I'm not a fugitive, nor do I belong to any particular place," she
stresses. Her tireless journeys from one place to another, usually lasting months,
with inkwells, brushes, and paints in her baggage instead of dresses, show that
Anna does not allow herself to be tied down to a prescribed role or place—either
as an artist or as a woman, to any city, nationality, or religion. "I feel I belong to
the world, without being bound to its frontiers. I'm Egyptian as much as
Armenian, as well as Indian, or simply Alexandrian," one of the rare sentences of
the artist that does not end in a question mark. This "I belong to no one," and the
rejection of transcendental truths seems to derive from fear of injuring herself
with imposed limits. "Really?" she growls at the person opposite, surprised and
somewhat in self-irony, as she fixes the other's eyes. She seems to be about to get
up at any moment and disappear in an indeterminate direction. The opposite is

the case. "That's interesting," she says politely, tapping a filterless cigarette on the back of her hand before lighting up.

That their only daughter would make no effort to ensure herself a conventional existence must have been clear since early on to her parents Antranig and Maria, from their daughter's reading fervor and her need to express her impressions with the pen. No sooner did her father pass on in 1968, but Anna also packed her bags and, with the excuse of a supposed invitation to a wedding in Beirut, she took her leave. From there she wandered through Syria and Turkey to Greece. "I needed an escape valve," says one who by no means comes from a strict parental home. Literature and painting remained closely joined, and led her onto the tracks of her revered English poet and illustrator, William Blake, who, in the eighteenth century created a world entirely his own with his verses and gravures. But the 24-year-old straight away traveled on to Canada, where she spent her next twenty years in Montreal, and finally she devoted herself to painting and poetry. It was only when her mother got seriously ill that she returned to Cairo. "If my mother hadn't needed me, I'd probably be in Pakistan or Cambodia," she sighs, a little sad.

On her forced return to Cairo, she chose a studio next to the Nile, on the giddy height of the terrace of a run-down building, and works here in two rooms cluttered with drawings. "I have a manservant who always messes everything up," she apologizes for the existing chaos. "I have no idea what he does with the drawings," she says shrugging, and passes her fingers though her untidy hair, which is graying on all sides. She takes the confusion and the disappearance of the drawings with self-ironical, dry humour. A helpless look in a gigantic old white plastic bag, in which she carries around her original drawings and important documents on her journey through Nicosia, Paris, and Amsterdam, shows she does not seriously blame the "manservant." "These bags are the ones Cairo rubbish collectors use to put papers in. I emptied this one for the journey. Very best quality!" she says, rejecting the offer of a suitcase.

As wide as the view of Muslim Cairo from her living quarters and studio is the scope of her work. This includes illustrations for the novels of Egyptian Nobel Prize-winner Nagib Maghfus, as well as own publications, such as "Anna's Cairo" (AUC Press, 2003), some sort of poetic geography beautifully written and illustrated by herself. The walls of the American University of Cairo are also painted by the former student there. However, what is most important for her right now is her project "Sacred Rivers," which she has been working on for a few years. Watercolors of wonderful sensuality done on handmade paper have arisen from the Nile and the Ganges, with her own poetic texts, which the renowned publishing house Fata Morgana (Montpellier) has published as a limited handmade edition.

Still, Anna would not be herself if she did not take her distance from this matter too. She was certainly more spiritual in past years than at present, she maintains. The constant everyday confrontation with Islam has not exactly reinforced her need of religion. "From morning to evening Allah here, Allah there," she says, regretting that the country on the Nile has lost its cosmopolitan character of former days. She rejects the making absolute of one's own faith, and favors more intellectual freedom. "I don't think everything in life comes from God, but that a great deal is our own responsibility. Whoever attributes every happening to God's will denies their own responsibility as a human being." Spiritually she feels tied to the Dalai Lama. "But I don't tell my patriarch this, or he'd excommunicate me and then who knows where I'd be buried," she says jokingly, and puffs at one of her innumerable non-filter Camel cigarettes, which have given her a rough, masculine voice. "On the other hand, who knows beforehand where they're going to die?"

With this mixture of curiosity and distance, accompanied by a strong will for freedom and the watchful look of a bird of prey, she observes the world with no more than a bundle on her shoulder and pen in hand, observes the course of the great mythical rivers and their symbology of eternity, travels through India by train in overalls and a lumberjack shirt, and draws the people in the compartments, crowded together and yet isolated from each other. Or she spends a couple of months in Cambodia to sketch the ruins of the fallen Khmer regime and allow the secret of the funerary temple of Angkor Wat to have its effect on her. Or maybe she is walking along the streets of Alexandria at this moment, reflecting the verses of its poets in sepia. So, ibis like, it says in her book, *Images of the Nile*, with her own poetry and watercolors:

> That day the sun disk
> Glowed red
> The white ibis turned
> Black
> Disappeared
> To stride across
> Past times
> Squatting on a tree
> It settled down
> And knew its earth well.

Note

1. Joachim Sartorius (ed.), *Alexandria*, Fata Morgana, Stuttgart 2001.

Film and Photography

24

SCREENING HISTORIES:
THE FILM-MAKER ATOM EGOYAN
(TORONTO)

Ian Balfour

The films of Atom Egoyan are edgy. Their visual texture is far from seamless and deliberately so, even when there is a beautiful transition from one moment to the next. Often one will switch from one kind of image to another, throwing the authority of the previous image into question. And this visual dynamic will complement and be complemented by a remarkable, layered story whose force depends as much on word and music as on the supposed primacy of the image.

Where did these compelling films come from?

Born in Cairo in 1960, Atom Egoyan moved as a young child to Victoria, British Columbia on the west coast of Canada and grew up there. A child of Armenian parents, he resisted after some time his mother tongue and while growing up he more or less resolutely opted for the path of what he would himself later call "assimilation" in the officially multicultural setting of Canada in the

1960s and 1970s. Growing up in Victoria the young Atom Egoyan was also without an Armenian community and without an Armenian church, which, together with the Armenian tongue, he considered the three traditional pillars of a more traditional Armenian society. As a young man, however, while a student of International Relations at the University of Toronto, he adressed Armenian history in thoroughgoing intellectual fashion, not least by writing an undergraduate thesis on aspects of the genocide and its aftermath. This was the beginning of a passionate engagement with the legacies of Armenian history and many vexed matters of identity, Armenian and otherwise.

The household Egoyan grew up in was, however, unusually conducive to the arts, with both his parents themselves being artists. Egoyan went on to study classical guitar and his sister Eve would eventually become a leading performer and proponent of contemporary piano music, especially in the experimental vein. It's no accident that Egoyan's films feature an acute attention to sound and music, rivaling that of a Godard.

Egoyan did not "train" formally as a film-maker but rather picked the craft up on his own, something that may have contributed to the startling originality of the early works. Those early films were understandably modest in terms of production values, though he found a congenial system of significant support from arts councils and government granting agencies in Canada that helped make some projects possible. Some early television projects, not least on *Alfred Hitchock Presents*, helped him hone his skills.

The early full-length films (*Next of Kin, Family Viewing*, perhaps up to and including *Speaking Parts*) are remarkable for their exploration of a variety of visual media, the interrelations of film and video. Both poles of the gaze—viewing and being viewed—are laid bare in a wide array of settings, personal, familial, cultural, and political, even in the narrow sense of the state regulation of filmic images. This results not in some sterile narcissism of the image reflecting on itself but rather in an interrogation of the status of the modes of viewing and being viewed, and their inextricable implication in even the seemingly most private situations. Along these lines, his most commercially successful film in the early 1990s was *Exotica*, which was driven in part by the dynamics of erotic seduction, not least in an institution (a strip club) dedicated to just that. Or *The Adjuster* would focus an unlikely figure of the insurance adjuster—not obviously a sexy subject—in order to follow how his unusual position in relation to the stories and lives of others (he needs to be able to know all kinds of "private" things in order properly to assess a claim of loss or damage) gives him a privileged vantage point, with which in turn viewers can—up to a point—identify.

One might imagine that a film-maker would be committed to the authority of the image, especially the filmic one. Yet, as much as Egoyan might devote his work to the power, truth, and beauty of certain images, the status of images—and of any given image—is far from secure. An almost dizzying multiplicity of kinds of images combine to give many of the films an extraordinarily variegated texture: photography, painting, super 8 home movies, video, television, surveillance footage, painting, and film. What is remarkable in Egoyan's oeuvre in this respect is that there is no particular hierarchy of media. It is not as if film is the final arbiter that tells the truth about all the other sorts of images. In one of the most famous films to take up the claims of different visual media, Soderbergh's *Sex, Lies, and Videotape*, the action closes with the destruction of all the videotapes that were formerly so crucial, thus enacting a kind of triumph of film over video. No such hierarchy prevails in Egoyan's work.

In the early films, Armenia and Armenian culture have a relatively shadowy presence. In *Family Viewing*, say, the specifically Armenian texture is hardly insisted on, visible sometimes in the home-video image of an Orthodox priest at a funeral or in the allegorical resonance of its hero's name. "Van" is a possible but not at all common Canadian first name and so one is invited to hear in it the name of the major Armenian city that had suffered the famous siege of 1915, later to be filmed by Egoyan's fictional film-maker, Edward Soroyan, in *Ararat*. With the exception of a short television show entitled *Looking for Nothing*, the matter of Armenia is confronted head-on mainly in *Calendar* and *Ararat*.

Ararat risks being didactic partly because it wants to inform an audience who may not be so knowledgeable about the history of the genocide and its aftermath, including its massive denial. So Egoyan deftly circumvents any merely didactic impulse by embedding anything that is of the order of information into charged interpersonal scenes. Thus when Ani, the art historian, is giving a lecture on the life of Arshile Gorky, the great modernist painter, the scene is far from a staid formal occasion.[1] The talk is interrupted by her stepdaughter, the girlfriend of her son (!), challenging her reading of Gorky in terms of her (the lecturer's) own fraught past and possible relation to the death of her first husband. A similar impulse and strategy are visible in *Calendar*, many of whose scenes feature information about this or that site—mostly but not all churches—in Armenia, but every such scene is implicated in a triangular drama between the photographer, played by Egoyan, the translator, played by Arsinée Khanjian, and the local Armenian guide, played by Ashot Adamian. What should be a more or less mechanical task of recording images—a photographer is commissioned to return with pictures for twelve months of a calendar year—is quietly heightened into a probing, anxiety-ridden drama of the first order. There is scarcely any statement uttered that is not marked by a (psychosocial) drama that can in no way be reduced to the "information" being conveyed.

Ararat is and is not a film "about the genocide." The extreme difficulty of the genre of the "Holocaust film" is evidenced by the fact that there are precious few examples of good films addressing the much-filmed destruction of the Jews by the Nazis (*Shoah, Night and Fog*). The task of a film about the Armenian genocide is arguably more daunting, given its "screening," that is to say, effacement or near-obliteration by so many official histories. Egoyan's own website (egofilmarts.com) does indeed describe the film as a "meditation on the Armenian genocide" and yet in interviews following the release of the film he also remarked that we should get away from thinking about it as a film "about the Armenian genocide." Both of these standpoints are true in their way. The film by no means sets out to tell the truth and the whole truth about the genocide. *Ararat* adopts any number of strategies that contribute to stopping short of that, even if the essential fact of the genocide looms large and sometimes is right before our eyes. Yet the film is (self-)reflexively a film of the making of a film, itself in its turn called *Ararat*. Moreover, that film within the film is organized not as some objective account of things "as they were" but is based on a forceful and authoritative but still "subjective" journal of the American missionary Clarence Ussher, now seen through the eyes of latter-day children of survivors and others in the Armenian diaspora and beyond.

"After great pain, a formal feeling comes," writes Emily Dickinson. Virtually every film by Egoyan is shaped by trauma or loss, their specters and their prospects, of which the immense loss of the Armenians at the hands and blades and gun barrels of the Turks is the most spectacular and haunting instance. Egoyan's preoccupation with loss derives, I think, not from some morbid fascination or some irremediable melancholy but from a sense that loss, and even the fear of loss, is crucial to how people experience and conceive of the shapes of their lives.

The Sweet Hereafter meditates, after the example of Russell Banks's novel of the same name, on the character and consequences of a group trauma, and one that entails one of the most harrowing sorts of trauma, the death of children in advance of their parents, a sequence that upsets our sense of the natural course of things. All the deaths in *The Sweet Hereafter* are untimely ones. This causes not just the emotional crises that unfold in mourning but also crises in how to make sense of one's life and how to tell the story of that life. A good many critics consider *The Sweet Hereafter* Egoyan's most achieved film to date. It garnered him the Grand Jury Prize at Cannes as well as Oscar nominations for Best Director and Best Adapted Screenplay. It seemed to have everything that a first-rate film from a major studio would have, without comprising an "indie" or independent sensibility. Offers came pouring in from Hollywood but Egoyan largely resisted its lure. In this, he is in solidarity with fellow Toronto film-makers such as David Cronenberg and Patricia Rozema. Egoyan indeed is something of a community film-maker, working closely and repeatedly with a familiar "stable" of actors (including his wife, Arsinée Khanjian), composers, and technicians.

Atom Egoyan is one of the formerly rare breed of writer-directors, the tradition that began with the formidable Preston Sturges. His early features (*Next of Kin*, *Family Viewing*, *Speaking Parts*) consist of original material, sometimes autobiographical though in the main not. But Egoyan sensed eventually that to continue on this path would be to risk repeating his "obsessions"—not too strong a word. So he opened himself to working more with screenplays to be adapted from existing novels: Russell Banks's *The Sweet Hereafter*, William Trevor's *Felicia's Journey* and Rupert Holmes's *Where the Truth Lies*. In all of these Egoyan walks a fine line between fidelity and invention, more concerned to honor the spirit than the letter of his sources. He is more than willing to create *ex nihilo* whole scenes, to alter major structural features of his pre-texts, and to omit what appear to be key scenes, even ones that seem to lend themselves to visual representation. A striking example of this is the scene of a demolition derby at the end of Banks's *The Sweet Hereafter*, which originally prompted Egoyan to think in terms of adapting the novel, only to find in the process of writing and filming that it would upset the visual and narrative economy of the film. Egoyan was also more than happy to work with an existing literary text that could not be altered in the least, Samuel Beckett's *Krapp's Last Tape*, a play that he had loved since he was a teenager (and so the project was a kind dream come true when the Beckett Trust turned to him to direct it). The material was congenial to him, not just for Beckett's verbal and conceptual brilliance, but also for the dogged attention to the recording of observations and to the technologies that make that possible.

Though best known for his films, Egoyan has worked with great success in other media, having to his credit a striking production of the opera *Salome* as well as his direction of a path-breaking production of Wagner's *Die Walküre*. He even authored his own opera, *Elsewhereless* with music by Rodney Sharman. Gallery installations have also proved a tailor-made medium for his explorations of the ramifications of technology and technologies in the shaping of our sensibilities, as in the show called *Hors d'usage*.

Egoyan's work displays a fascination with otherness, translation, and difference extending even to the gritty matter of how subtitles work (engaged most resolutely in a book he co-edited, *Subtitles: On the Foreigness of Film* (Cambridge, MA, 2004). *Calendar*, to take only one example of such a concern, features numerous scenes of "un-subtitled" dialogue in a film that is dominated by English and addressed in the first—but only the first—instance to an English-speaking audience. As the photographer who is the "hero" of the film has one date after another in his apartment, each prospective woman asks at a certain point to be able to use the phone and then conducts a flirtatious conversation with some lover or potential lover in a language other than English. None of this talk is subtitled. One scene filmed in Armenia displays an old man speaking Armenian and it too passes without subtitles. All of these are graphic illustrations of the limits of "our" comprehension, which may begin with words but can extend also to the enigma of images themselves. Egoyan's concern with translation dovetails with an ongoing fascination with what happens at borders, with what transpires when a person crosses from one "state" to another. From the early work to the late, but especially in *Ararat,* a good many crucial encounters happen precisely at border crossings, as in the Toronto airport to which Raffi returns thinking he is bringing back film shot in Armenia and having to account for himself and his history and the filming of *Ararat* to a customs officer. It is here that a certain legalistic "identity" is forcefully felt as an imposition or a constraint, even at the moment when characters still passionately embrace just those identities. In their exemplary staging of questions of identity, Egoyan's rich, layered stories continue to challenge us, to provoke us in words and images that remain to be seen and read—and seen and read again.

Note

1. So crucial is the story of Arshile Gorky for Egoyan that he and Khanjian named their only son Arshile. Something of the importance of this is captured in the short film Egoyan made called *A Portrait of Arshile*.

25

HOLLYWOOD IN DOWNTOWN CAIRO: VAN LEO, PHOTOGRAPHER (CAIRO)

Huberta von Voss

The bright lilac of the blossoming Judas trees contrasts with the city's mud-gray background, announcing the eternal return of spring in the land of the Pharaohs. Hundreds of families take advantage of the benign temperature this Easter Monday, and go to the zoo with their picnic hampers and spread their tablecloths in the shade of ancient trees. Mothers calmly keep an eye on their children's lively activity, and hand out the food, whether Sunnites, wearing their long *milleyas*, squatting on the ground, or Christian Copts or Armenians, in their Western garb. On this Christian and Muslim holiday it would seem that concord reigned between the confessions in this huge metropolis of 20 million inhabitants. On the

Nile the white sails of the feluccas swell in the morning breeze, and young men look on with yearning from the iron balustrades on the bridges joining the new western part of the city with the old eastern part.

From the quarter of Zamalik on the Nile island, the July 26 Street crosses the river and deeply penetrates the Old Town. Great old houses in art deco style are a reminder of past times, when Egyptians were oriented to the way of life of the European metropolis. At that time the street was named after the Egyptian king Fouad and housed a row of the fanciest restaurants and boutiques in the city. Its present name marks the date on which the last Egyptian king, Faruk, fled to exile in

1952. Little by little the luxury restaurants gave way to simple eating houses, and the exclusive boutiques to cheap clothes shops, their windows filled to capacity. Only on the fourth floor of number 18 has time stopped. The name van Leo figures in peeling letters on the bell box.

Here, outside the age-old lift, Dalida, the diva, must have wondered whether she wished to make use of the rickety vehicle to go up to famous photographer van Leo's, alias Levon Boyadjian, studio. Born in Egypt into a family of Italian immigrants, she returned to the Nile from Paris after an international scandal-sullied career in order to film with Egyptian film director Yussouf Chahine the melodrama *Le Sixième jour* (The Sixth Day), which became famous. Van Leo's photograph of her is one of the singer's last: she took her own life shortly after returning to the Seine. Whether Hollywood star Omar Sharif, the famous novelist Taba Hussein, kilted Scottish Commonwealth soldiers during World War 2, princely Saudi brothers in the mid-1970s wearing modern bell-bottoms under their white burnooses, or simply Mercedes, the lascivious dancer with her lips painted black and a cigarette in the corner of her mouth, just out from the night cabaret, all had to make the personal pilgrimage to van Leo's if they wanted to be eternalized.

From 1941 to 1998 he would personally open the door, inviting them to sit down in the reception room illuminated with electric light bulbs in his parents' house. He studied their facial features and carefully listened to the wishes of the stars, and others that wanted to look like one for once. He would then open the enormous double doors to his living room and invite his clients to take up a position on the simple dais on which they were to pose, without any assistant cameraman around to disturb the intimate atmosphere of the session. And then the precision work would begin. Van Leo illuminated his clients' faces with minute exactitude until a dramatic black-and-white contrast brought out the beauty of the face and disguised its less attractive aspects. Right from the time he was a child van Leo used to spend his weekly pocket money on photographs of Hollywood stars, in which he would study the lighting effects for hours. Thus, in the course of fifty-four years 19,000 takes and 16,000 negatives resulted, which today are housed in the photo archive of the American University of Cairo (AUC), which can be seen as a document of a bygone age.

When he was almost eighty and could no longer pick up the very heavy old enlarger he kept in the bathroom turned into a darkroom, van Leo's studio closed its doors for good, marking the end of an era of portrait photography in Cairo in which, from the time of photographer Legekian's arrival from Istanbul in 1880, the Armenians achieved preeminence, with artists like Archak, Armand, Vartan, and Alban. None of them, however, recorded so much on celluloid in the Cairo formerly open to the world in the 1940s and 1950s as van Leo, whose studio at the entrance to the artists' and night-life quarter was the unavoidable destination of Cairo's *demi-monde* with its dancers, actors, musicians, and singers.

"I was very good-looking as a young man," recalls the svelte eighty-year-old, in his turtleneck sweater, thick horn-rimmed eyeglasses, and black patent leather shoes, sitting some distance away on the reception armchair. More than 500 self-portraits prove that van Leo was not only handsome but also liked dressing up and, just like his clients, used photography as a means of metamorphosis: fearsome-looking bandits with prison numbers or drawn pistols; romantic-looking propeller-driven airplane pilots in leather jackets and wind caps, reminiscent of some novel by Saint-Exupéry; or cool, aloof beaus looking on the night world with the arrogant certainty that, if possible, they will outlive the observer. It was with one of these self-portraits that van Leo won the Royal Netherlands Prince Claus Award, and in this way gave rise to a whole series of retrospective exhibitions, books of photographs, documentary films, and prizes. The surrealist image shows van Leo as a young man with a shaven head: a three-quarters profile decisively looking toward the future, appearing in the background with a doubtful, pessimistic look, and in the foreground lying on his deathbed. The photo expresses van Leo's simple philosophy, "No matter who you are, prince or pauper, death awaits you at the end." Maybe it was this attitude of stressing the equality of human beings that enabled him, apart from his talent and commitment, to make a beggar look like a great philosopher or a dancing-girl in a revue like Scarlet O'Hara.

Despite all his later fame as a star photographer, life has grown lonely for this man, for whom, in his heyday, Cairo society had to wait its turn for days to have its picture taken. The stars and would-be stars that used to light up the sky in the metropolis on the Nile have long since gone out. Van Leo's career began with the arrival of British, Commonwealth, and Allied soldiers during World War II. The officers brought money to the city and the Entertainments National Service Association, ENSA, made sure the boys did not get bored in the shadow of the minarets. The oldest theater in the world, the Theater Royal of Drury Lane, arrived from London, but the more profane entertainments were also attended to, such as shots of French striptease artists and South African athletes. At first they were all photographed free of charge by young Levon, whose father had given him a camera as a present, and so he was allowed free publicity in theatre programs.

Levon's father, Alexander, emigrated in 1924 from Jihane in Turkey to Egypt with two-year-old Levon, and had one interest above any other: that his three children would be able to fend for themselves and not end up as employees like himself, who spoke seven languages fluently and, as a one-time British spy and high functionary of the Turkish railway, had irremediably lost his social position and, in his new Egyptian home, was forced to earn the hard bread of the immigrant.

Levon's elder brother, Angelo, soon teamed up with him, and the pair made a name for themselves. After a few years their pathways diverged once more, and Angelo moved to Paris, where he was able to set himself up as a photographer. Levon, the individualist and womanizer, who was never to exchange his freedom for a wedding ring, today looks back on his past with sadness. The country that harbored him never became his home. "For the Egyptians I've always been a third-class Armenian." (The second class was always the Copts'.) His kind of art never received wide recognition.

When Gamal Abdel Nasser was elected president of the young republic in 1956 and an ever-increasing Islamization of society, the economy, and culture was put in motion, life for minorities of other faiths, open to the world, soon began to get more difficult. Thousands of Armenians, Jews, Italians, Greeks, and Copts left the country. But the wish of those that stayed on for beauty, showing off, and naughtiness did not disappear, and satisfied clients took their pictures home with them, but with greater discretion than before. Hundreds of nudes, male as well as female, were taken over the years. Van Leo burnt them for fear of repressions after Egyptian Nobel Prize winner Nagib Machfus was attacked by Muslim fanatics.

"You know," says van Leo grabbing his walking stick, "I'm seriously thinking of marrying a pretty young woman to take care of me." He opens another portfolio full of pictures and starts to tell about the Saudi noblewoman of beautiful nails and hypnotic eyes; about the flower girl who wanted to look like Rita Hayworth; and his mistress, Ghada, of the melancholy eyes, whom he did not marry because she was Muslim, and he did not want her to change her religion for him.

On March 18, 2002, van Leo died, single, in Cairo. The above conversation took place a year earlier.

26

BEYOND ALL LIMITS: ON THE ART OF FILM-MAKER ARTAVAZD PELESCHJAN (MOSCOW)

Gerald Matt

Russian film theorist Oskana Bulgakova called Artavazd Peleschjan a marginalized eccentric, on the one hand for creating his work outside the cultural-artistic gravitational field of Western art (so ex-centric) and on the other because his work is unusual, convulsive, and displays a certain taste for bizarre pathos. The marginalized eccentric, in this case, is no pleonasm since, in the actual Soviet Union, Peleschjan arrived from the periphery, that is to say, from Armenia, and for a long time was an outsider in the Soviet movie and art world, determined to on produce films outside the mainstream.

In specialist circles, however, Peleschjan's genius was recognized early on, as his modest output is too individual and innovative for great film-makers like Jean-Luc Godard or Serge Daney to pass it by. In 1988 films by Peleschjan were shown for the first time outside the Soviet Union at a film festival in Rotterdam, followed by numerous invitations to other festivals. The art world also soon discovered his work as a stimulus for exhibitions dealing with moving images. The most spectacular was the show organized by Paul Virilio, *Ce qui arrive* at which one of Peleschjan's most important films, *Our Century* (1980–90) was presented. In the process he became famous among all the European connoisseurs, and finally the Ursula Blickle Foundation, in Germany, and the Vienna Kunsthalle exhibited a selection of his works.

In contrast, there still exists a widespread ignorance on the part of those that set the rules of the movie canon, who are not up to the level of his important role as a "missing link" between the heroic period of the birth of Russian film-making (Eisenstein, Vertov, Pudovkin) and today's vanguard.

Peleschjan, the taciturn loner, who prefers to let his work speak for him instead of resorting to words, has remained a solipsist with fully subversive intentions: a quiet fighter for an esthetic style that cannot be popular; a jagged, oblique mind that steers clear of all marketing criteria in the sense of Western PR categories—

which does not imply he is unaware of his own value: his battles for a suitable presentation of his works and adequate compensation for film and photo rights are legendary. What he likes best is to have the cash laid out in neat piles on the table of his modest Moscow apartment.

Artavazd Peleschjan is an old-fashioned modernist who catches hold of a loose end from the 1920s and hoists himself up on it—in spite of Soviet cinema trends of the 1960s. What he does cannot be placed in any category: he works with "found footage" and his own real-life takes without being a maker of documentaries; he tells stories without using the dramatic possibilities of films. His creed is the montage which he takes from Eisenstein and Vertov and redevelops, taking it to the limits of conscious perception.

Under the dry title of "distant montage" he shapes far-reaching narrations with internal correspondences and repetitive cycles which, in their esoteric angulation, are reminiscent of Bach's quadruple fugues or the structure of a novel by Arno Schmidt. Peleschjan, who once said he could not imagine his films without music, composes his series of images according to rhythmic criteria. He introduces certain pictures time and again like punctuation marks, he interrupts scenes, accelerates and brakes, develops bunches of motifs which he confronts with abruptly intruding counterimages. The film-maker works synesthetically, in a certain sense: he translates sounds into images, and images into sounds. And through the interplay of the two levels his works attain a frankly painful density. Poetry of movement: the beat of swan wings and the fowls' rise in flight in his ten-minute work, *Inhabitants*, appear several times as a leitmotiv, turning into ciphers in a movement that advances with no kinetic goal as an absolute objective, the beauty of the abstract, *belle et inutile*. Can one see in this a criticism of the progress myth prescribed for Soviet society? Peleschjan does not use actors in his films, but he does show people. In *The Seasons* he gives a view of Armenian life, of daily activities and ritualistic interchanges among the farming population. However, under the director's masterly management bringing the cattle down from the mountain pastures, stacking hay, individuals' manoeuvres against snow, hail, water turn into a chiaroscuro of light and shadow, of accelerated bodies and liberated matter.

The director builds monads of events which, through repetition and retrogression, come into ever new relationships of context and perspective. He creates his visual world out of the archaic reservoir of the struggle between human and nature, but transcends the banality of daily routine through an act of hyperstylization. In the script of his project, *Fata Morgana*, which he never filmed, this transformation of the very human into a supratemporal yearning for an unchanging personal management of things becomes specially clear:

> The tempest roared, but without being able to cover the radiance; and in the sand extended man's footprint—straight, goalwards, toward the light.
>   And somewhere, very far away, already as an echo, as lacking hope by now, desperate, muted, the voices could be heard: Turn back …! Turn back …! Turn back …!

The Romanian film-maker and theoretician Andrej Ujica, who has done a lot to reveal Peleschjan's work, asked the rhetorical question of why a peripheral country like Armenia could produce three significant film directors: Sergej Parajanov, Atom Egoyan, and Peleschjan, speculating that its frontier position, intellectual as well as geographic, sharpens concentration on what is one's own, and preserves one from triviality and passing fads. This must be understood metaphorically in the case of Egoyan, who was born in Cairo, the son of Armenian refugees, and went through his artistic socialization in Canada. In contrast, Parajanov and Peleschjan spent their formative years in their homeland, although they polished their art in a dialectic interplay with the "central esthetics," represented by the renowned Moscow cinema school, VGIK.

Artavazd Peleschjan, born in Leninakan in 1938, arrived in the Soviet capital when he was twenty-five. As a student until 1968 he was able to produce five short movies, and he was soon promoted as a talent many admired. Despite the physical distance, his Armenian past remained stuck to him, as eggshell to a newly hatched chick. In his work he only once dealt explicitly with the cruel history of his land, but with particular intensity. In *Us/Menk*, carried out for Armenian television and Armenfilm, the director narrates in his typical radically chopped-up style the genocide of one and a half million Armenians by the Turks, which foreshadowed the Shoah, the resulting exodus of hundreds of thousands, the first return to the Soviet republic after World War II, and the symbolic value of sacred Mount Ararat for Armenian Catholics.

Peleschjan's art can hold out even against history's traumas and catastrophes, not allowing itself to be flattened by their baleful nature. His films represent, their subject matter notwithstanding, modern esthetics in its most crystalline aspect, requiring the active participation of the spectator who does not wish to remain hovering at a superficial level. In these works, which attempt to communicate beyond words, it is a matter of rediscovering that pristine language prior to the Babylonian collapse of speech, which resulted in a division of the arts. "I believe in man more than in the language he speaks," says Peleschjan. This can also be attributed to Soviet ideology, which uses the verbal mainly to keep series of orders in circulation, and so keep people manageable in all their contradiction and exuberant irrationality. The Armenian director's art is opposed to such a partition and reduction of the existential. He is interested in delirium, excess, hubris, catastrophe—and the magical element in apparent trivialities. Politics is not his ostensible theme, but its manifestations in everyday life, its collective effect, interferences in nature, and the influence of technology make up the repertoire from which he digs out the elements to build his visual chain reactions.

In Peleschjan one finds, in contrast to a socialist ideology, profound skepticism toward a teleological philosophy of the world and man's capacity to rule it. For progress and catastrophe are, as Susan Sontag points out, nothing but the two sides of the same coin. In his film *Our Century*, which combines an apocalyptic stance and grotesque humor, Peleschjan questions this viewpoint. There are firestorms, crashing trains, phallically erect rockets, a countdown that, as if trapped in a back-and-forth sanding machine, always goes back to the beginning, and men at control panels—all the furniture of science-fiction fantasies and dreams of the future. Yet this collected instrumental energy leads nowhere: the gadgets burst into ridiculously splendid flames, serving infantile destructive urges, and the future implodes as the materials are held with wedges. This is the way Peleschjan goes about deconstructing the metaphorical "*Gestell*" (Heidegger) quite like Tarkovskij in *Solaris*. In the nonverbal space of the images the basic questions about the limits of human existence and enterprise are posed. The films are about triumph and catastrophe, protest and loss, and, finally, life and resurrection. It is not by chance that one of his first works is called *Beginning*, and his last two films, *End* (1992) and *Life* (1993), conceived as a diptych, are about birth and death.

In the age of the flood of television images, posters, video, and video telephones, pictures like Peleschjan's are striking. In contrast to the mass images of our day, which no sooner are they seen than they are forgotten, they are images that impress themselves in one's awareness. Peleschjan films are "epiphanies" of a *conditio humana* in which the situation is always special and aesthetically convulsive beyond the traditions of genres and the formal imperatives; and, precisely in its "splendid isolation," of a modernity that many classics in the history of films and videos leave out. In the age of the New World Order since September 11 they have acquired amazing currency.

It is no coincidence that Paul Virilio included Peleschjan in a series with contemporary young artists like Aeronaut Mik, Cai Guo-Chiang, Wolfgang Stähle, and Tony Oursler in his exhibition *Ce qui arrive*, which deals with catastrophes and the uncontrollability of the world. Nevertheless it would be an inadmissible simplification to place Peleschjan exclusively in an apocalyptic role. On the one hand, there are plenty of his works that, much to the contrary, express a principle of hope; on the other, he is interested in problems of structure and form more than questions of the contents and meaning of the existential paradigm. In the ideal case of a "distant montage" thought out to the end, the two categories join up in a sort of Hegelian synthesis and raise human possibilities to the hyperreal. "The method transcends those limits beyond which our conceptions, our laws of time and space, are no longer applicable: those limits beyond which those that are born don't know whom they're killing, or those that die, whom they're giving birth to."

Music

27

THE VOICE OF FRANCE: CHARLES AZNAVOUR, ALIAS VARENAGH AZNAVOURIAN (PARIS)

Pascale Hugues

Comment crois tu qu'ils sont venus?
Ils sont venus, les poches vides, et les mains nues
Pour travailler à tour de bras
Et défricher le sol ingrat …

Comment crois tu qu'ils ont aimé?
Ils ont aimé en bénissant leur premier né
En qui se mélangeait leurs sangs,
Leurs traditions et leurs accents.

Ils ont bientôt créé un univers nouveau
Sans Holocaust et sans ghettos.

How do you think they arrived?
With empty pockets they arrived, and their hands bare
To work with all their might
Tilling the ungrateful soil …

How do you think they loved?
They loved when they blessed their first child
In which was mingled their blood,
Traditions, and accents.

They soon created a new universe
With no holocausts or ghettos.

The small figure is very frail and yet very much alive. His step is light as he slowly crosses the stage. This famous song is often his opening number in recitals abroad. A song that resembles him. For Charles Aznavour, the monument of French song, is at the same time its revered ambassador in every country in the world—who sings of noble love. This embodiment of French cultural tradition was neither born French, nor is he a Frenchman by his own choice. Varenagh Aznavourian is French by chance; he has become French out of necessity. When he was born in Paris on May 22, 1924, his parents, who had fled from the Armenian genocide in Turkey, were just in transit through France. With their luggage unpacked, they were waiting for a visa to go to the U.S.A. However, the quota of

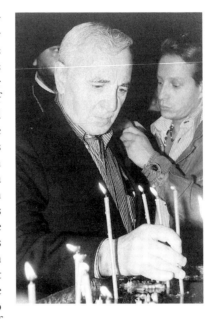

Armenian immigrants had been filled, and the family was refused the visa. So they settled in France. The midwife was simply unable to pronounce the name, which she considered too exotic for a baby. So she simply named him Charles—the most French of all names. Later, he would adopt it as his stage name.

Aznavour's father, Misha Aznavourian, was born in Georgia. His mother, Anar, came from a family of salesmen established in Turkey. Misha Aznavourian was an opera singer, and Anar an actress. The new arrivals opened a small restaurant in the Quartier Latin. Every evening the Armenian exiles would come to the Rue de la Huchette to listen to their own music and speak their own language. This environment had a profound influence on Charles and his sister Aida. Charles Aznavour, the singer with the astringent Parisian charm, did not deny or forget his Armenian roots. "I, who come from this graveless people," he sings. Even if he often sings with stormy passion, and its painful transience, he does not forget to honor his people.

Specially impressive is the text of the song he wrote for the sixtieth anniversary of the genocide, one of his most political songs about a genocide that took place with the knowledge of the international community, which refused to intervene.

> They died without really knowing why,
> Those men, women, children who wished only to live,
> With heavy gestures, as though drunken,
> Mutilated, massacred, their eyes wide with terror.

They called upon their God as they died
On the threshold of the church or at their front door,
A stumbling herd in the desert, advancing like a cohort,
Annihilated by thirst and hunger, weapons and fire.

No voice was raised in a euphoric world
While a nation rotted in its blood
Europe discovered jazz and its music,
The blare of trumpets covered the children's screams.

They died shamefully, without a sound
by the thousand, by the million, without the world shaking
Soon turning into little red blossoms
Which the wind covers with sand, and then forgetfulness.

Charles Aznavour, whose wax effigy is in the Grevin Museum in Paris—the pantheon of famous men—is amused by the personal cult surrounding him in Armenia. "There are two statues of me in Armenia, one in bronze 4 metres tall, and the other in stone, 4.5 metres. Those statues tend to deteriorate as the years go by. And just think of the wax. That certainly does melt!" On December 7, 1988, an earthquake buried more than 50,000 people. Deeply troubled, Aznavour began collecting donations to come to his people's aid in their need, founding the humanitarian organization Aznavour pour l'Arménie, which sent foodstuffs and clothing by air to the stricken region in the north of Armenia.[1] In early 1989 Aznavour teamed up with the prominent French film director Henri Verneuil, also of Armenian provenance.[2] Both appealed to their French musician and actor colleagues to support the relief program for Armenia. Ninety celebrities collaborated, composing a CD, *Pour toi, l'Arménie* (For you, Armenia), of which a million copies were sold.

Aznavour is the permanent Armenian ambassador at the UNESCO, a task he performs with great diligence in spite of his tours and his advanced age. He considers this commitment as self-evident. "I was born in France, but my parents were from Armenia, the country of my roots. I help Armenia the way Jews all over the world help Israel. That doesn't mean I feel more Armenian than French. If I were Breton, I'd help Brittany. I'm French of Armenian origin."

In May 2004, Charles Aznavour celebrated his eightieth birthday. The president of the republic sent him a congratulatory telegram. On the lapel of his jacket, a minute red button indicates he is a Commander of the Legion of Honor, a distinction personally conferred on him by Jacques Chirac. Out of the poor son of immigrants came France's showpiece. There are few French people as well-known abroad as him. The songs he wrote for his idols Maurice Chevalier, Juliette Gréco, and Edith Piaf were heard all over the world. When "la Piaf" discovered him in the 1950s and took him on as a kind of maid-of-all-work, she had no idea that her pianist, chauffeur, and secretary would one day become as famous as herself. Little Charles, with that certain something in his voice, had to struggle arduously to get there. He had his first success only in 1955 with his song "C'est la vie." Here he already showed his unmistakable mixture of melancholy and ironic coolness which kept him on the summit of world stardom for fifty years. Nevertheless he did not limit himself to composing and singing, but also stood out as an actor. He appeared in front of the camera more than sixty times for the big names in French cinema like René Clair, Jean Cocteau, Claude Chabrol, and François Truffaut. His last important appearance was in Atom Egoyan's film, *Ararat*, in which he plays the part of an aging Armenian film-maker who wants to shoot the "ultimate" film about the genocide of his people, a homage to all the Armenian film-makers that could have tried it, or did try it, or were prevented from doing so, like Rouben Mamoulian, Henri Verneuil, and Elia Kazan.

His new album *Je voyage* sold like hot cakes, and his faithful French public goes to his concerts as if they were going to a great national religious ceremony. The only thing is that he has become slightly deaf. His hair has gone white. And he no longer climbs stairs four steps at a time. But that is all: his voice has not developed wrinkles. He still has the mischievousness of a Paris street urchin. Small lively eyes look on at the world of today. Slender, he is seated, wearing a casual corduroy jacket, and he says his recipe is very simple: optimism, humor, and a balanced life have made an eternal youth of him. He is already planning his next songs, but "no rush." Charles Aznavour still has all his life in front of him.

Like his friend Edith Piaf, who opened the door to the United States for him, he grew up in the street and is no longer afraid of anything. He laughs as he says this, and yet his songs give him away. On listening to them one realizes he is not quite so untroubled as he makes out. Passing time, wilting youth, approaching death—all of them are the melancholy subjects that people his music. "For me time is an obsession," he says with his dreamy look. "Time is what torments me, because I get the feeling I no longer have enough left to do all I have in mind!" Yet Aznavour faces the fact that time is slipping through his fingers, turning his great age into a trump card. It is a good weapon for seduction. He knows this, and uses it. "Only in France are there such old hands as myself!" Aznavour is not the only member of the Old Guard that manages to fill concert halls. Those that were thought worn-out grandads—troubadours for old people's homes, with a load of old junk from the past, trodden underfoot by the dictatorial marketing of the "reality shows," by the factories of falling starlets with neither voice nor glitter— those veterans make a comeback with wholly up-to-date songs, which the public acclaims to the heavens. They have won back the French people that yearn for their roots and more solid values. That is the oldies' revenge.

Charles Aznavour is that thread of Ariadne through three French generations, one of those glues of national unity that show the transience of fashion, but the eternity of France, such as Charles Trenet or Juliette Gréco—for whom he wrote the legendary song "Je hais les dimanches." *Time* magazine has named Charles Aznavour the entertainment artist of the century. And for Germans he belongs in the same pantheon as Edith Piaf and Maurice Chevalier. His love songs are the expression of their somewhat naive fascination with neighboring France.

Aznavour weaves a tender bond—accessible, sensual, immediate. He connects generations, different ethnic origins and social milieus, and crosses borders by accepting everyone and excluding none. Be it granny or granddaughter, the professor or the baker at the corner, all of them hum the same "Ave Maria" Aznavour has sung to their hearts. Americans place Aznavour on the same pedestal as Frank Sinatra. The huge ICC hall fills up when he appears in Berlin to sing his heart-melting songs. And I remember an evening in Burkina Faso when the French envoy sang together with young African girls "Ne dis rien, mais laisse moi serrer ton corps que j'adore."[3] "I am a singer of the people," he declares. "Culture is what circulates in the street."

Charles Aznavour roars like a lion when it is a case of defending the variety of French songs. That is when he becomes a staunch patriot. He approached the very Senate, where he obtained the approval of a 40 percent quota of French songs on the radio.

> Quotas are important! A government that doesn't impose them murders its own culture. When "Lilli Marlene" became a world hit, it was the song itself that did it. But nowadays you have to give songs a hand. In France governments fight for our culture. You can't forbid other music. You have to allow for coexistence. I'm very combative, aren't I? But you have to be.

Aznavour apologizes for his firmness, but is sure he is right. "Young people must develop pride in their national inheritance. Without one's noticing this in French youth, they also have this. There are French bands that got to the first place in the States. French techno music is very advanced. And there are very famous French DJs in Berlin." And there is a Charles Aznavour, firmly anchored in his Armenian roots, and the most French of all French singers. A journalist dubbed this singular phenomenon the "Aznavourization of France."

Notes

1. Numerous projects were added later. Aznavour often donates the proceeds of his concerts to the foundation.
2. Verneuil was born at Rodosto, Turkey, on October 15, 1920, as Henri Malakian. His parents fled to Marseille. He wrote a successful novel on his childhood, *Mayrig* (Paris 1985), which he later filmed with Claudia Cardinale and Omar Sharif. He made numerous films with Jean-Paul Belmondo and Yves Montand. The winner of many awards, he died in Paris on January 11, 2002, honoured by multitudes.
3. "Don't say anything. Just let me embrace your body, which I adore."

28

Under the Stars: Accordion-player Madame Anahit on the Alleys of Beyoglu (Istanbul)

Christiane Schloetzer-Scotland

Suddenly … that sound. Amid the clatter of plates and the clink of glasses a long sound is heard, like a deep sigh. Then, a chord. At the tables heads turn, unsurprised and unhurriedly, but rather to greet an acquaintance who has placed herself in the narrow aisles. She is not tall. Her lips are painted dark red, and she wears an equally red rose on her lapel. The accordion now exhales, and Madame

Anahit plays a new sequence. The drinkers take up their glasses of raki. The music allows them to sink into themselves, seduces them, reminds them there can be no love without melancholy. But, by the time the glasses are empty, Madame has disappeared again, like a ghost in the night.

"I saw Madame Anahit," say the drinkers the following morning, and some even have their photograph taken with her before daybreak so as to hold on to the image, which seems to have come out of an Oriental fairy tale among the cheerful eaters and drinkers on the Nevizade Sokak. The Nevizade starts at the Istanbul fish market, like a thick side-branch loaded with heavy fruits. The rows of tables of the fish restaurants seem interminable, and leave only a narrow pathway free for people to pass. There is always noise here, and in the hubbub Madame Anahit used to appear with her accordion of pearly keys and played her favorite tune, "Under the Stars." Madame herself was a star that descended from another age into the quarter of artists and bars in Istanbul, Beyoglu.

At the end the accordionist needed her son Onnik Varan's support to make her appearances. Still, she did not wish to give up doing her nightly show—more to the point, she could not do without it. In short, this woman, out of the ordinary, never learnt anything but the accordion, with which she made a living and fed her children. When I saw her, I wanted to meet her, but soon after the Turkish newspapers reported: "Beyoglu has lost its voice." Anahit, who had hidden her physical ailment for a long time, died on August 29, 2003, at the age of seventy-seven. There were photographs framed in black on the tables along the Nevizade, and the mayor of Beyoglu sent a wreath. Yet only a handful of people attended the funeral service in the big Armenian church of Uç Horon between the fish market and the Nevizade Sokak.

"She was part of a minority within a minority," said one of her friends, Yetvart Tomasyan, looking at the tiny group of mourners. But she was at least honored in the newspapers, which published her photograph, with her dark hair always combed back, always wearing an elegant outfit, and her accordion at her chest. "She always dressed as if to appear on a stage when she went out," says Onnik Varan, her son. "She had four wardrobes full." Onnik was Anahit's right hand, her agent and helper. Since his mother died he has lived on the memory and what she left. It is not a lot. "I'm prominent, but I've got a hole in my pocket," Anahit gladly used to say. Any money she made, she spent. She could play every night, and the accordion would give her enough to eat, Anahit maintained. But this woman, who played tangos and tarantellas, never sat down at the guests' tables, even when she played for them. "I'm no 'meze' (side-dish) for your drink," she would tell the pests among the drunkards, so as to keep a distance, as she only drank cherry-juice and water with ice.

"My mother was a woman of great dignity," says Onnik Varan. If people gave her money, she would politely say, "May you come upon gold." People liked that. The accordionist recorded no disk or CD, as did her internationally famous colleagues, like Cher, or the sisters Ani and Aida Kavafian, who were born in Istanbul and moved to New York. In any case, Onnik Varan has not heard of them. There are only a couple of filmed takes of her. But she loved applause no less than other stars, even though her stage was the street. Now and again she used to complain about the accordion, "Ah, I should never have got into this."

Anahit Yulanda Varan was twenty when she heard a Greek, Yorgos, play the accordion on Büyük Ada, the greatest Island of the Princes in the Sea of Marmara, opposite Istanbul. From that moment on she fell in love with the instrument. She begged her mother so much that, finally, an instrument was bought for her at "Papa George's," a well-known music dealer in Istanbul. She began to practice fifteen hours a day.

Anahit's mother also had more than a weakness for music. She played the piano and this as a young girl on ocean liners that went to America. This extraordinary woman apparently mastered seven languages, as Onnik Varan recalls of his grandmother, a genuine Constantinopolitan, proud and free in her way of thinking. She was almost ninety when she died. Nor did she have an easy life. She raised her children single-handed. Of her father, who came from a respectable Armenian family of Istanbul and worked for the treasury, Anahit never had anything good to say. It was a household of women and female musicians Anahit grew up in.

The early 1950s in Istanbul were a period of national renewal. Istiklal, Beyoglu's fancy street, "smelt of perfume everywhere," as people that remember it say. Anahit lost her musician husband, and had to feed her child, later two. She began playing the accordion at weddings, and shortly thereafter in the famous Çiçek Alley, near the fish market, where people still ate and drank on upturned wooden barrels. In this alley, in which all the colorful Bohemians met, she became famous. Here she came night after night, until a fire destroyed the place in 1978. When the Çiçek was rebuilt, now more elegant and somewhat sterile, the old habitués kept away, and tourists began to arrive. The restaurant owners took on noisy trios, and there was no more room for Anahit and her "Stars."

She moved on to the Nevizade, which the *Istanbullular* had still not allowed themselves to be driven away from, and where poets and dreamers waited for the musician and her tangos to give flight to their dreams and interminable tirades. She did not always have a well-disposed public, but only those that "didn't know how to behave" had treated her as a *gavur*, infidel, in those grim September days of 1955, when the Istanbul mob rose up in fury against the Greeks, venting their wrath on other Christians besides. Sevin Okyay remembered this in the daily *Radikal*, when Anahit died. She herself, who had "never wished to make any distinction between Christians and Muslims," felt disappointed to see "people she had played the accordion for turn into wolves that same night."

At the editorial offices of the Armenian daily *Marmara Gazetesi* there was a smell of incense, not exactly usual in a journalistic milieu. But the building of the newspaper, which is published in Armenian and Turkish, gave directly onto the Uç Horon church. Edvard Aris had chosen the place for a meeting. "My mother was very fond of Edvard," said Onnik Varan.

Aris is an accordeon virtuoso, a graduate of the conservatoire in Paris, who plays on famous stages with orchestras, and on the Turkish state radio, TRT. However, if one is lucky, one can see Aris, who makes no distinction between serious and light music, appearing to play among the tables of the White Russian pub Reyans in Beyoglu. "I play everything except football songs, or the people get up on the tables and go wild," he says.

Edvard Aris must have felt the same compulsion for music as Anahit, which is why they understood each other well. He was born in Istanbul in 1945 and his only wish as a birthday present when he was still a child was for a harmonica. Thirty-six relatives came to his birthday party. That was a time when children were given mainly useful things, like woollen socks. But Edvard, who was worried his parents might scold him for being extravagant, whispered in his guests' ears his wish for the following year. "A year later I received thirty-six mouth organs, and not one single pair of socks," he tells, still pleased at his funny trick.

He played his way up while still in short trousers and, as a student, he participated in small bands that entertained the guests at the Kilyos beach, near the mouth of the Bosporus on the Black Sea. Aris today owns the largest collection of accordions in Turkey. But the short, plump man, who can scarcely keep still for a moment, and who can be imagined as "playing twenty-four instruments in twelve minutes," is also a talented musical missionary. This can be proved if one accompanies him to the Armenian primary school at Bomonti in Istanbul.

May 19 is one of those dates on which the Turkish Republic specially commemorates its founder, Kemal Atatürk. The date marks the beginning of the Kurtulush Savashi, the Turkish war of liberation. Reciting patriotic eulogies is obligatory in schools, including Armenian ones. "A country is such when people give their life for it," reads a teacher from a book. But Edvard Aris makes sure the routine ceremony at Bomonti has a special character to it. Forty-two children and a dozen teachers sit on plastic chairs in the simple schoolyard, and Aris plays in front of them in different combinations, always accompanied by two or three pupils. The children play on guitars and trumpets, drums, and accordions short pieces Aris has taught them. Every single child plays, despite the occasional false note. There is always enthusiastic applause. Carl Orff did not do it any better in his teaching activity than this kind virtuoso and philanthropist.

A girl in a pleated grey skirt with red knee-length socks and a white T-shirt comes up with a little accordion and sits down in front of everyone. Her name is Ani Varan, Anahit's granddaughter. Confidently she pulls the bellows and presses them closed again. The applause is resounding. Ani is seven, and her eight-year-old sister, Anahit, studies the piano with Aris. Twice a week Onnik takes his daughter to her piano lessons. Says Onnik, "I want them to learn that we owe everything we have to the accordion."

Aris has taken one of Anahit's two instruments for his collection. He proudly exhibits it in the schoolyard and soon puts it away, before it can suffer any damage. What is left of his mother's "very colorful life," which has not lost its meaning for Onnik Varan, is not much more than an accordeon, four wardrobes full of clothes, and the little apartment in Tarlabashi, a simple neighborhood not far from Çiçek Alley. "We always dreamt of better times," he says, "but we were never short of food on our table, and our mother also used to play for us, when we had a birthday party." Her clothes, among them eccentric flounced bathing costumes—Anahit was also famous for swimming in the Bosporus—were made for her by a seamstress. "She was çok Madame," a great lady, says her son.

Onnik Varan learnt shoemaking. His brother sells music cassettes. They both manage to get by. Anahit was married four times. Her first husband was also her fourth and, except one, they were all musicians. In addition there were platonic loves. "Hand me my makeup and my glasses so that I can read the paper," Anahit asked her son the morning of the day she died. For fifty years she circulated in the small area between posh Beyoglu, and Tarlabashi, quite gone to seed in recent times—fifty years of busking among fish, raki, and the smell of incense from Uç Horon, the church which, protected by a heavy brown wooden door, like a sacred island, opens out directly on the flow of business and exchange at the Istanbul fish market.

Anahit's grave is in the Shishli cemetery in Istanbul. The register of the family burial ground is from the Ottoman period. Anahit did not renew the entry in the republican registry. She preferred spending her money on the nicer things in life.

Commitment

29

WAYS TO IDENTITY: BERGE SETRAKIAN, PRESIDENT OF THE ARMENIAN GENERAL BENEVOLENT UNION (NEW YORK CITY)

Huberta von Voss

Boghos Nubar Pasha had everything a man of the nineteenth century might wish for in the Orient: a distinguished name, a title of nobility, and money. His father, Nubar Pasha, was born in Smyrna on the Ionian coast in 1825 as the son of an Armenian businessman. Thanks to useful family ties and his diplomatic ability,

Nubar Pasha had achieved the summit of power in Egypt, which was part of the Ottoman Empire at that time. Sent as the Egyptian representative to Constantinople, he extracted the Sultan's agreement for the completion of the Suez Canal, which was to open the sea route to India. Nubar was promoted to the rank of pasha—an unusual dignity for a Christian in the Ottoman Empire—and, after numerous ministerial posts, became Prime Minister of Egypt. His son, Boghos, studied in France like his father and received recognition for an invention he presented at the Paris World Fair in 1900. When he turned fifty-five six years later, he remembered his Armenian origin founded the Armenian General Benevolent Union, the AGBU, and a benevolent association to alleviate the needs of the Armenian minority in the land of his forefathers. In 1909, three years after its foundation, when 30,000 Armenians were victims of massacres in Adana, in Cilicia, the AGBU already faced its first great humanitarian challenge. Today, almost a hundred years since it was founded, the seventh president of what is now a worldwide organization, Berge Setrakian, can look with pride on many past successes. Most of them originated in his nation's needs.

The AGBU helped the survivors of the genocide to establish themselves in exile. In 1915–16, whoever was able tried to get passage on an oceangoing steamer from Marseilles. A bare quarter of a century later, the refugees of the Holocaust would anxiously crowd the same pier, in search of a passage to North America, Argentina, Brazil, or Uruguay. The refugees coming from the "old country," as the former homeland in present-day Turkey is still referred to, organized themselves in the place as the AGBU, when the organization still had no branches. In twenty countries, including Ethiopia, South Africa, Iran, North America, France, Greece, Lebanon, and Syria, schools were founded; here children learned Armenian and social assistance projects were financed with funds raised for the purpose, extending to cultural activities from the popular folk dances to choirs, readings, theatrical performances, and, in general, everything pertaining to Armenian culture. In time, communal centers were built, where Armenians get together mainly on weekends. "Wherever there are three Armenians, there are four parties," says Zarouhi Isneian happily. She comes from Plovdiv, in Bulgaria, where there is a centuries-old Armenian community. With financial backing from the AGBU, she went to the Melkonian school for diaspora Armenians in Cyprus. Today the 23-year-old young woman is studying in Berlin on an AGBU scholarship and actively participates in the Armenian community's dancing group. The whole idea nowadays is to win over this young generation so that the cultural heritage continues being fostered among the Armenian diaspora, which should be ready to help Hayastan—the original Transcaucasian Armenian motherland—to remain afloat with heavy financial contributions.

Berge Setrakian is not a man of poetic words. As a partner in an influential New York law firm, he is used to getting to the point. His eyes, behind gilded eyeglasses, are concentrated. Ten pencils with very sharp points are in his pencil holder, showing that this man, amid his untidy pile of papers, takes things seriously. The sun projects a monumental play of shadows on the nearby Chrysler

Building and the East River—in vain. Setrakian has no time to attend to the beautiful summer day. His monitor beeps continually like a heart pacemaker with each incoming e-mail. An official telephone call from Geneva immediately turns the American lawyer into a Lebanese Armenian. "Bonjour … yanni … let's do it." It is with this flexible mentality that he will lead the AGBU into the twenty-first century.

His predecessor, Louise Manoogian Simone, set high standards. Now she rules behind the scenes as the chairman of the board of this organization, whose capital reserves amount to around 258 million dollars and with an annual working budget of 34 million dollars (2004). "Louise," as everyone calls her, is a name one whispers in awe, in the same way one does not call Queen Elizabeth "Elizabeth Windsor." Far from the ancestral homeland, which many young people have never visited, the presidents of the AGBU satisfy the desire of many diaspora Armenians to have worldly leadership. Unlike his predecessors, such as Calouste Gulbenkian and Alex Manoogian, Louise's father, Setrakian is no self-made multimillionaire. But he is experienced and practical and has known the organization since his childhood in Beirut. His parents were themselves AGBU volunteers. There he met his wife, Vera Nazarian, who also comes from a family with several managing posts in the AGBU. "It's a family affair," as they would say in the States, where Setrakian has lived since 1976. "I owe everything to the AGBU," he says hoarsely, as though talking of the profits of a financial year. "All my Armenianhood comes from it."

As the father of two adult daughters, both raised in the U.S.A., he also knows, however, that the organization must be open to innovation. "The diaspora's changed. There's a young fourth generation that, for the first time, has had no physical contact with the country of its ancestors." This means not only Turkey but also the Middle East as a whole. There are between 70 and 80 percent mixed marriages on the East Coast of the United States. On the West Coast there are always fewer. "First of all, we're human beings, then Armenians. Marriages with non-Armenians are perfectly normal in view of integration," he says, which shows he is modern—because even today marrying an *odar*, as non-Armenians are called, produces major crises in some families. Setrakian mentions the names of some well-known families. "All the boys married non-Armenian girls. So what? That's human nature." On his cabinet there is a photograph of his pretty daughter, Ani. Has this tolerance had anything to do with her choice? "No. We were lucky. It wasn't a mixed marriage," he says, unable to hide his relief. "But she could also have married a non-Armenian," he adds, laughing. This marriage was also "sponsored" by the AGBU, where Ani met her present husband.

"I'm firmly convinced our possibilities of survival in all foreign countries are better than ever," declared Setrakian in a speech to the Los Angeles community. Some 600,000 Armenians live in California, most of them in Greater Los Angeles. "Our children and grandchildren are not simply Armenians who live in the United States, Canada, or France. They are 100 percent American, Canadian, or French. There's an independent Armenia they can see, accept, feel, and visit.

They can identify with it." The statement is simultaneously a request for backing for his new program, because under Setrakian's leadership, the AGBU continued contributing to its worthwhile Armenia and Karabakh projects, while at the same time continuing to maintain and increase its financial support to AGBU diaspora projects. "We're at an important crossroads in our history," says Setrakian in his Park Avenue office. After the Turkish massacres, the rest of the Middle East became a surrogate home.

> There were a lot of us, and our rights were respected. It was easy to retain our identity. For the first time now—thank God—we're not persecuted. But when we were, it was easier to preserve our identity. It's unfortunate we no longer live in our own kingdom because, when you're strong, it's easy to retain your identity. For the first time we don't live in the country of our ancestors, at least not the majority of us. Contact with the land gives you your identity. For the first time we live spread out all round the world among civilizations as good as, or even better than, our own. So ... which is our identity? This is why Armenia is so important.

The dexterous rhetorical construction shows how great an effort Setrakian must make to convince his own people. Among the diaspora, aid for Armenia enjoys approximately the same popularity as West German aid for East Germany did. One gives because it would be embarrassing not to, but all the time impatiently criticizing the lack of progress. The relation between *Spyurkahais* (Armenians abroad) and the *Hayastanzis* (those born in Armenia) gives rise to the same prejudices as between "Wessis" (West Germans) and "Ossis" (East Germans). Additionally, most of the diaspora Armenians speak Western Armenian, and to them the accent of the old motherland sounds as quaint as Saxon does to a Bavarian or the dialect of Georgia to a Bostonian.

After the devastating earthquake of 1988, in which 23,000 people perished according to official figures (nonofficial estimates place the toll at 80,000), and in the period after 1991, when the Soviet Union collapsed, the AGBU was unable to ignore the situation, stresses Setrakian. "From the start, Armenia was part of Boghos Nubar Pasha's vision." His first project was carried out for the benefit of Armenia, but with the happenings of 1915 the situation changed, and it was now the needy refugees of the genocide who urgently required help. Still, even during the Soviet period, the AGBU always endeavored to carry out its work in Armenia. "This is the country of our national inheritance. Political regimes come and go." With the AGBU's help, clinics, museums, monuments, and whole residential areas were built. After the new republic's independence, the AGBU helped build an American University and picked up the bill for the Philharmonic Orchestra. "We believe humanitarian aid ought also to include projects beneficial to the soul and the mind. People in Armenia are deeply attached to culture. Above all, during the years of the blockade, when the people suffered cold and hunger, it was fundamental to keep the Philharmonic going. We're proud of having done this."

Besides its cultural work, the AGBU closely cooperates with the seat of the Catholicos at Echmiadzin. "We encourage donors to build churches in Armenia. Of course there are numerous historical churches, but they aren't temples with adjoined communal centers. Spiritual values must reach the community for the people to unite." Additionally, the New York headquarters contributes to training clerics abroad.

The Armenian attitude regarding personal effort is clearly apparent in Setrakian's words about the actual area of humanitarian aid. It is important not to make it too central. "One way or another the people are going to get by." For the elderly, pensioners, and orphans, a soup kitchen was set up. Every day, around 1,200 old people receive nourishing food at six different centers. "To help is as hard as receiving help because, unless you do it with tact, dignity, and sensitivity, it's better not to do it."

Like all small nations living in the diaspora, the Armenians know their survival depends on the talents of its children. This is why the AGBU did not delay in establishing youth centers in Armenia, where 3,500 children between the ages of seven and sixteen can employ their time after class hours. Among other things, they learn music, painting, dancing, sports, and chess.

"How can we hold on to our identity?" is one of the key questions in Setrakian's thought. "The most important element is the Armenian language. But it's retreating, and it's going to be spoken less and less, whether we like it or not," he says soberly.

> Today there is a completely new definition of the Armenian identity. Do the children of mixed marriages stop being Armenian? How about those who don't speak Armenian? The answer is, No. We have to develop for the future a definition of what it means to be Armenian. We live in the DNA age. If we already give up, we're wasting our time in the diaspora. We have to water these plants.

Many of his compatriots, especially in the Middle East, will suppose being Armenian means speaking Armenian or having parents of Armenian roots. Yet what is more important in Setrakian's eyes is young people's commitment to their community, whether they are 100 percent Armenian or not.

At AGBU general headquarters, which functions in a nondescript building near Central Park, there is a bustle of activity. Here, some twenty-two full-time collaborators from different countries are in charge of coordinating the program on an international level. But the heart of the organization is its numerous volunteer members. There is an atmosphere of renewal since the younger generation organized itself as the Young Professionals. Here, the career-oriented make up a network to support each other in their studies, choice of career, and job seeking. Additionally, there is a cultural program suited to their own tastes. "Our events are aimed mainly at the younger crowd. In contrast to our parents, we no longer organize those big traditional galas," says Hrag Vartanian, born in Aleppo in 1973, who is in charge of the AGBU's Press Office. His friends laugh.

It is clear that globalization has shaped their identity as Armenians. "To be frank, I didn't like Armenia," says Hrag honestly about his first two trips to the country in the 1980s and 1990s. His most recent trip in 2004 changed his mind. Clever Meldia Yeseyan, born in Teheran in 1974, who now makes cultural films for the Metropolitan Museum in New York, did not find her visit to the "old country" decisive for feeling Armenian either. "We have our own idea of what it means to be Armenian," says Meldia. "Well," critically adds Monique, born in Jerusalem in 1977, who worked as a clothes designer for Oscar de la Renta and has never been in Armenia. "Maybe there is a certain vague fear about what one might find there." These fears are not shared by Ani Setrakian Manoukian, born in New Jersey in 1978. "All I can say is, 'Visit.' It's already great to hear everyone speaking Armenian in the street, the street names are in Armenian script, and the food's Armenian. All at once you realize you belong to a big group. It's a good feeling after being used to seeing oneself as the member of a minority." Maybe this experience of his two daughters Ani and Lara, who both worked as guides at holiday camps for orphan children in Armenia, is what makes their father Berge opine: "We must send more young people to Armenia. As soon as they get there, something happens to them. They suddenly realize what our country means." His new project is a further step in this direction. In the future, the Melkonian Educational Center in Yerevan will be offering 200 young Armenians from all over the world the opportunity to study for a semester in Armenia. "We're building better language labs, sports centers, and a pleasant environment. Young people need to get immersed in a completely Armenian environment. If we can manage that, it's going to help a lot."

30

DAILY BREAD OF RESOLUTIONS: HILDA TCHOBOIAN, PRESIDENT OF THE EURO-ARMENIAN FEDERATION (BRUSSELS)

Daniela Weingaertner

When Hilda Tchoboian has business to deal with in Brussels, she leaves her great blue wheeled suitcase in the rooms of the Euro-Armenian Federation. In these offices on the first floor of an old town house in Brussels giving onto the Jubilee Park are put in motion the press campaigns to keep the European public aware of the Armenian position: the incorporation of Turkey into the EU is not negotiable unless Turkey recognizes the dark side of its history.

The short, olive-skinned woman with her chiming gold jewelry and medium-length brown hair is an Oriental apparition. She accompanies her speech with her powerful little fingers, which underline each word. She thinks of herself as a European of Oriental roots, considering life in the diaspora to be the height of globalization.

By chance, directly opposite, on the edge of the city park, stands the biggest mosque in Brussels. While Hilda Tchoboian gives radio interviews and poses for a piece on the French television channel Antenne Deux, veiled girls walk by in front, on their way to lessons. It is a little as it was during Hilda's childhood in Aleppo, Syria, where the religious communities lived in close proximity, but knowing little about the rest.

The 53-year-old naturalized European is an international traveler for the Armenian cause. Today Paris, tomorrow Strasburg or Brussels, then to Washington and, once or twice a year, Yerevan. Her visits firmly join the widely spread diaspora communities. Just like the Armenian monks 1,700 years ago, who traveled through Europe to bring Christianity to the heathens, Hilda Tchoboian is also permanently on the move to ensure Armenian culture and history do not fall into oblivion.

La cause arménienne had already marked her life before she was born. Like almost all Armenian children in the diaspora she was made aware of being a descendent of survivors right from the cradle. When the Turkish government sent the Armenian communities on their long trek across the desert with the pretext of resettling them in Syria, her grandfather refused to leave. As a mechanic who dealt with keeping mills in working order, he became indispensable for the Turkish lords.

> My grandfather used to service all the mills in the town, and this is why he was allowed to survive. He and his three sons, one of them my father, worked practically like slaves throughout the war. As payment he received, for himself and all his family, two kilos of flour a day, and this is how they were able to survive.

Hilda Tchoboian recounts her family history calmly, not as having to repress her feelings so as not to lose control, but as someone that has accepted her life in the diaspora as well as her personal history. Compared with others, her father's family was very lucky. When new expulsions and massacres began after Turkey's defeat, her grandfather fled with his five children to the city of Aleppo in the desert, only 50 km distant from his home town.

They were able to take with them carpets and furniture, the manuscripts of the grandfather, who was in fact a writer, the family Bible, and the family tree. In this way the story was not, as it was for many in the Armenian community of Aleppo, an abstract tale of their own nation's Calvary: there were snapshots of happy times, old books, clothing, and other things one could hold in one's hand.

Hilda was six when a truck driver who ferried goods between Aleppo and the south of Turkey arrived to give them some news. "He told us which houses had been destroyed, which churches. They had turned one convent into a museum, another into a prison. I remember the bunch of keys grandmother extracted from her purse. The day they escaped she locked up everything and kept the keys."

Little Hilda did not then understand why her grandmother furiously shook the keys, while she cried and shouted. "I didn't understand what the man had told her. They'd had lands, pistachio plantations, and grapevines. My paternal grandfather owned extensive vineyards. My grandmother sobbed, 'My houses, my houses. What we've come to! We've left everything behind, and here we're refugees.'"

In the Armenian community of Aleppo each had a grim story to tell, the grandmother of who would later be Hilda's husband, for one:

Kurdish farmers hid them, and her baby was born amid the farm animals. The other fugitives told the mother to kill the baby, as it would cry and need nappies. That way the Turks would find them and kill them. But she refused to kill the infant. Her husband had been sent to war and that same day he was shot dead outside the town. She lived with this baby girl she saved till her last day, and the girl, her only daughter, was my husband's mother. Naturally, she never knew her father. But the usual thing is for people not to know where they come from. Each family of that period has similar stories. One doesn't know where one comes from. There's neither continuity, nor memories, nor keepsakes passed on from one generation to the next. There's a total break with the past.

When fifteen-year-old Hilda arrived in Grenoble to carry on studying there, she already had two distinct cultures in her baggage: the experiences and stories of the Ottoman Empire of her grandparents' time, and her childhood and youth in the Middle East, in the Syrian diaspora. Here there was religious tolerance, but at the price of the communities' living in total isolation from one another. A civil society cannot arise under such conditions, thinks Hilda. Now a third world, Europe, added itself to the others.

Her first impressions at that time were:

the elegant buildings and the orderliness of things, in contrast with the East, where buildings grow chaotically side by side. I arrived with my two sisters in 1968—that May 1968. We couldn't understand the demonstrators. The first thing I thought was that these French are never satisfied. They had everything, compared with what we only dreamt of having. They had every freedom, and they no longer wanted them.

As a student she worked in her free time at what she had absorbed in her cradle, participating in the Committee for the Defence of Armenian Interests in Lyon. Here was coordinated the work of all European organizations engaged in preserving the Armenian culture of that continent. As though not wishing to tie herself down to any particular spot, she divided her time between her studies at Grenoble and her work at the organization in the southern French city more than 100 km away.

When she graduated in international commerce, she got a job. A mere four months later she was offered the management of an Armenian cultural center in Lyon. "I accepted without hesitation, because that's what I wanted to do in my life. Although I'd studied international commerce, economy, and political sciences, I was much more interested in culture." And she is still active at the Cultural Center to this day, whenever her duties as chairwoman of the Euro-Armenian Federation allow it.

There exists a culture which was eradicated. To talk about this culture is to allow a dead man to revive. If one fosters Armenian culture, this is not free of obligations. This cannot be separated from the history of this culture. To defend Armenian interests is for me the same as defending Armenian culture, which was intended to perish alongside the Armenian people.

All facets of community life take place at the Cultural Center. There are language courses, a dancing school, art courses, and sports. By means of co-productions with cinemas, theaters, or other cultural associations they try to keep alive and make known the Armenian heritage. It is a meeting place, for instance between French and Armenian politicians, as there are Armenian parties living on in the diaspora all over the world. Other national groups have seldom achieved this. The exiled Armenian parties have built cultural centers and churches, and communication structures. Only the Armenian international benevolent organization AGBU has created a greater number of community institutions. She describes the program of the party to which she belongs: "The Dashnaktzutiun socialist party has as its objective a free, independent, and newly united Armenia. The independent state already exists. Free—well, I don't know about that. Maybe we'll get there some day." She laughs.

United, we are not.

When the party was founded, Armenia was divided between the Russian and Ottoman empires. Ottoman Armenia was completely wiped off the map. What remains is the part that was once Russian territory, with approximately a seventh of the original area last century. The final goal of the socialist party, then, is an Armenia within its former borders.

Nevertheless, it is not a matter of immediate urgency to reclaim the former territories from Turkey. It is much more important to require the Turkish government and people to recognize the historical facts once and for all. Only then, says Hilda Tchoboian, will Turkey be able to become a part of Europe. "Since independence, Armenia has followed the policy of offering its hand to Turkey. This is why the demands that arrive each year from Turkey are unacceptable. Turkey insists that Armenia pressure the Armenians of Europe and the U.S.A. We should take the genocide question off the agenda of national parliaments and international organizations."

The Euro-Armenian Federation has not the slightest intention of doing this. In the European elections of 2004 they published a list of politicians that filled the bill. These were the ones that included the Armenian question in negotiations with Turkey on acceptance by the EU. In a resolution of 1987, the European Parliament condemned the Genocide, whereas in 2001 the proposal that Ankara's evasion from its own history should be documented annually in the EU commission's progress report did not obtain a majority. These progress reports serve as the basis for entry into the EU. In autumn 2004, in December, the European Council will decide whether to initiate negotiations for acceptance.

Hilda Tchoboian is convinced Turkey has barely changed in the last 100 years.

As far as the state doctrine goes, from the end of the Empire to the present day Turkey has changed very little, hardly at all. Let's take the question of its treatment of minorities. The Armenians were exterminated almost completely. The Greeks were expelled. Only the Kurdish minority is left. No sooner were there no Christian minorities left then the Kurds were oppressed, deported, and massacred. The elimination of whoever is weaker, whoever doesn't belong to the body of the state, in other words, whoever is not considered a pure Turk, carries on today.

Many people in the Armenian communities of Europe are wondering whether it is not time to move further away—to Canada, whose government has recognized the genocide, or to the states of the United States that did likewise. They no longer feel at ease in a European Union that could extend to Anatolia in the medium term. Hilda Tchoboian, however, intends to stay. With her friends all over Europe she plans to carry on fighting for Europe to remain European. In the recently elected European Parliament she will launch a new move to impose the resolution on Armenia that ran aground three years ago.

Politics and Diplomacy

31

FROM DIAMONDS TO DIPLOMACY: VARTAN OSKANIAN, ARMENIA'S MINISTER OF FOREIGN AFFAIRS (YEREVAN)

Rainer Hermann

Vartan Voskanian, as his name originally was, could be a rich man in the Diaspora, as are his relatives. He could trade in diamonds in Los Angeles and live up to his surname, since the Armenian word *voski* means nothing less than "gold." By his name Vartan Oskanian already reveals two facts: that his family engaged in trading precious metals at some time, and that the Oskanians originally come from West Armenia, where names derive from one's occupation. In East Armenia, they come from the personal name of a family.

Today, most of Vartan Oskanian's relatives live in the United States, and many are engaged in the gold and diamond trade. When Vartan Oskanian also left for the U.S.A. in 1981, he eliminated the V from his surname so as to make it easier to pronounce. Unwittingly he moved away from the his ancestors' trade. Since the early 1990s he no longer deals in precious metals but in high diplomacy. Right after independence, he returned straight to Yerevan in 1992. Step by step he rose in the Foreign Ministry until, in 1998, he exchanged his U.S. passport for the Armenian, and was finally named Foreign Minister.

Armenia could hardly have found anyone more suited to the task, for Oskanian knows the whole of Armenian reality as few others do. He was born on February 7, 1955, in Aleppo, Syria; from 1973 to 1979 he studied in Soviet Armenia, and then studied and worked in the U.S.A. from the early 1980s on. In 1992, he returned to Yerevan, the capital of the newly independent Armenian Republic. Armenian identity is always made up of two elements: great Mount Ararat and, small in comparison, the smaller one standing next to it, which symbolizes Armenia and the diaspora. Oskanian carries both experiences in himself.

The genocide is also part of Oskanian's family background. His father's family came from the Anatolian town of Marash, and had survived the killings. His maternal family had already fled to Aleppo from previous massacres. For two generations in the first half of the twentieth century Aleppo, together with Beirut, was one of the two centers of the Armenian diaspora. As that commercial city was beyond the Turkish nationalists' reach, it accepted the refugees with great understanding and hospitality, and these gladly moved to Aleppo. It was precisely this center of trade that offered economic opportunities such as few other cities did.

And this is how Vartan Oskanian was born in Aleppo. It was not the Syrian state that issued his birth certificate, but the Armenian religious community in which he grew up, firmly integrated. He went to the Armenian school, played for the basketball team and was a member, as one of the best players, of the Syrian national selection. From early on he enjoyed reading. He used to read Armenian books published in Aleppo and Soviet Yerevan. Nor was this by chance since, at a certain period, the Armenians had introduced book printing in the Near East and, in the twentieth century, the Soviets turned Yerevan into the center of translation of the universal classics of literature into Armenian.

When Vartan was a youth, the Aleppo community still possessed a keen intellectual life, until increasing Arab nationalism and socialism began making life ever more difficult for the Armenians. Many moved to Beirut, which became the new temporary center for the diaspora. In Aleppo, however, young Vartan also read the classics translated in Yerevan and so firmly decided he wanted to study in the Soviet Armenian Republic, even though Stalin tried to have Armenian spelling modified, for which reason it is politicized to this day. In Armenia they determined that the outer world could not dictate what was correct and what was not. The diaspora, in contrast, is infuriated by the idea that someone might try to teach them spelling, who had kept the old (so the correct) form.

Vartan Voskanian left for Yerevan in 1973 and graduated as an engineer at the Polytechnic Institute. This showed he was not on the side of the diaspora, which had always rejected Soviet Armenia. He never became a member of the powerful diaspora nationalist party, the Dashnaktzutiun. He and his family were among those that increasingly set up ties with the Armenian motherland, even when it was part of the Soviet Union. Soviet policy was to attract diaspora students to Yerevan, hoping to acquire

influence in the diaspora, as the students would certainly go back to their old country some day. This attempt at brainwashing failed with Oskanian, as with many others. Instead, the Soviet opening up toward foreign students produced enduring close ties between Armenia and its diaspora.

Also present in Yerevan as a medical student in those days was the wife of the current Foreign Minister. She was also born in Aleppo, and they got married, as students, in Yerevan. When they left for the U.S.A., they shortened their name to Oskanian. His wife stayed with the rest of the family in Los Angeles while Vartan studied in Boston on three further occasions. He earned a master's degree in Engineering Sciences at Tufts University; then, at Harvard, in 1986, a mastership in Political Sciences; finally, in 1991, at the renowned Fletcher School of Law and Diplomacy, a third master's degree in Law and Diplomacy.

Amid his bouts of studying, and concurrently with them, Oskanian worked, first as an engineer and then in the trade he inherited from his ancestors. His uncle, an important wholesale importer of diamonds in Los Angeles, was especially involved in this tradition. He bought them in Belgium and resold them in the U.S.A. First of all Oskanian worked with him, and later he opened up his own firm in Los Angeles, trading in diamonds.

It was not by chance that the Oskanians were in Los Angeles. There is no town, except Yerevan, where more Armenians live, maybe half a million, and so they are more numerous there than in Moscow. They arrived as a result of the civil war in Beirut, but especially from the Soviet Republic of Armenia itself, as former president Reagan had got the Soviet Union to allow the first exit of Jews and Armenians, as a token of its "new human rights policy." The expatriation paperwork was lengthy, generally taking six years. Nevertheless the Armenians of the Middle East diaspora, who arrived in the Caucasian republic in Stalin's time, seduced by the invitation to return to their ancestral Armenian homeland, did not pass up the opportunity. Especially the Armenians took advantage of the chance to get out, exchanging their ancestral land for freedom. And this is how the Los Angeles community came to be.

Oskanian founded the monthly *Armenian International Magazine* there in 1990. Its first issue appeared the following year. His original purpose was to improve the network among the international diaspora. After Armenia's independence, its policy changed. Nowadays the magazine, published in Yerevan since 2002, keeps Armenia informed about the Diaspora, and vice versa, but with Armenia increasingly holding center stage.

Oskanian returned to Yerevan in 1992, previously transferring the business to his brother. Back in Armenia, the brand new diplomat laid the family tradition aside, but he did not completely lose sight of it. Armenia has certainly no diamond deposits of its own, but the Armenians were the diamond polishers of the Soviet Union. They were bought in Siberia, polished in Armenia, and then sent to every part of the empire. The term "Armenian cut" was already in use at that time. The stone was not cut in a round shape: with innumerable facets it acquired a shape that was roughly spherical. After independence, computers perfected this Armenian cut, and the consumer market expanded in the West. In this way Belgium became Armenia's most important partner, followed by Israel. The advantage of diamonds is that they require no exit corridor, since Armenia is practically landlocked. On one side, Turkey keeps its border with Armenia closed, and on the other, Azerbaijan.

This is the challenge for Foreign Minister Oskanian, in which he can bring his whole palette of experience into play. To begin with, he was deputy head of the Middle East Service for two years, then a similar period for North America, and two years each as Foreign Undersecretary and First Foreign Undersecretary. His career unfolded without interruptions, and the principal Armenian diplomat has found it advantageous to handle his foreign politics as an incurable optimist. He is appreciated in his country. People like his open, public politics, and the fact that he always keeps clean, honest, and on the people's side.

He employs his optimism and accessibility above all in his politics toward the Turks. He is in favour of establishing unconditional diplomatic relations. This does not mean, however, that Armenia will set aside its national memory or no longer commemorate the historical injustice its people suffered—as he said in 2002 in a speech in Istanbul, making it very clear to his listeners that the memory cannot be healed by denial, or the wound by questioning its existence. Conflicts cannot be solved when it is claimed the past is irrelevant. History is the basis of good neighborly relations as much as geography and topography. So, too, is Ararat, standing a mere 45 kilometers from Oskanian's office, yet ever unreachable for the Armenians, a permanent reminder of this.

Oskanian also considers the genocide a constituent part of the Armenian identity, but, in contrast to many diaspora Armenians, he does not see it as the only defining characteristic. Everyone needs something to identify with, and for many the genocide meets this requirement. Oskanian has gone through the experience of two diasporas. He knows that that of the Middle East keeps Armenians together, a lesson they learnt under the Ottoman *millet* system. For them the genocide is part of their individual memory. Instead, Armenians in New York or Los Angeles seem to carry the genocide in front like a banner. As they are no longer so closely connected with the Armenian community, they hang on that much more strongly to that part of their identity.

Not many diaspora Armenians returned to the Armenian motherland after the collapse of the Soviet Union—a few thousand, perhaps. Vartan Oskanian was one of them. In the main they came from the Middle East and Iran, less so from the U.S.A. and Canada. Armenia does not recognize dual nationality, so Oskanian gave up his U.S. citizenship. With his diplomatic passport, however, he is able to travel more extensively without impediments. His family's life is also centered in Yerevan, and the younger of his sons is in the last years of high school. The elder is studying, as did his father, at Tufts University in Boston. In this way the Oskanians have founded a new family tradition. It no longer has anything to do with gold and diamonds.

32

ARMENIA'S ATTORNEY ON THE BANKS OF THE SEINE: MINISTER PATRICK DEVEDJIAN, LEGAL ADVISER TO FRENCH PRESIDENT CHIRAC (PARIS)

Michaela Wiegel

It is January 18, 2001, a gray winter's day in Paris, but the man leaving the imposing Bourbon Palace seems satisfied. Patrick Devedjian, a deputy of the neo-Gaullist RPR party, has just finished participating in a memorable vote: on January 18, 2001, the French parliament unanimously recognized, in a brief legal text, the Armenian genocide of 1915. For Devedjian, a long campaign for the historical truth thus reached its conclusion. After 83 years' delay, on May 29, 1998, the Parliament attended to the subject of the genocide for the first time. The president's parliamentary fraction, which at that time went by the acronym RPR, had Devedjian among its speakers.

> I hesitated for a long time about participating in this debate … For me, this morning in the Congress, there was no right or left wing, but only Eternal France. I want to talk about this France … France is a special nation, and this is why today it's my family's home. For the Christians of the Orient, for every persecuted minority, France has always been a protective patroness.

His father, an engineer, fled from the Armenian homeland to France, where Patrick was born in 1944 in the royal city of Fontainebleau, on the outskirts of Paris. Devedjian does not say much about his childhood, except that he grew up motherless; that his father sent him to the Armenian school at Sèvres when he was eleven; that he felt lost. He was six when his mother died in a riding accident. Devedjian does not send his four children to an Armenian school. "What for?" he asks. He feels French and Armenian, but rejects what the French call *communautarisme*. After finishing his secondary schooling, he studied law and political sciences, and joined the ultra-right-wing association Occident. He bases

this membership on his conviction that Algeria should carry on being French. "As an Oriental Christian, I felt Christians were not defending themselves enough against the onslaught of Islam, and I was convinced France had no reason to be ashamed of its civilizing role in Algeria. I didn't want Christianity to capitulate to Islam again."

In 1970, he was admitted to the bar by the Paris Chamber of Attorneys, and at the same time he directed the philosophical and political magazine *Contrepoint* for Raymond Aron. How does he explain his turnabout from his juvenile extreme right-wingery to a liberal thinker like Aron? "As the passage from puberty to adulthood," he replies. He worked six years for and with Raymond Aron, whom he considers even today his *maître à penser*. In 1971, Devedjian joined the Gaullist party, known by its initials UDR. He met Jacques Chirac, who took down the young lawyer's name. In 1976 Chirac, on taking over the Gaullist party, sought Devedjian's advice in helping him to write up the statutes of the new party Chirac wanted to form. In this way Devedjian became one of the small circle of RPR founders. Chirac saw in him a gifted lawyer whose services he gladly made use of, a lawyer who, when not defending Chirac, also occasionally comes out in defense of the Armenian terrorists, who, as members of the group ASALA (Armenian Secret Army for the Liberation of Armenia), act against Turkish interests. Devedjian refused to act as a defense attorney only in the criminal proceedings against the authors of the attack at Orly airport, who set off a bomb outside the Turkish Airlines office in July 1983. "Killing innocent people goes against my principles." That same year he was elected mayor of the Paris suburb of Antony, a part of the city's "red belt." He gave the communists in the municipal council a hard time. "I've never sympathized with totalitarian ideologies like communism," he explains.

Devedjian helped Chirac, the mayor of Paris, the prime minister, and head of the party, to win twenty lawsuits. At the Chirac home he is better known than the majority, but does not go about publishing it. This relationship of trust was put to a severe test in 1995 when, in in-party wrangling, Devedjian very openly backed Chirac's rival, prime minister Edouard Balladur. The latter's family, like Devedjian's, was of Armenian origin. "But he's a complicated man, who doesn't openly admit it," says Devedjian. Nor was it their common origin that influenced his decision. "Balladur is an extremely intelligent man. I respect him," and this is despite Balladur's tendency to disclaim his Armenian origin, "which I consider unfortunate." In contrast to Balladur, Devedjian does not mind being considered Armenian. He makes frequent journeys to Armenia, although his family does not come from the Armenian Republic. But he refuses to join what in fact is the most important Armenian organization in France, the Committee of April 24. "I am and will be independent," he declares.

What Chirac cannot forgive others, such as for instance Devedjian's present superior, Nicolas Sarkozy's, "betrayal" in the election year 1995, has not led to a breach between the president of the nation and his legal adviser. When a wave of accusations of corruption broke out during Chirac's second government, Devedjian once again came out in his defense. Relations only got cool in the past few months, due to the increasingly public struggle for power between Sarkozy and Chirac. But Devedjian supported Sarkozy in the government—from 2002 to 2004 as deputy minister of local freedoms under interior minister Sarkozy, and from April 2004 on, as minister of industry of the superministry of economy and finance. In his spacious office in the bulky ministry of economy and finance, on the banks of the Seine, there is no reminder of Devedjian's Armenian origin. Nevertheless, the minister speaks proudly of his campaign to prevent Armenian history from falling into oblivion. He ascribes great importance to the parliamentary resolution on the genocide, also and precisely on account of Turkey's efforts to join the European Union. "I allow myself to remind people that the past can only be overcome by accepting it. A nation rises when it recognizes its errors," were Devedjian's words in the first parliamentary debate on the Armenian genocide. "It is true that we have had to wait till 1995 for a president of the nation to have found suitable words for the raid of Vel'd'Hiv (which resulted in the deportation of tens of thousands of French Jews). But this day was one in which France became bigger and better," added Devedjian, and appealed directly to the Turks that were responsible:

> Listen to the word of France, which is one of peace, and for your healing. If you recognize the Armenian genocide, this will free you of the temptation to commit yet another. I think of the Kurds, I think of Cyprus, and the last wall of shame, like that of Berlin, dividing a European capital. If Turkey wishes to become a part of the EU, it must begin by accepting its values.

Devedjian is against accepting Turkey as a member of the European Union. He no longer talks about the matter with President Chirac, who is in favour of the inclusion. "He knows I don't beat about the bush in this matter." In his opinion the Turks' denial of the Armenian genocide is something extremely serious. "Of my children's two grandfathers, one was deported by the Turks during World War I, and the other by the Germans during World War II. How should I explain the difference to them?" asked Devedjian in Congress. His wife, Sophie Vanbremeersch, is the daughter of a French officer deported to Buchenwald by the Nazis. Devedjian is very reserved about talking of his own history and that of his wife's family, appearing distant and constrained in his public appearances, as if constantly on guard. He evidently enjoys displaying his knowledge of history while, at the same time, he keeps it all on an impersonal level. In an interview his wife once said, "He's a sentimental man who protects himself with coldness." The French public knows the minister as a brilliant orator, as little reticent in expressing severe criticism of a political opponent as of internal party polemics.

"The genocide has consequences till this very day. It's impossible to divide the Turkish state's revisionism from its present position towards its own people. Human rights are trampled on, the Kurdish minority is oppressed, and there is the scandalous military occupation of Cyprus," said Devedjian on January 18, 2001. Denying the genocide is equivalent to the perpetuation of hatred. Devedjian criticizes the Turkish leadership for never having carried out a comprehensive "de-Nazification," or a debate on a social and historical level. "When Hitler asked in 1939 who still remembered the Armenian genocide, he adopted this as an argument to justify the Holocaust." As a result of his statements the deputy became the target of attacks, above all defamations on the Internet. He is compared with criminals, insulted as a disrupter of democracy, or an extreme right-winger. The minister is convinced those web pages are financed by the Turkish secret service. "I set an investigation in motion that proved its origin in the Turkish secret service," he says.

For the minister, episodes such as this are ample reason not to keep quiet in his fight for historical truth. France has closer relations with Armenia than is generally known. "The Armenian genocide organized by the Turkish state with the knowledge of Germany began on April 24, 1915. On May 24 France, Great Britain, and Russia sent a memorandum to Turkey 'In view of Turkey's new crimes against humanity and civilization.'" In the middle of the war France did not soft-pedal, describing the massacres of Armenians as "crimes against humanity," which became one of the first mentions of this principle of law. The secret treaty between France and Britain signed on May 16, 1916, by Sykes and Picot, recognized French administration of Cilicia, confirmed in 1920 by the League of Nations. Devedjian points out that people have forgotten the role of France, as a protective power over the Armenians, carried out a deeply moral role. For this reason it was no act of benevolence but the fulfilment of a promise that France recognized the Armenian genocide. "Whoever favours accepting Turkey into the European Union should at least have the integrity to demand that it cleanse its bloody hands." Regardless of how his political career continues in the future, he has pledged himself to remain the faithful lawyer of the land of his forefathers.

Patrick Devedjian left his post as a minister in June 2005 and continues to be a member of parliament.

33

IN THE MISSION QUICKSANDS: BENON SEVAN, EX-UNDERSECRETARY GENERAL OF THE UNITED NATIONS (NEW YORK CITY)

Huberta von Voss

Outside, the August sun scorches the dusty street, a heat that would make any New Yorker have turned on the air-conditioner long since. But the 200 collaborators at the UN general headquarters know that, at each mission, one forgoes the usual luxuries: they were taken to Baghdad. It is 4 p.m. on August 19, 2003. Benon Sevan, head of the greatest UN humanitarian food program, called the Oil for Food Program, lights a cigar. One more conference and at the end of two exhausting weeks he can at last return to his office in Manhattan, right opposite to the UN headquarter. Three colleagues are with him. A fourth is late. He is stationed in Baghdad where, so as not to have to do without all his comforts, he has brought his Italian coffee-machine with him. "Come, let's go to his office and have an espresso," suggests Sevan. "Get some coffees ready," he says jovially over the phone.

The four go toward their absent colleague's office. The instant they sit down, a van full of explosives blows up underneath the window of Sevan's office, turning the whole side of the building into rubble and ashes. On the floor above Sevan's office his friend Sergio Vieira de Mello is torn into pieces. The UN special representative and twenty-one colleagues die, and 150 are wounded, many of them seriously.

We met one year after the attack took place in his New York office. When he remembers it today, this 67-year-old man easily loses a grip on his emotions. "You can hear how people die, but when you know them personally and hold them in your arms, as they die or are heavily wounded," he says quickly. Then he bursts into tears.

He has already served in the United Nations for forty years. The fifteenth story over the East River is now empty. Of the more than 100 collaborators of the Oil for Food Program only he and a secretary are left on duty. The program, which provided food for Saddam Hussein's Iraq in exchange for oil, according to UN security resolution 986 of 1995, has been discontinued. The humanitarian program, for a total of 10 billion dollars a year, was the biggest in all the history of the United Nations. Sevan's task, to ensure that, between the corrupt dictator's interests and the international companies' profits, the benefits should reach the needy Iraqi people, was not an easy one. "Impossible," say some insiders today, after the dictator's disappearance. The humanitarian aid organizations, and also the UN, have known for years that the thousands of millions of dollars benefited not only the people. In spite of the gigantic volume of the transfers, infant mortality hit dramatic levels under Saddam's regime. The Iraqi leaders' bank accounts abroad grew ever fatter, as they would not allow the entry of goods without claiming their slice. Now there is ostracism, even of Sevan. His name figures on an Iraqi list of 270 individuals and organizations whom Saddam supposedly bribed so as to carry on diverting the profits of the program from his hungry populace to his international accounts. Also mentioned among these names are high-ranking officials of foreign governments. "Straight out of the mouths of hungry Iraqi children!" raged the New York press when the list of 270 suspects was published. At first Benon Sevan tried to dodge the flak, by issuing statements on his own. When the situation became ever tighter he asked a renowned law firm for advice and launched a series of statements to defend himself against the allegations. He declared the accusations groundless, challenging those that had made them to come forward and show the evidence.

Nevertheless, very soon after, it became clear the list was also part of a struggle of interests of old opponents. Conjectures about who could be behind the affair abound. Some suppose it is a small group of Iraqis, who, in collusion with American neocons, want to prevent the UN from going back to Iraq. Others claim it is the Americans, who want to weaken the UN and oblige its Secretary-General to be more accommodating. Behind closed doors, the investigation committee, which was set up without delay, is prosecuting the culprits of the distribution disaster. "Benon's hands are clean," says a high UN official, "but the affair was badly managed." And he adds drily, "Yet, if bad management now became punishable, we'd have to take the precaution of dismissing the half of our collaborators." He didn't know yet that another year later, the report of the so-called Volcker Commission would blame Sevan not only for "various management failures." The report continued, "Mr. Sevan's failures are all the more troubling when considered against his corrupt receipt of oil allocations from the Iraqi regime from which he profited." The Committee concluded in two reports that Sevan "compromised his position by secretly soliciting and receiving Iraqi oil allocations on behalf of a small trading company from which he corruptly derived nearly $150,000 of income."

However, Sevan hasn't stopped denying the charges since the day they covered the front page of the international media. As he puts it, he repeatedly requested the Security Council to give the UN secretariat more freedom in implementing the program. "They tied my hands and feet, and expected me to serve them a seven-course meal. No doubt we could have managed the program better if only they had let us," says one of his many statements. Looking back, he reflects, "We did the best we could under the most difficult circumstances imaginable, at times even risking our lives. In spite of all criticism, which now is noisy and often politically motivated, our work brought about a great change in the lives of humble Iraqis." In fact, the Security Council as well as the investigating committee were aware of the difficulties, but no one did anything.

For Sevan, besieged for weeks by the press, the possibility of being acquitted after the rash initial judgment is no longer important. "The double standard in all this makes me sick," he says, moving to and fro on his seat as if in a cage, among the cases awaiting removal, while trying to remain calm. On top of a cupboard a photograph of UN Secretary-General Kofi Annan gathers dust. "For Benon, with friendship and warmest regards," wrote his superior as a dedication. Sevan and Annan smile at each other. Today Sevan's clear facial features reveal the bitterness of this white-haired man, born in Cyprus in 1937. He considers himself the victim of a conflict in which chiefly the members of the Security Council behaved irresponsibly in disregarding his warnings of irregularities.

In his personal and professional life he has often experienced the fact that the truth remains hidden in political conflicts in which many players are involved. His mission in Afghanistan, which lasted almost five years, also served him as a training ground in power politics. Sevan, who grew up in the crooked side streets of Nicosia, brought along with him the right skills for managing a number of hostile groups and rival powers. Early on he learned not to get himself tripped up in the trap of different languages and mentalities. His grandparents, who brought him up, had been expelled from Adana and Zeitun by the Turks, and found refuge in Cyprus. Just like many of their compatriots from the Ottoman provinces, they knew no Armenian but were acquainted only with the alphabet. "My grandmother used to read the Bible in Turkish but phonetically written in Armenian characters," he says. When her eyesight had become very weak her grandson, proud of his education at the Armenian school, offered to read to her aloud. Years later, during his first semester at Columbia College in New York, he finally understood that "she opened the Bible on the Song of Solomon. In those days I found that text specially embarrassing. That a ten-year-old boy should say 'breasts' in Turkish to his grandmother was totally unthinkable," he recalls, and laughs. "I expected to read passages about God, Jesus, or the saints. So I skimmed over the text, leaving out all the problem words. My grandmother got upset: 'My child. What you're reading makes no sense.' I closed the Bible and went out to kick a ball with a neighbor's son."

On leaving the island after finishing his secondary studies at the Melkonian school, he spoke fluent Armenian, Turkish, Greek, and English. He later perfected his French with his wife Micheline, also a recently retired UN employee. The flexibility he acquired gained him his colleagues' admiration, but also their envy. For some he was a "cunning Levantine," for others a "go-getter." But he was always appreciated for his boisterous good humor. When he walked along the streets in the UN area in New York in the afternoon, many came up to shake hands with him. He has lived there since 1965, when he began working at the UN. "That's longer than a marriage," he says of the four decades. "It's been an interesting life, full of variety. I served in many different tasks." After the release of the Volcker Report this life has definitely come to an end. Sevan has left the Big Apple for good to avoid possible criminal charges.

Before joining the UN the gifted young man studied history and philosophy in New York thanks to several scholarships. He was an activist in student groups in favour of Enosis, the radical political movement that fostered annexation of Cyprus by the "motherland," Greece. His sympathy for the Greek cause was so marked that he renounced his British Commonwealth passport. Despite his political commitment, he attended lectures by Turkish guest professors, to the utter bafflement of his Armenian and Greek friends. He said, "One has to know how the others think. I can't hate people. We have more similarities than differences." Sevan is a man who permanently looks ahead. He always gave the interns that came to him via AGBU, the Armenian General Benevolent Union, a piece of advice: "Don't look on the genocide as a burden but as a source of strength. In spite of it, we didn't go down. We've survived, and we're doing very well. That shows we're strong."

During the forty years on the East River, he always felt a deep affection for Armenia. "When I started working for the United Nations in a special decolonization commission, I always thought about where Armenia, then part of the Soviet Union, would have its seat at the sessions, between Argentina and Australia." When the Catholicos of All the Armenians at the time, Vaskan I, visited the United Nations, Sevan gathered all UN employees of Armenian origin for them to meet the prelate. He apologized to His Holiness for his not having been allowed to speak in the plenary session, since Armenia was not yet a member of the United Nations. "But because he hadn't been allowed to speak in the general assembly, I had another idea: I was pleased to inform him that the seat on which he had sat is normally on the podium of the conference hall, and is reserved for heads of state that speak to the assembly." The Catholicos had to laugh. When three years later the first President of the brand-new Republic of Armenia, Levon Ter Petrossian, spoke for the first time before the United Nations, Sevan assured him that he was taking the place of the Catholicos before him.

One learns pragmatism the same as languages. His grandfather had always dreamt of going back to Adana in present-day Turkey. When the weather was clear one could see the outline of the lost home from the Turkish coast of Cyprus. "The day we go back home I'll buy you a black horse, son," his grandfather was wont to say. The present never existed for that generation of survivors, only past and future. Perhaps this escape from reality is also a reason why Sevan did not flee from it in many difficult moments. More than once he found himself in tight spots in Afghanistan. He proved his courage in April 1992, when he landed without runway lights in Kabul in a UN plane, with the task of rescuing President Najibullah. "When we disembarked, combatants came from all sides in the dark, with all sorts of weapons in their hands." Did he feel afraid? "No. The Afghans are tough guys. If one shows fear he'd best go away. They respect whoever doesn't show fear." After a few hours' negotiations, he and his collaborators got the green light to go to the UN office in Kabul, which had already guaranteed President Najibullah asylum. Such experiences became the inner yardstick for other tough battles. However, he may have lost his latest one.

34

THE MAN WITH THE MIRROR: THE ARMENIAN AMBASSADOR TO THE OSCE AND TO INTERNATIONAL ORGANIZATIONS IN VIENNA, JIVAN TABIBIAN (VIENNA)

Huberta von Voss

Once upon a time there lived an emperor who liked good clothes so much that he spent all his money on dressing well. One day two weavers, who were shrewd businessmen, arrived in the city. They did not let themselves be at all impressed by all the glitter and pomp. The astute weavers realized that, behind the emperor's vanity, there existed great insecurity, and they decided to make good use of it. "We will weave you an extraordinary cloth such as has never been seen in the world. But it will be invisible to anyone that is foolish," they told the emperor. The weavers made out that they were weaving cloth and, when the emperor arrived to try on the supposed garment, they dressed him with nothing and held a mirror in front of him so that he might see himself in it. And lo and behold! the emperor was naked. And because, in their vanity, neither the emperor nor his ministers and courtiers wanted to admit they were fools, the emperor went out naked.

Jivan Tabibian is like one of those weavers in Andersen's fairy tale, "The Emperor's New Clothes." He holds a mirror in front of others, as well as himself, and lo and behold! more than one of them are naked. This was the case of a Turkish colleague at the embassy to the OSCE in Vienna more often than the case of the emperor and his court. "The previous Turkish ambassador in Vienna never said the word 'Armenia,'" says Tabibian with a somewhat ironic indifference. "At the same time I answer with Turkish proverbs, which I translate into English for the rest." No doubt his composure irks the old generation of Turkish diplomats. "Instead, I win over the younger ones, because they see I have no complexes about being Armenian," he says drily. "I don't hand over the key to my identity to anyone."

Jivan Tabibian is not at home in only one world but indeed perhaps not even properly at home anywhere. His life career refutes every father's advice to his son to choose a clear pathway in order to finally succeed. Perhaps it is his early multilingualism that makes this nimble man in his late sixties seem still restless. It is tempting to open up ever new worlds when, besides Armenian, one speaks fluent English, French, Arabic, and Turkish, and feels just as comfortable in the Middle East as in Los Angeles, the Côte d'Azur, or the Caucasus.

Born in Beirut, he studied first at the American University of Beirut. From there he went to the U.S.A., to the elite Princeton University, where he received his graduate degrees in political science and international relations. He taught at several renowned universities, among them that of California (UCLA). Yet, his scientific pathway led him above all through different disciplines, which in his conversation he makes skillful use of in building unconventional houses of cards, amongst which disciplines, besides political sciences, interweave urban design, design theory, and community psychiatry.

Apart from this, he became a highly successful businessman as a management and marketing consultant, as well as in the film industry. Tabibian very quickly became a giver of inside tips in the circle of wealthy and difficult clients. One of these was the flamboyant multimillionaire Sir Jimmy Goldsmith, who in 1997 sent shock waves through the established parties with his anti-European stance. But movie actor and philanthropist Robert Redford has also asked Tabibian for advice. He contracted him in the early 1980s to draw up a plan for the Sundance Institute, a huge artist village in a formerly Indian canyon in Utah. "Redford is a complicated character with whom many others had ran aground," recalls Tabibian, who once told him over lunch: "Even I, Robert Redford, cannot have my cake and eat it, too." Like a bridegroom at the altar, Reford said "I do" as he was asked, and their collaboration began. This all led to the planning and realization of the Sundance Institute and the place, and its eventual incorporation of the Sundance Film Festival, now the most important independent film festival in the U.S.A.

Notwithstanding all his success, in the 1990s Tabibian set out in a new direction, and this had to do with his passion for good food. He opened a first-class restaurant in Los Angeles specializing in Venetian food, called Remi, an echo of Venice's rowboats and a homage to Harry's Bar, one of Hemingway's favorites. Like an Italian "godfather" that wants to smoke decent cigars in his own restaurant, Tabibian became a producer of cigars following a visit to Cuba. His brand is Don Jivan, and his picture with his goatee appears on the label. The cigars are of many sizes, called such names as Cervantes, Neruda, and Lorca in honour of some of his favorite writers. For ladies, he has a more slender variety called Mistral. The name of the series, Los Lectores—the "readers"—is in memory of the Cuban female and male workers, who, mostly illeterate, paid from their meager savings money to "readers" to read to them *Romeo and Juliet* or *The Count of Monte Cristo*. It helped them to bear the drudgery of rolling cigars. "Their story profoundly moved me," says Tabibian, thoughtfully smoking his Havana. He sends back the midnight espresso, which he finds not hot enough. Tabibian drinks it at just the right temperature. Pleasant things must also be just right.

"We were left alone with our dead, without knowing why we continue living," wrote the national poet of Chile, Pablo Neruda, in his memoirs. This is how Jivan's father must have felt, who escaped from the Turkish thugs together with his mother and brother. "My father grew cynical from all those experiences. He didn't believe in salvation through God. He was a man without illusions." The remainder of the extensive family of doctors from Cesarea did not survive. "They were fairly soon slaughtered on the road," he says laconically. His father, Stepan, in contrast, was adopted by a Turkish miller "as a pseudo-son and slave." Mills were always resting-places, and this is how Stepan found out that Turkish soldiers had "made a present" of his mother as a concubine to a Kurdish village chieftain. His mother had dressed up the younger son as a girl, and took him with her. She had a daughter with the Kurd, Sultana, or Sultanik in Armenian. Stepan saved each piaster, until his Turkish owner allowed him to go and search for and buy back his mother. The young man started out from the Syrian border and found his mother in a Kurdish mountain village. The four were able to escape to Beirut, where they arrived penniless, and there began struggling to survive. "My father was the first of his family that hadn't studied. But he accepted any job at all to feed his mother and siblings. We never lived in Bourj Hammoud," he stresses, and in his voice one can notice the injured pride of the exile. "I don't need any ghetto to protect my identity."

The origin of his aunt Sultana, who "was much more beautiful than the rest of the brood," was never talked about. "Neither of us knew she was a Kurd's daughter." In any case, not a single word was said about traumatic family experiences. "The subject was left in the freezer." Only later did he begin to assemble the pieces of the puzzle, without ever becoming obsessed by them. "I never assimilated their victim status. It wasn't transmissible suffering," is his technical explanation. His frequent vocabulary from deep psychology shows the point to which the situation at home later intrigued him, despite his utter "absence of self-pity." "My grandmother, like most of the women, never spoke about the outrages she suffered in order not to have to live through them again." His aunt Sultana never got over her provenance from an unwanted relationship, and became a deeply unhappy woman. As for his uncle, he was never able to leave his mother, who had saved his life. When she died, the uncle fulfilled a long-cherished dream, and went to Kaiseri (Cesaria) to see his paternal house once more. Shortly after, he died.

Jivan was the child of a divided world of experiences. His mother, who came from a cultivated bourgeois family of Istanbul, survived the genocide unscathed. "There there was no desert, no rape." On Sundays people went to the tea dance at the noble Pera Palace hotel, built at the turn of the century in art deco style for the passengers of the Orient Express. There, in the luxurious dance salon, the elite of the city rendezvoused to practice Western dances. Even Atatürk, the father of modern Turkey, under whose eyes Smyrna (present-day Izmir) was put to the torch in 1922 to expel the Ionian Christians that remained in Turkey, used to attend. This was when the mother's, Marie Beuyukian's, family also packed up. Their property remained behind, but the language went with them to their new home. "At home we always spoke Turkish."

When Ambassador Tabibian stands today at the door of his office in the Vienna Neubaugasse, he occasionally sees Turkish housewives wander round the nearby flea market—or should it be called a bazaar? It is already seven years since he got the call from Armenia in Los Angeles, offering him the chance of representing the young republic's interests at the OSCE. A man skilled in the management of complex issues, not least psychological ones was needed. The OSCE mediation in the Karabakh conflict had just floundered. Jivan did not take long to make up his mind. When Armenia achieved its yearned-for independence in 1991, Tabibian celebrated it with an article in *AIM* magazine, which carried the euphoric words: "I am no longer a refugee. It is the end of exile. I am an expatriate, an Armenian residing abroad." At last he was free of the obligation to explain to foreigners what it meant to be Armenian. Those that possess a country of their own have no need to do so.

But, as if this were too simple, Tabibian pulled out the mirror and held it in front of his compatriots.

> We do not have to go on making apologies and compromises. We do not have to count the number of times "Armenia," "Armenian" and "Armenians" are referred to in the international media; we do not have to scrutinize names to ferret out the weak of character who have adulterated their patronymic labels. We do not have to go on begging sympathy for our martyrs and telling the unknowing of our starving and mutilated pedigree. For it is clear that all nation-states have histories, wars and famines, triumphs and tragedies, heroes and villains, and struggles for their independence and territorial integrity.

Tabibian does not regret his choice. Still less, as he is enjoying life in Vienna with his wife Isabella, a 34-year-old pianist. His pretty Korean wife is an *odar*, or foreigner, Tabibian shrugs: "when I'm with her, I have a feeling of deep satisfaction." This already sounds a little weary, as though after a long journey he had finally arrived somewhere.

Life Images

35

COURIER OF THE CZAR: THE PETROSSIAN CAVIAR EMPIRE AND ITS OWNER, ARMEN PETROSSIAN (PARIS)

Gil Eilin Jung

The Rue d'Aubervilliers in the eighteenth *arrondissement* in Paris has nothing glamorous about it. Very distant from the Eiffel Tower, the elegant shops on the Rue Faubourg St. Honoré, the pleasant bars and restaurants on the big boulevards, it lies on an ugly stretch of an urban motorway, and houses industrial establishments of every sort. A large gray gate opens on to section CAP 18, a conglomeration of container yards, one next to the other like Lego blocks. In the

corner café the floors are being swept clean of the debris from the early shift. The people sit at wall tables in their short sleeves, having a cream coffee. In the gray building, which looks like a giant refrigerator, only the firm's logo announces that, beyond the modest front, something very promising is hidden, to wit, the international symbol of luxury: caviar.

The czar of rare delicacies, Petrossian, manages the distribution of the noble products of his emporium from here: French *foie gras*, *pata negra* from Portugal, smoked salmon, truffles, dark chocolate, champagnes, each product more expensive and refined than the next, but specially Russian caviar from the Caspian Sea, with a turnover of 40 million Euros. The thriving firm, with restaurants and shops in Paris, New York,

Los Angeles, and Las Vegas, started up in 1920 thanks to the genial inspiration of two brothers of a good family. Tradition has it that Mouchegh and Melkoum Petrossian, fleeing from genocide and civil war, left their home in Russia as young men and arrived in Paris, together with a wave of wealthy Russians: nobility, intellectuals, and artists, who found in the Paris of the crazy 1920s, the *années folles*, everything to satisfy their epicurean tastes, with the exception of caviar.

The brothers Petrossian achieved the impossible, namely to be the first enterprise established in France to trade with Russia, with which they enriched the self-indulgent French taste with caviar, the delicacy of delicacies. Despite the ups and downs of the civil war and the White Army in their homeland, the Russian embassy in Paris kept up a commercial section. The two Armenians, who had nothing to lose and everything to gain, presented their proposal in their most impeccable Russian, and were listened to. Years later Mouchegh Petrossian married the great-granddaughter of Lazarus Mailoff, the first producer of caviar in Russia. That got the rubles rolling in all the better.

In the Rue d'Aubervilliers there is a little office at the end of the passage, square, cosy in an old-fashioned way. It belongs to Armen Petrossian, the son and nephew of the founders of the company. There is a heavy desk on the left side of the room, and a small, round conference table on the right. At the back snorts an espresso machine. The contrast between the antiques and old paintings and the brass-ribbed walls of the 1970s is huge, but in general does not jar. The president is fifty-odd years old, and a trifle overfed … *embonpoint*, as the French say. He has a thick white head of hair, a pair of narrow eyeglasses on his nose, and below it a twirled moustache, which hints at a certain irony and eccentricity. Wearing a pin-striped suit and a bow tie, he smiles affably, and has big, dark eyes, with dark shadows below them. They have a friendly, though tired, look. Armen Petrossian does not look like the big international businessman he is, but rather a man whose passion is his profession, devoted to a firm founded over eighty years ago by his father and his uncle in conditions both strange and difficult.

"In our family it was the women that ruled the roost," says Monsieur Petrossian, with his dark, peaceful voice. The family home in Baku, today in Azerbaijan and formerly Russian, in which at one time the population was 60 percent Armenian, was a matriarchate.

My two Armenian grandmothers realized the danger of the Turks long before the massacre of our people began. They smelt the hate and ill-omen in the atmosphere, and understood the consequences it would have for us. It is due to the women's vision and skillful management that almost every member of my family got away from the Caucasus alive. But friends, acquaintances, people one loved stayed behind, and lost their lives in a brutal way in fearsome massacres.

The consequence was an unbelievable mass migration in stages. The Armenians' exit route passed through Iran, the Black Sea, Cyprus, Lebanon, Romania, and the north of Italy to France. The Petrossians split up: to travel all together was considered much too dangerous. Father and uncle left together, fleeing over Georgia and Iran, and ended up in Moscow. On the banks of the Moskva they studied—architecture and law. They remained there only until the beginning of the civil war and even there it became unsafe. From there they traveled to Paris.

Why Paris? For many Armenian families, including the Petrossians, their knowledge of languages came in useful. "In the better circles it was part of a good education to speak French," explains Armen Petrossian. In his family they "did not speak it flawlessly, but rather with difficulty, due to the lack of practice." But it was enough to get by in their new place of residence without the problem of a language barrier. French was the language of society, German very often the second language, and Russian the every day language. However, the initial stages in Paris were hard. "They had some savings, but only enough to have a roof over their heads." In the first wave of flights from their Caucasian homeland, in 1915–17, one was received by compatriots. When the second dispersion in 1917–18 and the Russian Revolution began, relationships had become mixed: "It was more natural and sensible to have good contacts with the French, Belgians, Germans, or Moroccans in one's neighbourhood instead of inflexibly insisting on remaining among one's own people."

Petrossian pensively stirs a cup of coffee. "When my father arrived in Paris, society was caught up in a process of change. There were many Russian aristocrats there, who had two things in common: they were wealthy, and they wanted to go back home. They didn't even consider staying in France. They spoke of two or three years of exile, not longer." All these members of the nobility, who were often customers of the Petrossian enterprise, all those multimillionaires from the East, the president says, now grinning to himself, had thought, "We'll just stick it out for a few years here in the West, leaving behind our hundred-room palaces at home, move into a nice little *hôtel particulier*—a modest city house with twenty rooms, and live as best we can." His father told him how those people carried on living extravagantly, as though nothing had changed, as if they had been back in Russia. "Money," says Monsieur Petrossian, "had only one use: to spend it. They never talked about it. Money was vulgar." All those people carried on believing in a return to Russia until 1925. "Then, it was all over." People that had previously enjoyed prosperity, power, and social standing stood before the ruins of their existence. There was nothing left; money was now everything. Faith and social standing vanished, and the way back was barred forever.

Through the window on the Rue d'Aubervilliers comes the whisper of passing cars. The second espresso, which Monsieur himself prepares, grows cold in the cup. "My father had a small apartment opposite our company, which for him was a kind of salon. Every afternoon and evening he received friends and acquaintances there. The door was open to practically everybody. There were always between ten and twenty people with him." In the business there was a certain Mikhail, a factotum of the firm. He was tall, imposing, broad-shouldered, competent in deliveries. Monsieur Petrossian reminisces, "When I was a child he used to sit me on his knee. He worked for the firm, but he was more like a member of the family, and he had been—which I didn't then know—one of the highest generals in the Czar's army."

One day, Armen Petrossian continues, a customer arrived at the pretty shop in the Boulevard Latour Maubourg in the seventh *arrondissement*, and he was dumbstruck when he saw Mikhail. The customer removed his hat, bowed, and said breathlessly and full of reverence. "Sir! My general!" "I remember it as if it were yesterday, how uncomfortable the situation was for Mikhail. It hurt him to be discovered like that", he remembers. The first female taxi driver to drive in this ultra-Parisian institution, was also a Russian noblewoman. "Ben oui," says the businessman in his impeccable Parisian French, "everyone knew her. She was one of my father's customers. She must have been rich, and lost everything-everything but her style. I remember her well. She used to come once a year to buy her caviar. That was something she wouldn't deprive herself of. We thought she was wonderful."

The pearly beluga, the delicate ossetra, the fine sevruga—when it is about a product of his Monsieur Petrossian lets his passion show. The Sorbonne graduate in political economy becomes effervescent. "I'm a gourmet. I love my job, and I feel constrained by my father's company motto: Quality, Innovation, and Tradition." Caviar is a "wonderful product," worth every cent in costs. He tried his first spoonful as a baby. "I must have been six months old. D'you know, babies adore caviar. It has a very strong taste, but the consistency is tender, soft." What Petrossian does not like is for people to buy cheap caviar and take it back home with them from their trips. Then they complain it has no taste. He rolls his dark eyes upwards. "I ask you! It's as if I bought my foodstuffs at the flea-market."

You don't play around with quality. The least you lose is your reputation. "Any Armenian who gets to be well-known for whatever reason has, barring personal differences, certain common traits: he wants to be successful, show that he can make a way for himself, wants to build something, become integrated, and stop suffering. He has the vigor, the fire that burns within him. He has taken up the challenge of his destiny." If anyone told him today, move camp, and start out from scratch in Mexico, he would do it "and make headway."

When Armen was born in Paris in 1949, his father was fifty-five. Young Armen later married Cécile, a Breton girl, with whom he had two sons in 1980 and 1982, Michel Serge Karen, and Alexandre Aran Cyril. Each has a French, Russian, and Armenian name. No, he says, he did not feel obliged to marry an Armenian to continue the line. "Chance, meeting, love are things written in the book of destiny. What is important is to achieve unity. And that's the way it happened." He knows of Armenian–French relationships that work, the same as any other couple. "It was never our intention to limit ourselves to ourselves," says Petrossian, understanding this as "a form of integration."

Nevertheless, there are traditions that are honoured, in the first place the Apostolic Church, which is many centuries old. The Paris church, opposite the Avenue Montaigne, was built by one of his uncles in 1910. "We decided freely when we got married, but on condition that all religious festivities, like weddings, baptisms, funerals should take place in our church. And our celebrations are always quite open and lavish, because essentially we don't celebrate within the narrow circle of our near and dear but with the most distant imaginable." Respect for elders is also written in capitals.

Armen Petrossian was a child when he heard about the genocide of his people. His parents told him openly and in neutral tones. "They limited themselves to simple facts, without elaborating. It was only later I realized anything else would have been too painful for them." An Armenian friend of the family was more explicit. He said he found it unbearable to talk about what really happened. It would be like reliving the terrible things he went through "and it would cost him his life to do so." Instead his parents explained it otherwise. "From them I only heard happy stories and little anecdotes from the time before the expulsions, of their previous life. That was their way of sidestepping and repressing to build themselves a second reality, so as not to be destroyed by the other."

In 1968, during the student revolts, the family lived in front of the church of Les Invalides. There were police vehicles all over the city, and even tanks. In 1962 the picture was similar, with the Algeria business. Mr Petrossian says quietly:

My father, who was an old man by then, said to me, "If this carries on like this, I'm going to leave France." I was very impressed, because he was saying it seriously. Do you understand? The flight carries on for us. It never ends. And my father says, "I've already lived four wars. I wouldn't survive another." That shows the mentality, the attitude, but also the tremendous force of character of many of us.

His father died on April 24, 1981, the official day of commemoration of the genocide. The son has tears in his eyes as he tells this. "Now that date is doubly painful for me."

On the floor of the cube-like office there is a wooden reproduction of the emblem of the firm. It is very pretty—a blue sailing vessel with swollen sails, surging in choppy high seas, proudly braving the storm, with the rising sun behind it, and advancing toward the observer.

This ship makes use of all its strength to carry out its struggle, but it doesn't retreat. It always goes forward. For me this has always been a symbol of the optimism that has been the hallmark of my family's history. Look ahead, for you go forward even when the road is hard. Life is a struggle. It's never still. It's always moving.

What does he consider himself: Armenian, French, European?

I'm a Frenchman of Armenian origin. You can't be both things. I'm not Armenian. That's impossible. I can't live in France and be Armenian at the same time. The Armenian part is still my origin. One represents a culture, carries a certain knowledge, a philosophy. I greatly respect the people of Armenia, but for me the situation is another. I don't live in Armenia but in France, with all its consequences. For me it's a great mistake to go abroad, live in the diaspora, isolate oneself, and pine for a distant homeland. I also think it's unfair to the country in which we found refuge.

There is much that is special in the Petrossian company. It is still independent of any large enterprise. As for the future, it would seem all options were open, specially as regards his sons joining the firm. "Whether they'll want to or not— things come as they come," says the father. "I'll never oblige the boys to do something they don't wish. Let them take their time to decide, and if they feel like joining, I'll be happy; but there's neither obligation nor expectation. I firmly believe each person has a predestination." As for the future of caviar, Petrossian has no worries. He smiles. "The special is needed in life to be able to put up with the humdrum."

36

END OF A LONG JOURNEY:
THE SEXTON MICHAEL STEPHEN AND
THE ARMENIANS IN INDIA (MADRAS)

Jochen Buchsteiner

The sexton is packing. In the corridor there are trunks and suitcases covering the pictures on the wall: portraits and buildings, reminders of the great periods of the Armenians in India. They are no more; and, with the departure of Michael J. Stephen, sexton at St. Mary's church in Madras, yet another bit of history vanishes.

You can see from the church façade that in recent years it has not had an easy time preserving the Armenian heritage. The pale yellow plaster is crumbling, and the main door and the windows look as if they were not very often opened. Who would one open them for? In Madras, which the Indians have been calling Chennai for a considerable time, there is no community left. Michael Stephen is, or rather was, the last Armenian left. St. Mary's, at number 60, Armenia Street, from now on will be in the hands of an Anglo-Indian family. Michael Stephen, whose family arrived in Dacca in 1903, still Indian in those days, returns to Bengal, Calcutta to be precise, where he will join forces with Sonia John, directoress of the Armenian Philanthropic Association.

He is leaving a few little secrets behind, the rare Bible of 1686, and the bell of 1754, whose builder engraved on it: Thomas Maers, in other words the maker of Big Ben in London. But, most of all, Michael Stephen is leaving a place in which Armenian history is engraved. Out of the community centered round the church the Armenians built in 1712, destroyed by the French, and then rebuilt sixty years later, there arose in 1773 the first constitution for a free Armenia, which at that time was under the domination of the Ottoman Empire.

In the same community arose a little afterwards Armenian journalism too, when one Haroutiun Shmavonian founded the first Armenian newspaper. Although the *Azdarar* existed a mere two years, from 1794 to 1796, it marked the beginning of a journalistic culture, which, from the end of the eighteenth century to almost the end of the nineteenth, gave rise to eleven periodicals in India alone.

The common history of Armenians and Indians starts much earlier, and not on the subcontinent but in the Caucasus. According to Zenobius Glak, a disciple of Gregory the Enlightener, a Hindu community settled in Armenia in 149 BC. In Zenobius' book, not published until 1832, in Venice by Catholic Armenians, it says that it was two Indian princes who founded the colony, having had to leave their country as a result of a failed *coup d'état.* The Armenians afforded the princes a "royal welcome," as Zenobius tells us. Among other things they were assigned lands in the province of Daron. Very soon after, the Indian refugees built temples and named their new city "Veeshap."

After centuries of harmonious coexistence, the immigrants disagreed with their hosts when, in 301, Christianity was adopted as the state religion. The Indians either had to assimilate, or else leave the country, and many of them chose the latter option. In spite of these difficulties, relations between Armenians and Indians were generally harmonious, as historical accounts confirm, from the Greek writer Xenophon down to the Armenian chroniclers of the eighteenth century.

The first sign of Armenians on Indian soil was a man called Tomas Cana or Kana, who arrived on the Malabar coast in southern India in 780. His place of origin is as little known as the nature of his mission, but the Christians of Kerala and Tamil Nadu commemorate the merchant and diplomat as a man who did a lot for the rebirth of Christianity.

One of the permanent religious achievements of the former Armenian immigrants is quite close to St. Mary's church. Atop Mount Thomas, near the airport, is the supposed grave of the apostle Thomas, who brought the teachings of the New Testament to India in the year 52. The first people to discover the sepulchre were Armenians, who took the Portuguese there in the sixteenth century. The 160 stone steps, which the Christian Indians still climb in celebration of St. Thomas's day, were hewn in the rock by the Armenian merchant Khojah Bedros Woskan. It was also he that, together with Edward Raphael and other Armenians, established the financial bases for the Moorat–Raphaelian school of Venice, which has educated generations of Armenians all over the world.

There are over 300 headstones to be seen to this day in Madras, among them the most ancient Christian sepulcher of the city, dating from 1663, are proof of a significant Armenian settlement in the seventeeth and eighteenth centuries. In other places the Armenians previously began to intermingle with the Indians. At Agra, where today the Taj Mahal is a reminder of the periods of glory of the city, there was as early as the sixteenth century the first large Armenian community. Its influence is reflected in the treatment accorded by the Mogul chief Akbar, who not only financed the first Armenian church on Indian soil in 1562, but liked to be surrounded by Armenians at his court. His wife Mariam, his doctor Juliana, and his supreme judge Abdul Hai, were all of Armenian origin.

Abdul Hai's son, whom Akbar gave the Muslim name of Mirza Zul-Qarnain, rose in his father's footsteps under Akbar's successor, Jehangir, and became a legendary figure. Jehangir not only favored "the Armenian" for his "intelligence and industry," but also made famous his musical compositions. Promoted to the rank of governor Mirza Zul-Qarnain used his power and wealth to support the Jesuits in India and finance Armenian churches in far-off Jerusalem.

No one danced with such zest among the religions or obtained such renown in the Mogul empire as Sarmad, the most famous Armenian in India. While Jehangir's son, Shah Jahan, the builder of the Taj Mahal, ruled in Delhi, Sarmad arrived by sea from Persia, and established himself as a merchant, like so many Armenians of the seventeenth century, at Sindh. In Jacob Seth's masterly book, *Armenians in India* (Calcutta 1937), Sarmad is described as a well-to-do entrepreneur, whose life began to cloud over when he became an inveterate devotee of the Hindu beauty Abhai Chand. From that moment on he roved around the country as a wandering fakir, which would hardly have raised eyebrows if he had at least worn the bare minimum of clothing; but, according to the sources, Sarmad went around completely naked.

Influenced by Sufis, he began to write poetry and to preach, and he soon acquired a certain renown as a "saint." In Delhi the Mogul ruler's eldest son came under Sarmad's spell. Prince Dara Shikoh spread the news of the miracle-working poet at the court and in the country. This close relationship was ultimately to bring misfortune on Sarmad, when the prince's younger brother Aurungzebe murdered his two brothers after Shah Jahan's death in order to take over the throne, and had nothing good to say about Sarmad. According to the legend, he summoned the nude poet right after acceding to the throne and slyly asked him if he still considered his brother to be Shah Jahan's successor. Sarmad supposedly calmly answered, "God has accorded him eternal sovereignty. My prophecy is not false."

Shortly afterwards Aurungzebe, the last of the great Mogul lords, condemned him to death. It is not altogether clear what pretext he used for this, whether Sarmad's odd behaviour or his tenets. His sayings are often quoted: "The mullahs say Mohammed entered Heaven, but Sarmad says Heaven entered Mohammed," a light enough blasphemy but probably enough for the offended ruler to condemn him to death.

Sarmad's works, written in Persian, belong till the present day to the subcontinent's Sufi literary canon. Although his tomb at the entrance of the Jama mosque in Old Delhi has drawn Muslim pilgrims for more than three centuries, the remaining Armenians of India whisper that Sarmad never left off being a Christian in his heart of hearts.

At no point were there more than 20,000 Armenians in India, which makes their well-documented presence even more remarkable. Not only were there Armenians in the highest levels of the Mogul empire, but they also rendered service under the British colonial power in very high positions. They were judges, doctors, officers. In the late eighteenth century, Colonel Jacob, an immigrant from Yerevan, was given command of 12,000 troops. He commanded the brigade with forty Armenian officers, having his headquarters at Gwalior, south of Agra, for no less than seventy years. That the officer, who died in 1850 at the age of 95, was thanked for this on his tombstone was only to be expected.

The Armenians were also famous for their skill in business. Now and again the British sought their company in order to profit from their knowledge of the Indian market. One who followed a remarkable path was Sir Paul Chater, whose career in Calcutta began around the time Colonel Jacob was buried at Gwalior. Chater specialized in finance, and he later became one of the most successful commercial brokers of Hong Kong. With the money he made in the Far East he backed the Armenians of India, having a number of buildings constructed, and creating a museum and a park. The little community of Calcutta is nourished by his donations till this very day.

Much of the history of the Armenians has gone by the wayside. Over the centuries hundreds of churches were established, favoured by the agreement of the East India Company of 1688 that, wherever more than forty Armenians lived, a church would be backed with money. There are no more than a dozen of these left. As their places of worship disappeared the faithful have also become fewer and fewer. If one asks Armen Baibourtian, the Armenian ambassador, how many of his compatriots now live in India, he can count them almost individually: three old ladies in Bombay, the sexton in Madras, who is now leaving, and a further two hundred in Calcutta. Baibourtian attributes the fall of the small but proud Armenian community at the beginning of the nineteenth century to the fact that the British perfected their commerce to such a degree that there was no room left for the Armenians. When India became independent in 1947, so many Armenians had left that Great Britain, in its retreat, had the boldness to offer those that were left British nationality. Hardly any took advantage of the offer.

It is not difficult to locate the last Armenians, however. One need only go to the Fairlawn Hotel in Calcutta, which many consider by far the fanciest guest house in Bengal. A certain Violet Smith, with her well-coiffed hair and black lipstick at eighty-three welcomes you at the reception. Her parents fled to India from Persia, via Afghanistan, to try and make a new start in the textile industry in Dacca. Violet arrived in Calcutta when she was eight, and seven years later her parents bought the Fairlawn Hotel. It was here that, during World War 2, she met her husband, a British major who arrived as a guest. She came back after years in England and Bombay, to take over her parents' hotel. She never felt comfortable in England, she says. Her accent and her lifestyle were not accepted, whereas she feels at home in Calcutta.

Violet Smith is in the center of the small but steadfast Armenian community's activities. Many events are held at the Fairlawn Hotel. Near the Academy there is still the Chater old people's home and three churches which, however, are seldom attended by more than forty people. Violet Smith feels protected by the Armenian community, from which she received the necessary help when she had to care for her husband in one of the hotel rooms for many years before his death.

Sonia John, the directress of the Calcutta Armenian Academy, is the person that keeps Little Armenia in Calcutta united. She is also close to eighty years old, and conditions have not become easier. Forty years ago the Academy and the Armenian school for girls, which is still based in a single building, had 200 pupils. In 1998, there were only six left. In view of this, Sonia John took notice of the changes that had taken place, and opened classrooms as well as the formerly successful sports club to non-Armenians. Today, there are sixty students at the Academy, which can think of the future thanks to Sonia John's foresight. The community has kept the school going for 180 years, she says, and there is no valid reason for it not to carry on existing.

37

THE SKEPTIC OF THE JAFFA GATE: KEVORK HINTLIAN (JERUSALEM)

Paul Badde

He would recognize an Armenian face among hundreds, Kevork told me 20 years ago; whereas for me, Armenia has always had just one: his. If anybody asked me what was worth seeing before travelling to Jerusalem, I would send them to him, and each of them, whether Christian, Jewish, or heathen, would say they had found him there, as I had said they would. One could rely on Kevork. For me he was the face of Jerusalem, more than any general, or bearded rabbi or archpriest.

I do not know when he was born although I have known him for a long time, during what was possibly the happiest period in the Holy Land in the last fifty years. No foreigner had heard of the intifada. It was the time of limbo. One gladly travelled to Gaza to eat good hummus or fish, without checkpoints, without barriers, walls, graves, without fear. But, because even then Kevork questioned everything with his ironical comments, I thought he was much more perceptive than me. He was a cynic of the old school, perhaps even a nihilist like one of those legendary Paris intellectuals, but in the Old Town of Jerusalem where Kevork, in contrast with the *rive gauche*, never had a retinue, or a Gauloise in the corner of his mouth or a mistress at his side. His arm was always loaded with newspapers from Egypt, France, England, Israel, or Lebanon in Arab, Hebrew, Roman, or Armenian characters.

I met him at a café at the Jaffa Gate at which I arrived by a devious route, to spy just a little into the Armenian convent whose forbidding walls produced magnetic curiosity in me. As I wrote later that day at the hotel:

> The quarter in which Kevork lives, comprises a sixth of the Old Town, a square area surrounded by walls on the top of Mount Zion, bordering on the south and west with the city walls, on the east with the Jewish quarter, and the Christian one on the north. Possessing the same imperturbability as the Jews, they too consider themselves a chosen people; and, like the Ethiopians, the connection of their church with the nation is almost seamless. Out of this history, the Armenian convent was sent straight from Ararat to Jerusalem in the remotest periods as the ark of their aspirations. Chronicles

of the Crusaders already describe the convent here in which Kevork lives: a former cloister, whose gate is shut every night, where laymen and clerics now live together as the patriarch's tenants, almost gratis, or even altogether free of charge, in the environs of the most expensive apartments in the world in Jerusalem's Jewish quarter. There are refugees living here with Kevork, in this land for which kings gave their lives. At the patriarch's feet riches accumulate, which pilgrims dragged to the summit of the Golgotha over centuries. "Blessed is he that leaves a keepsake on Zion," they held. Each gave what he was able (and the very best was just good enough for Jerusalem), for Armenians have a different way of looking at things than we do who, if at all, feel happy with souvenirs when we can take them back with us, or someone else steals them for us. Armenians often feel exactly the opposite.

I wrote the story as if about meeting a strange woman in a strange city. Then I added in abbreviated form what I was able to interpret from Kevork regarding the Armenian tragedy. For days he spoke to me about what I knew mainly as literature until then, about Franz Werfel's *The Forty Days of Musa Dagh*, from which there were some refugees even here in Jerusalem. Kevork spoke as if he had been an eyewitness, as though he had been present when his parents' and grandparents' generation were deported from their homes "toward the void." The echo of the footsteps of the deportation of millions pounded once more in the refugees and their children's temples in the convent. The memory of the monstrous "cesspit of death at Deir-es-Zor," and the putrefying "human manure" through which the columns of deportees, very far from Europe, dragged themselves during World War I never ceased in Kevork's skull. Cellars overflow with documents and witnesses' accounts of the molten butter that was poured into wounds, of the apocalyptic screams, the crucified, the amputations, the

horseshoes nailed to the soles of the feet, on the dam of corpses that obstructed
the flow of the Euphrates at Echmiadzin, on the deranged mothers that sang
hymns as they flung their children over cliffs, on the proverbial rape of his people.
"Aha! So you're wily Armenian rogues," and just like this many a priest, doctor,
or teacher was removed from the columns, and they then had their heads
squeezed in a vice until they shattered. Those were the days when Armenia
became a Utopia, which has only come back from the realm of utopias to reality
once more in the time I have known Kevork: out of the glorious Soviet Union a
mountainous region on the summit of Asia Minor that becomes the Armenian
Republic. Too late for Kevork.

"Jerusalem's my home," he said at our first meeting. This did not change with
his journeys to Yerevan. "The people there speak a funny Armenian," he said on
returning "home," to Mount Zion, the first time, where only a few neighbors
could understand his language, though they all speak at least three or four, a home
where none of the stone crosses on the walls is like the next. Why? "It's more
realistic," says Kevork. "Things never repeat themselves, so ... you never get the
same thing twice over. Neither is it ever the same cross." At a café near the
convent gate we order three mocha coffees. His friend Albert has joined us, Albert
Aghazarian, lecturer of history at the Bir-Zeit Palestinian University, behind
Ramallah, who spoke impassionedly about the "graveyard politics" that ravaged
the Holy Land. "What side are we on in these politics?" he asked me, bewildered.
"Have we got any choice? We're all slaves of national security! The land has turned
us into Palestinians! Even the Jews are Palestinians, though they don't know it
yet." Kevork diverted the conversation away from Albert's anger to the story of a
student from Ankara who had invited him for a cup of tea the week before. This
student of his wanted to know if he also believed what Armenians all over the
world said of the Turks. "What'd you mean by 'believe'?" replied Kevork. "We
have the witnesses, the documents." The student stared at him. "But then do you
think we're the same as the Germans?" Albert laughed. "Kevork, Kevork! Man ...
man is evil. But the Turks are wonderful men." Archbishop Boghazian, the
convent librarian, slowly tripped by us. When the old prelate disappeared into the
convent, Kevork said. "In Africa they say that each time a tribal chief dies it's as
if a great library burnt down. It'll be a catastrophe for us the day this man dies."

The archbishop has long been dead, and the patriarch, in whose service
Kevork was still employed at that time. So, too, the sexton with his heavy brocade
cassock smelling of mothballs. Albert Aghazarian, his friend, became an adviser to
Arafat at the Madrid conference, with which began the long since shipwrecked
Oslo process, and a yet longer career of frustration and awkward resignation. Each
time I arrived in the city I found Kevork at our old café at the Jaffa Gate, and I
always recognized him from behind by his sweater. I always looked for him first,
despite his analyses and forecasts not always being worth much, but even so this
made him similar to the shrewdest heads in Jerusalem.

What exactly was his work is something I never asked him. In the 1980s, he
cultivated a careless reputation as a successful womanizer. He was a loner par

excellence. Ten or twelve years earlier he had been writing a book on the role of the American Colony Hotel of 1917 and the battles of the Turks and Germans against the British for Jerusalem, as he told me that time in the patio of the legendary house. "350,000 British camels decided the fate of Palestine. And that's why," he said with a wink, "the hotel's become a center of rocking-chair journalism." I leaned back in my chair. What had he meant by this? We argued about West and East, Nagorno-Karabakh and Serbia, Saddam and Rabin, Islam and Israel. His positions were not very consistent, I fancied. Finally, he smiled at me. "I'm two hundred percent in agreement. That's exactly what I don't like." Now I believe it was a piece of nonsense with which, in his resignation, he wanted to manage me. What did I know already? In the period of greatest euphoria— around the time of the peace with Jordan—he just shook his head whenever I asked him for his opinion. "The country's forever too small for peace and the great expectations that are placed here. The number of suitors is too large. Just look at Jerusalem. Isn't it the only city people miss without ever having been here—millions of total strangers?" He smiled slightly. "Imagine that there were peace and they all came. Catastrophe. The world would stream in through the city gates. They'd trample Jerusalem underfoot. The country's really too small for peace. It would drown with visitors."

But that was not to be. Rather, it drowned once again in its violence. Those were the years I lived in Jerusalem, for good, I thought, and where Kevork always met me as on my previous visits, ever amiable, ever skeptical, ever with his enormous collection of newspapers under his arm as he went to, or came from, the convent, lost in thoughts, around half of which seemed reserved for the Armenian tragedy. He showed me the most secret corners in the maze which was the Old Town, and finally opened up the deepest cellar below the Church of the Sepulchre. In the storeroom of the baker Saladin he showed me still-standing arches of the portico of the destroyed basilica of Constantine from the fourth century, built in the architectural style of Jerusalem, and he invited me to some of the best flaky-pastry pastries of the Middle East. He led me past paranoiacally jumpy security guards to the Pope, who made an unprogrammed visit to the Armenians during his trip to Jerusalem. That morning the city was immobilized by traffic snarls. It was a miracle.

Yet, I always picture him as I saw him the first time I left, when I thought I would never again manage to return to the city of cities. We had met below the oldest pine tree of Jerusalem. "From this tree Archbishop Boghazian hears a little owl hoot each time one of us is going to die," he told me near the massive trunk, and waved toward the top of the tree where the wind was playing among the branches. "Did it also hoot before the murder?" I asked. He looked at me with compressed lips. I knew it had not been a murder that the whole town had been talking about for weeks, but a simple case of a stabbing: a knife in the hand of one Armenian in the heart of another, the result of an *amour fou*. At that time such a case was totally unheard of in the history of the quarter, when violence still caused shudders. In the convent a veil of shame and silence was drawn over the case.

Kevork leaned against the pine. In general, I only saw him smile with his eyes, but this time he looked at me fully. "We Armenians have no confession as the Catholics have," he said. "This is why we always sin openly." In their cathedral of St. James he had shown me, the day before, a miniature of Adam and Eve in the act of stealing the fruit from the forbidden tree—but both were clothed. Is it possible that the Armenians, after our expulsion from Eden, helped themselves from the tree of knowledge once more?

"My father never went to church," he said. "But he often told how, during our expulsion, a woman would suddenly run out of the column and head towards the desert. 'Where'd you want to get to?' the others would shout at her. 'To a grave,' she answered. 'Who's died?' 'God,' she screamed, in a way my father could never forget. Of course, she was off her head." He looked at me a moment, a bit embarrassed. "You know," he went on, "we're not solemn fools. Our faith is too big for us. That's why we can only join up, why only our church can believe." Now he had embarrassed me. I took his arm. "I don't know if I'll be coming back. But do take my story of you once I've written it, and keep it here somewhere. I'd also like to be remembered by you all, and have a keepsake in Zion."

That was twenty years ago. Kevork has surely kept my story of him among a pile of newspapers. On my last visit to Jerusalem, however, he was not there, for the first time. I searched for him in vain, at the Jaffa Gate, in the streets, all the length of the wall. An acquaintance said he was in the States, but had no further details to offer. Kevork has never owned a cellphone. The convent janitor said he was coming back the following day, or two days later at most. But he did not return. This troubled me more than any other troubling thing in that town that winter: the fear, the assassinations, the apathy, the new walls, the barbed wire, the despair, the hopelessness. Kevork seemed to have vanished, as though Jerusalem had lost its unshaven face.

38

"Excuse me, how do I get to the front?" The Brothers Monte and Markar Melkonian (Los Angeles)

Michael Krikorian

In October 1999, I was sent to Armenia to cover the election of the new Catholicos, often referred to as the Armenian Pope. While there, I tried rather feebly to communicate in Armenian. My favorite target of these crude conversations were Yerevan's cab drivers. With my photographer Mark Cross seated in the back seat, I stumbled through the ancient language as we were driven around the city. Whenever I got stuck, I would resort to my ace in the hole. I would ask the cabbie "Did you know Avo?"

The reaction was always ebullient. "Avo? I love Avo. I fought with Avo!"

Twice, cabbies, while still driving, took their hands off the steering wheel to embrace me. Once I had to grab the wheel to keep from slamming into a parked car. About two weeks into this adventure, Cross and I were in a cab heading back to Yerevan from still earthquake-ravaged Spitak. There was a light rain falling as we sped and screeched through several kilometers of downhill switchbacks. Mark tapped me on the shoulder and whispered in my ear, "Don't ask him about Avo."

Avo was Monte Melkonian, the adventure-book figure—intellect, terrorist, war hero—who hailed from California and lived a very different life from the one that may be expected. Unlike so many in this book who were scattered about the world and found their fame far from the homeland, Melkonian's legend, though partially cast in Lebanon, took on mythic proportions in Armenia and the battlefields of Karabakh in the early 1990s.

Born in the fertile San Joaquin Valley, Melkonian's brilliant star would burn out in a small village of Karabakh in 1993, where he died in battle at age thirty-five. Melkonian, credited with helping to organize and lead a ragtag army to victory over Azerbaijan, was so revered that he was laid to rest at the single highest point of the Yereblour Cemetery, Armenia's scarred burial ground for fallen soldiers. The president of Armenia declared Monte Melkonian a National Hero.

Avo's life has been chronicled in a memoir by his older brother, Markar Melkonian, entitled *My Brother's Road—An American's Fateful Journey to Armenia*, published by I.B. Tauris (2005).

For eight years, Markar Melkonian wrote, sweated, researched, pored over files, tapes, and memories to produce a book that he says rather glumly probably won't see a best sellers' list. "I could have written ten books on Monte," he said from his home in Los Angeles. "My brother was an amazing man."

Anyone familiar with Monte Melkonian's life would agree.

Monte Melkonian was born on November 25, 1957 in Tulare County. He was the third of four children—his sisters were Maile and Marcia—of Charles and Zabelle Melkonian. At an early age Monte displayed a tremendous intellect and maturity. He would eventually go on to master five languages—English, Spanish, French, Japanese, and Armenian—and speak passable Arabic, Italian, and Turkish, as well as some Farsi and Kurdish.

Brother Markar, who earned a Ph.D. in philosophy from the University of Massachusetts at Amherst, says it is difficult to pinpoint his younger brother's fascination with Armenian causes, but the spark may have occurred on a family trip to western Turkey to the village of Marsovan, his mother's ancestral home. Turks had taken over the house and Monte's father, a man who had knocked on the doors of strangers around the world, could not bring himself to go to the house.

In the book *The Right to Struggle—the Selected Writings of Monte Melkonian*, his brother, who edited it, wrote in a preface that "years later, Monte looked back on this trip as a turning point in his life ... this episode, as much as anything else, was responsible for his decision to identify himself first and foremost as an Armenian."

On the family journey—a fifteen-month trek through Europe, Russia, Africa, and the Middle East—twelve-year-old Monte began to formulate his philosophy.

"He thought 'We are like everyone else. People on the bottom. But we are survivors,'" said Markar. Later, when he became militant, Monte altered that to more of a "we're gonna kick the ass of the people who shit on us" way of thinking and acting.

"It's about time that we loudly repudiate the romantic conceit that 'My pen is my gun.' Pens are pens and guns are guns. There are more than enough 'intellectuals' in the diaspora. What we need are fighters, soldiers, fedayeen" (Monte Melkonian from "A Critique of Past Notions," *The Right to Struggle*).

In addition to acquiring a strong curiosity about his ancestors, Markar said that trip brought on a strong case of wanderlust. At the age of fifteen, Monte went to Japan as part of a student exchange program. But he extended his stay for one year, learning the language and martial arts, and traveling also to Vietnam. The liberation of Vietnam had a strong effect on him.

"Here was this small people that beat the empire," recalled Markar. "Wings of freedom were filling red sails. Something was in the air."

After graduating in 1978 from the University of California at Berkeley with degrees in archeology and mathematics, Melkonian passed on a chance to study at Oxford and instead headed for the Middle East. The Iranian revolution was brewing and Monte went to Teheran. He taught English and participated in the movement that eventually overthrew the Shah. That revolution only further convinced Melkonian that it was possible for Armenia to once again be independent.

> There exists no Armenian "race." There is only Armenian people, an Armenian nation. This is why we need to fight. The Armenian people in the diaspora are losing their identity as a cultural-national entity, succumbing to the centrifugal effects of cultural assimilation. If Armenians of the diaspora do not claim their right to live in their homeland they will gradually lose their common cultural identity. And if this happens, the white massacre of our nation will have succeeded." (From *Our Origins: True and False* by Monte Melkonian.)

In the fall of 1978, Monte made his way to Beirut to help in the defense of the teaming Armenian quarter of Bourj Hamoud and other neighborhoods from attacks by the right-wing Christian militia known as the Phalangists. The Phalangists were upset with fellow Christian Armenians for not joining in the battle against Muslims in Lebanon's barbaric civil war.

"Monte got a crash course in street fighting in Beirut," said Markar, who also went to Beirut and joined the militia to defend Armenians.

Markar said that many Armenians living in Beirut were suspicious of the two brothers from America who had come to help fight back against Phalangist attacks.

"Most people thought Monte was nuts," said Markar, a modest, powerfully built man of forty-seven. "They thought 'A guy from California, from paradise, what is he doing in hell?'"

Still, Monte and Markar were among those who did protect Armenians.

Around this time in his life, Monte met Seta Kabranian, the woman who would become his wife and comrade in his struggle. Monte the tough guy, who would stay up all night in the most dangerous neighborhoods in Beirut, grew silent around Seta.

"He was really shy around me," Seta said in a 1999 interview. She recalled the day Melkonian, twenty-one at the time, visited Seta, then fifteen, at her school. He gave her a quick, soft kiss on the lips. "Everyone at school was talking about that kiss."

By the spring of 1980, Monte had joined what was considered by many governments to be a hard-core terrorist organization, the Armenian Secret Army for the Liberation of Armenia (ASALA). Several Palestinian resistance organizations provided Monte with extensive military training. It came in handy in Lebanon and it would become very useful more than a decade later in Karabakh.

While in ASALA, Melkonian is said to have participated in several assassinations of Turkish officials in Europe. Toward the end of his time with ASALA, the organization was responsible for bombings that killed innocent people.

By 1983, ASALA was split into two feuding factions. After alleged supporters of Melkonian killed two close aides of Hagop Hagopian, ASALA's founder, things got hot for Monte. Hagopian's followers captured two of Monte's closest friends, then filmed their torture and execution.

Melkonian went undercover in France. In November 1985, he was arrested in Paris and sentenced to six years in prison for possession of falsified papers and an illegal handgun. Melkonian spent three years in French prisons at Fresnes and Poissy.

He then spent another eighteen months living underground, scrounging for a life with Seta at his side.

"We didn't have any money," Seta said as she talked about those tough times with Avo. "The FBI, Interpol, ASALA, they were all after us. We never stayed in one place very long. We were crossing borders. Selling Pepsi Cola bottles to buy bread. Sleeping on floors. God, those were the good old days."

As Seta sat in Dolmama, one of Yerevan's best restaurants, she was not joking. Her eyes turned shiny with wetness.

"People tell me now, 'Seta, you have such a lovely home.' But I would sell this home, give it away and ten others just like it to live in the old days with Monte."

This was a chaotic time. The Soviet Union was breaking up and all hell was breaking loose. With Seta's help, Melkonian managed for the first time in his life to get into Armenia. Not long after, Seta and Monte were married at the monastery of Geghart in August of 1991. Markar, who had not seen his brother in nearly ten years, was at the wedding.

"Armenia was at the crossroads then," said Markar. "Armenia was a complete mess. Corruption. The war in Karabakh was heating up."

Karabakh was a region of neighboring Azerbaijan which had a very large Armenian population and was a historical part of Armenia. Monte eventually began focusing his energy on Karabakh.

"If we lose Karabakh," the bulletin of the Armenian Karabakh Army Forces quote him as saying, "we turn the final page of our people's history." According to Markar, Monte believed if Azeri force succeeded in deporting Armenians from Karabakh, they would advance on Zangezur and other regions of Armenia. Monte saw the fate of Karabakh as crucial for the long term security of the entire Armenian nation.

Monte began fighting in Karabakh. But the men he was fighting with were a ragtag group, some wearing dress shoes with holes in the soles, some smashed on vodka and firing their Kalashnikovs wildly into the air in a drunken rampage. Back in Lebanon, Monte had been trained by battle-hardened Palestinian and Lebanese fighters. He was an artillery spotter in the 1981 Israeli invasion of Lebanon that foreshadowed the massive 1982 invasion. He was a veteran street fighter. He was trained in explosive techniques. And most importantly, Monte Melkonian was a fearless leader.

"Most of the soldiers, they tried to be like Monte, but that was impossible," said Albert Arakelian, who fought with Monte and now leads a military division in Yerevan. He clenched his fist to show words tattooed on his knuckles. In Armenian is written "Glory to Monte."

Melkonian first went into Karabakh to translate for a French journalist, Markar said. But soon he found himself in the thick of battle and accepted a position as commander of the region of Martuni in southeastern Karabakh.

There he reorganized fighters into a disciplined and effective fighting force. Under his command, his roughly 4,000 soldiers and fifty tanks successfully defended a mountainous region of 200 square miles and 28,000 people.

Monte's forces recaptured much land lost to the Azeris and earned a reputation as a disciplined, fierce fighting force. So many stories were told about Monte that many people believe he was at every major battle in the war. He was not. For example, he was not involved in the fighting that opened the Lachin corridor linking Karabakh with Armenia.

Still, Monte Melkonian was the chief military strategist who planned and led the operation to capture the region of Kelbajar, located between Armenia and Karabakh.

Markar, who has video footage of those battles, said it was an intense campaign through a rocky gorge with Azeri gunners firing from the high ground. "Monte just plowed right ahead."

Throughout the fighting, Melkonian is said to have maintained respect for Azeris, both non-combatants and fighters. In an interview taped shortly before his own battlefield death, Melkonian lamented the lack of regard Azeri leaders had shown for their own fighters. "It's a shame," he said, "that they send them against us with so little preparation to be killed like that."

In the spring of 1993, Monte and Seta were planning on taking their first real vacation. They had hopes of having a baby. They made reservations at a hotel getaway in Armenia. But, on June 12, shortly before he was due to leave Karabakh to spend some time alone with his beloved wife, Monte received word that a Soviet T-72 tank had been captured.

By now, Monte had become fascinated by tanks and was convinced they were the key to victory in Karabakh. So, whenever word reached him that a tank had been captured, he wanted to personally verify it. On June 12, he set off with his faithful driver Komidas and four other fighters, to the village of Merzuli to check out the Russian tank.

As they neared the village, they saw an armored personnel carrier with a turret-mounted canon and several soldiers milling about. Komidas asked the soldiers something in Armenian and by the bewildered look on their face he knew that he had stumbled on the enemy. A wild gunfight broke out: automatic weapons, the canon, hand grenades.

Monte fired from his rifle. A canon round smashed into a wall near Melkonian and a foot-long piece of shrapnel tore into his head, killing the hero on the spot. Several other people were killed or wounded in the gunfight but Monte's body was retrieved by the wounded Komidas and other Armenian fighters and taken to Martuni. The town would later be renamed Monteapert, or Fort Monte.

In an interview with the *Fresno Bee*, his father, who is now in the early stages of Alzheimer's disease, talked about Monte's end.

"We always figured he was going to die because he was always at the front," said Charles Melkonian from his Visalia home. "I am very proud of him, but I would rather have him alive."

Monte Melkonian was buried with full military honors on June 19, 1993. By all accounts, more than 100,000 people attended his funeral (some reports put the figure as high as 250,000).

Markar Melkonian wrote about his brother in the foreword to Monte's book The Right to Struggle:

"Monte—or Avo, his nom de guerre in Karabakh—was many things to many people. To an Azerbaijani embassy official in Washington, D.C., he was a "terrorist with a criminal background;" to the U.S. State Department he was a "threat to national security," to more than one village woman in Karabakh he was a 'saint'; to another unnamed Armenian quoted in the *New York Times*, he was "the best god we ever had;" and to the mothers of Monteapert he was the first person to thank for the fact that their children no longer had to huddle in basements for fear of rocket attacks.

Above all, Markar said Monte was "a teacher who taught by example. In the example of his life, he still offers us lessons—lessons about what is important in life, and about the possibilities available to even the most outgunned and beleaguered victims of aggression."

If you're ever in a cab in Yerevan, ask the driver about Avo. Just be ready to grab the wheel.

39

THE EVERYDAY LIFE OF A HERO: LEVON ARUTUNYAN, VETERAN OF THE KARABAKH WAR (YEREVAN)

Rainer Hermann

He looks older than he actually is. His drawn face is haggard and his dark eyes have a nervous tremor. But Levon Arutunyan was not born until 1957: at Artashat, 30 kilometers. south of Yerevan, where, on the other side of the Turkish border, the mighty Ararat rises to the sky as if wanting to carry the universe, and one understands why that mountain is so important for the Armenians. Westwards from here extend the wide plateaus of Anatolia, and in the south the Ararat valley leads to the Azeri enclave of Nakhichevan.

Levon Arutunyan can hardly be recognized in a photograph of previous years showing a sturdy man with a dignified expression, with firm cheeks and thick black hair. Today, in his ascetically shrunken face, his nose looks even larger. He never laughs. When he talks about himself he makes long pauses, as though reliving what he narrates. He covers his mouth with his hands as if what he tells could not be true. Time and again he hides his weary eyes behind his hands.

He began his life like so many other Soviet Armenians. He was twenty when he had to travel very far away for the first time. The Red Army sent him as a conscript to Vladivostok, on the Pacific. In 1979, he returned to his village and worked as a chauffeur and a farmhand. He was happy for almost ten years: he got married and devoted himself to his work. And then the Karabakh war broke out. First, a tremendous earthquake devastated northern Armenia. Then Karabakh claimed its independence. Forty years earlier, Stalin had handed over the region inhabited by Christians to Muslim Azerbaijan.

Idyll turned into war, and war into hell for Levon, as in 1990 the Azeris carried out attacks on the town of Artashat from the enclave of Nakhichevan, enclosed between Turkey and Armenia. Its citizens formed a militia to defend themselves even if only with rifles. The Red Army did not give the Armenians any help, as the soldiers and officers serving in the Caucasian regiments were mostly Azeris. They attacked the Armenian civilians and their militias. They also attacked other towns and villages in the wide Ararat valley, which the Artashat militia and tough men like Levon Arutunyan arrived to defend. "We had nothing but rifles, while the Azeris were well equipped," he said. No wonder: they had the Red Army to fall back on. Nevertheless, the resistance resulted in a cease-fire.

Shortly afterwards, the Azeris attacked the village of Vardanis in the narrow strip between Lake Sevan and Azerbaijan. The skirmishes lasted two years, and Levon now helped in the defense of the Armenians there. "We were told the situation in Karabakh was getting critical." At this period Armenia had no regular army, just volunteer militias scattered throughout the country, which came to each other's rescue. Levon was asked to go to Karabakh, the "black garden" separated from Armenia, which hardly had any weapons, and was unable to supply its own needs. Provisions were ferried by helicopters to the exclave surrounded by Azeris.

On May 18, 1992, Karabakh stopped being an exclave. First of all, the militias liberated the city of Shushi on May 8, and then they connected Karabakh to Armenia by means of the Lachin corridor. At that moment, Levon was serving in the north of Karabakh, in the region of the town of Martakert where, on June 12, the Azeris launched a great offensive. For the first time they used heavy guns, tanks, and airplanes. The guerrilla actions turned into a full-fledged war. On July 4, the Azeris conquered the town of Martakert. In a mere three weeks they took over the whole of northern Karabakh, and by September 1, were in control of half the exclave.

Levon was involved in the defense of a village north of Martakert. Before July 2, he had evacuated the inhabitants of a village before the Azeri advance. The whole day long, he and other militia fighters had to accompany the villagers through a nearby forest. There was no petrol. Whoever was unable to flee from the village was locked up in the church. The Azeris set it on fire. Only a girl of twelve survived. She told how her mother, hit by bullets, fell on top of her and covered her. The girl did not yet know her mother was no longer alive.

On July 2, 1992, the Azeris attacked with 1,500 soldiers, eighteen tanks, and three planes. They had no idea that only fifty militiamen were there to defend the village. It was only the day before that a hundred of the militiamen had been sent to other villages. The remaining fifty defended themselves only with handguns. "We wanted to gain time so that the population could reach safety," says Levon, without a trace of emotion. Not all of them were able to save themselves. Two

"Stalin Organs" fired on the village and killed the civilians. Before Levon's eyes a woman died in the hail of fire.

By noon, most of the inhabitants had gotten to a safe place. Levon, in an armored car, came under fire. He was hit by shrapnel in the legs and one hand. One of his index fingers is still dislocated, and his hand shakes as he talks. He remained lying in the grass for two hours. With only one hand he was unable to bandage himself to stop the loss of blood. That was when the Azeris entered the town, and four of them found Levon. They hit him again and again, dragged him 50 meters to a truck, and dumped him on the loading space.

By now the village was in flames, and the Azeris also threw three women that had not been able to save themselves onto the truck. The two elderly ones were covered in blood, as was the young one, whose clothes the Azeris had torn off. When the others tried to give her something to cover herself with, the soldiers kicked them. They threw stolen objects on the truck and drove to the village of Gerambo. There the prisoners were shoved off the truck. "The inhabitants threw stones at us, spat on us, and wanted to attack us with scythes, and the soldiers kept them away by striking them with their rifle butts."

The three women were taken to the soldiers' headquarters, and Levon to the hospital. They left him on the ground outside the entrance. The relatives of the patients had to pass by him, and they spat on him and kicked him. At nightfall they dumped him on a pile of leftover food in a stinky room. After an hour he was able to get to a room full of broken furniture where he remained three days, without medical attention. The wounds, however, had stopped bleeding. It was hot and stuffy in the room. On the fourth day someone came, who, without saying his name, bandaged his wounds.

The wounds hurt. Levon took off the bandages and saw maggots in them. He asked for water to wash them. In vain. Every day dozens of unwelcome visitors would arrive, only to spit on him. The task of the four guards outside the room was not to prevent this but to keep the prisoner from escaping. Levon was at the hospital for a fortnight and, on the morning of July 18, was kidnapped by some strangers, who took him to an Azeri village. A local family had lost one of the four brothers recruited as soldiers. Levon was the hostage with which to obtain his release. During all this time Levon had received no medication or a transfusion. This was not to change over the next months.

By chance the Red Cross heard about him and a representative visited him only on December 2, 1993, and promised to send him regular supplies of food, cigarettes, and medicines through the owner of the house. Needless to say, he never received those packages, which the house owner sold on the black market. As Levon's health worsened, the Red Cross insisted on sending him to the hospital. The family did not want this, but in spite of this Levon's swollen leg now received injections. He was cared for by Red Cross nurses when his temperature rose to 40°. The house owner called a Red Cross doctor, who discovered a piece of shrapnel in Levon's leg, and removed it. He recommended that Levon be sent by plane to Georgia to be given medical treatment. Otherwise his chances of surviving were minimal.

As far as the Azeris were concerned, that was out of the question. Levon carried on struggling to survive. The three brothers were still missing the fourth. Once they brought the head of an Armenian in a carrier-bag and showed it to Levon. "From the room in which I was held prisoner I could see cars going by with the heads of Armenians as trophies. The drivers were cheered as heroes. This pained me more than my wounds." Massacres and the heads as trophies are still haunting him.

On April 17, 1995, the Red Cross finally managed to get Levon transferred from his private captivity to the state camp for Armenian war prisoners at Gobustan, which was carried out two days later. This camp was the only one to which Azerbaijan allowed the Red Cross access. But in the days prior to Levon's arrival, six Armenians were bludgeoned to death there. There was no cause for this, but the apparent reason was that some of them refused to shut their eyes when the guards ordered them to go to sleep, according to some of the Armenian prisoners.

"Whenever a Red Cross representative came, we had a peaceful day." However, the organization's delegate never realized the prisoners were more emaciated every day. "When we were called to eat, the guards counted to ten, by which time we had to have eaten the bread and drunk the water," Levon recalls. If there was ever soup, it was like water with two pieces of charcoal in it. The prisoners' strength was dwindling. Many had to be helped to get back to their cells. They would faint. But they were still forced to carry the stones to build a new camp within the existing one. For their enjoyment the guards ordered the prisoners to fight one another. If they were not satisfied, they did it themselves.

Levon spent only twenty-three days in the concentration camp. May 12, 1995, was the first anniversary of the cease-fire. It was already a year since all the war prisoners should have returned home, but it was only then that the Red Cross was able to take Levon to Baku, the Azeri capital, and fly him back to his country in a small plane the following morning.

He is thankful to the Red Cross, which kept his hope alive. But it was his family that helped him get back to reality—his wife and three children, the youngest of them born three months after Levon marched off to war. The little girl did not recognize her father, and greeted the gaunt, emaciated figure as "uncle." Levon took up growing vines again. At last he laughs, for once. "To make wine."

40

THE MAGIC OF THE OPAL:
THE JEWELER VAROOJAN (JOHN)
ISKENDERIAN (SYDNEY)

Ron Knight

Today we witness people in many parts of our troubled world being displaced with virtually nothing and becoming refugees. Varoojan's story is about a talented young man from Palestine who took the initiative to seek a safe and secure future in Australia, a New World country that had captured his boyhood imagination. It is an object lesson about how a person can take action to exercise the fundamental human right of achieving the best they can through initiative and perseverance.

Underlying Varoojan's story are his father's "nightmare: struggles to survive after escaping from Ottoman Turkey in 1915, and the flight of his family as refugees from war-torn Jerusalem in 1947. These are persistent memories.

Varoojan was born in Palestine Jerusalem in 1938 to Armenian parents who were both from Aintab in Turkey. They had left Turkey separately to escape persecution from the Ottoman Turks in 1915, and met for the first time many years later in Jerusalem. They were married in the early 1930s. Varoojan was the third of five children.

His father Iskender Iskendarian left Turkey at the age of seventeen and lived first in Syria and then in Lebanon before making his home in Jerusalem. These were difficult times in that part of the world and life was a matter of surviving from one day to the next. "This experience had a profound impact on him and, at second hand, upon me," said Varoojan who today is a prominent designer and manufacturer of jewelry in Australia.

When he was a young boy there were many family occasions when his father would talk about his experiences. He would speak about the genocide of the Armenians by the Ottoman Turks and the various things that had happened to him during his struggles to survive in Syria and Lebanon. Varoojan said, "My father would talk non-stop for three or four hours to a rapt audience. You could have heard a pin drop. His stories were like reliving a nightmare and they made me aware that I could not take safety and security for granted!" Varoojan now has two grown-up children himself, Lisa and Garo.

Varoojan's father worked in the family goldsmithing business as a teenager and had learned how to refine and process gold and silver, and to manufacture jewelry. With his brother Haroutune he was able to establish a manufacturing and retail goldsmith and jewelry business in the Old City in Jerusalem. "This business was successful and my family was reasonably prosperous under the British Mandate until 1947, when we became refugees to escape the war between the Arabs and the Jews." This war resulted in the partition of Palestine and the creation of Israel. The West Bank was given to Jordan.

"At that time I was nine and attending the Armenian school in Jerusalem. I clearly remember the explosion and how all the windows in the school were shattered when the nearby King David Hotel was blown up." This was on July 22, 1946, the day Irgun-leader Menachim Begin gave the order to blow up the prestigious building that was the site of the British military command. Today, the King David Hotel, placed between the Knesset in the West and the Wailing Wall in the East, is supposed to be the safest place in Jerusalem.

When the sun spreads its golden light on the heart of Jerusalem today, the world leaders who stay in Israel's most famous hotel may easily forget that this quarter of town was once a bloody battleground in the Jewish struggle for an independent state. "I clearly remember huddling, scared, in the back of a shop with my father and my brothers and sisters, while a gun battle raged on the street outside. We had been on our way home from school when the fighting started."

"My father and uncle decided it was not safe to be in the middle of warfare and arranged to leave Jerusalem," Varoojan recalls. So they melted down the jewelry stock to make it easier to carry and, with only a few essential belongings, the two families hastily departed Jerusalem on the back of a truck to make a new start in Bethlehem on the West Bank.

Accommodation was difficult to find and the families (and many other refugees) lived for some time in a Bethlehem Armenian convent. Also, no one was interested in jewelry so the two families had a very difficult time starting a new business.

Varoojan was enrolled in the Terra Santa College and had to learn three new languages, Arabic, English, and Italian, at the same time. He managed well and became a good student. Geography and drawing were his passions. "My drawing skills were recognized by the Bethlehem City Council," he proudly remembers. But at that time the officials were not interested in pretty drawings. Instead, they paid him to do sign writing for bomb shelters in various parts of town.

Varoojan's two interests came together in geography classes.

> The teacher would call me up to draw maps on the blackboard while he spoke to the class. The map of Australia was easy to draw and my favourite. I was fascinated by the geography of Australia. It looked like a huge island surrounded by water that made it look safe. I dreamed of going there even though it was much too far away.

Years later he saw a documentary film in a local cinema about Australia and its blue waters, beaches, and people, which made the childhood dream more real.

But there was no space for dreams.

"I finished school at the age of eighteen prior to matriculation. For family economic reasons there was no chance of any further education. I would have liked to have become an architect or an engineer. Instead, I went into the family business of making jewelry."

As a small boy he was fascinated by the idea of making interesting shapes out of metal.

> I had watched my father and uncle at work and was eager to try for myself. At about eight I made myself a little workbench from whatever pieces of timber I could find. My father and uncle provided me with silver and tools … and some guidance. The products I finished were appreciated … with coins. But I was made fun of because of the way I hung out my tongue as I concentrated on my work.

Varoojan laughs in his resounding baritone. Later, during his early teens, his father arranged further training with a goldsmith friend during the school summer vacations. "I remember being paid wages—a few silver coins. They meant a lot at that age."

With this limited experience he started to make jewelry, often working out how to do things as he went along by trial and error. "If I wasn't successful I would try again and again, until I was satisfied. Nature had been generous to me in giving me talents: I was able to create new designs and had skills to turn my ideas into reality." Soon he was able to sell the pieces of jewelry he made to some of the better-known jewelry outlets and became one of their regular suppliers. "This gave me great satisfaction and there was no longer a shortage of money. I earned up to 100 pounds per week when the normal wage was only about five pounds per week." This prosperity enabled Varoojan to help his family and allowed him to think more and more about his own future. "Australia loomed large in my thoughts and the chance viewing of the documentary film on Australia led to serious inquiries that helped me decide what I wanted to do."

In September 1962, at the age of twenty-three, the day came to say farewell to his family and home. In Beirut Varoojan boarded the Greek liner 'Patrice' to head east with mixed emotions to face the unknown. The young excited man did not know that he would not see his mother again. After almost a month at sea, Australia appeared on the distant horizon. "We anchored at a distance and as I watched the approaching launches with the big, neat, blue-uniformed representatives of the Australian Commonwealth Police and Immigration Officials for the immigration formalities, I said to myself, I am in a safe place—a land of law and order." The schoolboy who loved to draw the map of Australia was about to set foot on the country of his dreams.

I will never forget that day. A representative of the Commonwealth Bank of Australia came on board the ship and invited passengers to open a savings account with even as little as one "shilling" (10 cents today) as a deposit. I handed him a bank check for 1600 English pounds (that would buy half a suburban house then). My check was replaced with a bankbook and nightmares until I arrived in Sydney and went to the Commonwealth Bank on George Street. To my great relief my money was there and it had already earned some interest!

Within a few days of arriving in Sydney a family friend introduced the young man to Freddie Neuman of Carina Jewellery. Mr Neuman introduced him to Ludwig Schmid, a master jeweler who had immigrated to Australia from Munich in Germany. He offered him a job in his jewelry manufacturing business. "I worked with Ludwig for nine months and I gained experience and learned to understand Australian English." The basic wage was about 14 pounds a week but Ludwig suggested he could do piecework to earn more money. "The pieces I made sold and my income multiplied. This was a very happy time and I still pay Ludwig an occasional visit."

The success of his pieces encouraged Varoojan, now John (he changed his name for the convenience of his clients), to start his own business in 1963. His early years were difficult and at times painful. Initially, business was very slow.

I made jewelry to my own designs and then tried to sell it to jewelry stores. But I had very little success. I wondered if there was something wrong with my goods, or was it with me? What I didn't know was that my designs were too creative and "before their time" for the conservative small retailers I had visited.

He did not have the courage yet to walk into a major jewelry showroom. "But I knew I had to and one day I forced myself to go in Percy Marks Jewelers, a well-known Sydney jewelry retailer. I introduced myself and opened my boxes to show my samples." Behind the glass counter sat the late Mr. Rolf Marks, a distinguished personality. "I didn't know how to react when Mr. Marks picked several items from the box and asked me to invoice them. I could not believe it. It was a substantial amount and my 'first' invoice. I regret I did not keep a copy." As Varoojan was about to leave Mr. Marks asked him about his origins. He said, "I remember the Armenians and the tragic events during the war of 1915 by the Turks." He had probably served with the ANZACs.

This success gave Varoojan the courage to visit the renowned Hardy Brothers, the Australian branch of the UK jewelers. who were suppliers by appointment to the British royal family. "I showed my stock to the late Mr. Hardy, who, much to my surprise, picked various pieces of jewellery from my box. He then asked if I could make mounts. When I said, 'Yes,' I was given some loose diamonds to make into solitaires." Australia began to look very much brighter.

At about that time the late Maria Neuman asked Varoojan if he would give her his stock for a few days to take to Melbourne, where she was going to visit clients. She came back with very little stock and a bundle of colorful checks. "I will not forget her," said Varoojan, still grateful.

Varoojan became fascinated by the opal gemstone and in 1964 made his first visit to Lightning Ridge, where the famous Australian black opal is mined. Australia produces about 75 percent of the world's output of opals. "My 'love affair' with the magnificent beauty and tantalizing colours of opal began at Lightning Ridge. I call opal 'nature's artwork.'"

For many years Varoojan has promoted "free-form" creative designs that take their shape from the natural shape of the opal. These designs are distinctively different from the calibrated standard shapes that waste valuable opal during the cutting and polishing process.

But life away from his family was not easy in the early years. "In 1965, I was shattered by the sudden loss of my mother and I would have returned home if the friends I had made here had not convinced me otherwise. Instead, my younger sister Teny and I managed to bring my father, who was unwell and lonely, to Australia to spend his remaining days." Before he passed away he said, "Son, I should have come to this country years ago."

Today, Varoojan is a proud grandfather of two and looks back with a feeling of gratefulness. "I have led a full life in Australia. I have been successful in the jewelry industry and have a happy family." His wife Sylvia is an Armenian who came to Australia from Cairo in Egypt. His daughter Lisa married Michael Ter-Minassian, a young Armenian man who came to Australia from the U.S.A. to take part in the AGBU (Armenian General Benevolent Union) sports competition.

"But, despite the passage of time and living happily in a faraway country, the Armenian tragedy still continues on as part of my emotional state of mind." During a visit to Australia, U.S. President Bill Clinton saw some samples of Varoojan's work at the jewelry store in his hotel and asked to see some more.

> I met with the President by appointment and he and members of his entourage bought some of my pieces. Subsequently, the President and I exchanged letters. My letter included the following paragraph:
>
> My name gives me away as being of Armenian origin, a son of a survivor of the horrific crime of 1915. We are indeed fortunate to be living as citizens of free, democratic and compassionate great countries like Australia and the United States of America. I do hope one day, perhaps soon, the Government of the U.S.A., with your assistance, will recognize the tragedy that befell our people in the years 1915 to 1923 as genocide. Perhaps then the living nightmare will leave us and we can continue to serve humanity as best we can, with peace of mind.

Varoojan Iskenderian has been recognized for his work with many awards including the prestigious "De Beers Design Award" for diamond jewelry in 1985, and the "Inaugural Lightning Ridge Opal Jewelry Design Award" of 2000. Recently, Varoojan was honored by being commissioned by the Jewelers Association of Australia to design and make jewelry to be presented to Prince Frederick and Australian-born Princess Mary of Denmark on the occasion of their visit to Australia in 2006.

41

¿Hablás armenio? Rosita Youssefian, Teacher of Armenian (Buenos Aires)

Josef Oehrlein

The schoolgirl begins with some difficulty, letter by letter, but she finally gets the meaning of the sentence. "Which of us has read Harry Potter?" Nobody in the hot, windowless classroom seems interested in the film hero. The teacher quickly steers interest toward what she intended to show with the question—to grammar. And, to illustrate the complex multiplicity of forms in the Armenian language, she writes another sentence in the light-blue copybook: "'I would not have thought that the president steals." But all politicians in general, should be carefully observed.' When I give a class a text, I have to simplify," says Rosita

Youssefian, the teacher. Not even in high school are her pupils able to negotiate the great Armenian literature. It is too difficult. This is why she prepares in advance the chapters to be seen in her lessons, and she herself makes up "little dialogues and tidbits" to explain rules of grammar. She has the both challenging and thankless task of teaching her pupils a complicated language they have absolutely no previous knowledge of, and which is of small use to them in their daily and later professional life.

Rosita Youssefian, forty-eight, is a teacher at the Marie Manoogian school, which, with 380 pupils of every age, belongs to the Armenian benevolent association UGAB (Unión General Armenia de Beneficencia), the Argentine section of the AGBU. The complex is located in the middle of an area in which the first Armenian immigrants settled more than a century ago. The quarter is called, not altogether appropriately, Palermo Viejo (Old Palermo, a part of the Buenos Aires quarter of Palermo), but the street, formerly Acevedo, in which the administration building, the church, and an Armenian restaurant are located, was renamed some time back "Armenia."

Rosita's father, Hovsep (José) Youssefian arrived in 1937, when he was sixteen. He was part of one of those great waves of immigration after the genocide of 1915. The grandparents had been expelled from the ancient Armenian city of Urfa in "historical" Armenia, and they first resettled in Aleppo. He arrived in Buenos Aires with one of his brothers, and was received into a nest conveniently prepared in advance. An uncle, who had emigrated to Buenos Aires shortly after the genocide, gave them lodging and a job in his textile company. Later Rosita's father moved to La Pampa, the countryside. He was used to the rural life, and even now, at eighty-three, he divides his time between country and town.

Rosita's mother was born in Buenos Aires, but is also of totally Armenian stock. The Kafafians were also swept to this far-off diaspora community. Rosita's grandmother was pregnant when she left. At the orphanage she was made to marry a youth while still practically a child, "so that the Turks would not carry her off," as Rosita explains. Until shortly before she died in 2001, her grandmother never wanted to give details of their flight. "She always burst into tears when we asked her about that." On the anniversary of her death in the winter of the southern hemisphere, her grandchildren gather every year at her grave in the British Cemetery of Buenos Aires. "Instead of chanting the Lord's Prayer in accordance with ancient custom, we sang for the first time a song in Armenian about a bird, which she taught us," explains Rosita. "The people that hear us must think we belong to some strange cult."

The story of the extended family is typical of nearly all the families of Armenian immigrants who settled and met once more, 14,000 kilometers away, in their new Argentine home as early as the first great persecutions at the end of the nineteenth century, en masse after the genocide, during World War II, and a few more even later. There was always a relative who covered the new arrivals' basic needs, who gave them lodging, and might even offer them a job. In the late nineteenth century and the first half of the twentieth, Argentina was an immigrant paradise. Arriving from everywhere, no one was a "stranger." Or else they were all "strangers" and found a way of living together. Argentina was a country *in statu nascendi*, which made assimilation easier.

However, there was a basic difference between Armenians and most other immigrants, with the exception of the Jews: no Armenian came to the River Plate willingly. Most other immigrants left their countries of their own accord, to seek out better living conditions, a new beginning, prosperity. "In the case of our parents it was the genocide and wars that ejected them from their countries."

The Armenian immigrants and their descendants, today a community of 80 to 100 thousand, were refugees, victims of persecutions. In the mixture of peoples that was Buenos Aires, they passed unnoticed. The city received them with open arms as it did all the rest, and the new citizens set themselves up here. Others went to the provinces. The Armenians are still a remarkably closed community, in which others are admitted with difficulty. The reason for this is the great cultural difference between their culture and others, and the difficulty in understanding it that non-Armenians often feel. Little by little, above all in the third and fourth generations, one can notice visible signs of dissolution. Rosita gives the example of her three daughters, whose friends are of Armenian and non-Armenian families. "Fifteen years ago this would have been unthinkable. Before, Armenians only married other Armenians. Today, no one obliges them in any way."

The policy of arranged marriages and the close proximity of the families fostered the Armenian community's unity for decades, as did the church, which is also losing ground. Ever fewer churchgoers attend the Cathedral of St. Gregory the Enlightener, built in the Armenian style opposite the UGAB center. "For young people the $2\frac{1}{2}$-hour Sunday services in ancient Armenian, a language they don't know, or only understand with difficulty, are simply far too long." And the priests are inflexible when it comes to the prescribed rites.

A few years ago a poll among 168 community youngsters between the ages of fifteen and seventeen in Buenos Aires showed that practically all of them—98 percent—considered themselves mainly Argentine. In only apparent contrast to this, an equally overwhelming 91 percent were firmly determined to have their children learn the Armenian language. To be Argentine and feel Armenian is no longer a contradiction. Whereas, the immigrant generation preserved its Armenian identity intact and refused, or was unable, to integrate, the results of the research show that the intermediate generation felt undecided with regard to the two nationalities. For present-day youth this conflict no longer exists.

Rosita gives her class on "Armenian Culture and Tradition" in Spanish. She quickly goes through the national epic, David of Sassoon (Davit in Armenian). In the most flawless Porteño accent she talks about the beauty of the noble and valorous Chandut Chatun, who forever falls in love with David. She tells this with such relish that she herself seems to become the lovely young woman.

Rosita studied Armenian in Armenia. In Argentina this would have been impossible, as there is no chair of Armenian language or culture at any university. The two languages have had practically no influence on each other. Spanish does not possess a single word derived from Armenian—not even the cant of Buenos Aires, *Lunfardo*. Amongst themselves, Argentines of Armenian origin use a kind of jargon. "Whoever really wants to be Armenian has to go to Armenia," declares Rosita, and admits she herself sometimes thinks of going back to the land of her forefathers. Unfortunately, her enthusiasm for Armenian language and culture has so far not led to any of her students going to study Armenian in a university.

Argentine society regards its Armenians with benevolence. They are a capable, hard-working people, according to popular opinion. This carries on unchanged in spite of occasional celebrities with a surname ending in -ian managing to come out in scandalous headlines, thanks to shady deals.

The Armenian community has given Argentina a series of extraordinary personalities in politics, the arts, and medicine. Composer and conductress Alicia Terzián enjoys worldwide recognition. A well-known figure in present-day politics is León Arslanián, for many years the able minister of security in the conflict-torn province of Buenos Aires. Some "prominent" Armenians occasionally drop in on the local Armenian community. "But the majority of them don't actively participate in community affairs," comments Rosita. They belong, like so many other citizens of Armenian origin, to the numerous Argentines whose origins have dissolved in the great melting pot of nationalities.

42

PORTRAIT OF SURVIVAL: REFLECTIONS ON THE LIFE OF VAHRAM S. TOURYAN (PASADENA)

Lorna Touryan Miller

I grew up listening to firsthand accounts of suffering and death associated with the Armenian genocide, which were told and retold by adults that surrounded me in my neighborhood, church and the larger Armenian community. My father lost seven of his nine family members between the years 1915 and 1919, while half of my mother's family was killed during the same years. My parents moved in and out of countries five times before settling in Pasadena, California, in the United States.

On the surface, my father, Vahram Touryan, was the model immigrant citizen. He dedicated his life to serving others as the pastor of a small Armenian church, where he was a social worker, civics teacher, chauffeur, and all-around handyman. He took life seriously and found meaning in his work, as well as comfort and joy in his seven children—which was his way of replacing the seven siblings he lost in the genocide.

The night hours were not as kind to my father. It was common to hear him walking about restlessly in the middle of the night. During these hours he often was tormented by memories from his childhood. He countered these feelings by spending time reading, studying, and praying. Nightmares were also common. I especially remember the time he woke up with his knuckles bleeding from hitting the wall in an apparent conflict with a Turkish captor.

Vahram was born in Darman, in the county of Keghi in the northeastern part of Turkey. They lived a comfortable life in a town that was inhabited entirely by Armenians. My father's father was a successful merchant, who traveled regularly to nearby villages on business. In 1915, on one of his routine tours he was sought out and killed for no apparent reason. At the same time that the news of his death reached the family, Turkish soldiers appeared in the town and confiscated any arms that Armenians owned and took up residence among families. Simultaneously, leaders and influential men from the community were arrested in

the middle of the night, imprisoned, and killed. Younger men were forced to join the army and once on duty were separated into work battalions and then killed. The rest of the townsfolk, mostly women, children, and the elderly, were ordered by the Turkish government to leave their homes to be relocated due to Turkey's involvement in the war. With no further explanations given or sufficient time for them to prepare, the family set out for a journey of uncertain duration and to an unknown destination. Once on the streets, more families joined them until they realized outside their town that the entire population was being deported.

After a day's walk away from towns, Turkish gendarmes informed the deportees that they should leave their valuables in a pile to appease bandits. Not only did Armenians watch the looting of the few belongings they could carry, but they were ambushed several days later. Men opened fire on innocent children, women, and the elderly, many of whom were shot dead, while the rest quickly scattered. Vahram, a child of seven or eight, became separated from his family, fell to the ground, and waited while others ran around him to avoid the bullets. When the shooting stopped and all was quiet, he got up and ran to take cover behind a large rock. He described what happened next: "Before I could catch my breath, a hefty Kurd appeared before me [Kurds in the region were often instigated by Turk leadership to do the looting and killing]. He ordered me to take off my clothes and shoes and hand them over to him. I had no choice but to comply. I sat there dazed and shaken, but grateful that my life had been spared."

While he sat there, Vahram witnessed several incidents that added to his confusion: a middle-aged Armenian man appeared from behind the rock where he had taken cover. Several Kurds rushed toward him, pinned him to the ground, and stabbed him repeatedly. Somehow this large and powerful man managed to break free and, bleeding heavily, started to run. But another man noticed him, took aim with his rifle, and with a single shot, knocked him to the ground. On a rock in the middle of a shallow river, he saw an abandoned infant crying. In retrospect, he wondered if that baby had been placed there in an act of mercy or left in a moment of desperation as the child's mother fled the shots of perpetrators.

Vahram then looked around in search of someone he might recognize. Much to his delight he spotted a classmate, who told him that his whole family had been killed, including his grandfather, who had been protecting him. Uncertain what to do, Vahram suggested that they kneel down and pray, so they said the Lord's Prayer together. Feeling somewhat strengthened, they then got to their feet, and he began searching for his family.

Eventually, Vahram miraculously found the remnants of his family: his mother, two younger brothers, and an older sister, who had been wounded in a struggle with two men. An old woman told them about the fate of another of his brothers, who had been abducted by a Turk while standing over his grandfather's dead body.

Soon, others joined them from their town and once again they began to move in a caravan under the supervision of the gendarmes. Contrary to their hopes that what they had just experienced was an isolated incident, they noticed an increasing number of corpses on the roadway, and over the next few days Vahram witnessed scenes that he would ponder for the rest of his life. For example, he noticed a baby being snatched from his mother's arms and a young girl being pulled from the grasp of her mother. He also recalled an aunt giving birth to her first child out in the open, without a bed or midwife. The next day the women of the caravan urged her to abandon the infant. Vahram watched her wrap the child in rags, place him in a cave, and walk away. But she had taken only a few steps when she returned to fetch her child.

Vahram's security of being with his lost mother and surviving siblings was short-lived. After the caravan of survivors was once again forced on its death march, at a fork in the road his sister was directed one way by a soldier who was intent on taking her as a bride, while the rest of the family followed their fellow villagers, never to be seen again. Fortunately, his sister, who had been placed on the soldier's horse, managed to hold on to Vahram, or otherwise he too would have perished with the rest of the family members. The soldier took the two to his home and presented the sister as his bride and Vahram as a grandson to his own father. Ironically, the solder who had ordered the attack on their townsfolk and now had saved their lives, was later himself killed in a feud. But his family adopted Vahram and his sister in honor of their son. Upon their insistence, the family promised to find their mother and bring her to them. Years later they heard that in fact the mother and some of their siblings were found and separated from the caravan, but on their journey toward them they were killed while resting under a tree.

Vahram with his sister lived in his new "grandfather's" home for two years. He learned to speak Turkish and converted to Islam as a prerequisite for being a family member. The home was comfortable with plenty of food to eat, and soon a genuine bond formed between Vahram and his Turkish sisters. He became a star pupil in his Turkish school. His sister, being older, was less happy. She was keenly aware of their Armenian identity and would often watch numerous caravans of deported Armenians from a distance, pondering the fate of her mother.

While becoming accustomed to life in the Turkish family, several incidents occurred that ignited his conscience, even in his adult years. One event was the brutal killing of a young Armenian girl who was brought to the house from a caravan of deportees. The beautiful girl was ill with dysentery, which became progressively worse. While Vahram's sister nursed the young Armenian girl, the Turkish sisters decided that she would not recover and that she should be killed. They ordered their male servant to perform the task. Vahram recalled the servant taking the young girl a short distance from the house and then hearing what he described as a "heartrending wail" as the servant clubbed her on the head. Vahram was tormented by this incident and could not reconcile his sisters' behavior with his respect for them.

He also recounted another event that haunted him as an adult. Two cousins of his Turkish sisters amused themselves by robbing Armenian caravans that passed through the valley below. One of these young boys returned one day and described how they had found an Armenian mother with an infant in her arms. The elder cousin, along with some friends, killed the mother and then asked the younger Turkish boy if he wanted to kill the baby. This lad told Vahram how he kept striking the infant, but hit as he might, the baby continued to cry and moan, refusing to fall silent.

Vahram also remembers seeing orphans from the caravans who had somehow made their way to his town. He specifically remembered two emaciated siblings gathering a bundle of sticks, probably to sell for a loaf of bread. An older Turkish boy chased them, stole the bundle from their hands. Vahram ran after the Turkish fellow, took back the bundle of sticks, and joyfully returned it to the weeping and distraught orphans.

After the defeat of the Turks in October of 1918, the well-publicized plight of survivors brought millions of dollars of aid and relief personnel to Turkey. Orphanages were either established or reopened in different parts of the country. Hearing about these developments, Vahram's sister planned their escape from the Turkish home. He, however, wasn't convinced that they should leave and resisted her efforts. Finally, the two left with hopes of being reunited with family members and entered an orphanage operated by American missionaries in a nearby city.

In the orphanage, Vahram was once again in an Armenian community, where he relearned his mother language and converted to his childhood faith. There he continued his education and learned a trade and, when the orphanages were asked to leave the country in 1922, most of them were taken to countries in the Middle East. Vahram first went to Greece and then to Beirut, Lebanon, where he was reunited with his sister. Tragically, his only surviving sister died of pneumonia, leaving him all alone at age sixteen without a family, relatives, or a country. The death of his sister was a blow to Vahram. With her parting, he lost all ties to his past.

My father remained in Beirut, married another survivor, and settled in Jerusalem. His reconciliation with the loss of his seven siblings was to have seven children of his own. He became a pastor among Armenians and dedicated his life to comforting others.

Reconciliation for survivors of the Armenian genocide of 1915 has been a struggle for nearly ninety years. In the face of official denial by the Turkish government, survivors have had to seek their own personal reconciliation. For my father, this was a lifelong process of healing and re-creating a new life.

Perhaps the healing first began in the orphanage, when children began to share their stories with each other and discovered that they were not alone in their confusion. It was there that they could piece together what had happened to their nation. But it wasn't until my father married and had his own children that he grasped the scope of the tragedy of his past on the one hand, and at the same time became comforted through his new family.

My father cried easily, especially when we went to the cemetery the day after Easter, as was the custom, to visit the dead. Out of a family of eleven his sister was the only one who had a grave. At her graveside, my courageous and brave father became instantly vulnerable. Her burial stood symbolically for the rest of his family members, who had died unceremoniously.

It was inevitable that some day I would return to my parents' stories and try to understand what really happened. While raising my own two children and taking a break from my profession, I began a project with my husband that resulted in 100 interviews with survivors, most of whom were living in Southern California, and the eventual publication of a book. What began as a ten-week interview with my parents turned into a fifteen-year immersion in survivor stories that challenged my belief in the goodness of humanity and led to many melancholic hours of transcribing, as well as a lingering sense of hopelessness in the possibility of justice.

It was a particularly difficult task because my own two children were the ages of those whose stories I heard day in and day out. I was tormented by the thought of my children going through such horror and tragedy. The years I spent on this project was due to my obsession with an injustice I could not explain. It was also a way of understanding my parents and my people as a nation, scattered all over the world, adjusting to cultures foreign to them and losing parts of their identity to the host country.

We each have had to find personal reconciliation in the absence of the possibility of social reconciliation, which demands telling the truth of what happened—an acknowledgment by the perpetrators who to this day deny vehemently that this was an intentional genocide. Armenians' obsession with the genocide, now several generations later, is due to the fact that there has never been closure to this inhumanity and, therefore, no healing for either nation.

Yet I have become aware that, despite our resolve that "never again" shall genocide be tolerated in the world, three additional genocides have occurred in the twentieth century with the full knowledge of the rest of the world.

My husband and I first wrote the book, *Survivors: An Oral History of the Armenian Genocide* (Berkeley – Los Angelos and London, 1993), as a way of allowing the stories to tell the truth. Now, we have turned our attention to the Rwanda genocide, where much healing and reconstruction of society is still a critical need. Just as my father was orphaned at age eight with thousands of others, so in Rwanda we have connected with a group of orphans who head households of siblings under impoverished circumstances. Unlike in the case of Armenians, where there was an incredible outpouring of humanitarian help after the genocide, Rwanda, a small and poor country, is already abandoned by the world.

Upon reflection, my passion for the work that I have done on the Armenian genocide, and the work that I do now in Rwanda, is a way to counter the injustice done to my father and to thank those selfless and courageous people who went to the aid of Armenian orphans. They housed them in orphanages, fed and clothed them, as well as giving them an education and life skills to make them self-sufficient. Most important, however, these men and women gave the children hope and the start of a new life by loving them through their actions during a phase of their young lives when they were most vulnerable.

43

GRANDE DAME OF THE MYTHS: ARCHEOLOGIST NINA JIDEJIAN (BEIRUT)

Huberta von Voss

When Nina Jidejian sits down at her age-old typewriter in the morning, the sun rises over Beirut. Way up in the eastern hills of the elegant suburb of Yarze, the dainty eighty-year-old sits at her desk as on a throne, from which she can look out on the whole of her kingdom through the panoramic window: directly north of Beirut is the fabulous seaport of Byblos, which, across the Mediterranean, smiles at its southern sisters, Sidon and Tyre, whose ports, just like Beirut, used to receive conquerors and merchants with open arms. Whether Egyptians, Assyrians, Babylonians, Persians, Romans, Caliphs, or Crusaders—they all left their imprint on the Levantine coast. In the midst of all this, at a dignified

distance from the zestful sea, beyond the mountains of Mount Lebanon, rises imperial Roman Baalbek, former Heliopolis, the City of the Sun, amidst the orchards and fertile fields of the Bekaa plain. Throughout this region soaked with history, archeologist Nina Jidejian, who in forty years of tireless work has produced an irreproachable body of knowledge on numerous finds in this Cedar State, reigns supreme. Since the late 1960s, she has written twenty books on archeological deposits of antiquity, and anyone that sees her vivacious light brown eyes will perceive that the energetic grande dame of the history of ancient Phoenicia intends writing many more books.

No one but she knows how she manages her meticulous research amid the maze of papers, photographs, and folders arrayed piled high around her splendid ancient typewriter. Amongst these stacks of papers and tubes of gum, one discerns that here, as in the manufactories of yore, everything is handmade; and it is precisely this very modest style of working that Nina Jidejian best characterizes, although any visitor arriving at her bungalow at the end of a private road lined by conifers and olive trees might well imagine something else. Yet, instead of the comfort appropriate for the widow of a doctor, a famous surgeon, guests are received with the cordial but austere modesty of a couple who were not concerned with material things. "I like to travel light," she stresses, "and when Yervant was alive it was the same." The reasons come from way back.

As children, both were acquainted with what losing wealth and prestige meant to their families. Yervant, born in Aleppo in 1906, was the third son of a highly respected family of businessmen without whose knowledge and influence no deal was carried out in the legendary souk of that city, which was still part of the Ottoman Empire. Yet, when the government of the Young Turks commenced its persecution of politically and economically influential Armenians, the prosperous existence of the Jidejians collapsed like a house of cards. His brother's political activity in the Dashnak party also led to Yervant's father's arrest, and he was sentenced to death.

The mother, who had already lost two infant daughters, fled with a minimum of luggage, taking her three little sons to Beirut. There, like so many other Armenian refugees, she rented a tiny room near the sea, sold her life insurance, and attempted to obtain her husband's freedom through middlemen. Four years later she achieved it, having sold all the family property; and Yervant's father arrived in Beirut with just a piece of cloth wrapped round him. Under his arm he brought a charcoal drawing another prisoner had made for him of a photograph of Yervant. He felt special affection for this son who, at the age of three, was seriously ill with typhus and got better only when his mother, very religious, made a pilgrimage to Jerusalem. Arriving to witness the new poverty of his family, the father, morally destroyed, died soon after in the arms of his already teenager son.

Yervant kept the drawing which, today, modestly framed, hangs at Yarze, as well as the deep conviction that money as such is of no value, and health is much more important than anything else. He decided to study medicine, and so his profession was a vocation right from the start. "Yervant also made a great name for himself in research. More than anything, he wanted to be useful in his life, not to become famous but for people to respect him," says Nina Jidejian. Both were idealists, Yervant as a healer, and Nina in recovering the past from oblivion.

She met her husband, eighteen years her senior, on arriving in Beirut to visit her elder sister. Beautiful Mary got married in the early 1940s with the member of a well-to-do Maronite family. It was a time of awakening. Lebanon had declared independence in 1943, with which the French protectorate came to an end. Nina, at home anywhere and nowhere, took a great liking to the pulsating

Levantine city and the handsome surgeon, who treated many of his patients for free. After spending their childhood on the east coast of the United States, in Boston, Nina and Mary spent their teenage years in Teheran, where their father, a businessman, had settled. Mihran Nazaretian's family had had close links with Persia for a long time, as in their old home, not far from Aleppo, they had been honorary consuls of the Shah. The prosperous Nazaretians had been one of the foremost families there, and every time the vali traveled to Aintab, he stayed with them. "That was a great honor in those days," remarks Nina, with a certain pride. Nevertheless, she is not one of those people that spend their lives regretting the loss of trivialities. "We lost all our property, but what's property? Money buys neither health nor dignity."

Dignity, according to the disciplined archeologist, who only began her studies in the fourth decade of her life at the American University of Beirut after many years of social engagement, means not only independence from material things, but a very special link with cultural identity and spiritual autonomy. "I possess a very strong sense of being Armenian, without ever having spoken good Armenian." She knows many of the approximately 200,000 members of the Armenian community in Lebanon criticize her for never having carried out any study on Armenia, but Nina allows no one to influence her choice of subjects. Presently the prolific authoress, who has received many decorations, among others the Order of Mesrop Mashtoz (named in honour of the inventor of the Armenian alphabet) from the Catholicos in 1999, the highest national Order of the Cedar of Lebanon (Commander rank) in 2000 from the president of the republic, and in 2001 the highest Lebanese literary award, the Prix Saïd Akl, is embarked on writing a biography of her husband and also a book on archeology for children. The latter work is designed to serve as a means for her only daughter Denise's four children, who live in France, to discover the rich world of the myths of antiquity. She knows that, when interest in history is awakened, there are no national barriers. Thus she is making secret preparations for her grandchildren, who may soon want to find out a lot more about the history, legends, and myths of the Armenians, and is diligently studying Armenian with an old school textbook. "But don't let on," she jokes, "so that it's a surprise."

44

A PERFECTLY NORMAL STORY: ALFRED AND OPHELIA MOURADIAN (BERLIN)

Jochen Mangelsen

His back a little bent, face showing age blotches, he is seated in front of me at a small café in Yerevan. From his village in Karabakh he has brought a bottle of mulberry brandy. He himself does not take alcohol, but for a visitor from Germany it is apt. He drinks tea and, amid the clouds of a strong cigarette, Varo begins his story about a man whom, in fact, I should know about a lot better than him: Alfred Mouradian, my father-in-law. "I would have snuffed it, was almost dead," he describes his suffering as a Soviet soldier in a German prisoner-of-war camp. "Mr. Mouradian got me out. He rescued so many of us. He was a good

man." His eyes fill with tears, but the old man is not ashamed. And those tears reflect the image of a man I was familiar with until the day he died but, as I was later to discover, who was pretty much a stranger to me.

I met the family in the 1960s. Actually it was the elder daughter I met, a young Armenian woman from Berlin wearing a self-made Chanel-type costume, a student, an able talker with a biting wit. She introduced me to her family. Her mother, Ophelia, would cook a tasty garmir pilaf every so often, and tell old stories; her father, Alfred, frequently away on business trips to the Middle East, amused himself with his favorite pastime, comparative linguistics, and he was a respectable dabbler in this area. He never told old stories … A perfectly normal family.

A perfectly normal family? It was only later, when I began researching the two of them for a historical novel, that I got to understand what a perfectly normal Armenian family means, with the normal destiny of any Armenian family. Alfred Mouradian was from Amassia, in the Ottoman Empire. His ancestors, among them an old line of German Swiss, were mill builders and grain merchants. As a child he lived eight happy years, after which nothing was ever the same again: through the window he saw below an unfortunate crowd of defenceless women and children that soldiers were expelling from the town, among them a boy with a red school cap on his head: his best friend. Alfred saw the cap bobbing around on the horizon. This was his image of the genocide. His mother was able to get away to Constantinople with her sons, Alfred and Alfons, but for almost all the other relatives and, finally also for his father, there was no exit. The latter carried on taking care of the business and the Armenian orphanage. There he was found and shot. The family traveled on to Berlin, where they had to find emergency accommodation in a basement, but they were alive and in good health.

Ophelia Nazarian should have been the spoilt daughter of a landowner in the Urmia region. Her grandfather Enakolopian, a general in the Persian army, with the honorary title of Parvis Khan, tried to prevent his daughter Aroussiak from marrying the intellectual Artashes Nazarian, but in vain. When World War I broke out and, on the other side of the Turkish–Persian border, the massacres began, Ophelia was six. What followed was an Odyssey, an escape full of adventures with ever new dangers: Yerevan, Tiflis, Yesentuki, Kislavodsk, once more Yerevan, Baku, Moscow. Who held power, and where? Who persecuted whom? If the Russian Revolution succeeded, would we survive the famine? Would Armenian independence hold out? Ophelia's father published a periodical at the time. It was increasingly banned, and he had to go into hiding. He tried to carry on publishing it with another title, and was arrested. Even as a deputy in the first parliament of Armenia he only briefly found a safe place. And Ophelia? She was an adventuress who lived through all those events, which she later narrated with such gusto. She had the energy her mother lacked. As a young child she already took care of her brothers and sisters. She sold newspapers for her father, and made coffee for people at the health resort in the park. If necessary, she peddled Chinese silk her father got from somewhere. Finally, Moscow. That was her place. Here she could dance! She began learning Armenian folk dances, and was invited to perform in St. Petersburg, as the crowning point of her teenage career. But there was no question of staying on the banks of the Moskva. So, Berlin.

Somewhere along the Spree River, perhaps at an Armenian community picnic, they looked in each other's eyes longer than the usual. Alfred had set up a wholesale cigarette business to feed his family and finance his studies in political science. For years Ophelia had been sewing silk underwear and night garments in a sewing establishment, and then she ran a simple soup kitchen for students. Both of them went in for dramatics, and this is the way a little novel-like romance started up. Will you ...? And yes, they got married, had two daughters, a perfectly normal family. Or wasn't it?

The death brigades had ravaged his family, but he survived. And what motivated Alfred Mouradian was to devote his life to the Armenian cause: to shake the public into awareness, inform the people, demand recognition of the genocide, organize Armenian life in the diaspora. He had been active for quite some time in the Armenian Academic Union of 1860, and the German–Armenian Society, whose revival in the early 1970s was in no small degree due to his efforts. And, needless to say, he was active in the Berlin community all his life.

After the war Alfred had to start from scratch again. For a few years they lived in Teheran. On returning to Berlin in the 1950s, he immediately went back to his Armenian affairs. The communities of the prewar years were orphaned, dissolved as legal associations, and inactive, and he decided to revive these bodies. By the time of the fiftieth anniversary of the genocide, this was already under way in Berlin and, shortly after, the same happened in Hamburg. Alfred Mouradian was then one of the founders of the Zentralverband der armenischen Vereinigungen in Deutschland (ZAD, Central Union of Armenian Associations in Germany). The Armenians in the country were to have an official voice. In this he was ever more the initiator and *spiritus rector*, but personally he always preferred remaining in the background.

Time and again he connected German scientists with Beirut or Jerusalem and with the catholicosate of Cilicia. In this way he established an important informal link for personal and institutional communication between the communities at home and abroad, universities, churches, and firms, and through this network obtained, among other things, a line of scholarship for young Armenian theologists. These were then able to study in postwar Germany and also carry out their priestly functions there for the first time.

In the meantime, Ophelia was a little eclipsed by Alfred. She helped in the communities, but dreamt of having a career of her own, and of missed chances. An exile: "If only we'd been able to stay in Moscow ..."

One chapter in particular remains in the dark; the scientific research has not been carried out. There are two doctoral theses being prepared on the subject: Dancing with the Wolf. Alfred and Alfons Mouradian were already engaged, at the beginning of World War II, in a risky game with great personal involvement. Together with other German Armenians they were called upon by the Ministry of the East to locate Soviet Armenian soldiers in the prison camps. With growing impatience Alfred urged his helpers on. There was no time to lose. Each hesitation, each day lost, would cost lives. This is how he saved thousands from dying of hunger and disease. Not infrequently it was Ophelia who first comforted the youths, and then set a good plate of home-made food before them. At that period she had already had her first daughter, and she often felt left aside by her husband, who was mainly concerned with the prisoners. The men became members of the German army's Armenian Legion. This way they at least had a second chance to survive the war. Many of these 40,000 legionaries were later able to go to the U.S.A. with the help of the Mouradian brothers, and others to France; but the majority were sent back against their will to the Soviet Union, where the severest punishments awaited them as "traitors." Nevertheless, the odd exception, if he was lucky, went back to Armenia or Karabakh, like Varo, whom I met at the café.

Facets of an unknown life. Nearly sixty years after the war ended, over a cup of tea and a cigarette, this old man added a couple of colorful new brushstrokes to the family portrait. "Mrs. Ophelia gave us courage at that time, when everything was so black. A strong woman. And Mr. Mouradian … I have to thank him that I survived." Way past eighty years old, back a little hunched, he rises, kisses my daughter's hand, and boards the first minibus. We'll drink the mulberry brandy later, to his health.

Part III

Symbolic Places

45

SWAN SONG IN THE HOLY LAND: THE ARMENIAN QUARTER IN JERUSALEM

Joerg Bremer

Jerusalem remains the second Armenia. One can easily forget its all-pervasive background of faith and religion. Secularization, persecution, political and economic problems are the burning issues of today, which even threaten to mask the obvious. Also, there is no sense in limiting the meaning of Jerusalem merely to mosaics in monasteries surviving from Byzantium's age of splendor, or the tenth-century stone crosses on the outer wall of the Convent of St. James, weathered in the intervening ages. Ask any Armenian in Jerusalem, and they'll say, "I'm here because I belong here. After Armenia, this is my home."

More to the point, with their pride in belonging to the most ancient Christian people, the Armenians of the Holy Land say Armenia's Christian identity is nurtured by the fragrant scent flask of holy events, as Gregory of Nicaea once put it. Thus one perceives that Armenia could not exist without Jerusalem. Bishop Aris Shivanian, Patriarch Torkom Manoogian's wise adviser, sets his roots in the origins, in the long breath of history, and remains only briefly in the present, as though already seeing the Armenian community of Jerusalem as a thing of the past. Meanwhile, this weary patriarch watches over his inheritance, which seems to swallow him up, a child of the deportation born in the desert near Baghdad in 1919. Manoogian lives in history's books, priests' prayers, and poetry of the classical period.

Liturgy is the holy language of timelessness, turning the daily routine into magic, and pointing to life after death. It spreads out, also, in the grandiose nave of the cathedral of St. James, "the Brother of the Lord" and first bishop of the city, which was built in the early fourth century by the founding father, Eusebius. But a national liturgy also leads the Armenian community once a year along the asphalt and dirt of the streets to the Armenian cemetery on Mount Zion. The patriarch, shuffling along with tearful eyes, leads the procession, as though heading the woeful march of deportees year after year, yet again to suffer, die, and hope.

In this way it is legitimate to speak of the closeness of Armenia and "Palestine," and of its inheritance of Jerusalem. Time and again, usually over centuries, Armenia and Jerusalem were parts of the same empires: Cyrus the Persian's, Alexander the Great's, the Roman and, finally, the Ottoman. This fostered attachment. To this may be added the intense correspondence between Dionysius of Alexandria and Meruzanes of Armenia in the year 254, or that of St. Euthymius, an Armenian bishop of Mitilene, with whom there occurred an expansion of the desert monks' "spiritual field" from Egypt to the Holy Land in the second half of the fifth century. This Euthymius was the teacher of St. Theodosius and St. Sabas, father of the "liturgy of Jerusalem," which has also endured in the Western churches down to the present. Armenian, Syrian, and Greek hermits established monastic life modeled on the "laura" (monastery) of the anchorites who lived in the solitude of the roads, to the brotherhood behind cloister walls, first of all, just as protection for "beardless" young monks and the elderly, who would have met their death in their caves and huts. Euthymius is the typical anchorite that must go through monastic school before taking to the desert in order to avoid the hierarchy of the cities.

After the Persian invasion of 614, Greeks and Armenians seemed to be the main partners in the reconstruction. The former Armenian Metropolitan became the Patriarch. Omiads and Abasids both guaranteed the rights of the churches. The Arabization and the retreat of Greek were much faster than the conversion of the population to Islam, which happened very gradually. In this sense it is hardly a case of tolerance in its modern sense: the Muslim lords who came from the desert needed the Christian citizens to administer their empire for them through their communes, and to build them their first mosques.

Under the Fatimids after 972, the Armenians enjoyed special protection, and were promoted to high office at the Egyptian court. History records four grand viziers. Until two centuries ago, the Patriarchate extended from Jerusalem to Egypt—the Holy Land within its ancient frontiers.

The Frankish crusaders considered the Armenians almost contemptible foreigners at the beginning, the same as Greeks, Jews, and heathens; but for political reasons an alliance was soon formed between the Armenian king of Cilicia and the European lords. In this way it was possible for the Armenians of Jerusalem, Gaza, Cesarea, Acre, and Tyre to maintain their position and, to a certain degree, establish links which the noble families reinforced through marriages. In this connection Queen Melisenda, the daughter of King Baldwin II, must be mentioned, but above all, the Armenian princess Morphia, "a woman of great wisdom, experienced in affairs of state, who succeeded in excess of the limitations of her sex," as Bishop William of Tyre put it. After her husband Fulk of Anjou's accidental death, she managed the state for the son of both of them, but also as a builder of cities and a patroness. This Armenian woman is to be thanked for St. Anna's church in Jerusalem, on the traditional site of Mary's place of birth. When the church was consecrated in 1140, Melisenda's youngest sister became the abbess of the church and cloister.

Despite the closeness of Franks and Armenians, the Eastern church evaded the prohibition of the Muslims, who very soon recovered power. Saladin expelled the Western Christians but, following the conquest of Jerusalem in 1187, he allowed the 2,000 Armenians of the city to carry on living there, and recognized the rights of Greeks and Armenians to the holy shrines. In 1300, the Armenian king Hetum II, allied with the Mongols, reigned in Jerusalem for a brief time. He financed the restoration of the Armenian churches after the Turkish attacks of previous years, and brought stability back to the city. The Ottomans ruled Armenia and the Holy Land from 1516 till their defeat in World War I. There were Armenians all over their empire. The Jerusalem community sent a vicar as ambassador to the government in Constantinople, and envoys to every corner of the empire to talk about Jerusalem's fame and encourage people to make pilgrimages there, or for money and luxuries.

Thanks to this, Jerusalem became the repository of Armenian art. From Bombay and Crimea, from Isfahan and Cracow, Armenians sent treasures, embroideries from Smyrna and Constantinople, manuscripts and liturgical lamps for St. James's cathedral. The chronicles of pilgrims, who endured all sorts of rigors, are impressive. "But a journey to Jerusalem begets wealth in Heaven," says an invitation to pilgrims of 1727. "Confess thy sins, write thy will, abandon thy evil ways, be thou modest and silent." In the meantime, the "Armenian quarter," in which all these pilgrims were lodged, grew. The cloistral city turned into one of burghers under the patriarch, who, as monarch and superior, administered justice and property. In 1833, the Patriarchate opened the first print shop in Jerusalem. Armenian tile-makers constantly replaced the majolicas of the Muslim Dome of the Rock, and stonecutters provided similar ornaments for the inside of the German church of the Ascension on the Augusta Victoria. Till the present day there are Armenian photographers in the Old Town, who opened the first studio in the Holy Land in 1857.

With the fall of the Ottoman Empire and the Armenian genocide put in motion by the Young Turks, contact was broken between the central Armenian region and the Holy Land. At the same time, Jerusalem became a magnet for survivors. Up to 20,000 Armenians lived in Palestine during the mandate. A similar number that fled when the communist Soviet regime harassed their homeland likewise found shelter in the Holy Land. However, this began to give way little by little after the foundation of the state of Israel in 1948. Eight thousand Armenians resettled in Lebanon, which seemed politically more stable. The Six Days' War in 1967 unleashed new emigrations. In 1990, there were still some 4,000 Armenians living in Israel, three quarters of them in Jerusalem. After the first intifada and the disorders starting in autumn 2000, the number shrank yet further. Today, the Armenian presence in Jerusalem is calculated at less than 2,000. Altogether there are today only five Armenian families still living in their traditional homes in West Jerusalem.

This skeleton community is not facing only political insecurity and economic collapse. Legally, these citizens in remote areas of Israel count as Palestinians, and this is how the Israeli authorities treat them. They are considered a security risk, and have all the difficulties in entering and leaving the country that the Arabs must endure. Besides, the Armenians are pained at Israel's official negation of their genocide, even though historians, the press, and the radio have been airing the subject since long ago. But above all, the Armenians, used to mobility and internationalism in the borderless expanse of the Ottoman Empire, now find themselves, in Israel, cut off from communities from Beirut to Teheran.

The once proud Armenian quarter in the Old City of Jerusalem is now in decay. More than anyone else it is Israelis who use the main street to get from the Jaffa Gate to their Jewish quarter. Graffiti hostile to the Armenians or the genocide appear in ever-increasing numbers on the walls of houses. In the diverse "peace negotiations" between Israelis and Palestinians, the quarter was disposed of without the least consideration. In one division of the city it is to be adjudicated to the Israeli part, whereby it would be separated from the other Christian quarters of the Old City. The patriarchs rose against this in unison, but the quarter, with its large properties, is in danger. While the community owns around 16 percent of the Old City, it is only 3 percent of the population. Above all it is the Jewish quarter, bursting at the seams, that would be interested in purchasing the Armenians' land.

However, on the Western side it is also the Armenians—after the Greek Orthodox Church—who are the wealthiest proprietors. In this way, the patriarch is frequently pressured to accept lavish offers in order to replenish empty coffers. And hush-hush deals in real estate take place. Whereas the Catholic Church cannot sell property or lease it on a long-term basis without Rome's consent, the Armenian and Greek patriarchs can dispose of theirs as they wish. The Armenian community, politically weak, is in danger of becoming a tool of Israeli interests. Without too much trouble the Israeli army was able to take over land in 2002, and put up a border fence against Bethlehem, at the expense of Armenian property. The land in the valley opposite the gate of Zion, where Judas is supposed to have taken his own life after the betrayal, has been Armenian since 1350. There are Armenian graves there, and a church from the time of the Crusades. In spite of this, Israeli bulldozers removed that earth so as to carry out projects of their own. The Patriarchate seems a mere spectator. It presented the city with no building plan of its own, in order to carry out its own projects.

The road of commemoration of the genocide leads from St. James's cathedral to the Armenian cemetery on Mount Zion. At the entrance there is a half-built Armenian church, a ruin of decay and forgetfulness. It is already 30 years since the Israelis revoked the building permit. The city declared it had other plans for that historical complex. Instead, the city claims all that is needed is to present a new application. Yet, what good would a new building permit be? Money is certainly in short supply, and possibly hope is too.

46

LAST STOP: THE DESERT OF DEIR-ES-ZOR

Nouritza Matossian

Footprints on the Mind

Dust rises up from the flatness all around us twisting into sand ropes and spiral columns. I drift on the threshold between sleep and waking. The sun glares, high up. I stare into the dust again. My eyelids fall shut. It has been this way for many hours. I am very aware of the limits of my own body. Four strangers in a Mercedes are driving me across kilometers of the Syrian desert. I have no picture of our destination. It is a name. To my countrymen it has a breath of disaster. Let me try it on you. Have you heard this name?

Der Zor. Some say the correct name is Deir-es-Zor. Dry, isn't it? If you have heard it, chances are you are from the Middle East or Syria or you know the Middle East. It won't send a shiver up your spine. Unless you are Armenian.

My companions are gentlemen in city clothes. They too have fallen silent. Not only because of the noonday heat, dust. We are all hushed by the pictures that are going through our minds. We look out of the car windows at the straight flat line of the horizon. Reddish dry earth with a few scrubby thorns here and there, it goes on and on unchanging. But I know that each one of us is seeing different images. People in rags, women with their heads tied up in kerchiefs, children, and old people in a long staggering line, shuffling along as far as the eye can see. I close my eyes. They appear closer. Dark eyes here. A child dragged by a mother there. Only when I open my eyes, the close-up disappears and I see the line again weaving into the distance.

It's nearly noon. We will drive another three hours at least. Along the straight road, desert creeps up on either side. Black-robed barefoot women pad across the stony earth carrying baskets high on their heads. A sign announces Al Raqqa. Cement buildings, dirty streets, shabby shopfronts and dusty black-clothed people winding between cars and bicycles. Wagons pulled by mules drag vegetables. Al Raqqa, Al Raqqa. What was it I heard about this place? My friend's father was found here as a little boy. I never knew his story until after he died. I had the chance to ask him but we avoided the subject like an obscenity. I am too late. Several decades too late. He always told jokes and we laughed. When he was near death the horrors returned and he would run away from home to roam the streets.

I have come to Syria to find the route along which my relatives walked.

Aleppo, September 10, 1916

About Herrera is a small locality north of Meskene on the bank of the Euphrates. It is the most complete desert. On a small hill 200 meters from the river are confined 240 Armenians under the surveillance of two gendarmes without pity, who leave them to die of hunger in most atrocious sufferings. The scenes which I witnessed surpass all horrors. Near the place where the carriage stops, women who had not seen me arriving, were searching in the dung of horses barley for seeds not yet digested to feed on. I gave them some bread. They threw themselves on it like dogs dying of hunger, took it voraciously into their mouths with hiccups and epileptical tremblings. Instantly, informed by one of them, 240 persons or rather hungry wolves, who had nothing to eat for seven days, precipitated themselves towards me from the hill, extending their emaciated arms, imploring with tears and cries for a piece of bread. It was mostly women, children and about a dozen old people.

(August Bernau, Aleppo Agent of the Vacuum Oil Company of New York, September 10, 1916, U.S. State Department Record Group 59, 867.4016/302)

Unknown Relatives

I have come to Aleppo to give a talk in my mother tongue, Armenian, on my biography of the American Armenian artist: *Black Angel, The Life of Arshile Gorky.* Armenian descendants of the deportees fill the hall and listen with emotion to the story of an Armenian survivor who became a leading painter in America. From the stage I look at faces from my father's birthplace, Aintab. How many unknown relatives are here?

But for an accident of fate I might have grown up in Aleppo myself. I would not have written this book which was a result of my migration to England and education, far away from my ancestors.

I walk past high stone walls through the narrow streets of the old city the next day, the seventeenth-century Armenian church, the bazaar, wondering how it had looked in 1915, overrun with exhausted refugees from the marches.

"Euphrates, Graveyard of the Armenians"

Aleppo was the destination of the deportees from western provinces. The Young Turks' official plan of 1915 was to deport and exterminate 2 million Armenians by outright massacre in the six Armenian provinces Sivas, Diyarbekir, Harput, Erzerum, Bitlis, Van, and the heavily populated area of Trabzon. Those who had not been killed in their hometowns and villages were deported on forced marches over the Amanus Mountains and by trains to the deserts of Mesopotamia, crammed into cattle trucks without sanitation and forced to pay.

Around the railway stations chains of concentration camps were organized by the Ottoman government for hundreds of thousands of deportees, as well along the Euphrates toward Deir-es-Zor. In charge of the operation was the official Abdulhad Nuri. The Armenian victims were divided between twenty-five concentration camps located in the north of Aleppo and mostly along the line of the Euphrates. Turkish death camps like Auschwitz, Bergen-Belsen … Their secret objective was total extermination.

In these death camps, without food and water, exposed to extremes of heat, the starving, dehydrated deportees would die of hunger, if not of typhus and cholera. The German Consul in Aleppo, Walter Rössler, quoted a deportation Commissar, "We want Armenia without Armenians." Aleppo, the Syrian center for commerce, where the German Baghdad railway met with the Syrian French network, was the hub of the German military transportation. The Turco-German Alliance had resulted in the modernization of the Turkish Army under Baron von der Goltz, who in 1915 became the Commander in Chief of Turkish forces in Mesopotamia. Some of his soldiers later became senior *Wehrmacht* officers in Hitler's army carrying out the Jewish Holocaust in Russia.

> There are special wagons on the Baghdad railway, designed for the transport of goats and sheep, separated in the center in such a way that there is a lower and an upper level, so that animals can be loaded on two levels. Into these wagons the deportees were stuffed, like animals. It is impossible to stand, they can only sit, and even that is hardly possible, because the wagons are so overcrowded. Men, women and children, the able-bodied and the sick, all together are transported in this way for days. The sick die en route, while pregnant women give birth. What I learnt here in details, I had been told already previously, in Eskisehir and Konya. But although this report left a profound impression, it was overshadowed by all the dreadful things I saw and heard later on.

> (Ernst Christoffel, *From Dark Depths: Experiences of a German Missionary in Turkish Kurdistan during the War Years 1916–1918*. Berlin-Friedenau: Christliche Blindenmission im Orient e.V., 1921, p. 10)

Arriving in Aleppo on foot, some of the lucky ones with money settled for a time before moving on to safety, but for the hundreds of thousands it was the final stop before an interminable journey to Deir-es-Zor. Thousands who had tramped here in the hope of surviving were robbed, raped, tortured and sold as slaves along the way.

The Ghost Sister

A niggling memory of a family story now fell into place. My great-aunt, then a girl, had been captured by the Bedouin. She was spotted many years later by her relatives in the market. Her face stamped in blue tattoos and dressed in Bedouin robes, she was selling goats. They called out her Armenian name. She turned around. They tried to get her back, but she refused to leave her children behind and melted into the crowds.

My own mother was named Satenig after a beautiful queen. Years later I found out that my grandmother had had another daughter before her. This beautiful little girl also had golden hair and a pale complexion. Grandmother Hadjigul was a young woman with a small son and daughter, forced to march from their home in Kayseri, under the eye of the Turkish soldiers. My grandfather was in the Turkish Army being bastinadoed. Grandmother marched with thousands of others. She kept her daughter beside her. Every morning she dipped her hand in the ashes of the cold fire and rubbed the girl's face black, to hide her beauty from the Turkish soldiers. One evening the child squatted on the ground playing in the dirt. She heard horse's hooves. Above her a Turkish officer on horseback asked her name. All the warnings she had received were for this day. "They'll kill you. Cut you up. Those 'zaptiehs' will murder you … " She was dumbstruck. Then she ran and ran. That night on her makeshift bed of rugs she lay in a fever. Her golden hair was drenched with perspiration. Her green eyes, like my mother's, never shut. "She never said a word." Mother said, "She did not recover. She died of fright!" Each time she heard her name did she think of Satenig, her ghost sister too? Mother gave birth to me on April 24, the day Armenians commemorate the genocide.

A Pilgrimage with Strangers

My hosts picked me up at 4 a.m. to take me on a pilgrimage to the shrine of Deir-es-Zor, where thousands of Armenians had been forced to march. In an air-conditioned car we drive across these same burning steppes where the caravans had marched. When we reach the lush Euphrates River the car pulls up. We splash our faces with cool water. But the caravans had not stopped to drink water. They had been herded into the water to be drowned. Next to me the Armenian doctor says, "There were so many thousands of bloated bodies in the water that the local people refused to eat fish for years."

Aleppo, June 5, 1915

American Consul Jackson concluded, "It is without doubt a carefully planned scheme to thoroughly extinguish the Armenian race."

(Jackson to Morgenthau, Aleppo, United States Official Documents on the Armenia Genocide, Vol. 1, 1993)

Deir-es -Zor Church

I enter a new church, dedicated to the two million dead Armenians. Downstairs in a yellow stone shrine filled with light, bones of the dead lay on a bed of sand under glass, sanctified by seven altars. A column from the center pierces the ceiling emerging through the open dome in which the sunlight gleamed in a brilliant shaft. It seems clean and impersonal. How many uncles and cousins had I lost? I recall the stories I had blocked out in childhood. Complicated emotions well up in me. In the cave-like museum a power strike makes it impossible to see the display. By torch and candlelight we peer at photographs on the wall, black-and-white images. A terrified young girl with a baby in her arms ran across an interminable desert. Starved naked women, with breasts hanging from their ribs looked strangely dignified. Each time I shine my torch in the dark, it picks out another horror. I am hit by waves of nausea. Swarthy Turkish soldiers swagger alongside severed heads of their Armenian victims arranged in a pyramid. I recognize historic photographs credited to the German sounding name, Armin T. Wegner. They now hang in Deir-es-Zor, the very place where they had been photographed, eighty-five years ago. How come a German and an ally of the Turks had lingered at these unbearable scenes to take pictures that dignified these naked victims of atrocity?

A Just German

In April 1915, following the military alliance of Germany and Turkey, Armin T. Wegner, a volunteer, was sent to the Middle East as a member of the German Sanitary Corps. As second-lieutenant in the retinue of Field Marshal von der Goltz, commander of the Sixth Ottoman Army in Turkey, he traveled through Asia Minor on the route of the Armenia death march.

> "The roads are lined with the famished and suffering Armenian refugees, like a weeping hedge that begs and screams and from which rise a thousand pleading hands. We go by, our souls full of shame …
>
> I have just returned this very minute, from a walk around the camp: hunger, disease, and desperation shout out at me. Everywhere the smell of faeces and decay. From a tent the laments of a dying woman. A mother, who thought the dark violet badges on my uniform were those of the Medical Corps, came toward me with outstretched hands.

Taking me for a doctor, she clung to me with all her strength, to me, unhappy me, who had neither medicine nor bandages, for it was forbidden to help her.

All this is nothing compared to the hordes of orphans, which increase day by day. On the edges of the camp, rows of holes in the ground covered with old rags, girls and boys of all ages were sitting, head after head, abandoned and reduced to animals, starved and without food or bread, without any human aid whatsoever, packed tightly one against the other and trembling from the night cold, holding in their frozen hands pieces of wood still smoldering to try in vain to get warm …

All the mountain valleys, all the river banks are filled with these camps. This flood of outcasts, hundreds of thousands of refugees drags itself along the Taurus and Amanus passes.

(Armin T. Wegner, *Weg Ohne Heimkehr*, Ras-el-Ain, November 26, 1915)

While his commanding officer Baron von der Goltz stared from a safe distance through field glasses, fearful of catching typhus, Wegner rode into the death camps with his camera taking photographs, which would become priceless proof of the secret extermination carried out by the Ottoman government. He smuggled dispatches and photos and broke the news with the help of the American Embassy, risking punishment and death. A just German, he would also protest the persecution of the Jews by Hitler.

Aleppo, October 16, 1915

On the 52nd day they arrived at another village; here the Kurds took from them every thing they had, even their shirts and drawers, and for five days the whole caravan walked all naked under the scorching sun. For another five days they did not have a morsel of bread, neither a drop of water … their tongues were turned to charcoal.

(J.B. Jackson, American Consul General at Aleppo, October 16, 1915; U.S. State Department Record Group 59, 867.4016/225)

The Second Phase

The "second phase of genocide" did not really begin until the end of spring 1916 and ended in autumn with the massacres of Deir-es-Zor and Ras ul-Ayn with over 250,000 deaths … At the end of a horrific march into the desert, those who had survived the tortures of the journey and the depravity of the soldiers were pushed into a vast cave, fires were lit at either end and they were burned to death. Just a few children escaped death. They survived by cannibalism.

To the Sinking Desert

That evening I returned to the church to speak to Armenians living in the dusty town of Deir-es-Zor, children of the few survivors. At first they are shy of talking of their parents' suffering. They stressed how honorable many Muslim Syrians had been, often adopting Armenian children to bring them up as Christians, and marry them to other Armenians. "They were much kinder and more decent than the Christians who sold us to the Turks."

In the moonlit churchyard a schoolteacher whispers, "I'll take you to a spot under the bridge where the plants smell of blood from the numbers of bodies that blocked the river there." A burly man, Vartan, warns of a place in the desert where his father, a little boy, saw his parents slaughtered. "The desert constantly sinks; so many bodies are buried there. It is called 'the Place of the Armenians.'"

Next day I drive to Markade, a wind-swept hill gifted to the Armenians by the government. A stone chapel clings to the desolate slope. The Syrian guard insists on scraping at the parched earth with a sharp stone. Just a few inches deep, thigh bones and human remains come up to the top. My feet sink into the crumbling soil. I flinch as I step on the unsanctified bones of my ancestors. These are the killing fields Vartan's father had fled. The dead will not rest. They keep coming up to the surface to demand justice.

47

Gangway to Life: The Armenian Quarter of Bourj Hammoud in Beirut

Victor Kocher

At the board table in a building in the center of the Armenian quarter of Bourj Hammoud, they go straight to the point. The view, though from a fourth storey, gives right on to the newest motorway, which here rests on concrete pillars and brutally divides the whole quarter in two. There is no room on the table for plates or cutlery due to the pile of minutes and other papers on it. This is supposedly a working lunch of the Armenian Relief Cross—Lebanon but few mouthfuls interrupt the discussion on marketing, viability, cash flow, and other matters relating to a new project of the Armenian Red Cross Association. In an atmosphere of sober calm these ladies devote their attention to their intense work serving the community.

"'When my grandparents arrived in Lebanon in 1920 after the genocide in Anatolia and Cilicia...'" says chairwoman Seta Khedeshian with a smile. "That's how the story begins for every Armenian here." The tireless Mrs. Khedeshian allows herself a little dry humor. In Bourj Hammoud she has served on practically every imaginable committee related to social service, schools, clinics, old people's homes, and orphanages. She leaves others to ponder on the extraordinary motivating power that comes from the collective memory of a genocide. Her art is procuring funds from international and religious aid organizations, UNO organs, diplomats, NGOs, and the Calouste Gulbenkian Foundation in Lisbon. With 25,000 dollars from an embassy in Lebanon she developed a permanent production of foodstuffs in less favored regions of Lebanon, and with the proceeds from traditional Armenian embroidery she set up a distribution network for artistic embroidery, which includes moneymaking outlets, an idea that has also been adopted by the Lebanese authorities and the Palestinians.

Bourj Hammoud is the safe haven in which innumerable genocide survivors found refuge. France, the colonial power in the Levant, first of all planned to send Armenian deportees—meaning some 150,000 starving people—back from the

Syrian desert to Cilicia, as a belated resurrection of the Armenian kingdom south of the Taurus mountains. However, in 1921 France handed over Cilicia to the Turks once more, which led to a definite Armenian exodus. The transfer of the sanjak of Alexandretta (now Hattay) to Turkey in 1939 added further refugees. Whoever did not get to Aleppo by train traveled to Beirut by sea. The Lebanese authorities assigned the asylum-seekers the suburban region north of the River Beirut, and in particular Bourj Hammoud, to settle in. As the colonial governors regarded the Armenians as a welcome reinforcement to the Christian communities in the land of the cedars, they granted the refugees, numbering some 200,000, who spoke a non-Semitic language and had a church of their own, full Lebanese citizenship in 1924.

Before long the Armenians, who manufactured cheap shoes, accustomed the Lebanese not to go barefoot any longer. This was just one of the immigrants' successes. In the neighboring industrial quarter of Dora many Armenians of Bourj Hammoud found jobs, and in time the Armenian craftsmen expanded their workshops into factories. Family enterprises were more numerous here than among the other Lebanese. Official censuses in 1967 have the Armenians as owners of 14 percent of all Lebanese manufacturing companies with five or more employees; 90 percent of them were in Beirut and Bourj Hammoud. Famous were the tanneries, shoe and clothes factories, and the enamellers. In the early 1970s, 67 percent of all the jewelers in Lebanon were Armenians, and in Beirut so were 85 percent of photographers, 26 percent of tailors, 23 percent of pharmacists and dentists, and 9 percent of the doctors. In the carpet business they owned half of the Lebanese total, and 46 percent of exchange houses. There were at least a hundred Armenian millionaires. "Till the civil war we were the leaders everywhere," notes Mrs. Khedeshian. "After that the great brain drain began, with the Armenian elite emigrating to the States." The destruction of the old city center, the second largest Armenian settlement in the country, caused the community considerable losses for the first time. They suffered a second blow in the last stage of the war, when the anti-Syrian general and prime minister Aoun bombed the Christian militias in the middle of the Armenian residential and industrial area. Despite this, the Armenian community escaped the worst by maintaining neutrality toward the expansionist Christian leaders. The stream of immigration, however, continued unabated even after the war ended, owing to a persistent economic crisis.

Today, Bourj Hammoud is anything but a ghetto, everyone stresses, although at least half its inhabitants are still Armenians. It is rather a wheel of fortune for world trade. An old teacher amusedly recalls that, in his youth, the people in the quarter spoke only Armenian and, if any Arab family moved in, their children straight away learnt Armenian, and not the other way around. Since then many Armenian families have moved to better and quieter residential areas further north, like Antelias, Zalqa, Dora, Rabieh. Some Armenian schools followed in their footsteps. The business center of Bourj Hammoud, with its great glass fronts and shopping malls can be compared with the Hamra commercial quarter in

West Beirut. The little branch of Crédit libanais at the Place de la municipalité is the one that does most business of all this bank's branches. The secret is its directoress, Arpie Tcheboukdjian, and her half-dozen Armenian employees. Customers trust them from the word go, as they are attended in their own language, as if it were their own family. Along the Arax Road there is an array of boutiques, shops that sell leather goods, electronic appliances, and simple junk shops. "And today the assistants even speak Arabic," states a Beirut resident. Only in the more remote streets can one find the somewhat run-down old four-storey houses, with clothing hung out on the balconies, whose ground floors have been let, without exception, to printers, paint shops, shoemakers, or small restaurants.

In one of these alleys lives Bishop Kegham Khacherian, head of the Apostolic Armenian Church in Lebanon. In his quiet wood-panelled office he talks of his double role as spiritual pastor and temporal authority. Obviously Bourj Hammoud has a civil administration with a mayor, but the church holds sway over numerous Armenian schools and most social and charitable institutions. The church congregations elect, following an Armenian national constitution of 1863, an advisory council from among their members, whereby there is only one priest among their seven deputies. This advisory council, in turn, nominates the pastors and diverse executive committees, made up sometimes of clerics, others of civilians, who manage finances, properties, schools, and other community activities. Within this structure there is also a religious tribunal which, as in the other religious communities of Lebanon, regulates all family matters in accordance with official civil law: marriages, divorces, adoptions, inheritances, and guardianships. In state institutions the Armenians now have a stable representation, thanks to the 1989 Taif Peace Treaty. In the 128-member parliament, Orthodox Armenians have five seats and the Catholic and Protestant Armenians one seat each. Besides, they hold at least one ministerial post.

Bishop Kegham has no ready answer to the question of Lebanese Armenian identity. "Many say, 'I'm 100 percent Armenian, but I'm also 100 percent Lebanese,'" he explains, borrowing Charles Aznavour's statement with regard to his relationship to France. "But no person is 200 percent anything. We must be a little more honest with ourselves." The church is unwavering in the strict tradition that an Armenian man can marry only an Armenian woman of the same congregation. However, the bishop recognizes that nowadays 30 percent of marriages are mixed. Besides, by its vigorous backing of schools, the church guarantees a solid attention to Armenian language, history, and culture. Still, the number of Armenian schools has markedly decreased. In 1975, there were still 21,000 pupils at fifty-seven Armenian schools. Since 2002, there have been only 8,000 at thirty-three schools. School heads blame emigration for this, as well as parents' economic straits, as Armenian schools are private and top-level and, therefore, charge fees, as opposed to state schools. Moreover, there are many third-generation Armenians who consider Arabic more important for the future. Bishop Kegham finds it natural that a country which, more than eighty years ago, gave the Armenians refuge should now regard them as ordinary Lebanese citizens.

He is by no means the only person against the cultural assimilation and uprooting of Armenians. "We can and want to participate fully in the Lebanese state," says a teacher, "but at the same time we carry on being full-fledged Armenians. Lebanon is my country. I wouldn't even think of going to live in Armenia." Events since 1991 show that there was no tendency to go back to Armenia, but rather a flood of emigration to Lebanon from an economically caved-in Armenia. When they visit Caucasian Armenia, the Lebanese Armenians, mostly of Cilician origin, have noticed profound differences in language and mentality. The community in Lebanon has its own, Mediterranean identity.

The head of the Apostolic Armenian Church, Catholicos Aram I, embodies higher resolutions. He has nothing more to do directly with the affairs of the Lebanese community, although he knows them very well as former bishop of Bourj Hammoud. "Here in Lebanon is the core of the Armenian Church," he states at his seat in Antelias, north of Beirut. And he simply declared 2004 the Year of the Armenian Family, so as to combat erosive tendencies. With all the dignity of a 1,700-year-old ecclesiastical institution, he crosses the catholicosate courtyard, scepter of the Trinity in his hand and wearing his ample black cowl, in the company of nine bishops and archimandrites, to pray at St. Gregory's cathedral. After all, he is the custodian of the right arm of St. Gregory the Enlightener, who in the year 301 converted the Armenian king Tiridates, with which the Apostolic Church initiated by the opostles Thaddeus and Bartholomew produced the first Christian state. When in 1930 the catholicosate followed its flock and moved from Sis, in Cilicia, to Antelias, it became, in the liberal climate of Lebanon, the irradiating world center of the Armenian Church. The Lebanese state, which actually encourages religious communities to accentuate their peculiarities, also stimulated the catholicosate to rebuild and preserve the Armenian nation.

But in addition to the head of the Antelias church there is a second catholicos of the Apostolic Armenians in Echmiadzin, near Yerevan, who has made himself particularly noticeable since 1991. The schism took place in 1441, when the Caucasian Armenians felt they were being left aside by the catholicosate, which at that time was in Cilicia, a war zone; and so they nominated a second catholicos. No one tried to oppose the rule that in holy Echmiadzin, seat of the first head of the Armenian Church, there could not reside a subordinate patriarch. Besides, the Armenian Church has a patriarch in Jerusalem, who defends the not insignificant rights to the Holy Sepulcher; and another in Istanbul. This inflation of ecclesiastical heads was undoubtedly justified in previous centuries owing to the worldwide diaspora, but in the age of globalization its usefulness is less patent. Catholicos Aram I avers that both catholicoses observed the principle of the *primus inter pares*, and in this way were independent of each other, but had to act in coordination. What he describes as "certain differences" between them is seen by other lower prelates as an attempt by Echmiadzin to claim theological superiority over Antelias. Official protocol recognizes "pride of place" to Echmiadzin. Lately there have also been tensions between Antelias and the

Armenian Catholic patriarch of Bzummar, in Lebanon, who also adopted the title of "Catholicos." An intervention at the Vatican made clear that the Pope recognizes only one patriarch among the Catholics of Lebanon.

The catholicos of Cilicia, to whom almost the whole of the Near East, the Mediterranean, and North America subordinate themselves, underlines his position as the church's center of gravity. Among other things, Aram I, as moderator of the World Council of Churches, fosters ecumenical understanding. "In addition, this center is a living testimony of Armenian survival after the genocide by the Turks, of the resurrection, and of rebirth." With his commitment to justice and peace, the catholicos does not include only the painful details of the Middle East peace process, but also the genocide. "Forgiveness for this crime is perfectly conceivable for us," he says, "but only after its authors recognize it, that is, an official acknowledgment of the genocide by the Turkish government."

48

STRUGGLE FOR SURVIVAL: FRANZ WERFEL AND THE ARMENIANS OF MUSA DAGH

Hannes Stein

How do I get there? Behind me, white as chalk, is a churchyard over which flutters a red flag with the Turkish crescent. Before me I see a row of Armenian crosses embossed like reliefs on the outer wall of the church. Below the last of them there is an inscription in Armenian characters, which I can hardly decipher. Isn't this an M? And doesn't the middle letter remind one of a Greek sigma? And the last one—doesn't it look liked a chopped-off H? A gust of wind blows across the graveyard, and the strange characters sort themselves out and make sense: Musa Dagh, Mount of Moses. It was surprising, almost startling, when a roof with a crucifix appeared among the treetops. We had driven through humble villages with their mosque minarets rising aloft, and now, instead, this dream-like vision: an Armenian church! I rub my eyes. Who would have thought that precisely here, on the coast of the Turkish province of Hattay, there remained some remembrance of that expunged Christian race?

The Armenians were the victims of the first modern genocide. The Young Turks eliminated a million and a half of them. They were burnt alive; they had their heads split open with hatchets. Finally, the tiny remainder yet alive was dispatched to the Syrian desert. Talaat Bey and Enver Pasha were the two brains of the progressive Ittihadist regime that planned it. "The destination of the deportations is the void," Enver laconically wrote down on a telegram form.

Here, however, on the Musa Dagh, 5,000 Armenians from seven villages were able to defend themselves. On a large white cloth they painted a red cross, under which they wrote: "Christians in distress," and hung it facing the sea. They resisted the deportation and even captured two Turkish howitzers. Most of the combatants were rescued from Moses' mountain. In September 1915, French and British warships took them on board and ferried them to a safe haven, but I would never have heard of this had a Bohemian Jew called Franz Werfel not woven these events into a grand novel, *Die vierzig Tage des Musa Dagh* (The Forty Days of Musa Dagh).

Right from Antioch I began to feel uneasy. It was from here that, in Werfel's story, ever more gendarmes and soldiers started out to subdue the Armenian rebels, which meant Musa Dagh had to be fairly near. But how was I to tell which of the tree-covered coastal hills was the right one? To get out of the taxi and simply ask was unthinkable. After all, the present Turkish government denies the genocide, so the revolt couldn't have taken place. But when we got to the village of Samandagh, everything became clear: green and unconquerable stood Musa Dagh in the spring light. Only, I had imagined the side facing the sea would be more rugged. The taxi drove along country lanes. Were there no paved roads to the mountain? The driver rolled down the window and asked two schoolgirls in blue tunics. Finally a man with a moustache and smoking a cigarette joined us in the taxi, and guided us. The tarred road twisted up the mountain. A couple of kilometers further on we stopped near a house. Another passenger got in and flopped into the back seat with a sigh.

I catch the word *mukhtar*, a village mayor. The *mukhtar* is chubby and has kind eyes. On the belt of his bleached jeans he has a cellphone. While we climb the mountain the men chat away in Turkish. All at once my heart misses a beat: I hear the word *ermeni*, Armenian. I hope this doesn't cause discomfort, I think to myself, but just then a mirage appears before us, firm and solid, as the sole token of reality: the crescent flag.

I enter the church there on my own. It's practically bare. In front of the altar there is an open book on a lectern, a Bible in florid Armenian characters. I allow the thin paper to slip between my fingers and I think of Werfel's novel. On rereading him I realized just how Jewish he was. Werfel filters the true story of the Armenians' resistance through a Hebrew prism: the chronicle of the exodus. Forty days of resistance, forty years wandering in the desert.

Werfel describes the exodus from Egypt, from fate-imposed passivity. The social order in his novel is extracted from the Torah with a firm gouge. One a political leader, the other, a spiritual leader, they guide the fighting chosen people: of course, they are Moses, the prophet, and Aaron, the high priest. But it goes even further, I think, as I leaf through the foreign Bible. Gabriel Bagradian, as Werfel's hero is called—Gabriel, hero of God—is, just like Moses in the Bible, a stranger who grew up far from his people. He was so eager to be "an abstract man, the essence of a man." It is possible that, at the same time, Werfel painted here the typical assimilated German Jew.

Is it a general rule in esthetics that genocides can only be described indirectly, making use of the odd exception? Thus *The Forty Days of Musa Dagh* is not mainly about the deportations, but the rescue of 5,000 people. Nevertheless, we have to know something about the deportations for this rescue to be exciting. In *Schindler's List* we find something similar. This film is not about the normal, about anonymous deaths, either, but about an almost fabulous rescue. Yet perhaps the similarity is just coincidence. I shut the Bible.

Outside on the church porch the men are laughing. The *mukhtar* casts a large stone at a blindworm, but the creature survives. My amiable taxi driver squashes its head with the tip of his shoe, catches it by the tail, and flings it far away. Are these men evil?

From this height one sees, as with telescopic eyes, the plains: fertile land, houses, a river. That, in the distance, must be Syria. Behind it, Lebanon. After that, the great border fence, where Israel begins. My friend Benny Katzenelson, the socialist kibutznik, told me he and his comrades read Werfel's novel in the 1940s as a Zionist pamphlet. Not surprising. After all, it's about an ethnic-religious minority who fight, their back to the sea, against an overwhelming Muslim majority. When in World War II the Wehrmacht threatened with its advance on Palestine, the clandestine Jewish army intended to take up positions on Mount Carmel and from there launch a guerrilla war against the Germans. The code name of this operation was Musa Dagh Plan. Clandestine copies of Werfel's book are also supposed to have circulated in the Nazi death ghettos.

Suddenly a door opens in the house in front of the church, and a bearded man wearing a very white shirt comes out, hugging a pretty woman. The *mukhtar* goes over and greets them effusively. Then he looks at me and says, *Ermeni*. Are there still Armenians living on Musa Dagh? The man with the beard asks me if I speak *russki*. No, I don't know Russian. Behind the couple an older woman appears in the doorway. By signs I understand she is the man's mother. She points at a very bent old man with two days' stubble and a lambskin cap, who goes past the house. "*Mon père.*" Is this possible? Can that man be her father? Maybe he was a child then. Where was he in 1915? What did he live through? Where is this family from? We have no common language. We remain standing in the sunshine, smiling futilely.

Armenians live on Moses' mountain once more.

From today on, it is impossible to read *The Forty Days of Musa Dagh* without seeing a forewarning of the Third Reich in it. Nor is it an ancient massacre or pogrom that Werfel depicts, but a modern genocide organized with bureaucratic coldness.

In an unforgettable passage the German pastor Johannes Lepsius has a meeting with Turkish war minister Enver Pasha. The war minister is not at all an imposing figure, but rather small and childlike. Still, Lepsius straight away sees in him the "Arctic look of the man that has 'overcome all sentimentalism,' the face of a man beyond guilt and its punishments; the precision of a handsome face belonging to a race he knows not, but which leaves him breathless; the monstrous, almost innocent naiveté of total atheism. And what a power he possesses, that one cannot hate him!"

The faces of the people around me have no trace of that Arctic frigidity. They have laugh creases, moustaches, gentle brown eyes. In the meantime we have arrived at the next village, the taxi driver, the fellow with the ever-smoldering cigarette, and myself. In the village's minute square we are received by the local *mukhtar*. With his bushy, walrus-like white moustache he looks like a South

American "patron." We are honored with a sky-blue checkered tablecloth on a wooden table. Chairs are pulled up. Would we like tea? A river flows by near the square. On the bank there is a bronze bust of Kemal Atatürk, above which, once again, the pretty red flag of Turkey waves. A gnarled, century-old oak, split by lightning, projects its shade on us. One of the men shins up an orange tree like a young boy and plucks juicy, acid fruits for us from its branches.

It's green here, green and peaceful. Franz Werfel is absolutely right in saying Paradise is reflected on the Musa Dagh. I stir cube sugar in my tea. And as I do not understand what the men around me are talking about (I only catch the word *aleman* from time to time), and because I am encapsulated in my foreignness, an abstract man, an essential man, I pronounce in the back of my head a pathetic little speech. I say in silence:

> Dear Turks, you aren't inhuman. A blind man with a white stick can see that. You're kind and hospitable. You've invited me to tea and oranges, and you were just as hospitable as today, and more, in your history. When the Spanish Catholics expelled the Jews in 1492, the High Porte opened its doors and admitted the refugees. And during World War II you kept neutral only pro forma, for the truth is that you took in many emigrants from Nazi Germany, giving them a place of residence and work. This will never be forgotten.

I sip my tea and continue:

> But for this very reason it's terribly stupid that your government wants to hide the bloodstain on your shirt. Look at Germans. They committed the worst genocide ever. After 1945 they never disputed it (which would hardly have been possible), but paid a bit of compensation; and many, who were not guilty themselves, felt genuine remorse. Has this harmed them? Quite the contrary: nowadays Germans are liked more than before. Denying the genocide does you no credit. It diminishes you.

Can the *mukhtar* read my thoughts? He smiles at me, showing his teeth under the walrus moustache. I return the smile and lick orange juice from my fingers.

> But there is a much more important reason for you to stop acting once and for all as though the Armenian genocide had never happened. Franz Werfel wrote in the margin of the manuscript of his novel: "Don't attack the Turks," and strictly kept to this. He also tells about those that were against the Ittihadists. He tells about Turks who hid fugitive Armenians, and fed them with cheese and milk, behaving like humans. These heroic facts must finally be brought into the light! But they remain in the shadows because your government denies the genocide.

There are little piles of orange peel on the blue tablecloth. The tea glasses are empty. I have kept my speech quiet till its end, and now we must leave. Smile creases, moustaches, gentle brown eyes. I shake hands with each. *Salam alaikum,* I say, peace be with you.

Next Wednesday is April 24, 2002. That day Armenians round the world commemorate the forgotten, negated, sunken genocide that Enver Pasha and Talaat Bey's willing perpetrators carried out in 1915. "The destination of the deportations is the void." The Armenians are like prisoners, captive in the pain and bitterness of their lonely memory. Only the Turks have the key to this prison, no one else. Only they can free the Armenians from their loneliness.

And here goes a firm recommendation: Till April 24, 2005, there is plenty of time to film Franz Werfel's great novel, *The Forty Days of Musa Dagh*. The original scenario, which I've visited, would be ideal. Perhaps Steven Spielberg would like the material. The best, however, would be for a Turkish film-maker to direct it.

49

AN EYE FOR AN EYE: THE ASSASSINATION OF TALAAT PASHA ON THE HARDENBERGSTRASSE IN BERLIN

Tessa Hofmann

A man—a "gentleman" in the parlance of the period—of forty-seven, discreetly elegant, wearing a gray ulster, strolls unhurriedly towards the zoo down the bustling Hardenberg Street in Berlin around 11 a.m. on a Tuesday. He does not notice a young fellow crossing the street near the Conservatory of Music, who catches up with him around the Fasanenstrasse, and allows him to go by. Even less does he see that the youth pulls out a pistol from his right pocket, and taking careful aim from behind, knocks him over with a single shot, as if it were an execution. The gentleman in the overcoat crumples to the ground, the top of his skull opens, and a woman faints. Others pursue the gunman, who tries to escape down the Fasanenstrasse. Further passers-by join the chase and they drag the author of the crime to the nearest police station, beating him "as though gone berserk." A witness describes it later: "One gentleman beat him on the head with a key time after time. People were shouting, 'Stop that crook!' He got thrashed some more at the police station. His first words, in broken German, were, 'I Armenian, he Turk. Not damage Germany!'" All this transpired on March 15, 1921.

The Victim

The victim, Mehmet Talaat (1874–1921) was the former chairman of the Central Committee of the Turkish nationalist party Ittihat ve Terakki Cemiyeti (Committee of Union and Progress, commonly known as the Young Turks) and, as Turkish interior minister (1909–February 1917), together with war minister Ismail Enver, and that of the navy, Ahmet Cemal, a member of the ruling Young

Turk triumvirate from 1913 on. In these capacities he was, together with Enver, one of the politicians most responsible for the extermination of the Armenians of the Ottoman Empire during the war years of 1915–16, an event presumably planned before the war, in which a million and a half of the 2.5 million Armenian inhabitants, according to the German Embassy's estimate of October 4, 1916, were massacred, or died of starvation, exhaustion, and disease on the death marches dressed up as deportations.

Right after Turkey's capitulation, Talaat and other Young Turkish leaders fled the country on a German gunboat. Talaat and the "killer doctors" Nazim Bey Selanikli (1870–1926) and Bahaettin Şakir (1878–1922) found refuge in Berlin with the knowledge and blessing of the German authorities. Nazim had been Secretary General of the Young Turkish party Ittihat ve Terakki Cemiyeti, and Şakir, secretary of the Central Committee. Talaat arrived in Berlin on November 10, 1918, where he lived under the alias of Ali Saly Bey (Mehmet Sait Bey) in a nine-room apartment in Charlottenburg and carried out very intense political activity; Dr. Nazim moved there some time later. As a self-exiled diplomat and politician, Talaat put himself unconditionally at the disposal of Turkish nationalist opposition leader Mustafa Kemal, and even made contact with the Soviet Russian leadership through the communist chief Karl Radek, in prison in Berlin at the time, as well as with the British government. A German Red Cross passport enabled him to travel to Denmark, Sweden, Switzerland, and Italy and, in 1919, to Holland where, at the Congress of the Second Socialist International, he challenged the accusations of the Armenian participants, and led the chairman of the Congress to make pro-Turkish statements.[1]

The moment the Ottoman ambassador in Berlin, Rifat Paşa, heard of Talaat's arrival, he contacted the German authorities to obtain his arrest and extradition, as the Ottoman government, pressured by the military defeat into starting criminal proceedings in 1919 and 1920 against dozens of Young Turkish leaders and lower-ranking officials in special military courts, requested the German government in 1918 and 1919 to extradite Talaat. German Foreign Minister Dr. Wilhelm Solf turned down both requests, partly because of Talaat's loyalty to Germany: "Talaat has been faithful to us, so our country remains open to him."[2] In Constantinople a Special Military Court condemned Talaat to death *in absentia* on July 5, 1919. for war crimes and the "extermination of the Armenian people of the Empire." But the balance of power very soon tilted in favor of the opposition government of General Mustafa Kemal ("Atatürk"), who proclaimed a general amnesty for all the Young Turks on March 31, 1921.

The Author of the Crime

The failure of international and national efforts to call the Young Turks to account for the mass murder of the Armenians and other Christian peoples of the Ottoman Empire led surviving members of the Dashnaktsutiun Party, former allies of the exiled Young Turks of the opposition, to set up revenge (*Vrej*—"Nemesis") groups, which, in 1921–22, assassinated a total of ten Young Turks, as well as a number of Armenian collaborators in hit-and-run operations.

The first in this series was Talaat's assassination by Soghomon Tehlirian (1897–1960, also written Tehlerian, Teilirian), a Protestant Armenian from the Erzincan area, who lost all his family in the massacres and, in contrast to later avengers, was captured after the deed. Neither during the preliminary interrogations nor during the criminal trial, which took place on June 2 and 3, 1921, at a Berlin district court, was it known that Talaat's execution had not been Tehlirian's first act of requital. At a conference in Constantinople in April 1919 Tehlirian found out that the list of the Armenian elite arrested on April 24, 1915, had been drawn up for the metropolitan police chief, Bedri Bey, by one Harutiun Mkrtchian. He became Tehlirian's first victim. After Talaat's assassination, Tehlirian did not kill anyone else, but lived quietly, first in Bulgaria, and then the U.S.A.

The Prussian justice ministry, as well as the Foreign Office, exerted a discreet influence in Tehlirian's trial in 1921. They reduced the number of testimonies for the defense, and limited the time and content of the process in order to defuse its political explosiveness. In this way it was possible to avoid a public disclosure of the political background of the case, and base it on Tehlirian's insanity at the moment of its perpetration. Despite such manipulative tactics, the process turned into a trial of the victim and his former government, thanks to the depositions of Dr. Johannes Lepsius, a pro-Armenian German, and two genocide survivors. The trial ended with the jury's sensation-making acquittal of the defendant—one of the main reasons for lay juries being replaced by professional judges very soon after.

Apart from this, the Talaat case in Berlin gave rise to a whole series of other basic legal questions. Following the verdict, the *Berliner Allgemeine Zeitung* carried the headline: "Germany So Far Governed by Law. Are Exotic Peoples to Settle Their Private Accounts on German Soil?" As from November 1920, a sovereign Armenian state no longer existed in which the Young Turk leaders might have been brought to trial at an official tribunal., Tthere was absolutely no similarity with the MOSSAD investigator, Peter Malkin, who in 1960 tracked down Ricardo Clement, alias Adolf Eichmann, in his Buenos Aires hideout, and kidnapped him to make him respond before an official tribunal in Jerusalem for the murder of six million Jews. Likewise, a permanent international court able to judge the greatest of conceivable crimes, genocide, would only come into being seventy-seven years after the incipient preoccupation with human rights in 1921, a shamefully long time in the history of International Law.

One of the spectators at the trial was the German Jewish jurist Robert M.W. Kempner (1899–1993), deputy chief U.S. prosecutor from 1945 at the Nuremberg international war trials. In 1980 he wrote about the importance in political law of the trial against Talaat Pasha that he had had the opportunity to observe as a law student while living in Berlin at the same time as Talaat.

The murder of 1.4 million Christian Armenians by order of the Turkish government was the first programmed genocide of this century … Armenian student Tehlirian's action drew the world's attention to a specially important evolution in the right of peoples: After the Armenian atrocities of the First World War began, there were brave men who openly opposed this genocide in the name of the interests of humanity. They did not let themselves be put off by the absurd claim that a foreign state must not interfere in the internal matters of another sovereign state … The way from this holocaust, to which at least 1.4 million Christian Armenians fell victims, to the one that produced 6 million Jewish victims took a mere 20 years … In this way there is a wide arc between the first intervention of Henry Morgenthau Sr. during the Armenian atrocities, and the Holocaust … It is even wider, extending to the basic principle now recognized that any crime against humanity, even if a state approves it, can be opposed, and indeed must be, by any other state or its citizens .

Many observers, especially right-wingers, began to worry about the dangerous consequences of Tehlirian's acquittal[3] and saw connections between the assassination in 1921, the acquittal of its author, and later political assassinations. When on May 25, 1926, the Smolensk Jew, Shalom Schwartzbart, murdered the chief of the Ukrainian army, Symon Petliura, who, as president of the Ukrainian republic's ruling junta was responsible for the massacre of Jews, national-socialist ideologue Alfred Rosenberg draw a parallel with the Berlin process in the periodical *Der Weltkampf* (The Global Struggle), which he edited. In his article Rosenberg praised Talaat Pasha for his pro-German bias, minimized the genocide, and complained, like previous commentators, that the outcome of the process could well serve as a model for other attempts:

Even during the World War, Armenians were leaders in espionage against the Turks, just as the Jews were against Germany. This forced that faithful ally of the German Empire, Talaat Pasha, to take strong measures against them, in which certain excesses were unavoidable … After the defeat in 1918, Talaat lived in the capital of the country he had been faithful to, and was murdered here. Nevertheless, the main newspaper publishers in this country carried on criticizing him after his death, protecting his murderer, and demanding his acquittal. And indeed this was the decision of the Berlin tribunal. The Jewish press of every hue celebrated it, describing his absolution as 'the only possible verdict.'

In Turkey, where the reality of the Armenian genocide is officially denied and minimized, a translation into Turkish of the protocols of the Berlin trial in 1921 was published in early 2003, but at the same time the Turkish Deputy Minister of Justice who came to Berlin "to research archives" stated that Turkey was interested in a new trial of the case, or a revision of the process. Talaat's remains in the Turkish cemetery in Berlin were exhumed in 1943, and in the presence of then German ambassador to Istanbul, Franz von Papen, placed in a Grave of Honor on the Hill of Liberty in Istanbul. To this very day Turkey officially accords the genocidal Young Turks a personal cult as patriots, which prevents all critical research of the Armenian extermination as the "founding crime" of the

Turkish Republic. However, the nationalist newspaper *Hürriyet* complained of
the depravity of youths who, in their nocturnal rambles, disrespectfully piss on
the graves and leave syringes lying around.

Scene of the Crime: Charlottenburg

During and after World War I members both of the Armenian community and
the Turkish lived in the Charlottenburg area, which, for this very reason, became
the venue of assassinations on a further two occasions. Thirteen months after
Talaat's elimination, on the April 17, 1922, in the vicinity of the Uhlandstrasse in
Charlottenburg, *"Vrej"* avengers Arshavir Shirakian (1900–73) and Aram
Yerkanian (1898–1934) executed Cemal Azmi, who, as the former governor
general of Trebzon was the "butcher" of the province, and Bahaettin Şakir, who,
as a member of the Central Committee of the Young Turks and a high official of
the Special Organization, was responsible for the extermination of the Armenians
of the eastern provinces. The group managed by Shahan Natali and Hrach
Papazian in fact intended to do away with the entire Ittihadist leadership exiled
in Berlin. This time, as in all subsequent *Vrej* actions, the perpetrators were able
to escape. The victims, Cemal Azmi and Bahaettin Şakir, rest in "graves of honor"
in the Turkish cemetery of Berlin, as a commemorative plaque in Turkish on the
Columbiadamm states, where the union of Berlin Turkish workers built at its own
expense a luxurious mosque, at the entrance of which are the "graves of honor."

At the place of the crime it is less easy to find historical continuity. World War
II air raids modified the street plan and numbering of the Hardenbergstrasse.
Number 17, where Tehliriáan finished off the former minister with his
Parabellum in 1921, no longer exists as it was then. Aramaic youths danced
outside the present Chamber of Industry and Commerce following a public
commemorative meeting seventy-four years after the event, as Talaat was the
politician also responsible for the extermination of that nation in the fateful year
of 1915, which, coincidentally, was that of the manufacture of Tehlirian's weapon.
Since 2005, Turkish nationalists gather in commemoration of Talaat's
assassination.

These settlings of accounts only made the headlines again fifty years later
when, on January 28, 1973, a 73-year-old Armenian, Gurgen Yanigian, shot dead
two Turkish diplomats in Santa Barbara, California, in revenge for the
elimination of his family in 1915, and to make his young compatriots "wake up."
The double murder at Santa Barbara was no longer an act directed at high-
ranking fugitives among the Young Turkish politicians, who anyway had been
condemned to death by Turkish tribunals. The bureaucratic collaborators, and
those that had carried out the practical details, were long since dead—often
through suicide, execution, or assassination in their own country, or as victims of
Armenian acts of revenge. Instead, Yanigian's crime is more a link between the
original executions of the *Vrej* commandos, and the "journalistic terror" of various

Armenian secret organizations from 1975 to 1985, of which the Armenian Secret Army for the Liberation of Armenia (ASALA) was the most notorious. In spite of differing political orientations, these groups followed the common objective of fighting against the "crime of silence," which preceded the later official denial by Turkey. Their campaign was successful: whereas the murder of over a million Armenians in World War I had no news value, the serial assassination of dozens of Turkish diplomats produced constant headlines.

Notes

1. *Türken in Berlin 1871–1945: eine Metropole in der Erinnerungen osmanischer und türkischer Zeitzeugen*, edited by Ingeborg Böer, Ruth Haerkötter, and Petra Kappert, with the collaboration of Sabine Adatepe, Berlín/New York 2002, p. 199.
2. Quote from Vahakn N. Dadrian, *German Responsibility in the Armenian Genocide. A Review of the Historical Evidence of German Complicity*, Cambridge, MA, 1996, p. 217.
3. Dominik J. Schaller, "Die Rezeption des Völkermordes an den Armeniern in Deutschland, 1915–1945" in *Der Völkermord an den Armeniern und die Shoah*, ed. Hans-Lukas Kieser and Dominik J. Schaller, Zurich 2002, p. 537.

50

INCH PITI ASEM? WHAT SHOULD I SAY? THE TSITSERNAKABERD GENOCIDE MEMORIAL IN ARMENIA

Mark Grigorian

I never thought one has to prove the fact of the genocide. I think I knew from my early childhood: what happened in Turkey in 1915 was genocide. I just grew up with the feeling and knowledge that my nation passed through that inhuman, nightmarish, shocking experience—Armenians were killed en masse, because they were Armenians.

Now, when I am in my forties, I often reflect: what does the genocide that happened many years ago mean for me, what place does it occupy in my self-perception? The easiest thing to say would be that it is one of the most important, constitutive parts of my national self-identification.

The shock of the genocide was so big that probably every Armenian continues to feel it. And I am a carrier of that feeling, even though no one from my family was a survivor. However, among husbands and wives of my closest relatives there are three descendants from families that were slaughtered in 1915.

And, when I am trying to understand, what does the notion of the Armenian genocide—the *Yeghern*—mean to me, what connections and associations does it bring forward, my first thought is about the memorial to its victims built on the Tsitsernakaberd hill in Yerevan.

That means I became aware of the genocide, started to think and feel it, when I was more than seven, because I was seven in 1965, when the public in Armenia started for the first time to discuss it openly and the intelligentsia began to think about a monument. And of course, I do not remember the uprisings, which demanded that Armenians be given back their—our—history and be granted permission to mark the fiftieth anniversary of the tragic events of 1915.

Neither did I know that the then first secretary of the Communist Party, the factual leader of Armenia Nikita Zarobian, gave in to the demands of the people, and went to Moscow to talk to Nikita Khruschev: "Either he will permit, or I will resign," he said before departure.

The permission was granted.

I knew about that many years later, from my uncle, a well-known painter Sarkis Muradian, who together with poet Paruir Sevak played a great role in the Soviet Union's concessions to the Armenian requests. Such a concession was almost impossible for that country and that time. Why did Moscow allow fellow Armenians to mark that day, while the USSR did not officially recognize the fact of the genocide, and even the fact of massacres? I do not know. Maybe it was due to geopolitical reasons, because the Armenian–Turkish antagonism could be an excellent seal to the border with Turkey, a member of enemy-bloc NATO?

Maybe the powers gave in to the pressure coming both from inside the country and from the Armenian diaspora?

Whatever it was, marking the day was permitted, and even more—we could build a monument to the victims of the unrecognized genocide.

I remember how at the end of the 1960s on an April 24 evening my parents took me when they as a part of a big company of adults and children went to Tsitsernakaberd. The monument was not yet finished.

It was dark. One of the adults, I believe it was Jim Torosian, the then Head Urban Architect of Yerevan, lighting the blocks of basalt with a flashlight, explained what the monument would look like. I remember him telling about the high stele, consisting of two parts and symbolizing the unity of Armenians in Armenia and the diaspora. He was speaking also about the sloping walls, symbolizing the twelve provinces of the Ottoman Empire, vilayets, which suffered from the genocide.

I did not know the meaning of the word "vilayet". But I remembered for the rest of my life the explanation I heard on that dark April night. And I remember that part of that company were Sarkis Muradian, the author of the painting Last Night. Komitas," and Paruir Sevak, the author of the poem "Ceaseless Belltower."

These two works of art were for my generation, the symbols of the genocide. Muradian's painting is done with a red-brown palette. In the foreground is the composer Komitas, sitting half-turned by his piano. One of his hands is on the keyboard the other feebly droops. Behind him, in the dark, barely seen, is the face of the Turkish officer who came after him.

The great Armenian composer Komitas did not die during the genocide. He was arrested and then deported. But the horrors and sufferings he saw were so immense that his mind gave up. He became insane. Komitas was taken to Paris, where he stayed for nineteen years in a madhouse. He died in the asylum.

The poem "Ceaseless Belltower" is about the life of Komitas. And the genocide. "Paruir and me—we were writing about the same events," Sarkis Muradian used to say.

Before I became fourteen, my parents would not allow me to go with my friends to the memorial on April 24, worrying that I might be lost in the crowd. But, of course, I was leaving the school with my friends during the lessons, knowing that no one would be punished for illegal absence on that day.

We were walking by the concrete slabs, which were laid down on the alleys in the park on the Tsitsernakaberd hill. We were a part of a human flow. The people were walking—everybody alone, but nevertheless all together. Talking in a low voice, smoking. The eyes looking somewhere inside—concentrated, tragically. It was so wonderful—to feel that I am Armenian, like everyone else surrounding me, feel my unity with men and women, young and old, silently walking by my side. We were united by the place and time, and more—we all were Armenians: part of the nation that suffered and revived.

And, like an illustration of our unity, upon the hill resounded the gentle voice of the fabulous singer Lusine Zakarian singing songs by Komitas and the Mass by Ekmalian. "Surb-surb"—"Saint-saint"—sounded upon the hill.

I had a strange feeling. Yes, I understood that the very ritual of pilgrimage on Tsitsernakaberd was tragic—we were commemorating a hundred thousand of our compatriots. But there was something solemn and sublime. I had a great feeling: I am Armenian. I am different from the people surrounding me, but I am like them. And that is good.

I had the same feeling years later, during the Karabakh rallies. It was very sharp on a particular day in November 1988, when a crowd was standing on the square in front of the opera house in Yerevan. I was in that crowd. We were waiting for news from the opera hall, where an extraordinary sitting of the Supreme Soviet (the legislature) of the Armenian Soviet Socialistic Republic was held. The deputies were due to announce Karabakh as a part of Armenia. It was late at night. Suddenly, a rumor came that Moscow had declared a state of emergency in Yerevan accompanied by a curfew. Some time later, tanks appeared in the streets.

But we were there, feeling the power of our togetherness. That evening the Soviet troops did not harm anyone.

And another recollection—again years after. In the cold, hungry April of 1993, when Armenia was under total blockade, I was present at a meeting in the office of the Yerevan mayor. One of the problems to solve was how many gas cylinders would be enough to secure the "eternal fire" in the memorial of the victims of genocide, so that the people could, as always, come and lay flowers on the monument. The required amount was provided. The "eternal fire" was burning that day.

It was a long time, almost all my school years, that Cilicia, Marash, Zeitun, Arabkir were for me just parts of Yerevan, the same as Kanaker, Nork, or Third District—*Yerrord Mas.* I did not know that the names repeat the names of the regions in the Ottoman Empire that were Armenian before the genocide.

The book edited by historian professor Mkrtich Nersesian *Genocide of Armenians in the Ottoman Empire,* became a very important milestone for me. I saw it by chance on a shelf in one of the reading halls of Matenadaran—the Institute of Ancient Manuscripts—where I was reading books about miniatures illustrating the Armenian medieval manuscripts.

The book by Nersesian is a collection of documents and eyewitnesses' testimonies. I opened it and immediately forgot about miniatures and manuscripts. I was reading that dreadful chronicle of the events at the end of the nineteenth and beginning of the twentieth century.

From that book I learned that systematic exterminations of Armenians began in 1896. I learned about the heroic defense of Mush, the Zeyuntsis. Then I read about 1915. I was more or less ready to see descriptions of atrocities and barbarities. But an order issued by the central powers stunned me. It said that the Turks who are sheltering Armenians should be equaled to Armenians and treated like Armenians. That means that the men had to be killed on the spot and the women and children deported to the desert of Deir-es-Zor. Or killed. Almost certainly raped.

Before that I was leaving out how often my acquaintances, telling the stories of their grannies, were saying that they were saved thanks to Turks—their neighbors. The story had different shapes—sometimes it was the youngest son of a big family, who was saved by the compassionate neighbors, sometimes the daughter, whom her mother gave to the neighbor at the very last moment, sometimes a boy who was visiting a friend when the thugs came upon them.

But, before I read about that order, the genocide was very simple for me: Turks were slaughtering Armenians. All Turks were slaughtering all Armenians. Now I realized that the reality was more complicated, and the Turks more diverse.

Many years later, in the summer of 1988, I was helping the well-known Armenian author Samvel Shahmuradian in his work on the book *The Sumgait Tragedy*. Samvel was giving me cassettes with recorded stories told by Armenians, victims of pogroms in Sumgait, and I had to put them on paper. Among the horror-striking stories was one about a young Azeri woman who gave shelter to several Armenian young girls. When the thugs started to break her door down demanding the girls, she took a big kitchen knife, then opened the door: "You want blood? Here it is!" Saying that, she slashed her leg with the knife. The thugs left.

These two episodes showed me that even in the most difficult periods of life and history there are people who preserve in themselves forces to resist the pressure of a faceless crowd of thugs and killers, and who still maintain compassion and dignity. And I understood that these qualities are higher than ethnic differences.

Years passed by. In the winter of 1999 in Yerevan, a book called *Armenia and Turkey. What Then?* by Vladimir Grigorian, my father, was launched. Understanding that the recognition of the genocide is the main obstacle of Armenian–Turkish relations, my father suggested that the two governments have to start concentrated efforts to solve this very complicated moral, historical, diplomatic, and juridical problem.

During the launch, a former Communist functionary, a person well known in Armenia, took the floor. The main idea of his very emotional speech was that no relations with Turkey and Turks are possible until the government of that country recognizes the genocide. His speech was met with applause.

I was listening to the applause and thinking that the problem of the genocide is much deeper and more complicated than we see it in our everyday life. On the one hand, there is the moral imperative: the crime against humanity must be condemned. Penitence must follow the crime. That will inevitably help Turkey to become a real European nation. Not so much in the political sense, but from the point of view of values.

But who should confess? It is not really plausible that the modern Turkey should be considered responsible for the crimes of the Ottoman Empire.

Plus, during the past more than eighty years, several generations of citizens of Turkey have been born who are sure that there was no genocide. And the propaganda machine is continuing to work. Recently, I saw on the website of the Ministry of Foreign Affairs of Turkey a page saying that one and a half million Armenians could not be killed, because the Armenian population of the Empire by that time totaled in about three hundred thousand—about the number that survived after 1915. That means no one was killed!

Ironically, the government of Robert Kocharian, which made the recognition of the genocide a cornerstone of its foreign policy, is not demanding Turkey to recognize it. What is that? A carefully tailored diplomatic strategy, or a confession of their own weakness?

Instead, Armenia continues a policy of confrontation with Turkey using the Russian military presence and Russian weaponry as a shield. However, national confrontation cannot be a clue to solving the problem of the genocide. Even more—it can be solved only together with the Turkish side. We have to talk to each other about the genocide, discuss it, argue, search for solutions, and find them, because the problem has gone deeper than a moral issue, and gained many other aspects, which have to be addressed.

But at this moment, we have only the hard line of the Turkish and Armenian powers. However, refusal to recognize the genocide hinders not only the development of Turkey as a European nation, but—and this is very important— holds back development of Armenia, slows down our integration into the regional community, is an obstacle in the resolution of the Karabakh problem.

Whether we want it or not, the biggest and most economically powerful immediate neighbor of Armenia is Turkey. And the problem of the genocide along with the Karabakh problem is very important in order to gain stronger positions in the region, establish normal relations with the neighbors. We have to trade with Turkey, and not to fence ourselves off from it.

So what should we do? Forget about the demands of recognition of the historical fact of genocide? No. But act in a diplomatically clever way, calmly, and, what is most important, starting from the interests of Armenia—nothing more that a small Caucasian country.

Many in Armenia believe that the recognition of the genocide is first of all in the interests of the diaspora, because they, being the immediate heirs of the victims, are more interested in that.

"It is easy to be a citizen of the successful and flourishing America and demand recognition of the genocide," many in Armenia would say.

> They should try first to live here in Yerevan, where there are no jobs, and when there is a job, then the salary is late for months, where a handful of oligarchs is growing more and more rich, while the majority of the people does not have cash to buy daily bread. Let them try our bitter bread, when the men are going to work in Russia, and the women and children are staying at home without the breadwinner.

> Instead, we have more important problems: we must develop the country, secure jobs for everyone, raise the economy … But no contacts with Turks!

Apparently, there is no logic, because there are contacts. Many in Armenia wear Turkish jackets, almost every household uses Turkish products, and hundreds of Armenian young women are, in desperation, going to Turkey to sell themselves. Yes, no logic, but loads of emotions, which in the past were unofficially supported by the Soviet powers, and now are backed by the administration of Robert Kocharian.

There should be another way. We should show to the Turkish government that Armenia is interested in searching for a solution. I am sure: official refusal of territorial claims against Turkey would move us significantly closer to the recognition of the genocide. We should open the borders (well, the government is eager to do that—the problem is somewhere else), agree about confidence-building measures, start cultural exchange.

And we will have the possibility to drive from Yerevan in the morning, go directly to Ani, spend a day in the medieval capital city of Armenia and come back in the evening. We will be able to spend our summer holidays on Lake Van or enjoy the pleasures of Istanbul.

But not yet …

In the beginning of 1997, I had the chance to go to Istanbul. The ship was approaching the bay of Golden Horn when I started to feel severe pain in my stomach. It was so acute that it twisted and rolled me. We were in Istanbul for twenty-four hours. All that time I was suffering from the pain. I did not know where the pain came from, what it was about. However, I could not miss the opportunity to have a walk in the city, see Aya-Sofia, the Blue Mosque, wander around the famous bazaar … But the pain was always there.

However, as soon as the ship unmoored, the pain stopped. I thought and understood what that was. The subconscious, animal pain came because I was feeling with my whole being the death of the Armenians who became victims of the genocide. Something in the very depth of my ego was reminding me: this is the city of the genocide, though I was trying to think positively: this is the famous city, the former capital of the Byzantine Empire; hometown of Grigor Zohrab, an excellent writer of short stories, Misak Metsarents, a most delicate lyrical poet-symbolist …

But something hammered in me: Zohrab became a victim of the genocide, Metsarents suffered and died from an illness that developed after be was stabbed in his back. He was stabbed on what we would call today "ethnic grounds."

And my feelings reminded me of a Russian poet Osip Mandelstam's visit to Sushi in 1930. His wife wrote in her memoirs that Mandelstam could not eat in Shushi, where the entire Armenian population was exterminated as a result of the Turkish–Azeri attack in 1921, because he felt Armenian blood in the bread.

And another poetic reminiscence. A well-known Soviet poet, writer, and composer Bulat Okudzava, descending from a mixed Georgian–Armenian family, was writing in Russian. He died in 1997. One of his last short poems was called "Bowing my Head Before the Memory of Victims of Genocide." It was written in Istanbul.

> Midnight on the Bosporus. Time of silence.
> But in the Istanbul darkness that's great and numb,
> Cries of my betrayed ancestors are heard …
> Inch piti asem! Inch piti anem? (in Armenian—What should I say! What should I do?)

There, I had the same feeling.

But there are other possibilities. And I remember how a string quartet from Ankara performed the works of Komitas in Yerevan. It was really stunning. Komitas—the composer, whose mind could not bear the horrors of the genocide. And they were met by an ovation.

EPILOGUE

THE DICHOTOMY OF TRUTH AND DENIAL AND THE REMEMBRANCE OF A COURAGEOUS TURK (TORONTO)

K.M. Greg Sarkissian

Background: The Need for a National Research Center

In the late 1970s, a small group of Armenians, absorbed with questions about their history, their identity, and their future as a nation, came to the conclusion that there was a crucial need for a place to think critically about the Armenian reality. These individuals, propelled by deeply felt intellectual concerns, and compelled by a strong desire for change, set about conceptualizing an institution that would provide a forum for free and critical thinking about contemporary issues affecting the Armenian people, through a process that is analytical, scholarly, and detached. Taking into account the impact of rapid changes in modern society, including advances in technology, in an ever-shrinking world, this process would include the continual and systematic reexamination and reevaluation of their reality. This forum would facilitate intellectuals and the community at large to raise substantial questions about contemporary Armenian history and identity, and help develop new perspectives on vital issues, both current and future. Among its primary goals would be for the Armenian people to express their history in their own voice and define themselves (and not let others define them); to understand the forces and factors that have brought them to where they are today; and to help educate and involve the people in a higher level of discourse, without claiming to have all the answers.

The trauma of the genocide had become such an overriding concern for the Armenian people, especially in the diaspora, that generations later they were still in crisis mode, thinking only about survival. Intellectual responses in this situation were considered a luxury. The tendency was rather to take action of some sort, but without clearly strategizing what those actions should be. In the

Armenian tradition, the intellectual had been relegated to the role of a teacher in the classroom. It had been forgotten that the intellectual has a dual role, both to develop the theoretical ideas and to provide for their practical applicability. This group, however, saw it as essential that the intellectual reassert his/her role as thinker in society. In order to understand and deal with the trauma, it was essential that Armenians understand what happened during the genocide, how it happened, and why it happened. It was essential that scholars and intellectuals research and analyze these subjects and make their findings known.

Since such a large proportion of Armenians have lived outside of Armenia proper for centuries, which was further exacerbated by the genocide and mass deportation in 1915, it was also crucial to address and understand the diasporan experience. What does it mean to be Armenian when you have not lived in Armenia for generations—in some cases for over five hundred years? What are the markers of Armenian identity—language, religion, a nation-state? Can one have more than one cultural identity? If so, how do they interact? Is one cultural identity dominant? If so, what are the implications of this? And what can be the role of the diaspora in projecting and working toward the future of the nation? The group was cognizant of the fact that there are some outstanding examples of individuals who had been born in diaspora, but had gone on to have a tremendous impact on their homelands. (Theodor Herzl, for example, a Hungarian-born Jew, went on to become the founder of the Zionist movement, which ultimately led to the founding of the State of Israel in 1948 and its policy to encourage the return of Jews to "the promised land." Mahatma (Mohandas) Gandhi, an Indian living in South Africa, went on to lead India to independence in 1947.) It is noteworthy that the nineteenth-century renaissance of western Armenian literature and language flourished in Istanbul, far from historical Armenia. In 1918, the declaration of independence of the first Armenian Republic was made in Tbilisi, Georgia, instead of Yerevan. In the 1940s, when Soviet Armenia was under the threat of being converted from a Soviet republic to an autonomous region, Armenians from all over the diaspora responded to the call and flocked to repopulate the country in order to prevent this loss of statehood. Even though Armenians were living in a wide variety of countries and had a wide variety of local experiences, they still had numerous issues and concerns in common. It was essential for Armenians to understand their Diasporan experience, and to confront such vital issues as assimilation, loss of language, intermarriage, the preservation of their culture, and the struggle for genocide recognition and for an independent homeland.

In dealing with contemporary Armenian reality, it would have been impossible not to deal with the presence and influence of Armenia, which represented for many the idea of a homeland, a cultural and spiritual center, and the guarantor of nationhood for all Armenians. At the same time, owing to the influence of the cold war and its effects on communal politics, Soviet Armenia was also a source of serious friction between various elements of the Armenian community in the diaspora. There was a conflict of views as to whether the security, economic viability, religious freedom, and cultural identity of Armenia was better preserved as an independent country with a market economy, or as part of a denationalized, centrally planned empire.

The group felt that those in the diaspora had a special responsibility to fill a certain void. In the homeland—then under a communist regime—the Armenian mind was active but could not have open access to information or express and share its thoughts freely. In contrast, those in the West had open access to information and the freedom to think and express themselves, and also the ability to provide the support structures to enable scholars to think and work. This afforded the possibility of creating a formal organization to deal with the numerous, vital issues related to the genocide, diaspora and Armenia.

The Founding of the Zoryan Institute

With all this as a background, Jirair Libaridian conceived the idea of an institute in the late 1970s. He, Garbis Kortian, Nora Nercessian, and I were involved in the initial stages of the project and nurtured the idea, which gradually became a reality. And so, in 1982, we, along with a small group of people, established the Zoryan Institute for Contemporary Armenian Research and Documentation in Cambridge, Massachusetts. Soon, others joined us, such as Varouj Aivazian, Alvart Badalian, Levon Charkhoudian, Levon Chorbajian, Salpi Ghazarian, and Khachig Tölölyan, to name only a few. We were particularly attracted to Cambridge, a center of research and learning, by its vibrant intellectual life nurtured by numerous major universities in the area. As our activities grew very quickly, so did our group of staff members and volunteers, and our network of associated scholars. In just a few years, we had thriving offices in Toronto, Los Angeles, and Paris.

The Work of the Zoryan Institute

In 1983, the institute launched the Oral History Project as a unique source of information on the social history of the Armenian communities in Turkey, both urban and rural, before, during, and after the genocide. Some 700 survivors' oral histories have been recorded on video and audio tapes in such cities as Los Angeles, Boston, New York, Toronto, Montreal, Beirut and Yerevan. To stimulate new thinking and new approaches to complex issues in the Armenian experience, the institute has organized nearly a dozen international conferences, and hundreds of seminars and lecture series in partnership with universities and academic institutions. In 1986, it launched the Open University program, to share the results of its research with the community at large, in several cities in North America and Europe. Over the past twenty-two years, the Zoryan Institute has accumulated a wealth of archival materials relating to the Armenian genocide, including the personal papers of missionaries, government officials, diplomatic and military correspondence, intelligence reports, land deeds of deported Armenians, photographs, eyewitness accounts, survivor memoirs, and a wide variety of artifacts. Since its inception, the Zoryan Institute has published forty-one books and periodicals in six countries and five languages. Deserving of special mention is *Diaspora: A Journal of Transnational Studies*, which commenced publishing in 1991. This award-winning periodical is a forum for the analysis of the contending "others" that pose cultural, political and economic challenges to the hegemony claimed by many nation-states and addresses a wide range of phenomena encompassed by the terms diaspora and transnationalism. These publications have been groundbreaking in their content and their approach, and many are now classics in their field.

From the beginning, all of the institute's programs incorporated a strong comparative element, whereby the Armenian experience was studied in relation to the experiences of other nations and within a global context. At the same time, they incorporated an interdisciplinary perspective, analyzing issues from a variety of points of view, such as history, political science, sociology, law, etc.

In 1991, as a result of restructuring—after Dr. Libaridian took the position as Director of the Department of Research and Analysis of the Presidium of the Parliament of Armenians—the institute shifted its administrative center to Toronto, while the Cambridge office remained as the center for archival management and research support. When Vahakn Dadrian became Zoryan's Director of Genocide Research and George Shirinian became Program Coordinator in 1999, there was renewed activity in genocide and human rights programs, and renewed emphasis on documentary research and comparative genocide studies. Scholars from around the world intensified their work with the institute on specific projects: Taner Akçam from Turkey, Yair Auron from Israel, Wolfgang Gust from Germany, Eric Markusen from Denmark, Lorne Shirinian from Canada, Roger Smith from the United States, and many others. These scholars have been responsible for original research and the publication of numerous books in North America, England, Germany and Israel in collaboration with the institute. One particularly memorable achievement was the International Conference on "Problems of Genocide," held in Yerevan in April 1995, and cosponsored by the Republic of Armenia's National Commission on the Eightieth Anniversary Commemoration of the Armenian Genocide and the Zoryan Institute. Twenty-eight experts from around the world gave papers and participated in discussions of numerous cases of genocide, with a particular emphasis on comparative genocide. The conference proceedings were published by Macmillan and issued in 1999 as *Studies in Comparative Genocide*, a pioneering book in the field.

Establishment of the International Institute for Genocide and Human Rights Studies

Recognizing that there was a serious gap in the university curricula regarding the study of genocide from a comparative perspective, the institute, with the help of a committee of scholars and volunteers, launched in 2001 a unique course titled the Genocide and Human Rights University Program (GHRUP). Annually, up to twelve of the foremost experts in genocide studies come together with about two dozen students from around the world in an intensive, 65-hour, accredited seminar. The purpose of this course is to train a new generation of scholars to undertake the study of genocide at an advanced level. Along with a comparison of other case studies, such as the Jewish Holocaust, the Cambodian genocide and the Rwandan genocide, as well as the exploration of many other themes, there is a focus on the Armenian genocide as the archetypal genocide of the twentieth century. In 2003, Zoryan established a special division, the International Institute for Genocide and Human Rights Studies, whose sole mandate is to oversee the GHRUP and extend the program to other universities.

As a result of the success of this course, a partnership between the University of Minnesota and the Zoryan Institute has been established. The University of Minnesota, through its College of Liberal Arts, the Institute for Global Studies, and the Center for Holocaust and Genocide Studies, adopted the Genocide and Human Rights University Program developed by the Zoryan Institute. The same course is offered now in Minneapolis and Toronto, fully accredited by the University of Minnesota.

Observations on the Present

The Zoryan Institute has come a long way in the past twenty-two years, as a result of a great deal of effort by the members of its Academic Board of Directors, associated scholars, the staff, and the hard work of numerous dedicated volunteers and supporters. Zoryan's work is not just an intellectual exercise. It is designed to serve as a basis for developing and planning practical concepts related to the nation's future. Reflecting on where we were at the time Zoryan was established compared to today, it is evident that the Armenian reality and the world around it have changed radically. Today, the Soviet Union is gone; we have an independent Armenia, the Republic of Nagorno-Karabakh, and a prosperous and vibrant diaspora. As a nation-state, we now have the opportunity to define ourselves, to shape our own future, and to make our place among the family of nations on our own terms. There is no limitation on what we can achieve, except our own imaginations and our willingness to think.

Considerations for the Future: Armenian–Turkish Relations

In 1995, I shared a very personal story publicly at the International Conference on Problems of Genocide in Yerevan. My personal story tells of a Turk, Haji Khalil, my grandfather's business partner, who had promised to take care of his family in case of any misfortune. When my grandfather was hanged by the Turkish authorities and the deportations of the Armenians began, Haji Khalil kept his promise by hiding my mother's family in the upper storey of his house for almost a year. The logistics involved were extremely burdensome: there were seven people to hide, food for seven extra mouths to be purchased, prepared, and carried up undetected nightly and this had to suffice until the next night. Khalil's consideration was such that he even arranged for his two wives and the servants to be absent from the house at least once a week, so that my grandmother and her family could bathe. When two of the children died, he buried them in secret. He took tremendous risks and his situation was precarious, because his servants understood what was transpiring. Had he been caught sheltering Armenians, he would certainly have shared their fate. Luckily, his household was loyal and discreet, and therefore I was one of the very few children of my generation and in my neighborhood to grow up with uncles and aunts, all of whom remember Haji Khalil, the righteous man. This is in contrast to my father's story, who was orphaned at the age of eight, his father hanged, his mother raped and killed, and of nine children in his family, only he and two brothers survived. The dichotomy of the nightmarish genocide perpetrated by Ottoman Turkey, and the memory of Haji Khalil became the obsessions of my life. This internalized duality taught me that truth and justice cannot be had easily; they must be searched for. The conflict and questions I felt remained with me as I migrated to the U.S.A., studied engineering, and became a businessman. The desire to pursue the truth and to share it with others led me to join hands with a childhood friend and to establish the Zoryan Institute for Contemporary Armenian Research and Documentation.

The story of Haji Khalil attracted the attention of the only Turkish scholar attending the conference, who came in order to share his analysis of why there is silence in Turkey about the genocide. His paper about the taboo on this subject in Turkey and the challenges to the state of Turkey accepting this reality, as well as his very presence in Yerevan, was strong testimony that there are those in Turkey who know the facts of the Armenian genocide and are willing to take a stand for truth, based on the principles of universal human rights.

The next morning, when all the participants in the conference attended a mass in memory of the victims of the genocide, I approached Taner and asked him to join me in lighting two candles: one for the memory of my grandfather, lit by him, and one for the memory of Haji Khalil, the righteous Turk, lit by me. The emotional bond at this moment was so overwhelming that we embraced each other and became committed to working together to bring about a change in the hearts and minds of both of our peoples for reconciliation. We hoped that one day they would have warm, neighborly relations, just as we were embracing as two human beings. Taner and I have since become convinced that the best way to achieve this would be to facilitate a dialog by making key information available for both societies. We firmly believe that only through dialog, based on truth, can there be reconciliation between our two peoples.

Therefore, the Zoryan Institute is collaborating with the University of Minnesota to support a long-term research project entitled "Creating a Common Body of Knowledge," conceived, created, and run by Taner Akçam. The objective of this project is to create a common body of shared knowledge by making a wide range of documentary sources available to Turkish civil society and Western scholars, in Turkish and English, on the history of the events leading to, during, and immediately after 1915. The broader goal is to facilitate an informed, rational discourse on the issue between Armenians and Turks, hopefully leading to dialog and the normalization of relations between these two peoples.

Through such scholarly activity, the dichotomy I have felt throughout my life regarding Turks and the Armenian genocide may begin to be resolved. Accordingly, I want to extend my hand to the people of Turkey and ask them to remember that, though at the end of the Empire the Ottoman state was led by mass murderers, it also had its Haji Khalils. It would honor the memory of those righteous Turks if the successor state of the Ottoman Empire would acknowledge the overwhelming truth of the Armenian genocide and express sincere regret, so that the healing process between our two peoples may begin.

Key Dates in Armenian History

Fifteenth to thirteenth centuries BC

First mention of a state on the Armenian plateau: Hayassa in the triangle formed by the present-day towns of Erzinjan, Erzurum, and Trebizond. Thence the self-denominations of *hai* (Armenian) and *Hayastan* (Armenia).

Mid-ninth century to 640 BC

Kingdom of Urartu (whose own name was: Byainili), centered at Lake Van.

520 BC

The Persian Achemenid king Darius I mentions "Arminia" in an inscription as the tenth satrapy of his empire.

Around 190 BC

Foundation of the Arsacid dynasty. Artashes I declares independence from Seleucid dominion. According to Strabo, Armenian became the official language.

95–55 BC

The Arsacid king Tigran II (the Great) Artashuni vastly extends his frontiers. Around 78 BC Armenia achieved the greatest extension in its history, from the Caspian Sea up to the Mediterranean, with the inclusion of Cilicia, from the Tauruses of Cilicia to the east of Mesopotamia, with which it became Rome's greatest rival. In 66 BC the Roman general Pompey defeated Tigran, who became a vassal of Rome.

AD 52

The Parthians conquer extensive Armenian territories.

AD 53–428

Royal dynasty of the originally Parthian family of the Arsacids (Arshakuni). Tiridates I (Trdat) is king.

301

Grigor Lussavorich (the Illuminator) converts King Trdat III (the Great). Christianity is adopted as the state religion. Thus Armenia is considered the oldest Christian state. Grigor (Gregor, Grigoris) is the first Catholicos, whose seat is in Echmiadzin. More than a decade later (313) Christianity is declared the official religion of the Roman empire.

387

First partition of Armenia, in an Eastern part assigned to the Sassanid Persians, and a Western one that was a dependency of Rome.

405

Mesrop Mashtoz creates the national, 42-letter alphabet. In 433 the Bible is translated into Armenian. The fifth century is considered the Golden Age of ancient Armenian literature, whose greatest figure is the historian and poet Movses Khorenatsi.

May 26, 451

General Vartan Mamikonjan falls fighting the Persians at Avarair, in which the Christian faith of the Armenians is successfully defended. Vartan is one of the most popular names nowadays. The day is celebrated as St. Vartan's.

451

First schism of the Christian church at the Council of Chalcedony. Due to the battle of Avarair the Armenians were unable to attend. In subsequent synods (Dvin, 505–6 and 554) the Armenian church rejects the Council's decisions. In this way it belongs, alongside the Syrians, Copts, and Abyssinians, to the so-called pre-Chalcedonian or "ancient oriental" churches.

591

In the partition of Armenia between Persia and Byzantium, most Armenian territory becomes a dependency of Eastern Rome.

640–885

Armenia is conquered by the Arabs and ruled by Arab governors.

885–1045

Bagratid (Bagratuni) Armenian dynasty in northeast Armenia. The kingdom of Shirak rises. Ashot III is crowned in the city of Ani (961). The city becomes a powerful fortress and, thanks to its favorable location, an important trade center. For the Armenians, this city of "forty gates, a hundred palaces, and a thousand churches," destroyed many times, and nowadays in Turkey, has a legendary significance. The royal architect, Trdat (born *c.* 940) gained renown far beyond the city limits, and was put in charge of restoring the dome of the Hagia Sophia in Constantinople. In 1046 Ani is destroyed by the Seljuks. The population flees with its prince, Ruben, to Cilicia.

908–1021

Armenian Ardsruni dynasty in southwest Armenia. The kingdom of Vaspurakan rises. The residence is on the island of Aghtamar in Lake Van. From 927 to 969 the island is the catholicos's seat. The area around the lake, nowadays part of Turkey, develops into a center of medieval architecture. Today the architectural remains are in danger of falling into decay. The tenth-century church of Aghtamar is one of the Armenians' most important architectural monuments. The small kingdoms of Taron, Artsakh, Kars, Küriakan (Lori), Taik, and Sünik rose at this same period.

1064

Seljuk sultan Alp Arslan lays waste the capital of Vaspurakan, the most important Armenian kingdom. A mass flight to Lesser Armenia and Cilicia follows. Numerous Armenian communities establish themselves in East Europe, amongst others in Crimea, Moldavia, Galitzia, Poland.

1071–1236

After the Seljuk victory against the Byzantines at Manzikert, in the north of Lake Van, Armenia comes under Turkish rule for the first time.

1080

Prince Ruben of the Bagratid family, who has fled from Ani, founds a barony in the north of Cilicia. The surrounding crusader states accept the subsequent extension of his sphere of power. In 1175 Levon Rubenjan is crowned as King Levon I. 1175–87, Ruben III consolidates the kingdom of Cilicia. In 1226 the Hetumids replace the Rubenids. In 1230 Cilicia becomes a vassal of the Seljuk sultanate of Ikonium (Konya).

1198

Prince Levon II Rubenjan, thanks to his merits in the Third Crusade (1189–92) and the instigation of German emperor Henry IV, is crowned as King Levon (Leo) I in the cathedral of Tarsus by the German archbishop of Mainz, Konrad Wittelsbach. Many royal families congratulate him. The Byzantine emperor makes a present of a crown. Levon's kingdom, which quickly flourishes, is modeled on the crusader states of Western Europe. Latin and French are spoken at the court.

1200–36

Northeast Armenia undergoes an economic and cultural renaissance under the protection of the Georgian empire.

1236

The Mongols conquer Armenia. They ravage Ani.

1266

The Mamelukes invade Armenia.

1292

The Mongols capture Catholicos Stepan. The seat of the catholicosate is moved to Sis, in Cilicia.

1342–75

The Lusignan family of French crusaders, based in Cyrenia (present-day Girne, in the Turkish part of Cyprus), receives the throne of Armenian Cilicia.

1375

The Egyptian Mamelukes conquer the capital of Armenian Cilicia, Sis.

1386, 1387, and the 1390s

The fearsome Mongol chieftain Tamerlane (Timur Lenk, Timur the Lame) devastates Armenia.

1410–1502

Domination of Armenia by Turkoman tribes.

May 29, 1453

Ottoman Sultan Mehmet II Fatih (the conqueror) takes the Byzantine capital, Constantinople.

1472

The Safavid Persians put an end to the Turkoman domination of Armenia and subdue most of the Armenian territory.

1487

The Ottomans conquer Cilicia.

Fifteenth and sixteenth centuries

Numerous deportations of Armenians to Constantinople, where their artisans' skills are needed.

1511

First Armenian printing house in Venice.

August 23, 1514

Battle of Persians and Turks at Caldiran. Ottomans obtain half of Armenia. Sultan Selim I settles Kurdish nomads in his new possessions.

1555

Partition of Armenia between Ottomans and Persian Safavids.

1580

Ottomans lay waste the plain of Ararat and Karabakh (Artzakh).

1590

Ottomans and Persians make peace. Persian Shah Abbas I yields extensive territories in the Transcaucasus to the Ottomans.

1603

Abbas I continues his conquests and takes, among others, Tabriz, Nakhichevan, Yerevan, and Erzurum.

1604–5

Around 300,000 Armenians are forcibly deported to Persia. Near Isfahan is founded the Armenian settlement of Nor-Jura (New Julfa), which develops into a prosperous trade center. The local Armenians are accorded equal rights to the

Muslim subjects. The Armenians of Persia subsequently obtain the monopoly of the silk trade.

1616–39

New struggles between Ottomans and Persians on Armenian territory.

1639

Treaty of Diarbekir: second partition of Armenia between Ottomans and Persians, who are left only with the khanates of Yerevan and Nakhichevan in East Armenia.

From 1664

Emigration of numerous Armenians from Nor-Jura to India (incl. Madras, Calcutta).

1701

Armenian monk Mekhitar of Sebastia, 1676–1749, founds an order dependent on Rome at Morea, whose official denomination is Congregatio Monachorum Antonianorum Benedictinorum Armenorum, and which observes the rules of St. Benedict. When the Republic of Venice loses Morea to the Ottomans, Mekhitar flees to Venice with his brethren. There they are given in perpetuity the island on the lagoon of San Lazzaro (San Lazzaro degli Armeni), where they build a cloister. In 1789 an important book print shop is established on the island. In the eighteenth century San Lazzaro became the core of the renaissance of Armenian culture.

October 1827

Russia conquers East Armenia.

1839–76

Tanzimat (Reform) Period. The Ottoman sultans repeatedly declare equal rights for the Christians, but do not suppress the *millet* system, and subject minorities to oppressive taxation.

June–July 1878

At the Congress of Berlin, the six European powers negotiate after the Russo-Turkish war. Russia is given the Armenian regions of Kars and Ardahan (which it retains until 1917). The treaty obliges the Ottoman sultanate to carry out reforms in its "Armenian provinces" (Art. 61). The promises of reform, obtained for the first time in an international treaty, were not fulfilled, which led to great disappointment among the Armenians.

Until the end of the nineteenth century

Foundation of Armenian liberation organizations, citizens militias (fedayeens) and parties, who demand more rights and, in part, national autonomy. Amongst these: in 1887 the Hnchakan Kussaksutiun, in Geneva, which favored total Armenian independence from Russia and the Ottoman empire, without discarding acts of terrorism as a means of attaining its aims. Area of influence: mainly Cilicia and Constantinople. In 1890, Hai Hebaghojakan Dashnaktsutiun (Armenian Revolutionary Federation, accepted by the Second Socialist International) in Tbilisi. Area of influence: mainly the Russian–Ottoman frontier. In 1921 Ramkavar Asatakan Kussaktsutiun (Liberal-Democratic Party) in Constantinople.

1894–96

Under Sultan Abdul Hamid II (1842–1918), who, in this way, comes to be known as the Red Sultan, numerous pogroms are carried out against the *ermeni millet* (with some 300,000 victims). The massacres under Hamid encourage membership in the new Armenian parties. In 1896, twenty-five dashnaks occupied the Ottoman Bank in Constantinople, threatening to blow up the whole building if their political claims were not met. The massacres reached their high point throughout the country. Around 100,000 Armenians fled to Russia, the Balkans, the United States, and Europe. Many Armenian villages were destroyed.

April 1909

Pogrom against Armenians in Cilicia (30,000 victims).

March 1915 to February 1917

The party of the Young Turks' government, Ittihat ve Terakki Cemiyeti (Committee of Union and Progress) reacts to the ongoing collapse of the Ottoman empire with a policy of racial homogenization (Turkism, Turanism, Panturkism). In systematically planned massacres, approximately 1.5 million Armenians died, which was around two thirds of the total Armenian population of 2.5 million. A large number of Armenians flee, for instance, to Beirut, where they settle in the Armenian quarter of Bourj Hammoud, and in Anjar (Bekaa plain).

May 28, 1918

Declaration of independence of the Armenian Republic by the Russian government of Yerevan.

1918–20

At Baku the Azeris, with the blessing of the Turkish conquerors, slaughter 30,000 Armenians. In 1920 Turks and Azeris carry out massacres against the inhabitants of Shushi (Karabakh), in which some 22,000 Armenians are killed.

1919–21

The so-called "Istanbul trials" (Unionist processes) are first-time attempts, inspired by the Allied powers, to court-martial statesmen and military accused of war crimes. With the thirty-one ministers of the war cabinet who were members of the Committee of Union and Progress, and many bureaucrats, officers, and functionaries, there takes place an apparent trial of the main genocide culprits. Among the defendants are, for instance Talaat Pasha (former Grand Vizir), Enver Pasha (ex-War Minister), and Jemal Pasha (ex-Navy Minister). These were condemned to death *in absentia*, but evaded both trial and sentence by absconding to Germany. Only subordinate bureaucrats were tried. On March 31, 1923, Mustafa Kemal (Atatürk's) government proclaimed a general amnesty for all those accused of planning the massacres.

August 10, 1920

The peace treaty of Sèvres assures the Armenian Republic the regions of Van, Bitlis, Erzurum, and Trebizond. But, even before the treaty can be implemented, Armenia is occupied by the Red Army, and attacked by Kemal Atatürk's nationalist government.

March 15, 1921

Soghomon Tehlirian shoots Talaat Pasha, one of the main artificers of the genocide, dead on the Berlin Hardenbergstrasse (Charlottenburg district). The trial, at which survivors and eyewitnesses of the genocide testify, ends with the acquittal of the accused.

March 16, 1921

Moscow makes the historical Armenian region of Nakhichevan a protectorate of the Azerbaijan soviet.

July 5, 1921

Karabakh, also a historical Armenian region, is placed under Azerbaijan's administration.

September 1922

Mustafa Kemal's Turkish army burns down Smyrna. Some 100,000 people, Armenians, Greeks, Assyrians, and Jews, die in the conflagration. This fire marked the end of a thousand-year history of the Greeks in Asia Minor. The city was renamed Izmir.

1922–36

Armenia is part of the Soviet Union as a Transcaucasian Socialist Soviet People's Republic.

July 24, 1923

At the Lausanne peace treaty, the victorious Western powers in World War I fall back on their guarantee of an Armenian state in Western Armenia (east Turkey) or Cilicia. Armenians were to be tolerated in Turkey merely as a religious minority, not as an ethnic group.

1929–30

Deportation of 25,000 Armenian farmers (alleged kulaks) to Siberia as a consequence of forced collectivization.

1936–39

In Armenia 300,000 people are victims of Stalinist "cleansing." There are also massive arrests, summary trials, and banishments.

April 24, 1965

In the first mass demonstration of the Soviet Union on the occasion of the fiftieth anniversary of the genocide, some 200,000 people in Yerevan demanded the return of the historical Armenian regions of Western Armenia (eastern Turkey), Nakhichevan, and Artzakh/Karabakh. As it happens, the party and government leaders of the Soviet Armenian Republic were, at Moscow's nod, removed from their posts as a consequence of the demonstration, but the building of a monument to commemorate the dead was authorized at Tzitzernakaberd ("fortress of swallows"). It was inaugurated in 1967, and became a national shrine for pilgrims.

1975–1983

Armenian terrorist organizations, the main one being ASALA, carried out a number of bloody attacks, mainly against Turkish institutions and diplomats, in protest against the international "crime of silence." Forty Turks, nine people of other nationalities, and thirty Armenians died in the attacks. ·

Since 1983

International institutions are beginning to recognize the Armenian genocide as a historical fact, so as to wean the Turkish state from its negationist ploy and force it to acknowledge the fact. The initial push came from the World Council of Churches in 1983. In 1985 the UN subcommittee of human rights published a report on the genocide. The parliaments and senates of Argentina, Australia (New South Wales), Belgium, the European Council, the European parliament, France, Greece, Italy, Canada, the Russian Federation, Sweden, and Cyprus followed suit. On January 29, 2001, France officially recognized the genocide. Turkey reacted with sanctions. In the States, Turkey was only able to prevent recognition through assiduous lobbying.

1988–90

The local soviet of the autonomous region of Mountain-Karabakh (Nagorno-Karabakh) decides in February 1988 its secession from (Soviet) Azerbaijan and annexation by (Soviet) Armenia. Beginning of mass demonstrations in favor of greater national autonomy. Many people die in anti-Armenian pogroms in the Azeri towns of Sumgait, Kirovabad (Ganje), and Baku. Most Armenians (some 350,000) flee from Azerbaijan, and the Azeri minority abandon Armenia (some 200,000).

December 7, 1988

A devastating earthquake destroys the north of Armenia and buries 23,000 people, according to official data. (Nonofficial estimates are much higher: 50,000–80,000.) A flood of international aid, often coordinated by diaspora Armenians (like Charles Aznavour, Kirk Kirkorian, among others) palliates the suffering.

September 4, 1989

Azerbaijan begins blockade and embargo against Armenia. In 1992 Turkey joins in in the measures, so that the eastern and western borders of the country are closed. The provision of energy and the economy collapse. The population spends a freezing winter without heating. The continuing social crisis produces further mass emigrations. According to estimates, between 700,000 and a million people left the country.

August 4, 1990

Levon Ter Petrossian is freely elected as first noncommunist president since 1920.

April 6–June 6, 1991

In Operation Ring, Azeri and Soviet troops expel some 10,000 Karabakh Armenians from twenty-five villages, settling Azeris in their place. Serious human rights offenses are committed (kidnaps, torture) .

September 2, 1991

Reacting to Azerbaijan's exit from the USSR, Karabakh declares itself an independent republic, together with the northern region of Shahumjan.

September 21, 1991

In a popular referendum, Armenia declares its independence from the USSR. National holiday.

December 10, 1991

98.2 per cent of voters decide for the independence of Karabakh from Azerbaijan.

December 1991 to May 1994

Azeri and Armenian troops fight in Karabakh.

Since 1992

The OSCE seeks—unsuccessfully for a long time—to establish peace measures in the Karabakh conflict. Both sides are inflexible.

1994–1995

Political crisis within the Armenian Republic. Numerous members and sympathizers of the opposition Dashnaktzutiun party are arrested. The traditional party is banned by presidential decree. Thenceforth, including the next government, repeated offenses against press freedom.

September 22, 1996

Disputed reelection of Ter Petrossian as president. Tumults give excuse for repression of opposition parties and their deputies. Around 200 people suffered temporary arrest.

October 27, 1999

In an armed attack against the Parliament eight politicians are killed, among them the president of the Parliament and the prime minister.

February 25, 2001

Armenia joins European Council.

August 11, 2002

In "presidential" elections in Karabakh, not recognized internationally as an independent state, Arkady Ghukasian is reelected with 89 per cent of the ballot.

March 5, 2003

Election of Robert Kocharian as president for five years. International observers criticize the elections on account of the noticeable absence of women, and the attempt to pressure voters and manipulate results

September 29, 2003

Armenia finally abolishes the death penalty.

February 19, 2004

During a NATO course in Budapest, an Azeri participant kills a sleeping Armenian colleague with a hatchet in vengeance for the Armenian expulsion of Azeris. The incident leads to an aggravation of the Karabakh conflict at government level.

April 2004

German Foreign Minister Fischer visits Armenia and places a white carnation on the genocide monument at Tzitzernakaberd.

December 22, 2004

The Netherlands recognize the Armenian genocide.

April 21, 2005

Poland recognizes the Armenian genocide.

June 17, 2005

In June 2005 the German Bundestag indirectly recognizes the Armenian genocide, recommending Turkey to come to terms with its past.

GLOSSARY

Armenian:

It is still considered the extant language closest to original Indo-European. There are two principal quite distinct dialects of it: Eastern Armenian, spoken in the Caucasus, whose consonants are soft and dilated,
e.g. Vardan Margarjan, and Western Armenian, common in the diaspora, with hard, short consonants, e.g. Vartan Markarian.

Autocephaly:

Independence of the popular oriental Orthodox churches according to ecclesiatical law.

Catholicos:

Greek term for the head of an autocephalous church. The Apostolic Armenian Church has had two catholicoses since 1441, owing to an internal disagreement: the "Catholicos of All Armenians," whose seat is in Echmiadzin, in Eastern Armenia, and the "Catholicos of the High House of Cilicia," whose original seat was in Sis, Cilicia, and from 1929–30 has been in the Beirut suburb of Antelias. Jurisdiction over the dioceses spread around the world is divided between them, although the Catholicos at Echmiadzin is *primus inter pares*.

Dashnaktzutiun:

Usual abbreviation of Armenian Revolutionary Federation, founded in 1890 in Tiflis. It is the principal traditional Armenian party. The complete name in Armenian is Hai Herapokhakan Dashnaktzutiun.

fedayeen:

Arab term used for an Armenian paramilitary.

Haik:

First prince of Armenian race, who left Mesopotamia, as he did not wish to be a subordinate to the chieftain, Bel. Considered a direct descendant of Noah, Haik shot Bel dead with an arrow in a duel, and founded his own lineage in the "land of Ararat." Geographically this is in historical Urartu, south of the Van basin.

Hayastanzíi:

Armenian term for a native Armenian or long-time resident.

Ittihat ve Terakki Cemiyeti:

Turkish for Committee of Union and Progress, whose members were also known as the "Young Turks" and "Unionists." Absolute government from January 1913 to October 1918. In English sources, often abbreviated as CUP.

Massis:

Armenian name of the Greater Ararat, symbol of Armenia, since Noah's Ark came to rest "on Mount Ararat" (Gen. 8:4), with which the survival of Creation was ensured. Next to the Greater Ararat (5165 m) is the Lesser Ararat (3925 m). As the mountain has been on Turkish territory since 1921, the Ankara government demands that it be removed from the Armenian escutcheon. Yerevan replied that the crescent moon can be seen from everywhere, yet is part of the Turkish flag.

millet:

Arabic and Turkish word used in the Ottoman empire for a number of non-Muslim communities (Jews, Greeks, Armenian–Apostolic, Catholic, and Protestant.)

spyurk:

"Diaspora" in Armenian.

spyurkahai:

Armenian born or living abroad.

ADDITIONAL READING MATERIAL

Documents and Eyewitness Accounts

Bryce, James (ed.) and Arnold Toynbee (comp.). *The Treatment of the Armenians in the Ottoman Empire, 1915–1916. Documents Presented to Viscount Grey of Falloden by Viscount Bryce. Uncensored Edition*, ed. Ara Sarafian for the Gomidas Institute. Princeton, NJ, and London 2000.

Davis, Leslie A. *The Slaughterhouse Province. An American Diplomat's Report on the Armenian Genocide, 1915–1917*, ed. Susan K. Blair. New Rochelle and New York 1989.

Gust, Wolfgang (ed.), *Der Völkermord an den Armeniern 1915–16. Dokumente aus dem Politischen Archiv des Auswärtigen Amts*. Springe 2005.

Lepsius, Johannes (ed.), *Deutschland und Armenien 1914–1918: Sammlung diplomatischer Aktenstücke*. Reissue of the version published in Potsdam 1919. Bremen 1986.

Morgenthau, Henry. *Ambassador Morgenthau's Story*. Preface by Robert Jay Lifton, Introduction by Roger Smith, epilogue by Henry Morgenthau III, ed. Peter Balakian. Detroit 2003.

Toynbee, Arnold. *Armenian Atrocities. The Murder of a Nation*. London 1915.

Scientific Literature

Akçam, Taner. *Dialogue Across an International Divide: Essays Towards a Turkish-Armenian Dialogue*. Publ. by Zoryan Institute. of Canada. Toronto 2001.

———. *From Empire to Republic. Turkish Nationalism and the Armenian Genocide*. London 2004.

———. *Armenien und der Völkermord. Die Istanbuler Prozesse und die türkische Nationalbewegung*. Hamburg 1996. New edition, Hamburg 2004.

Auron, Yair. *The Banality of Indifference. Zionism and the Armenian Genocide*. New Brunswick, NJ, 2000.

———. "Jüdische, zionistische und israelische Reaktionen auf den Völkermord an den Armeniern," in Hans-Lukas Kieser and Dominick J. Schaller (eds), *Der Genozid an den Armeniern und die Shoah*. Zurich 2002, pp. 577–591.

Balakian, Peter. *The Burning Tigris. The Armenian Genocide and America's Response*. New York, 2003 and London 2004.

Balayan, Zori. *Between Heaven and Hell: The Struggle for Karabakh*. Yerevan, 1997.

Bauer, Yehuda. *Die dunkle Seite der Geschichte. Die Shoah in historischer Sicht. Interpretationen und Re-Interpretationen*. Frankfurt am Main 2001.

Chorbajian, Levon Patrick Donabédian, and Claude Mutafian. *The Caucasian Knot: The History and Geo-Politics of Nagorno-Karabagh*. London and New Jersey 1994.

Chrysanthopoulos, Leonidas T. *Caucasus Chronicles, Nation-Building and Diplomacy in Armenia, 1993–1994*. Publ. by Gomidas Institute. Princeton and London 2002.

Dadrian, Vahakn N. "The Role of Turkish Physicians in the World War I Genocide of the Ottoman Armenians" *Holocaust and Genocide Studies*, vol. I, no. 2, 1986, pp. 169–192.

―――. "Genocide as a Problem of National and International Law: The World War I Armenian Case and Its Contemporary Legal Ramifications," *Yale Journal of International Law*, vol. 14, no. 2, 1989, pp. 221–334.

―――. *The History of the Armenian Genocide: Ethnic Conflict from the Balkans to Anatolia to the Caucasus*. Providence and Oxford 1995.

―――. *German Responsibility in the Armenian Genocide: A Review of the Historical Evidence of German Complicity*. Watertown, MA, 1996.

―――. *The Key Elements in the Turkish Denial of the Armenian Genocide: A Case Study of Distortion and Falsification*. Cambridge, MA,1999.

―――. "Children as Victims of Genocide: The Armenian Case," *Journal of Genocide Research*, vol. 5, no. 3, IX, 2003, pp. 421–37.

Des Pres, Terrence. "On Governing Narratives: The Turkish–Armenian Case," *Yale Review*, 75, Summer, 1986, pp. 517–31.

Goltz, Hermann, and Klaus E. Göltz. *Rescued Armenian Treasures from Cilicia*. Wiesbaden 2000.

Gust, Wolfgang. *Der Völkermord an den Armeniern. Die Tragödie des ältesten Christenvolkes der Welt*. Munich 1993.

Hofmann, Tessa (ed.). *Der Völkermord an den Armeniern vor Gericht: Der Prozeß Talaat Pascha*. 3rd edition, enlargement of the Berlin 1921 edition. Göttingen 1985.

―――. (ed.). *Das Verbrechen des Schweigens: Die Verhandlung des türkischen Völkermordes an den Armeniern vor dem Ständigen Tribunal der Völker*. Göttingen and Vienna 1985.

―――. (ed.). *Armenier und Armenien: Heimat und Exil*. Reinbek 1995.

―――. *Annäherung an Armenien: Geschichte und Gegenwart*. Munich 1997.

―――. (ed.). *Verfolgung, Vertreibung und Vernichtung der Christen im Osmanischen Reich 1912–1922*, Münster, London, and Berlin 2004.

Hosfeld, Rolf. *Operation Nemesis. Die Türkei, Deutschland und der Völkermord an den Armeniern*. Cologne 2005.

Housepian Dobkin, Marjorie. *Smyrna 1922. The Destruction of a City*. London 1966 and New York 1998.

Hovhanissian, Richard G. (ed.). *The Armenian Genocide in Perspective*. New Brunswick, NJ, 1986.

―――. (ed.). *The Armenian Genocide: History, Politics, Ethics*. New York 1992.

―――. *Remembrance and Denial: The Case of the Armenian Genocide*. Detroit 1999.

―――. (ed.). *Looking Backward, Moving Forward: Confronting the Armenian Genocide*. Somerset, NJ, 2003.

―――. (ed.). *Armenian People from Ancient to Modern Times*. New York 1997 and London 2004.

Kaiser, Hilmar. "The Baghdad Railway and the Armenian Genocide, 1915–1916: A Case Study in German Resistance and Complicity," in Richard G. Hovannesian (ed.), *Remembrance and Denial*, Detroit 1999, pp. 67–112.

————. *At the Crossroads of Der Zor: Death, Survival and Humanitarian Resistance in Aleppo, 1915–1917*, with Luther and Nancy Eskijian. Publ. by Gomidas Institute. Princeton and London 2002.

————. "A Scene from the Inferno. The Armenians of Erzerum and the Genocide, 1915–1916," in Hans-Lukas Kieser and Dominick J. Schaller (eds), *Der Genozid an den Armeniern und die Shoah*. Zurich 20002, pp. 129–86.

Kevorkian, Raymond H. (ed.). *Arménie entre Orient et Occident: Trois mille ans de civilisation*. Paris 1996.

————. "Ahmed Djémal pacha et le sort des déportés arméniens de Syrie-Palestine," in Hans-Lukas Kieser and Dominick J. Schaller, *Der Genozid an den Armeniern und die Shoah*. Zurich 2002, pp. 197–212.

Kieser, Hans-Lukas. *Der verpasste Friede. Mission, Ethnie und Staat in den Ostprovinzen der Türkei, 1839–1938*. Zurich 2000.

Kieser, Hans-Lukas, and Dominick J. Schaller (eds). *Der Genozid an den Armeniern und die Shoah. The Armenian Genocide and the Shoah*, Zurich 2002.

Koutcharian, Gerayer. *Der Siedlungsraum der Armenier unter dem Einfluß der historisch-politischen Ereignisse seit dem Berliner Kongreß 1878. Eine politisch-geographische Analyse und Dokumentation*. Berlin 1989.

Kuper, Leo. *Genocide: Its Political Use in the 20th Century*. New Haven 1995.

Lang, David Marshall. *Armenia: Cradle of Civilization*. London 1968.

————. *The Armenians. A People in Exile*. London and Boston 1981.

Leverkuehn, Paul. *Posten auf ewiger Wache. Vom abenteurlichen Leben des Max Erwin von Scheubner-Richter*. Essen 1938.

————. *El eterno centinela. Sobre la emocionante vida de Max Erwin von Scheubner-Richter*. Buenos Aires 2004.

Matossian, Nouritza. *Black Angel. A Life of Arshile Gorky*. London 1998, 2001 and New York 2000.

Melson, Robert. *Revolution and Genocide: On the Origins of the Armenian Genocide and the Holocaust*. Chicago 1992.

Miller, Donald E., and Lorna Touryan Miller. *Survivors: An Oral History of the Armenian Genocide*. Berkeley, CA 1993.

————. *Armenia: Portraits of Survival and Hope*, Berkeley (CA) 2003.

Mutafian, Claude. *La Cilicie au carrefour des empires*, 2 vols. Paris 1988.

Nersessian, Vrej. *Treasures from the Ark. 1700 Years of Armenian Christian Art*. London 2001.

Nichanian, Mark (ed.). *Writers of Disaster. Armenian Literature in the Twentieth Century*, vol. 1: *The National Revolution*. Gomidas Institute, Princeton and London 2002.

Power, Samantha. *A Problem from Hell. America and the Age of Genocide*, New York 2002.

————. *Problema infernal. Estados Unidos y la edad del genocidio*, Mexico 2005.

Schabbas, William A. *Genozid im Völkerrecht*. Hamburg 2003.

Schaller, Dominik J. "Die Rezeption des Völkermordes an den Armeniern in Deutschland, 1915–1945" in Hans-Lukas Kieser and Dominick J. Schaller (eds), *Der Genozid an den Armeniern und die Shoah*. Zurich 2002, pp. 517–55.

Smith, Roger W., Eric Markusen, and Robert J. Lifton. "Professional Ethics and the Denial of the Armenian Genocide," *Holocaust and Genocide Studies*, vol. 9, no. 1, 1995, pp. 1–22.

Tamcke, Martin. "Zum Beieinander von Shoah und Völkermord an den Armeniern bei Armin T. Wegner," in Hans-Lukas and Dominick J. Schaller (eds), *Der Genozid an den Armeniern und die Shoah*. Zurich 2002, pp. 481–92.

Ternon, Yves. *Tabu Armenien. Geschichte eines Völkermordes*. Berlin 1988.

———. (ed.). *Visions of Ararat. Writings on Armenia*. London and New York 1997.

Walker, Christopher. *The Survival of a Nation*. New York 1980.

Weitz, Eric. *A Century of Genocide: Utopias of Race and Nation*. Princeton, NJ 2003.

Winter, Jay (ed.). *America and the Armenian Genocide of 1915*. Cambridge, MA 2003.

Zürcher, Erik J. *Turkey: A Modern History*. New York 1998.

Travellers' Accounts

Arlen, Michael J. *Passage to Ararat*. New York 1975.

Bitow, Andrej. *Armenische Lektionen: Eine Reise durch ein kleines Land*. German translation by Rosemarie Tietze. Frankfurt am Main 2002 (censored and abbreviated version published in the Soviet Union 1972).

Keheyan, Garo. *Yearning for the Sea*. Nicosia 2000.

Mandelstam, Ossip. *Die Reise nach Armenien*. Translated from the Russian by Ralph Dütli. Frankfurt am Main 1983.

Marsden, Philip. *The Crossing Place. A Journey Among the Armenians*. London 1993.

Nansen, Fridtjof. *Betrogenes Volk: Eine Studienreise durch Georgien und Armenien als Oberkommissar des Völkerbundes*. Leipzig 1928.

Wegner, Armin T. *Fünf Finger über Dir: Bekenntnis eines Menschen in seiner Zeit* (Notes of a Journey through Russia, the Caucasus, and Persia in 1927/28), Stuttgart and Berlin 1930, reedited in Wuppertal 1979.

Novels and Autobiographies

Arlen, Michael J. *Exiles*. New York 1970.

Balakian, Peter. *Black Dog of Fate*. New York 1997. (*Die Hunde vom Ararat*. Vienna 2000, Frankfurt am Main 2004.)

Captanian, Pailadzo. *1915. Der Völkermord an den Armeniern. Eine Zeugin berichtet*. Transl., ed., and prologue by Meliné Pehlivanián. Leipzig 1993.

Gregorian, Vartan. *The Road Home. My Life and Times*. New York 2003.

Hilsenrath, Edgar. *Das Märchen vom letzten Gedanken*. Munich and Zurich 1991.

Hofmann, Tessa, and Gerayer Koutcharian. *Die Nachtigall Tausendtriller: Armenische Volksmärchen*. Berlin 1983.

Housepian Dobkin, Marjorie. *A Houseful of Love*. London 1954.

Kricorian, Nancy. *Zabelle*. New York 1999.

———. *Dreams of Bread and Fire*. New York 2004.

Mangelsen, Jochen. *Ophelias lange Reise nach Berlin*. Bremen 2000.

Werfel, Franz. *Die vierzig Tage des Musa Dagh*. Vienna, 1933. 14th ed., Frankfurt am Main 2003.

———. *The Forty Days of Musa Dagh*. New York 2003.

Links

www.zoryan.org
www.armenocide.de
www.armenian-genocide.org
www.gomidas.org
www.cilicia.com
www.agbu.org

NOTES ON CONTRIBUTORS

Taner Akçam was born in the province of Ardahan, Turkey. In 1976 he was arrested in Turkey for publishing a political students' magazine and condemned to ten years imprisonment. Amnesty International recognized the 23-year-old as a political prisoner. After a year's captivity he managed to escape to Germany, where he was granted political asylum. From 1988 to 2000 he carried out research in sociology at the Institute of Social Research in Hamburg. In 1995 he obtained his doctorate in Hanover with the thesis, "The Turkish Nationalist Movement and the Armenian Genocide within the Framework of the Processes of the Military Court at Istanbul *(1919-1922)*." Since 2002, he has been a guest lecturer at the University of Minnesota, in the United States. The main points of his investigation are the Armenian genocide and Turkish nationalism.

Paul Badde is a historian and journalist. Since 1980, he has worked for the *Frankfurter Allgemeine Zeitung*, and is an editor and journalist of that newspaper's magazine. From 2000 on he has been an editor of *Die Welt*, first as a correspondent in Jerusalem, and now in Rome and the Vatican. Additionally he has written several books: *Jerusalem, Jerusalem* (Berlin: Volk & Welt 1998); *Die himmlische Stadt* ("The Heavenly City," Munich: Luchterhand 1999); *Maria von Guadalupe* (Berlin: Ullstein 2004). A worldwide success was the work he rediscovered in 1993 *Jossel Rakovers Wendung zu Gott* ("Josl Rakover Talks to God") by Zvi Kolitz, which he translated completely for the first time and published in 1996 (Zurich: Diogenes 2004). His last book, *Das Muschelseidentuch* (Berlin: Ullstein) appeared in October 2005 and contained his report about the even more sensational rediscovery of the "Veronica," the most ancient and authentic portrait of Christ.

Ian Balfour is a professor of English and of social and political thought at York University in Toronto. He is the author of several books of literary criticism, including *The Rhetoric of Romantic Prophecy* (Stanford UP 2002). He co-edited, with Atom Egoyan, *Subtitles: On the Foreignness of Film* (MIT 2004) and with Eduardo Cadava, *And Justice for All: The Claims of Human Rights*, a special issue of *South Atlantic Quarterly*. He has taught as visiting professor at Cornell, Williams College, Stanford and the Johann Wolfgang Goethe Universität in Frankfurt am Main. He has recently been a Visiting Scholar at the Getty Research Institute in Los Angeles and is currently completing a book on the sublime and editing a volume of essays on the work of Jacques Derrida.

Yehuda Bauer is one of the best-known Holocaust researchers in the world. From 1996 to 2000 he was director of the International Institute for Holocaust Research of the Yad Vashem Holocaust Center, of which he is presently an academic adviser. He is professor (emeritus) of the Hebrew University and a member of the Israeli Academy of Sciences. On January 27, 1998, he made a noted speech in the German parliament for the day of commemoration of the victims of National Socialism. In January 2000 he was the main academic adviser at the Stockholm International Forum on the Holocaust. Heads of state from all around the world attended this international conference organized by the Swedish prime minister Göran Persson, to give advice on the history lessons of the whole world, together with scientists and nongovernment organizations. Part of the debate on genocide, its criminal punishment, complicity, and denial was the Armenian case. The last of the four conferences, called "Preventing Genocide," took place in January 2004. (www.preventinggenocide.com)

Joerg Bremer studied in Freiburg and Heidelberg, and then got his doctor's degree from Werner Conze with a work on modern history. He later spent a time at the Institute of Administrative Studies in Speyer, and then at the Fletcher School of Law and Diplomacy in Boston. Since July 1978, he has been a writer on politics for the *Frankfurter Allgemeine Zeitung*, which he represented in Warsaw between 1981 and 1986, then in Lower Saxony, and since 1991 in Jerusalem, where he lives with his wife and three children. Bremer is a Knight of the Order of Saint John, and is active in the Protestant community in Jerusalem. He has written several books on Poland and the Holy Land, such as *Israel und Palästina*, a cultural history, published by Hirmer (2000).

Jochen Buchsteiner is the Asia correspondent of the *Frankfurter Allgemeine Zeitung*, and lives in New Delhi. He has previously worked for the federal weekly *Die Zeit* covering foreign and domestic politics in the German capital. He has recently published the book *Die Stunde der Asiaten* (The Asian Hour. How Europe is being marginalized), published by Rowohlt (2005).

Vahakn N. Dadrian studied mathematics, philosophy, history, and international law in Berlin, Vienna, and Zurich. He obtained his doctor's degree in sociology from the University of Chicago. From 1970 to 1991 he was a permanent professor at the State University of New York. He held a research appointment at Harvard, and has been a guest professor at the Massachusetts Institute of Technology (MIT) and several European universities. He directed a large research project on the genocide, financed by the H.F. Guggenheim Foundation. Since 1999, he has been the director of genocide research at the Zoryan Institute, in Cambridge, MA. He is presently engaged in a research project lasting several years on the Armenian genocide. He has dug in the German Foreign Ministry archives around twenty times for the primary sources dealing with the Armenian genocide. His knowledge of several languages—Armenian, Turkish, English,

French, and German—has been of great help to him in this connection. He has published numerous books on the sociological, historical, and international law aspects of the genocide.

Mark Grigorian has written and edited ten books on journalism in the former Soviet Union, as well as numerous publications on the Karabakh problem, Armenian domestic politics, and the situation of ethnic minorities in Armenia. He graduated in 1989 in Russian linguistics. He was elected a councillor of Yerevan city from 1990 to 1995. He began his journalistic career in 1993 as subeditor of a magazine in Russian in Yerevan. He became subeditor of the weekly *AIM* (*Armenian International Magazine*). Since 1998, he has been president of the NGO Cooperation and Democracy, which deals with the media and human rights. In 2002 he was one of the three founders of the Caucasus Media Institute in Yerevan. He emigrated to Great Britain following an assassination attempt in October 2002, in which he almost lost his life. There he works at the BBC as chief broadcaster for Central Asia and the Caucasus.

Wolfgang Gust is a journalist in Wentorf, Hamburg. From 1965 to 1993, he was a writer, editor, foreign correspondent, and department chief of the news magazine *Der Spiegel*. He is the author of books and articles on the Armenian genocide. He has collected Foreign Ministry documents on the genocide, which can be visited on the Internet at *www.armenocide.net*. He has recently published a widely acclaimed collection of documents of the German Foreign Ministry on the Armenian genocide (*Der Völkermord an den Armeniern 1915/16. Dokumente aus dem Politischen Archiv des Auswärtigen Amts*. Zu Klampen Verlag, Springe 2005, 675 pages ISBN 3934920594). The volume will come out in English too.

Dorothea Hahn works as a correspondent in France for *taz, die tageszeitung* (Berlin) and the news magazine *Facts* (Zurich). From 1983 to 1986 she wrote for the Mexican newspaper *Unomasuno*. From 1986 to 1988 she was the local editor of the *Berliner Morgenpost*. She then joined the international staff of *taz (die tageszeitung)*, and since 1995 has been writing from Paris.

Rainer Hermann has lived in Istanbul since 1991. He studied national political economy and Islamic sciences in Freiburg, Rennes, Basle, and Damascus. In 1984 he graduated in economics, and obtained his doctor's degree in 1989 on the modern history of thought in Syria. He was a functionary of the Bundesagentur für Außenhandel (German Federal Agency for International Trade, bfai) and correspondent of its magazine, *Nachrichten für Außenhandel*, in Kuwait until the invasion by Iraq. In 1991 he moved to Istanbul for the bfai, and since 1997 has been a correspondent of the *Frankfurter Allgemeine Zeitung*.

Tessa Hofmann, D. Phil., MA, graduated in modern philology (Armenian and Slavic languages/literatures) and sociology. A resident of Berlin, she has worked at the Institute for East European Studies at the Free University Berlin since 1983. She is author or editor of thirteen books about Armenian history and culture. Since 1979, she has been a voluntary worker for various human and minority rights NGOs (Society for Threatened Peoples; president of the Working Group Recognition—Against Genocide, for International Understanding). Her work focuses also on the implementation of respect for general human rights and minority rights in the Near East and the Caucasus. She has been given numerous honors by academic institutions of the Republic of Armenia and by Armenian diaspora organizations.

Pascale Hugues lives in Berlin, where she has worked as German correspondent in Germany for the French news magazine *Le Point* since 1995. Her articles and notes also appear in German newspapers (*Tagesspiegel*, Berlin). She is the authoress of several films distributed by ARTE, and of the book *Deutsches Glück* (Stuttgart, DVA 1999). From 1983 to 1989 she worked in London, first for the BBC, then as the correspondent of the French magazine *Libération*.

Gil Eilin Jung graduated from the Axel Springer school of journalism. She worked for three years as a political correspondent in Bonn. Later she was a foreign correspondent in Paris and London for different papers, among them *WELT*, *SZ-Magazin*, and *RTL-Television*. She lives as an independent writer in Bremen.

Ron Knight trained as a scientist in New Zealand, Scotland, and the U.S.A. and has a Ph.D. in physics and an MBA. He emigrated to Australia to take a research position with the Australian Government but soon acquired management and advisory roles, including drafting responses to technical questions asked in the Australian Federal Parliament. He spent time in Washington D.C. as an Australian diplomat to the U.S.A. and Canada, covering energy resources and nuclear safeguards issues. He participated in international safeguards negotiations and in the 1980s led Australia's participation in an international study of safeguards arrangements. On leaving the government he formed a marketing communication and public relations consultancy with his wife, Marjorie Anderson, to provide communication services for high-technology businesses and educational institutions. Currently he teaches in the School of Professional Communication at the University of Canberra.

Victor Kocher studied classical and Arab philology. For four years he was a delegate of the International Red Cross Committee in the Near East. He has written for the *Neue Zürcher Zeitung* from 1983, and since 1992 has been its Near East correspondent, based in Cyprus. He translated, together with Georg Brunold, Mohamed Choukri's, *Das nackte Brot* (Nördlingen: Greno 1986). He is the author of *Der neue Nahe Osten. Die arabische Welt im Friedensprozess* (Publishing House of the Neue Zürcher Zeitung 1996).

Michael Krikorian lives in his native city, Los Angeles. Till February 2004, he wrote for the *Los Angeles Times*, as a crime reporter. He specialized in reports on black street gangs. His portrayal of Big Evil, a notorious gang leader, was highly praised. From 1998 to 2000, Krikorian worked for the *Fresno Bee* newspaper, where he was nominated for the Pulitzer Prize for his reports. He traveled to Armenia in 1999 for the paper, to write about the election of the catholicos. During his stay Prime Minister Sarkissian and seven government officials died in an assault. Krikorian was the only Western journalist in Yerevan. He is presently working on a book about Los Angeles street gangs, and a novel about a journalist who, like himself, specializes in criminality.

Jochen Mangelsen is an independent writer in Bremen. He was previously a writer on culture in Hanover, and Radio Bremen press chief. In 2001, the Bremen publishing house Donat brought out his novel about an Armenian family, *Ophelias lange Reise nach Berlin*, a literary interpretation of the fate of Alfred and Ophelia Mouradian's family.

Nouritza Matossian was born in Cyprus and studied philosophy, music and theatre in England. A writer and actress, she lives in London. After publishing her biography and study of the Greek composer Iannis Xenakis (1981) she co-produced a BBC2 documentary, "Something Rich and Strange" (1991). She spent twenty years investigating the life of the Armenian American painter and published the authoritative biography *Black Angel, The Life of Arshile Gorky* in 1998. She also wrote a solo theater piece, *The Double Life of Arshile Gorky*, which she performed around the world (the Tate Gallery, London; the Whitney Museum, New York; the Edinburgh theater festival, Paris, Iran, Cyprus.) Her book inspired Canadian film-maker Atom Egoyan's movie *Ararat* with the female lead role based on her (see *www.arshile-gorky.com*). From 1991 to 2000 she was Honorary Cultural Attaché at the Armenian embassy in London. Nouritza Matossian speaks nine languages, is a human rights activist, gives frequent conferences, writes for international magazines, performs, and broadcasts for the BBC.

Gerald Matt lives and works in Vienna and since 1996 has been director of the Vienna Kunsthalle. He also acts as curator for numerous group and individual exhibitions of contemporary art at home and abroad, with their accompanying catalogues (e.g. Matthew Barney, Love/Hate, Flash Afrique, Anri Sala). Besides, he is the editor and author of different publications on contemporary art and cultural administration (e.g. *Kulturmanagement leicht gemacht*, 2003). Gerald Matt was contracted to carry out a number of studies related to the organization and reorganization of museums, for instance the Bolzano Museum of Modern Art (2001) and the Vienna Museum (2002). He founded, together with Dr. Wolfgang Fetz, the Vorarlberg art society, Magazin 4. He teaches cultural administration at the Institute of Applied Art and the Institut für

Kulturmanagement (IKM) of the Vienna University of Music and Figurative Art. He is the curator of the exhibition Unser Jahrhundert. Artavazd Peleschjan (2004), which was held at the Ursula Blickle Foundation and the Vienna Kunsthalle, together with a complete catalogue with numerous illustrations (Bielefeld: Kerberverlag), containing articles by Jean-Luc Goddard, Gerald Matt, François Niney, Artavazd Peleschjan, and C. Wulff.

Josef Oehrlein, Dr. Phil., since 1999, Latin American correspondent of the *Frankfurter Allgemeine Zeitung.* He lives in the capital of Argentina, Buenos Aires, on the perimeter of the former Armenian immigrant quarter. Previously he wrote for the *FAZ* magazine for thirteen years on cultural life in the Rhine-Main area. He is a Romanist, and the author and co-editor of books on Spain.

K.M. Greg Sarkissian grew up in the Armenian quarter of cosmopolitan Beirut. During the turbulent 1960s he moved to the U.S.A. The young engineering student got involved in student movements and social issues. In 1982 he was one of the three founders of the Zoryan Institute for Contemporary Armenian Research and Documentation in Cambridge, Massachusetts. In 1984 he created the Canadian Zoryan Institute in Toronto, and in 1988 helped in setting up the Paris branch of the institute. During his presidency the Zoryan Institute has published over two dozen monographs on the Armenian genocide and in the field of comparative genocide studies, and the award-winning *Diaspora: A Journal of Transnational Studies* was created. The institute also sponsored several major international conferences, including two on the consequences of the devastating earthquake of 1988 in Armenia (Paris, 1989, and Yerevan, 1990), as well as on the Armenian genocide (Yerevan 1995) and the Karabakh movement (Cambridge, MA, 1998). In 2002, the institute created, in conjunction with the International Institute for Genocide and Human Rights Studies (IIGHRS), the Genocide and Human Rights University Program at the universities in Toronto and Minneapolis (Minnesota, U.S.A.). In 2005, the IIGHRS conceptualized and helped organize a major international conference in Yerevan, "Ultimate Crime, Ultimate Challenge: Human Rights and Genocide," and in January 2006 launched *Genocide and Prevention: An International Journal* in partnership with the International Association of Genocide Scholars and the University of Toronto Press.

Christiane Schloetzer-Scotland was the *Süddeutsche Zeitung* (*SZ*, Munich) and the *Tages-Anzeiger* (Zurich) correspondent for Turkey, Greece, and Cyprus from Istanbul from 2001 to 2005. She previously worked for the *SZ* as the correspondent on parliamentary affairs in Berlin and Bonn following protracted activity as correspondent at the state parliament in Munich, among others for the *Deutsche Presse-Agentur.* She was previously an independent radio reporter. She studied communications and economic geography in Munich. She currently works in Munich as the deputy editor for foreign affairs at the *Süddeutsche Zeitung.*

Hannes Stein wrote for the *Frankfurter Allgemeine Zeitung* and *Spiegel*. He lived for a long time in Jerusalem, where he became acquainted with the Armenian community. In 1995 he published, with Richard Herzinger, the book *Endzeit-Propheten oder die Offensive der Antiwestler* (Reinbek: Rowohlt). In 1998 *Moses und Offenbarung der Demokratie* (Rowohlt) appeared, and in 2004 the best-selling *Endlich Nichtdenker! Handbuch für den überforderten Intellektuellen* (Frankfurt: Eichborn). Since 2001, Stein has been a member of the editorial board of the renowned literary weekend supplement, *Die literarische Welt*.

Lorna Touryan Miller directs the Office for Creative Connection created by All Saints Church in Pasadena, California. She is also business manageress of New Vision Partners, an interreligious philanthropic society with a global outlook. She is the daughter of two survivors of the Armenian genocide. With her husband, professor of theology Donald E. Miller, she published the book, *Survivors: An Oral History of the Armenian Genocide* (San Francisco: University of California Press 2003). Lorna Touryan Miller and her husband have just concluded an oral history project in Rwanda. This was carried out in collaboration with the AOCM (Association d'Orphelins Chefs de Ménages) and AVEGA (Association of Genocide Widows—AGAHOZO). This is an attempt to document the experiences of survivor children that are heads of families, and widows that survived the genocide. Lorna Touryan Miller has given conferences on the Armenian and Rwandan genocides in several countries, and she participated in a congress in Germany aimed at promoting dialog between Armenians and Turks.

Hrag Vartanian was born in Aleppo, Syria, and grew up in Toronto, Canada. He is a writer, critic and cultural worker. He is a staff writer for *AGBU News* magazine, *Brooklyn Rail* and *Boldtype*. He serves on the board of *Ararat Quarterly*. In his writings he deals with the issue of pluralism and identity in a global context. He lives in Brooklyn, N.Y.

Huberta von Voss is a writer and journalist in Berlin. She studied political sciences, history, and Romance languages with a scholarship from the Friedrich Ebert Foundation. On graduating she worked as a correspondent for various newspapers in the German capital. Later she was press spokeswoman of the German parliament. From 1997 to 2002 she lived with her husband and three children in Beirut and Nicosia. Publications and translations include Nadia Tuéni, *Jenseits des Blickes*. Poems in German and French (Freiburg in Breisgau and Zurich: Herder 2000; Berlin: Schiler 2004), and Alexandre Najjar, *Die Schule des Krieges*. Berlin: *Das Arabische Buch*, 2001. She received an honorary doctorate from the Armenian Branch of the International Academy of Science of Nature and Society for her book on the Armenians. She is currently working on a book on child poverty in Germany.

Daniela Weingaertner has been the EU correspondent since 1999 of the Berlin newspaper *taz, die tageszeitung* in Brussels. Before that she worked for fifteen years as a magazine writer for several television companies, and prior to moving to Brussels at the parliament office in Bonn for the television channel Deutsche Welle. As EU politics impinge increasingly on local politics, the items on the agenda of each of them are similar. In the new center, policies related to refugees and immigrants are one of the main issues. The stories of individual lives are always fascinating—even if daily life in the translation business is dominated by the challenge to explain complex norms and resolutions to her readership.

Michaela Wiegel has worked since early 1998 in Paris as a correspondent of the *Frankfurter Allgemeine Zeitung*. The center of gravity of a reporter's activity is domestic and foreign politics which, in centralized France, is necessarily focused on the capital. To this must be added articles and reports about the "provinces," on social change, and everything else that makes Germany's most important neighbor so different. She trained by attending the Paris "Sciences Po," and Harvard University, at Cambridge. As a freelance journalist she has worked, among others, for the Paris ARD television studio, for the Berlin *Tagesspiegel*, and the *Wochenpost*.